MILES FRANKLIN
Franklin at Talbingo,
at Brindabella and Thornford, near
attended a one-teacher school. In 1906 Miles Franklin went to
America and until 1915 worked for the National Women's
Trade Union League of America in Chicago. During the Great
War she served as a hospital orderly in Macedonia. Afterwards
in London she began writing as 'Brent of Bin Bin'. She visited
Australia twice in the 1920s and in late 1932 returned to settle.
Miles Franklin died in Sydney in 1954, shortly before her
seventy-fifth birthday.

Among some twenty books by Miles Franklin are three
Australian classics *My Brilliant Career* (1901), *All That Swagger*
(1936) and *Childhood at Brindabella* (1963).

JILL ROE spent her early years on Eyre Peninsula. She is a
graduate of the University of Adelaide and the Australian
National University. She was a founding member of staff of
Macquarie University, Sydney, where she is now associate
professor of history. After several books on the history of
Australian urban and social policy, she published a history of
theosophy in Australia. Among her many contributions to the
Australian Dictionary of Biography is the entry for Miles
Franklin, on whom she is now preparing a full-scale biography.

IMPRINT
lives

My Congenials

Miles Franklin & Friends in Letters

VOLUME TWO 1939–1954

EDITED BY
JILL ROE

The State Library of New South Wales
in association with

Angus&Robertson
An imprint of HarperCollins*Publishers*

AN ANGUS & ROBERTSON BOOK
An imprint of HarperCollinsPublishers

First published in Australia in 1993 by
CollinsAngus&Robertson Publishers Pty Limited (ACN 009 913 517)
A division of HarperCollinsPublishers (Australia) Pty Limited
25-31 Ryde Road, Pymble NSW 2073, Australia

HarperCollinsPublishers (New Zealand) Limited
31 View Road, Glenfield, Auckland 10, New Zealand

HarperCollinsPublishers Limited
77-85 Fulham Palace Road, London W6 8JB, United Kingdom

National Library of Australia
Cataloguing-in-Publication data:

My congenials: Miles Franklin and friends in letters.

   Bibliography.
   Includes index.
   ISBN 0 207 16925 X (v.1).
   ISBN 0 207 17860 7 (v.2)

   1. Franklin, Miles, 1879-1954 – Correspondence. 2. Novelists,
   Australian – Biography. I. Roe, Jill, 1940- . II. Franklin, Miles,
   1879-1954.

A823.2

Cover photograph of Miles Franklin soon after her arrival in America.
Mounted on a one-cent lettercard to her sister Linda. 1906,
(Franklin Papers III, Mitchell Library. State Library of NSW)
Cover designed by Nicole Court
Typeset by Midland Typsetters
Printed in Australia by Griffin Paperbacks

5 4 3 2 1
95 94 93

Contents

ILLUSTRATIONS

ABBREVIATIONS

ABC	Australian Broadcasting Commission [now Corporation]
AFL	American Federation of Labor
ALP	Australian Labor Party
ANP	Agnes Nestor papers (CHS)
A&R	Angus & Robertson, Sydney
ANU	Australian National University
BA	*British Australasian*
BCON	*British Commonwealth Occupation News*
BL	Battye Library, Perth
BP	E H Burgmann Papers (NLA)
CHS	Chicago Historical Society
CLF	Commonwealth Literary Fund
DCP	Dymphna Cusack Papers (NLA)
DDP	Dorothea A Dreier Papers (Archives of American Art, Washington)
DT	*Daily Telegraph*, Sydney
EC	Evatt Collection, (The Flinders University of South Australia Library)
EDP	Eleanor Dark Papers (NLA)
FAL	Fawcett Library, City of London Polytechnic
FAW	Fellowship of Australian Writers
FC	Furphy Correspondence (SLV)
FL	Fisher Library, University of Sydney
FP	Franklin Papers (ML)
GC	Grattan Collection (HRHRC)
HLC	Henry Lawson Collection (FL)
HRHRC	Harry Ransom Humanities Research Center, University of Texas, Austin
IMP	Ian Mudie Papers (SLSA)
IWW	Industrial Workers of the World
JKMC	J K Moir Collection (SLV)
KBP	Kate Baker Papers (NLA)
LC	Library of Congress, Washington DC
L&L	*Life and Labor*
MA	*Meanjin* Archive (Baillieu Library, University of Melbourne)

MAP	Mary Anderson Papers (Schlesinger Library, Radcliffe College, Cambridge, Mass.)
MBC	*My Brilliant Career*
MDP	Mary Dreier Papers (Schlesinger Library, Radcliffe College, Cambridge, Mass.)
MDR	Margaret Dreier Robins Papers (University of Florida Libraries, Gainesville, Florida)
MEF	Mary Fullerton Papers (NLA)
MHP	Muir Holburn Papers (ML)
MHR	Member of the House of Respresentatives
ML	Mitchell Library, Sydney
MLA	Member of the Legislative Assembly
MUA	University of Melbourne Archives
nd	no date
NHTPC	National Housing & Town Planning Council, London
NLA	National Library of Australia, Canberra
np	no place
OBE	Order of the British Empire
OP	Leonora O'Reilly Papers (Schlesinger Library, Radcliffe College, Cambridge, Mass.)
PBC	Miles Franklin Printed Books Collection (ML)
pm	postmark
PP	Palmer Papers (NLA)
RGH	R G Howarth/Miles Franklin letters (ML)
RIP	Rex Ingamells Papers (The Flinders University of South Australia Library)
RR	Raymond Robins Papers (State Historical Society, Wisconsin/ University of Florida Libraries, Gainesville, Florida)
RSC	Rose Scott Correspondence, Scott Family Papers (ML)
SC	*Southern Churchman*
SLSA	Mortlock Library, State Library of South Australia
SLV	La Trobe Library, State Library of Victoria
SMF	Stella Miles Franklin
SMH	*Sydney Morning Herald*
VGP	Vida Goldstein Papers (FAL)
VKP	Victor Kennedy Papers (SLV)
WILPF	Women's International League of Peace and Freedom Papers, Swarthmore College Peace Collection (Jane Addams Collection, University of Illinois, Chicago Circle, Illinois)

WSPU	Women's Social and Political Union
WTUL	Women's Trade Union League
WTUL	*Papers of the Women's Trade Union League and Its Principal Leaders*, RPI microfilm edition
WTUL (LC)	National Women's Trade Union League of America Records, Library of Congress

INTRODUCTION TO
VOLUME 2

'I'm alright when I have a congenial friend,' Miles Franklin once wrote to Mabel Singleton, companion of the expatriate writer Mary Fullerton in London. To Dymphna Cusack, a later friend and literary collaborator in Sydney in 1939, she wrote 'creative activity and congenial and stimulating association with one's fellows is the nearest to happiness one can get.' More crustily, to a literary protégé of the 1940s she asserted 'One oz. of congenial friendship is more warming in the cold and a better float in stormy seas than tons of vice and debauchery.' In later life what mattered most to Miles Franklin was Australian literature—and congeniality. At seventy, it pleased her to think, as she put it to Adelaide poet Ian Mudie, 'I can still enjoy my congenials.'

This volume contains a selection of letters by and to Miles Franklin during the last fifteen years of her life, from 1939 to 1954, ending with her last known letter, to Sydney children's artist Pixie O'Harris (3 September 1954). It is the second of two volumes of selected Franklin correspondence and follows directly from the first, which covers the years from Miles Franklin's birth at Talbingo, NSW in 1879 to her mother's death in Sydney in 1938.

Unlike the first, this second volume spans a relatively short period of time, fifteen years compared to nearly sixty. This is because extant correspondence is not spread evenly over Miles Franklin's lifetime. As outlined in the introduction to volume 1, the great accumulation of Franklin correspondence began when Miles Franklin returned to Sydney to live in the early 1930s after nearly two decades in Chicago and London, and there is a preponderance of letters from the 1940s.

The volume opens with a chapter of letters dating from World War II (chapter 7 'Our best traditions'), followed by the longest chapter in the two volumes, chapter 8, 'The waratah cup', a reference to Miles's legendary cup and saucer which favoured guests were required to take tea from, and concludes with a brief chapter containing letters from the last two years of her life (chapter 9, 'If I live'). In some respects Miles Franklin's last years are her most interesting. She corresponded with such a wide range of people in Australia and beyond, so quaintly and characteristically termed 'my congenials'.

In this, as in the prior volume, many letters are of necessity edited. Editing has been of a technical character only, with space and flow the main considerations. For further information on the principles followed the reader is referred to the introduction to volume 1.

The volume concludes with a checklist of letters and an index of names which encompass both volumes. All letters reproduced in the volumes appear in chronological order on the checklist, which is arranged according to chapter, and within chapters by year. Biographical information about correspondents is to be found in the index of names. A brief bibliography notes other published sources of information about Miles Franklin's life and letters.

7 OUR BEST TRADITIONS: 1939–45

'Believe me I am quietly doing what I can towards maintaining our best traditions as far as possible even in war time.'

MILES FRANKLIN TO IAN MUDIE, 21 APRIL, 1942

(FP)

Miles Franklin at home, with sunflowers (ML)

B ut for the onset of war, 1939 might have been an *annus mirabilis* for Miles Franklin. It began with a refreshing summer holiday up the country. Mid-1939 saw the publication of the sesquicentenary satire co-authored with Dymphna Cusack, *Pioneers on Parade*; and a second Prior Memorial Prize, for the biographical essay *Who was Joseph Furphy?* written in association with Kate Baker, in residence at Carlton during the first half of 1939 for the purpose. Miles even obtained support from the Commonwealth Literary Fund for further work on it in 1940. Also, Tom Inglis Moore agreed to coedit a selection of Mary Fullerton's poems. For Miles Franklin the outbreak of war in Europe on 3 September 1939 was a grotesque resumption of the 1914–18 conflict, at once a relapse into barbarism and a cruel setback for her own work and for Australian culture. Two European wars in a lifetime seemed an unbearable blow. She does not seem to have mentioned to anyone that on 14 October 1939 she turned sixty.

Even in remote Australia, where the 'phoney war' of late 1939-early 1940 seemed especially phoney, the war increasingly impinged on daily life. With war came censorship, and refugees were seen in the suburbs. P R Stephensen was loud for 'Australia First'. But after the fall of France in June 1940, when Britain stood alone, attitudes changed. The battle of Britain, July–August 1940, was probably a turning point for Miles Franklin as for many others. She worried about friends in England, especially frail Mary Fullerton, and wondered how best to serve at her age. In time, she would even have a good word for Winston Churchill. Hartley Grattan's visit in September cheered her up. The selection of Fullerton's poems was completed. A new friend of 1940 was West Australian writer Henrietta Drake-Brockman; also retired botanist Richard Baker, who gave her the waratah cup and saucer, subsequently reserved for favoured guests (see Chapter 8).

Richard Baker died mid-1941, a mainly dispiriting year. Due partly to Kate Baker's anxiously proprietorial attitude, Miles was unable to face the Furphy manuscript. Nothing came of her efforts to publish the Fullerton ('E') poems. She worried about her own health, especially in winter, and wondered if she had been 'boned', a colloquialism derived from the technique in Aboriginal magic of willing an enemy to die by 'pointing the bone'. The war dragged on in the northern hemisphere; and there was political drift at home, where a conservative coalition was replaced by Labor in October 1941. Miles worried about morale, and Japan, with Mary Fullerton the chief beneficiary of her uninhibited views on public affairs as usual. By now she was in contact with and supportive of many local women writers, Eleanor Dark for example, also Jean Devanny (the self-styled 'Red Menace', in Queensland in 1941). Important new 'congenials' were Adelaide poet Ian Mudie, and Sydney children's artist Pixie O'Harris (see chapters 8 and 9). In 1941 her Australia First friend S B Hooper gave her a year's subscription to a new literary journal *Meanjin*, the flagship of cultural nationalism in Australia for a generation.

Suddenly in 1942 everything changed. Pearl Harbor had been attacked by Japan on 8 December 1941. The fall of Singapore occurred 15 February 1942. The Japanese bombed Darwin on 19 February 1942. By mid-March 1942 Australia was part of the SW Pacific theatre of war under US General Douglas MacArthur, who established his command in Australia on 18 April 1942. These events marked the end of the British Empire in Australia. With the end of the empire went the Australia First movement, swept away by ugly and illegal means in March 1942. Some supporters were interned, Stephensen for the duration. What Miles Franklin called 'our best traditions' were highly apposite to a tricky situation. Paradoxically 1942, which began with the death of her last surviving brother, Norman Rankin Franklin, and ushered in a new phase of the war, also brought improvement on the professional front. Miles's work was in demand on radio and in the new literary journals, *Southerly* as well as *Meanjin*. On 5 September 1942 she delivered the oration at the Fellowship of Australian Writers' annual pilgrimage to the Henry Lawson statue in Sydney Domain. Outlets for 'E's poems also materialised. Miles hazarded that maybe after thirty years modernism was settling down. In October 1942 she greatly enjoyed a weekend with Dymphna Cusack in Newcastle, where she met up with Nettie Palmer's brother Esmonde Higgins, and the young bohemians Harry Hooton and Godfrey Bentley.

Alice Henry died in Melbourne on 14 February 1943, aged almost eighty-six. Her death broke Miles's only local link with her American career, and ended a fascinating but elusive, and so far as extant correspondence goes, largely unarticulated relationship. As Alice Henry's literary executor, Nettie Palmer invited Miles to participate in a memorial volume but Miles could not manage it, neither for love nor money. Early 1943 she resumed work on the Furphy manuscript ('the albatross'), spurred by rumours of paper available for books; and, cheered by a comparison with Thomas Mann's *Buddenbrooks*, was again angling for American publication of 'Brent' volumes. It was however Angus & Robertson, in the person of esteemed— and congenial—editor Beatrice Davis, which came to her aid. Through 1943 she assiduously promoted 'E', persuading Douglas Stewart at the *Bulletin* to a second volume, and making contact with young poets Muir Holburn and Marjorie Pizer. With her other pet poet Ian Mudie winning a prize in 1943, Miles had cause for satisfaction. She urged young friends in the army in the north and the Pacific to make the most of literary opportunity; and she sent a strong message to the Joseph Furphy centenary celebration. This war, with its unanticipated American dimension, was not necessarily a setback, after all. In September 1943 she went to Victoria for the graduation of her airman nephew Norman John Franklin at Point Cook, her (and his) last immediate relative and an increasing source of anguish.

In March 1944 Miles Franklin visited her 'native fastnesses', including Brindabella. In May there was talk of reissuing *Old Blastus*. The 'unforgivable' war in Europe rolled on. In private, to Bishop Burgmann, Miles reflected somewhat zanily on the changing world order heralded by war in the Pacific, where Norman Franklin now served. Partly due to her two poets, also due to the new market for Australian fiction created by the war, her optimistic nativism revived. Mid-year, she took the 'Ern Malley' exposé, of literary modernism as practised by Adelaide poet Max Harris and the so-called 'Angry Penguins', in her stride. At the same time, her hostility to 'examination passers' increased: she never forgot upsetting references to her work in CLF lectures delivered jointly by younger Sydney writers Marjorie Barnard and Flora Eldershaw at Sydney University the following year, and she was outraged by Colin Roderick's D Litt proposal, a two volume anthology of Australian writing. Differences between Sydney and Melbourne writers—noticed in a letter from a new 'congenial' Frank Ryland—helped ensure that her principled opposition proved ineffectual. In November 1944 Angus & Robertson published the Furphy essay, retitled *Joseph Furphy: The Legend of a Man and his Book*. Kate Baker accepted her share of the royalties.

Miles was obliged to give way to Roderick. There were bigger fish to fry in 1945. With the end of the war in sight, and 'reconstruction' the dominant mood, writers feared a postwar flood of foreign books. Early 1945 the Fellowship of Australian Writers established an Australian Book Society, with Miles organising the first selection committee. The Fellowship also surveyed Australian books in Sydney bookstores (apparently the germ of *Call Up Your Ghosts*, a play written jointly with Dymphna Cusack which shared a prize in Melbourne with another by the young Ric Throssell). Towards the end of the year, there was a Tariff Board inquiry into the problems of the publishing industry—Australian literature being tried for its life, said Miles. In 1945 Miles also wrote a children's story about Sydney's Royal Easter Show, which she percipiently compared with the Melbourne Cup; and publication of *My Career Goes Bung* seemed imminent. Rising interest in an Australian drama brought theatre people, such as Catherine Duncan, into contact with Miles Franklin, whose perspectives and opinions delighted many younger people. In 1945 two more congenials died, the irreplaceable Margaret Dreier Robins and 'dear little G B Lancaster'.

Ever alert to international issues, Miles did not miss the ambivalence of the atomic bomb as a means of ending the war with Japan in August 1945. She had little faith in the 'new order', much less Australia's Asian future. It was enough to know that European friends had survived. Still, she thought of herself as 'a sane kind of optimist'; and her extraordinary vitality was intact. With soldiers discharged—but not Miles's nephew, still needed in air transport—and the interned released, the world was 'teeming with movement'.

26 Grey Street
Carlton NSW
Good Friday night
[7 April 1939]

My dear Mabel, Jean and Mary, I'll write to you all together. . .

Well, today poor old Tubby Lyons passed away. Very suddenly. I am sorry for the family's grief. Each of us goes through it—little spell of something like joy or success and then the pangs and shadows. I don't think it will make much difference politically. We'll get another similar mediocrity. And I was very sick of her in public, boasting of her breeding power and saying the poor ought to have large families—a woman who was reared Protestant to go over to RC dogma has no thinking capacity, but she had a lot of personal capability and smartness which made her a great phony success—a woman for the masses. She was like Alice Grant Rosman's novels—the first delightful and surprising, the second, one begins to yawn, and I haven't read a third. . . .

By the way I have just been writing Mary's name on a list. Alice Henry written to by some body for a list of twenty names of Aust women writers, asked for my list. She had put Mary Fullerton and so did I and so did Kate Baker. She had also Alice Grant Rosman and D Cottrell—I objected to these two and Ethel Turner and M G Bruce—such slush. Why, a little girl of eight to whom I gave a copy of *Seven Lit Australians* in Chicago turned up her nose at it—said it was like *Little Women* only not half so good. . . .

The Furphy letters are very interesting to me but I wonder how much they would interest anyone who did not know him. It would take a lot of hard work, and sheer genius, perhaps, to make the interest go beyond the few who know and appreciate his worth to Australia. K B adored him like a Suttee widow, but she has no literary faculty whatever. ...

Angus and R have my novel in hand. I hope it will come out soon or the point of it will be lost. Cousins (A and R manager) said he had five people read it and they were all in fits of laughter. Cousins said 'I don't know any Australian book the least like it.' It is a new field I am pioneering.

They are booming from London a thing called *Happy Valley* by Patrick White. I call him a lost Australian. His book is by Joyce out of D H Lawrence. It is set in my country Kiandra which is the only town with snow so that the people tunnel from one house to another and the little towns with Chinamen but I know those places and that sort of copulation at sight between all sorts of people never occurs as far as I know. ...

8th Ap. Well, I see by the paper this morning that Italy has invaded Albania and Albania refuses to be gobbled by the Roman Empire. I hope it won't set all Europe blazing again. The only ally for England is Russia but the British Fascists and their hankerers like Chamberlain and all that privileged crowd would rather risk losing all than giving in to the possibility of such an experiment in democracy. I wish Australia could be free from Europe and let them fight it out among themselves. If we cd remove the British population out here—funny exile it would be for those royalties and other parasites which the Londoners worship; and the creatures out here do too, because they are sedulously trained by church and press and have nothing else in their pates. America has sense to stand aloof. ...

In this connection I am more than thankful for that book *Three Guineas*. It shows just as Mrs Gilman did that war is a madness of men. Women aren't hardly allowed into such a sacred thing except to clear up the mess. The argument against giving women the vote used to be that they couldn't fight. It would be better if the vote was taken from everyone who could fight, and the others be allowed to vote only for themselves to fight or not to fight.

Well, we're busy with Lyons lying in state in the Catholic Cathedral, and the big Royal Agricultural Show which always fills Easter. Archbishop Mowll and his predecessors are against Holy Week being thus desecrated by a holiday and had a procession against it this year. I don't know—it seems like a broken match on the current to me. The church has never been anything but an obstruction to me.

I took Miss Baker on Thursday. She was entranced. Something for the poor old soul to see, as she cannot hear. My brother and others went yesterday, all grumbling about the same old show. But I said think of us all sitting there in comfort looking at the glorious cattle and horses and the produce, year after year, without being sacked by Mussolini. ... Australia is a wonderful place if the people only had brains and alertness to keep it so.

[unsigned]

7.2 *From Michael Sawtell, Sydney*
Source: FP 32

Emerson Society
12A Victoria Arcade
3 July 1939

Dear Madam

I have been meaning to write to you for 22 years. In 1917 I did 7 months in Parramatta jail, for a political offence during a big strike at Broken Hill. Whilst I was in jail, I read almost every book in the library, & amongst the books, was a copy of your book *My Brilliant Career* which I remember was highly recommended by Henry Lawson. I read the book through several times whilst I was in jail, & although I can hardly remember what the story was about, the book made a great impression upon me, & I intended to write to the author when I was released from Jail. Well I never did. Then I almost forgot the name of the book, & the author, but an old bush friend of mine Billy Miller who has been in the NT for 52 years, & who is a great reader of the classics & the best books, told me that *All this Swagger* is a great book, by Miles Franklin. That awoke memories of your other book, then the other evening at the Lawson evening I heard Frank Dalby Davison mention

& praise your *My brilliant Career*, & also to-day I saw your name coupled with Miss Cusacks, in the Womens page of the *SM Herald*, & I determined at last to write to you.

I would like you to know that real bushmen praise your books. Very few men in Sydney to-day (or Australia for the matter of that) know more about the big bush than Billy Miller or I. Billy Miller told me that your book was about the bush in the early days in New South Wales (*All this Swagger*) & he said it also touched upon 'poddy dodging' which is a NT & Kimberly name for cattle stealing. And old Billy also said if Miles Franklin knew the real big bush, she would write a wonderful book about the life that we know so well.

Although I never read novels or stories now, I read essays philosophic, metaphysical & occult books, but because of my old bush experiences I do like to hear that some one is able to write a good bush book.

On thursday the 13th at 8 oclock I am going to give a talk at 'Pakies' upon reading in the bush. I wonder if it would interest you, my old friend Billy Miller will be with me.

I apologise for my belated praise of your book, but it is sincere never the less.

Sincerely yours
Michael Sawtell

7.3 To R G Menzies, Canberra
Source: FP 32

Carlton
July 5 1939

Dear Mr Prime Minister

I am sending you a copy of my latest, which is in the nature of a coalition. It is nice to have a PM with a name that indicates that an insight into the place of literature in life need not be unexpected nor incongruous. In the deepening complexities of existence the state and quality of Australian letters bid fair to become a barometer of this continent's condition as a place for desirable citizenship as against mere military vassalage.

If you have time for so light a novel as the said *Pioneers on Parade* I hope it will amuse you and draw attention to some of the undertones and overtones of what is at present national emotion rather than considered thought.

With greetings and good wishes for you in your hefty responsibilities.

[unsigned]

7.4   To Kate Baker, Melbourne
Source: FP 9A

Carlton
July 16 1939

Dear Katy O'Baker E
Private and Confidential

So we get a little prize after all, of £100. But you must not say a word till next Wednesday's *Bulletin*, Aug 23, as it is not for publication till announced in that issue.

I'll tell you the facts. Mr Prior asked me to come in and see him this morning, and I've just returned. Green, Davison and Esson agreed in their report which was that *Lachlan Macquarie* got the prize, and that *Who was Joseph Furphy?* was highly commended. They told a few people this, and that is how I heard it over a week ago, and wrote to you.

Mr Prior tells me that when this report was submitted to him, out of experience he has had, he insisted that some outside referee should be consulted to see that the Macquarie book would hold water. It was sent to Ida Leeson at the Mitchell to let loose herself or other historical experts upon it, and the MSS was returned with many pencilled notes, in fact as being in an unfinished condition. So the judges had to sit again. And their second report was that *Joseph Furphy* shd get the prize of £100, without accumulations, and the accumulations shd be carried forward to next year and thus give Mr Ellis time to finish his work and gain the £300. So that is that, my dear.

I am so glad, for your sake. Congratulations on your belief.

I wanted Mr Prior to join me in a telegram to you, but he said that would let the cat out of the bag before next Wednesday, but he said that I could write to you. So, we can each wear a secret grin as we go about our chores, and be ready to see our friends surprised when the day comes.

Also we must be ready to spring off our tails like good kangaroos with the finishings-up. I expect you have found lots of flaws in the composition which you must let me hear about. Mr Prior wants it for the *Bulletin* as soon as possible. I forgot to ask him how much he would give.

Mrs Stewart has to see it and Sam and much pother ahead of us yet, so take care of yourself. I congratulate you and we'll have much to tell interviewers and give lectures upon, you in Melb and I here.

So our work has been recognised to some extent and now we must climb higher with it. I do wish I could see you for a yabber about it.

My love as always
[unsigned]

7.5 *To Mary Fullerton, London*
Source: FP 119

August 9 1939

Dearest Mary

I saw Tom Inglis Moore yesterday and gave him that clipping about his poems that you sent from the *Sunday Supp*. I jogged him about my poet, and we have decided to make a selection. He is to edit them and write a poetical preface. He really is deeply interested in poetry, and must know something about it to write such dashing poetry himself. I shall write a human preface something like that article in the review I sent you. The former editor of it was at tea too with us and he wants some more poems for the magazine. That will bring them to life again. I hope something comes of it. Tom complains that what restrains him is that often the best ones are too, *too* much an echo of Emily Dickinson. He remarked, tho this spoiled them, in a way it was nevertheless high praise because he reckons Emily the greatest thing known in woman poets.

I shall keep on nursing him. I think he is my best bet. Now, as soon as we begin on it, I know the trouble with anonymity will come up and he will want to know have you had anything else published. Now tell me what I am to do.

Shall I say that here is another analogy to Emily—a poet so shy that it wd not publish at all—like Emily—but only upon my persuasion and promise of anonymity, and try to make it a mystery. I am quite game to say in the days when the truth comes out, if I am still alive, that *I understood* the feeling that there was no hope of the academic cliques seeing anything but the flaws if they knew the poet.

I am going to copy all the latest poems, for Tom will want to see them too. He said he wd go over his notes that he prepared at the time he and I were going to speak, but my mother's passing finished me. I am still finished.

Pioneers on Parade is making lots of people very cross—the English-garrison-minded are trying to down it. Dear Bishop Burgmann loves it. Made his registrar boom it over the diocesan broadcast, and wrote me a lovely letter. Says he wants to know what the offspring will be like. I say he can decide, as he will christen them; all got up in the tremendous robes that the boys have to carry the wings of. (That is an unacademic sentence.)

I send you samples of reviews, Adelaide was contemptuous and so was Brisbane. Inky enlarged his paper on purpose to come out in a roar in opposition to F E Baume in *Sunday Sun*, Baume could not leave it for old Napier and Adam McKay, but himself took the field to damn it. They say he has a daughter about to come out, and McKay has one who hovers ready to genuflect anywhere there is a title, and they are hoping for great things when the Royal Duke comes, and into this hopeful aura I barge with the ploughing of a new furrow.

You will have had *Pioneers* by now.

[unsigned]

Honey Ditches
Seaton
23 August 1939

Dear Miss Franklin

It was kind of you to send me *Pioneers on Parade*, but I fear
you will think me ungrateful for it when I tell you that it deeply
disappointed me. How you, who wrote *All That Swagger*, came
to be associated with such a novel, I cannot imagine. It might
have been written by Two Smart Girls in the Upper Fifth, who
have the habit of snarking at all their teachers and taking small
girls into corners to tell them the facts of life. By the time I
had reached page 80, I found myself impatiently turning to the
end to see how many more pages there were, and I heard myself
exclaiming, 'My God, another 184 pages of sneers!' I found
the last forty pages unreadable and only skimmed them
hurriedly to see what you had done with your people.

If it is your ambition to be the Ethel Mannin of Australia,
go on writing this sort of stuff, but don't expect anybody of
discernment to take you seriously. Apart from a small amount
of flippant smartness, which eventually becomes boring,
Pioneers on Parade has no merit whatsoever. It is stupid and,
you must forgive me for saying, vulgar. My first feeling was
that someone was taking your name in vain, so difficult did
I find it to believe that you had any connection with it. The
characterisation is poor, the style is sloppy, and the whole
outlook of the book is mean. The political sentiments expressed
in it are Early Street Corner. Your hero, Greg Moore—for I
suppose he is the hero—is a mixture of erotic errand-boy and
Bright Hope of a Back Street Debating Society. The only piece
of furniture, physical or intellectual, he seems to possess is a
soap-box on to which he climbs every time he wants to make
a remark. The incident.in which he figures as the second Ned
Kelly . . . really, Miss Franklin, really! Take a look at the conversation of this sour bellied ass as reported by you and Miss

Cusack at the bottom of page 59. In this country, a man who talked like that would be relegated to the remoter street corners so that he might orate to six small boys and one large girl, all of them under the delusion that he was a Punch and Judy man. His sort are ten-a-penny at the Marble Arch.

What happened to your sense of humour and your sense of character when you wrote the first four lines on page 192? They are supposed to represent the thoughts of Prim, a useless little slut, no better, if no worse, than Lucy. Well, were her hands gnarled and chapped? Would she have supported the rigours of winter without a murmur, when she might have avoided them with the help of an Esse stove? What, in God's name, has happened to your mind. Your other work had made me feel that you had the perceptions and the potentialities of a notable writer, but this sorry stuff, which might have been written by any disgruntled Hardboiled Hannah on a New York tabloid, makes me feel dubious about your future. If you continue to write books like *Pioneers on Parade*, I can foresee a time when your and Miss Cusack's entrance into any assembly will be greeted with murmurs of 'Here come the Sisters Sourgut, snarking as usual!' You are evidently at a critical point in your career, and I warn you, as solemnly as I can, that if you continue to write smarty-smart novels like *Pioneers on Parade*, you will soon cease to be worthy of any person's serious notice. If this book is the result of collaboration with Miss Cusack, for heaven's sake, cease to collaborate with her.

I would not write to you in this strain if I did not believe that you still have the perceptions and potentialities of a notable writer, and I hope that the shock of receiving such a letter as this will make you pull yourself together. You will probably loathe the thought of me for the rest of your writing life, but if I succeed in sending you back to the author of *All That Swagger* and making you set fire to the collaborator in *Pioneers on Parade*, I shall bear your loathing with equanimity; for I shall have done a good thing.

Yours very sincerely
St John Ervine

Box 2119L GPO
26/8/39

To Miles Franklin and Kate Baker
My dear colleagues

I do want you to know how terribly pleased I was to hear that you two won the Prior Memorial. And with such a type of book.

That's the sort of job, in my opinion, that does our writers credit. I hope to have the pleasure of thanking you personally for such a contribution to our literature.

For writers such as myself, people who find themselves torn between twin loyalties, people who find the vastest satisfaction in fighting to retain the freedom for writers such as yourselves to continue to work—well, dear colleagues, such recognition does give us satisfaction.

May I offer you, not only my own congratulations, but the congratulations of the Communist Party for your contribution to the history and achievements of Australia, which are the history and achievements of its people. We know that the writer of *All That Swagger*, in conjunction with Kate Baker, could not do otherwise than make a splendid thing of such a work as that which has won the Memorial Prize.

Sincerely yours
Jean Devanny

Carlton
Aug 30 1939

Dear Jean Devanny

I knew that your letter would be full of kindness and that is why I opened it at once. I became so immersed in its over-generous praise that I missed my cue, and seemingly my manners too, sitting there unconscious of what was going on.

I have sent your letter to KB knowing she will enjoy it.

But, my dear, I must point out that I am torn between half a dozen loyalties, that I forsook literature until a few years back and gave all my youth, my love years, financial security and everything else to the struggle for freedom consumedly, and only now when there is nothing but confusion and I am no longer able to work and rage for 36 hours in the 24 per diem have I turned back to my one great abiding love—*Australia*—our magic land, and am trying before the night cometh to lay a wreath however weedy and inadequate on the altar of my adoration.

I am glad for KB's sake of the recognition of merit contained in the Memorial Prize. Otherwise she would have thought that my design and handling of the material which she has so devotedly collected, was at fault.

Thanking you very much for your generous appreciation

Sincerely
[unsigned]

6th Sep 1939

Dear K B OBE

Well, there goes everything that you and I and our ilk cared
for, in another eruption of all that is male! Twice within our
lives is too much. . . .

Thank goodness we had our Furphy adventure before this
happened and that it came to a triumphant fruition. It could
not have been done at all without eager enthusiasm and it would
be impossible to feel that in face of the present situation. I am
so happy that we did it. You were a heroine to come over, and
I'm glad that I weathered the responsibility. It pulled me away
from my sense of desolation.

I suggest that during these lunatic days, if you can put your
mind to it, that you should write another volume yourself
recording those things that we had to eliminate from this
volume. Such for instance as the detailed account of the
unveiling of the monument at Yarra Glen, etc, etc. You could
give it to the Mitchell or a Melb library and it wd be there
for those that come after us. . . .

I wonder how Furphy would have reacted to war. He was
lucky that at least his work had peace to mature in. War might
so easily have swooped on the world to deflect his leisure from
it. The Boer War came and went during the passage of *Such
is Life* through the press, but that was merely a skirmish
compared with present warfare.

I am glad you are settled in a comfortable room. I have felt
for some time that I must go over to see Miss Henry. I don't
know if it will be possible now.

Oh dear, if it cd only end swiftly before the whole world
is maimed again.

Yours as ever
Miles

Carlton
Oct 4 1939

Dear H N

I feel impelled to write to you in face of the same old war
bursting out on us again. Heartbreaking, isn't it? This time I
shall not be at the Front traipsing among wolves and Serbs and
such. I shall rest on the laurels of ladies in their fifties and keep
the home fires going. In your business you will be up to your
eyes. I have been asked to do something, which if I can pull
it off will make me very happy. . . .

Our air mail has soared to 1/6 again. Too much for me as
I do not feel I have anything important to say, and the space
had better be left for the rich and profiteering. And you may
be away in USA or heaven knows where.

One of our little theatres is putting on Shaw's *Geneva*. It
is a great success. Just hits the times to perfection. Have you
seen it? I recall the time I inveigled you to Shaw's *Heartbreak
House* after the war—and the time you took us to hear Harry
Tate. George Roby is out here eyebrows and all cavorting with
old diggers.

I don't think the younger generation has realised the war here
yet. There is quite a deal of opinion to the effect that it is worth
it to have stopped Kent and his missus from being foisted on
us. I was not won to them by the reports of our rare jarrah
flooring being torn up at Yarralumla to put down some other
kind to match the intruder's color scheme.

It is the same war entirely. Winston Churchill responsible
for the Gallipoli *gaspillage* still at large and crowing over the
short wave radio about the wonders achieved. Long before this
reaches you the situation will have changed utterly, may it be
for the better. . . .

Yours for old association's sake
[unsigned]

Carlton
Oct 14 1939

Dear Mr Moir

I shd be delighted if Mr Moyle wd review *Pioneers* for *Bohemia*.
I seem to remember that his was one of the generous reviews.
Messrs Angus and R sent you a copy of *Pioneers* yesterday and
you can use it for this purpose if you will be so kind.

Even the *SMH* has come out with a sharp editorial demand
for an apology for the way Mr Menzies was treated in a news
release of vital import to us, so a few more of them may
understand the need for books like *Pioneers* before long. By the
way, in *Swagger*, by implication, I advocated that we become
a nation of airmen. I dislike standing armies and cd never idolize
professional soldiers, but a nation of citizenry roused to protect
themselves is a different thing.

If we could fly everywhere we would be in a position to turn
into defenders when necessary, and also, this would be the way
to overcome the vast expense per capita of roads through the
centre: and without such roads invaders would have a sorry
chance of taking over. . . .

Sincerely, and thanking you for your interest.

Miles Franklin

Carlton
Dec 28 1939

Dear, dear M E D

You don't know how nice it was to get your message today.
I don't know when or how the mails go these days, so I'll drop

this in the box, and hope it reaches you some time before the year has a beard on it.

The enclosed card about our *ornithorhynchus paradoxus* came to me from the NW end of our continent from a place called Yeelirrie Station, and I pass it on to you in the expectation of it being interesting. I fear, however, that there *is* a danger of its extinction. As a child, my native streams were full of them, now there is scarcely one.

It is indeed a weariness of the flesh to be confronted with a relapse of the same old war, even with that egregious Churchill crowing like a demented rooster on his midden. How I wish the belligerents would submit to the arbitration of the neutrals *now*. It would be a far better settlement than they will get years hence, with much of male youth slaughtered and all of the populations demoralised and debauched by war. If it cost a few millions to send representatives and hold conferences it wd be money well spent, and cheap, compared with war.

Here it is all so peaceful. I wish I could give you some of the peaches in my back yard. Immense white cling-stones with pink blush skins which are a perfect example of the complexions which used to be like peaches and roses, naturally. Such funny summer weather here—hot days and icy nights that are good for sleeping. I have not got a radio. I do not want to hear these terrible hooting speeches of the militarists and the politicians, bankrupt as they are, both of statesmanship and sanity.

So it was you sent me the lovely catalogues of the New York Fair. When I had seen them I sent them to a little girl who is very clever but an invalid. She looks to me for books and such. I wish you would sometimes stick a stamp on the book magazine of the Sunday paper when you are done with it. It keeps me in touch with USA, which I feel is drifting away.

I am busy with my literary work. I am finishing a biography of our leading writer, Joseph Furphy. Have gained for it the Prior Memorial Prize for the best contribution towards Australian literature for 1939; and the Govt has also given me a Commonwealth literary fellowship for it. I have to do some more research and finish it in a manner worthy of the kind notice it has already attracted. Furphy's novel is out of print or I shd send you a copy for bed-side reading.

I had a lovely letter from Mrs Robins and must write again—but the heart goes dead. I am so grateful therefore for the comforting message of your Christmas greeting. My Father always used to point me to that text 'Be still and know that I am God'. My pet Bishop, Dr Burgmann of the Goulburn See, used a paragraph from Shaw's *Saint Joan* for his Christmas card this year.

My dear love to you and to all my friends, as you see them. How far and far away, like fairy land, is that lovely summer we had together at Shawandassee in Connecticut. I missed your sister Dorothea. She never forgot me and was always so affectionate and remembering.

Stella Franklin

7.13 *From Henrietta Drake-Brockman, Perth*
Source: FP 33

Cottesloe
Feb 22nd [1940]

Dear Miles Franklin

A very pleasant surprise & very much appreciated. I had given away all my copies of that book, & know it is out of print—so am indeed happy to have a signed one. Some day, if I *ever* come to Sydney I shall maybe bring *Pioneers* across to get autographed too—I am beginning to feel I have quite a valuable collection of autographed first editions, people have so often been pleasant enough to give me.

I wouldn't be likely to forget meeting you: as I said in my letter to A & R (quite apart from interest in Miles Franklin writer) wit is such a rare thing in Australia that one is immediately pricked into sitting up & taking notice. I am glad you are working so hard & producing so much. I seem to be so submerged in growing family (believe me they take *far* more time as they grow up, & I did think it would be otherwise!)

A youthful portrait of West Australian writer Henrietta Drake-Brockman (Dorothy Welding, ML)

and so depressed with the stupid war & so censored by having a husband actively engaged in both the Civil Service and the army (what is left for me to 'have a go' at?) that my work has been moribund—

Regards, thanks, & lots of good wishes
Henrietta Drake-Brockman

K P S is in some ways sorry she is not joining you—but *I* am very glad she is staying here!

7.14   *To Dymphna Cusack, Bathurst, New South Wales*
Source: FP 30

Carlton
7 Mar [1940]

Dymphna my darlint, I was uplifted by your beautiful letter and its love of our siren Australia. That's right. The Gestapo can't do all it thinks fit here yet. We still have the behaviour if not the minds of a free people. The Corio bye election was a message to Menzies about conscription and a few things. You shd have heard some of the mothers talk about how they did not want to send their boys to the European shambles.

I hope you are feeling well and rested. I must see you when you are down at Easter—not long now. I have a document from Angus and R which looks painfully as if we had not yet cut out our hundred pounds. We must sit up some more interest.

I called on Jean Shain and she said she had had to get two copies of *Pioneers* to satisfy her clamoring clients. If she had had two hundred it wd be more to the point. I never saw one copy of it displayed anywhere and it was hardly ever mentioned. The book shops are rankly English Garrison. Not one single Aus book in Mullens window until Myra Morris's novel came and they gave it a facet of a window from top to bottom and big printed slips outside like an auction sale, which revived my spirits. I went to a number of libraries and saw no evidence of Australian literature and only in one book shop did I see

Australian books—*Man Shy*, Idriess and a few others. It shows that the Australian spirit as essenced in books must be powerful and deathless to persist and peep out now and again under the clouds and mountains and rivers of alien books all pushed by the sellers. Yes! let us go to. We must push *Pioneers* or if it does not sell it will be a clog on our next efforts. . . .

A queer situation met me in Melbourne. Baker OBE because I got that lit fellowship to help with the expenses immediately took a panic that I was going to concoct a fresh book and that she would not get sufficient recognition. Wrote to the Govt men and slandered me to everyone in Melbourne. I thought all would be well when I explained but not she still goes on fearing that she will not be the only one in the spot light. She has a grandeur delusion that she was the sole solace and grand inspirer in Furphy's life, a position not sustainable when the papers and other evidence are examined. It shows the poor soul is not much of a judge of character to have suspected me without even writing for an explanation after she had worked with me and saw the MSS. However it was a most salutary shindy. I was so enthusiastic and so full of admiration for her courage in face of deafness and increasing years that I was overly generous in painting her. I shall now be judicial. It was a surprise to find her feet were so large and of such *inferior* clay. It was as funny as that Angus and R poster in which your name was put so small that I seeking to put the limelight on another should myself be accused of hogging it. Oh well, poor little soul, it is her breath of life and I shall do everything compatible with literary and biographical proportion and perspective to let her retain her heroineship. I must however find out the facts of the situation before I proceed further. I can't be plagued by an amateur, suspicious and ignorant of all literary procedure. . . .

It was freezingly cold in Melb—fur coats were all the go. At Lake Cooper we had great big fires at night. It was lovely in the caravan. I slept in the car and waked up to see the stars and so many birds—black swans, duck, coots, sand-pipers and cranes right beside me. Oh lovely, lovely! and to see all the Furphy reunions and the wonderful country! Oh yes my darling daughter—it is good to be pitched out into our lovely, lovely land. People with the writing gift could spend a lifetime anywhere thinking about the land and learning the people and their idiom etc. . . .

Hoping to see you soon dearie, love from

[unsigned]

7.15 To Henrietta Drake-Brockman, Perth
Source: FP 33

Carlton
Ap 29 [1940]

Dear Henrietta D-B

I was so delighted by enclosed (par from *SMH*) to see that you are keeping our (empire) end up. You certainly are in high and highbrow company with Tagore, and the delight of diversity.

Yes, the demented war is paralysing to all human effort. You are in a tight corner as to freedom of pen but if we could make our minuses our plusses we'd be invincible, as Danny remarked when he used his wooden leg to empty his pipe. You have opportunities by reason of your official circle to do things impossible to the rebels so we must all keep bashing at whatever noxious insects we can hit for self-respect's sake. All the young talent coming up will be wasted again so we still have to carry on for them as well as for ourselves another debauched and wasted generation.

I struggle like a fly in tar but get no time and have no strength to achieve much. Angus and R are reprinting *Swagger* and rang up this week to say everything had been done now and they had forgotten to let me have proofs. I went weak at the knees from the blow—I had so wanted to improve on the *Bulletin* printing. Authors have the legal standing of illegitimacy in Australia, if that?

I wish you could hear how St John Ervine slangs *POP*. I chuckled at his whacks. If the book were as negligible as he thinks he wd not need to bash at it so fiercely. So I sent him some extracts from a letter received from a member of one of

26

the big clubs here whose signature I cannot decipher.

So long. I must get dinner, and mend socks and other things.

Good wishes and kind regards
[unsigned]

7.16 To Eleanor Dark, Katoomba, New South Wales
Source: FP 26

Wed morning May 8 40

Dear Eleanor

Sorry this is still hanging. I toiled to the Committee last night because of free speech. They quibbled about even that broad principle—tadpoles in a stagnant pond will never grow to frogs with powerful voices in anything but cheering a pugulist. There are a lot of oddments there now unknown to me—may have written masterpieces that I've missed—doubt it, as never except in rare exception such as Kipling does an outstanding creative literary mind and reaction go together.

They are still deferring (this is private of course—committee business must not be told outside), so Margery and Flora and I signed this coming out. (By the way the controversy was on a lovely manifesto submitted by Margery.) To send such letters will aid not deflect or diffuse more official pronouncements by writers. We shall need to keep persistently nagging at this question not make one hullabaloo and then let it lapse. So I send it back to you to get one or two of the names. They will all think it more entertaining to be asked by you than by me, I'm sure. I don't know Kylie's address. Dymphna's is High School Bathurst. She will stay a night with me in holidays. If you have it back then I cd get her name and post. X Herbert with a woman to hang on his every breath and not a chore or care in the world has found his work so sapping that he is away somewhere under doctor's orders. I wish he could follow in my tracks for a day and exercise might harden him as well as frustrate him.

To get back to point. It's not people like us that we want

to sign this thing (tho we must proclaim our view). If we cd get Dame Mary to lead the list you don't know what a triumph that would be and too much honor for her. If you get the others I'll undertake to call on her and coax her.

At any rate go ahead some way and I'll do what I can. Any letter will be a step in the right direction.

I meant to say that one of the oddments piously said we shd send no resolution to the Govt on Free Speech as a war was on—another said that such a resolution might make us lose our organization and position as writers. My God, Eleanor think of that for servile mindlessness. But this is private.

Can't you write a novel showing the non-existence of the Australian mind through colonial servility and through lack of exercise—it has atrophied. I'd try myself but I am so weary— much more broken down than Xavier I'll swan if I cd give way to it and your rapier mind cd make it entertaining.

Yours impatiently
[unsigned]

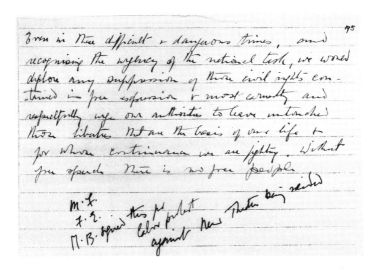

Draft protest against a raid on the New Theatre, Sydney, 1940 with the initials of Miles Franklin, Flora Eldershaw and Marjorie Barnard (source: FP *volume 46, ML)*

601 St Kilda Road
25th May 1940

Dear Miles

Miss Newsham rang last night. She has been very busy arranging for Miss Henry's move to a nursing home near Malvern, & has actually settled her into a room that was unfurnished. So she has all her own things round her, including her books. It is: St Ronan's, Adelaide Street Armadale. . . .

Terribly anxious times. It's quite a privilege to be concerned with someone whose life is just a matter of quiet arrangements, like Miss Henry or my mother. In these days, so far, the people for whom I'm most grieved *here* are the refugees, their anti-fascist reasons for being here at all not recognised, & their fears for everyone's future based on appalling experiences. I have a class of about fifty, for English—or rather for Australian affairs. I have had to abandon my rather historical syllabus in view of present events.

What a brilliant pamphlet that is of Stephensen's on Stephens! He is so curiously in Stephens' own vein, a sort of literary son, in 1940. I wish I had known Stephens better. Hugh McCrae brought him to see me once in Melbourne; but afterwards he was annoyed by me—some misunderstanding, he thought I was a well-off & influential person, because he had visited me in my aunt's large old house. So when I couldn't handle the *Bookfellow* for him (he sent me many fat receipt books) he thought I was smug & didn't write again for eight years or so, until he was publishing a new Neilson book. A gorgeous person he was really: I'm afraid he had many dis-illusionments & I was sorry he had to include me amongst them.

Well, if you write to Miss Henry at that address, it will seem more like home to her. Miss Newsham says she's more tranquil & can now read a little.

Good wishes; & promises to keep you in touch with your friend Alice Henry

Nettie Palmer

Carlton
May 31 40

Dear Nettie

I'm so grateful to you for keeping me informed of Miss Henry: I know the burden even one extra letter can be. Needless to say I have been writing to her about twice a week since the moment you informed me that she was deposited at the hospital, so she must have forgotten that she received the letters. She is so restless, it makes it hard for herself and nurses.

I am rather amused by your tale of A G S's discrimination against you as a plot: he was very exacting. A pity in this instance, as he surely would have had delight in you. After him no one held the floor more worthily than yourself. We have had many brilliant critics but they did only sporadic work—you were more continuous. P R S's paper on A G S is certainly vivid. He has real ability as a journalist.

It must be interesting to be among the refugees: some of them must have suffered. Have you come across the kind which is filling—for example—one of our suburbs? They are engendering great bitterness. They are refugees, or trade as such, but they have sufficient means to buy for cash blocks of flat buildings which at a minimum would run well into four figures, as all the provision and fruit shops. As one Australian put it last night, 'My two poor boys have enlisted to go overseas and these (animals) come here and dig in protected and easy. When my lads come back silly from what they have been through over there, they'll have no places.' Also many complaints that these refugee shop keepers always weigh over the amt asked for and charge a penny or so extra. The people are banding together to accept nothing beyond the exact weight ordered.

A year or two ago I sat down beside a certain Dr something employed at the Uni who first thing said that the govt here was quite right to keep Kisch out they shd have not let him land at all. In my early days in the USA I knew hundreds of refugees from Ghettos and pogroms. In five years the males had citizenship and votes and were industrious in opposing votes for the women of America, women whose mothers had borne their children under hard conditions and pioneered the prairies.

I am for religious liberty (tho I regard certain religions as fascism) but the Jews go beyond religion and reduce intermingling with gentiles to miscegenation. Can you give me an answer to these problems.

Another example. The fine needleworkers from Vienna make beautiful things and our elite love to purchase them because they are helping the dear refugees and the things are so cheap. The trade unionists cannot get at these sweated workers and undersellers of local labor because the refugees all swear that they are highly paid and fully satisfied tho the evidence is quite different.

Where is your daughter now, or did she return? I am sick at the paranoia of slaughtering all the blue-eyed fair-haired youth, German or British, and those slavering hordes of Islam and Mongol thought breeding and breeding. There is no rest for the foot of the soul these days.

Yours
[unsigned]

7.19 To Katharine Susannah Prichard, Perth
Source: FP 21

Carlton
June 6 1940

Dear Katherine Susannah Prichard

Did you see in *Pioneers on Parade* I made Prim say that all the good Australian writers were in WA or dead. I had you and Henrietta D-B in mind. I like rolling out your names— no Essie and Bessie and Sissie about them but some good Boadicea body in them. Furphy also spent the last of his life in Perth. I am finishing up the biography of him—you will be surprised to find I give you honorable mention in its pages.

I heard you were coming to live with us and my heart was lifted, but I hear your plans were changed. By the way, do you know of our grand Commonwealth Literary Fund and the fellowships it awards. I got a half one—great lift. Xavier Herbert is revelling in his chance to do his second novel as he wishes and so is Frank Davison. It occurs to me, are you rich— if not why not at once get a fellowship. It is not a dole or a pension or any of those things that annoy us—it is something to be proud of and we are so desirous of having the first class writers helped by it—have to watch it doesn't get down in standard. So do come in with us. This is confidential—private please, but your name would be grand to help the thing along. In these mad days we shall need our writers more than ever and want to keep this fund going.

Communicate with Mr H S Temby, Sec Commonwealth Literary Fund, c/o Prime Minister's Dept, Canberra. Mr Temby is so nice and approachable—no fuss and feathers or airs at all.

Excuse me taking up your time but in these days one clings to the thought of friends who are congenial. How is all going to end. Shall we be able to help or shall we be merely straws on the wind as the poor boys are a bit of debris in that horrible old Europe.

My love and good wishes
[unsigned]

Carlton
June 30 1940

Well Mary my darling, T M and I had a lovely meeting over
the poems. In arrangement he had placed 'Lion' for the first
as the poet had ruled out 'Process'. You can imagine how I
chuckled and poked it at him. He winked at me at last and
I had to be content with that. He says the grandeur of it worked
on him. I find that with intuition I can jump a lot of hard
work—it's great to have intuition as well as brains!!!!!

Well my dear as the hours roll around in our day I fit them
to your night and wonder with all my heart what sort of a
night you are having. Then I go to a neighbor to listen-in and
feel like a nurse watching who is glad the night has passed so
well.

I send this. It may reach you. Hitler may have stubbed his
blitz krieg toe on something long before it gets a week away
from these shores. All the women in our street are making
pyjamas or socks to keep the men dressed. I remember those
lovely socks and pyjamas last war. I had the distributing of
them to the poor worn Serbs—they were sent to our hospitals
there when our own men left Lemnos. Some of us are going
in for a few hens—all to help with the food supply as the blight
of Hitler settles down on Europe in the cold weather.

I'm afraid I'm not strong enough to go to the Front this time
and would only be eating up the food and cluttering the
horizon, but if things tighten up I'll go and cook or something
for our own army here. I feel that for those of us who are not
tradesmen or nurses or such the wisest thing is to keep life going
normally as much as possible—keep the home fires burning sort
of business. Life has to go on.

We are having such a mild winter so far. I have not needed
a fire all this week. I lit one and we all complained of being
over-hot.

You will remember my lovely trip to the Furphy country.
Instead of going back to West A Sam and his wife have stayed

33

at Lake Cooper and are taking on the old farm where his grandparents came in 1868 so the nice grandson who was living in it could enlist. Charlie Furphy was such a dear, so gentle and yet he felt he had to go. He is a bachelor so has no family to leave behind. Sam is 61 and is delighted to be doing such a grand thing as running a farm in this crisis. He had retired and feels right in things again now. Always wanted to be a farmer but he was apprenticed to the foundry. It is lovely for me as I feel they have not gone right out of reach.

I must not fill up the mails with too much stuff. We can't say much for fear it might go astray and tell too much.

Much love my dear to you and Jean and Denis and Eileen

Miles

7.21 *To May and Phil Meggitt, Cheshire*
Source: FP 34

Carlton
July 6 1940

Dear Girls

Where are you and how are you? Right in it I know. May as nurse and Phil as teacher. I wish you would come with the children to Australia and I could see you. I have a spare room to put you up and it would be joy to see you once again.

I'd be glad of an occasional newspaper. We are so far away from the centre of things and I suppose news can't be told for fear of informing the enemy.

We are having a warm dry winter and are past the shortest day which means that in Europe the short days are coming which may help to defeat Hitler. Of course we know no facts out here but England has most of the French fleet is the latest. It does seem if the French had only stuck to the British they could have cleared up the Mediterranean. I wonder if the French think they ever can get free. I always fit our time here to yours over there and wonder what sort of a night England has had.

All our men are enlisting. My brother and nephew live with

me; the nephew is under age, but hankering to join up—poor boys, it seems terrible that all the male world has to go mad at intervals. We all missed our chances after the last war. I hope we shall make a better fist of the peace this time.

I have a lemon tree heavy with ripe fruit at the back door: the guavas are just done and the loquats are coming on. I am sitting by a fire made of sunflower stalks and the wood pruned from a plum tree, and all is so quiet and peaceful. Not a sound in the street, no apprehension of raids and every shop full of butter and sugar and all sorts of food. I hope we will be able to help Europe in the ghastly days that must come.

I have not written many books since I saw you. . . . I am editing and arranging a friend's poems now. It seems futile work in face of the war din in Europe, but culture will survive war, and poetry still be a national need.

I shall help in every way I can as things go on. There is a great crowd rushing to serve in every capacity at present, and it is better for us older ones to keep as much of life normal as possible. We are all looking forward to having some British children and hope their parents will come later to take them home and in some cases to stay altogether.

Do let me hear from you. My dear love and happy remembrance of our times together in the war and after. Remember me to Mrs Meggitt and Miss Evans.

[unsigned]

7.22 *From Tom Inglis Moore, Sydney*
Source: FP 29

Thornleigh
Mon night, July 15 1940

Dear Miles

Finale! Hallelujah! Hurrah! Thank Gawd! and other expressions of chortling. Herewith the Preface to Poems by 'E'. I'm awfully sorry that I can't rejoice equally in the job itself. I've said most of the things I wanted to say—leaving the Spring

Books, Superintendent Gulls & the Undoing Violets etc as scraps of largesse for you—but I'm afraid the writing is only f.a.q.—if that!

What with the B—war, enlisting, moving, shifting furniture, laying linoleums (a helluva job which has kept me cussing on the kitchen floor most of today) etc, I haven't been able to prosecute the Preface with those undivided energies & last ounces of effort imperative at this critical juncture of the campaign for 'E's' victory. I'm sorry. Excuse me. Please run your eye over my long-winded (Eight pages no less!) panegyric & tell me frankly & Franklinly what to cut out & amend. Let me know when you are ready to put the boot in, & we'll hold another session. In the meantime I'll try to finish making my suggested list of the order for the Poems to bring that along. Hope the typing is going OK. Will be called up for the AIF on Aug. 6, so the sooner we meet the better.

Taut à toi
Tom

7.23 To Alice Henry, Melbourne
Source: FP 11

Carlton
July 17 1940

Dearest Pops

I am so glad to have two letters from you; while I was trying to spring off my tail with one—very feeble, tail and all these days. First of all let me remark how happy you are to have Isabel. If I could win the Irish sweep (without having a ticket, by the way) I'd immediately invite Isabel to be my secretary for a year hoping she would accept and that her family could spare her.

The *True Thomas* by Wood has returned accompanied by Hillman's story. It looks most enticing. How well I remember that early photo of Sidney. . . . Before I can start Sidney I must finish the *Life* of Havelock Ellis because I have to return it. I find it very interesting and very sad—shows how the generation immediately above me is all gone or going—and it is the generation immediately preceding us that makes the whole roof of existence. You will remember Mrs Ellis in Chicago. I think she was honest; but never attractive to me physically or personally so I turned her over to Ethel Mason as much as possible. I remember Miss Addams invited me to Hull House to meet her and combat her very English criticism of America. It was very funny. I remember the nights with her at the Little Theatre with Margery Curry Dell et al.

What a lovely thing Olive Schreiner was, but in the volume of her letters I gathered that Ellis had made a great mess of her life. Had she used half the energy in writing her novel that she wasted in blithering to him about the writing of it it wd have been out in its day instead of assembled by her wonderful husband after her death when its tide had passed. I always thought of O S as a girl of my own age because I did not read *African Farm* till I was twenty but I see she was a grown woman before I was born. I wish I had Editha to discuss this life with. I remember what she said of Ellis, with which I agree. I combat many of his pronouncements. I never cease missing Editha.

A big roll of clippings has just come in the door. . . . Considering the lack of all justice and logic in men and the sequaciousness and docility and servility of women I dunno how this world will work out or how it can be discovered to be anything but a limbo where the throw-outs were chucked by some master of creation. However, we are helpless.

Love and good night
[unsigned]

Carlton
Sept 17 1940

Dearest Mrs Robins

I am sending this little note to keep the life lines open, as there is a mail tomorrow.

Please send me a portion of the Sunday papers now and again—no matter how old—stick a stamp on it and do not worry whether there is a mail or not—it will get here some time. I so want to hear what the American women are doing about plans for some sensible way of life when this lunacy which is devastating Europe and Asia comes to an end.

I wish I had that quotation from a speech by Mr Robins wherein he said something to the effect that in spite of the rapacity and brutality of men the women managed each year to save a few children and rear up another generation.

Of course as the struggle grows more brutal the air will be more and more poisoned and we shall not be allowed to utter a sane thought at all.

For the present we try to keep the way open for freedom and constitutional civil rights. We (that means the Fellowship of Australian Writers of which I am an executive member) participated in a cultural conference. It was held in our Club Rooms by a central delegate body to which we are affiliated. I enclose our programme. It was very inspiring because our cultural leaders took part. Mr Cleary, head of our National (that means Government) broadcasting stations opened in a splendid pronouncement.

Many people had to be turned away from the public meeting at night. . . .

I have not had a letter from one of our fraternity for some time. One from dear Mrs Post was the latest. I hope you all are well. By one or two reviews of Elizabeth Robins's book it must be delightful. She was of course always the double artist—actress and author.

> Dear love and hoping to hear from you
> Stella M Franklin

I wrote to M E D some time ago and sent her some book if I remember. I hope she is well.

7.25 To C Hartley Grattan, Sydney
Source: FP 23

> Carlton
> Sept 18 1940

Dear C Hartley Grattan

What a delight it is to have you here again before your contacts have withered by separation—to me a special satisfaction that I did not have to wait as long as I generally have to for what I foresee to swing into operation.

You may remember one Sunday at Palm Beach I was asked as to my political orientation and you helped me out of my nebulosity. That awakened me from drifting and though the war increased and for a time caused a relapse into confusion I now have my mind clear and it will be interesting to compare notes in a real talk before you go.

An American review of *Propaganda for War* caused me to have it specially imported. I read it with tremendous interest in as well as experience of its sources at work. I wonder are there any other copies out here. Minds are too sealed by Britain to read it now, but it would be a light on American outlook and some of the reasons for it. It prepared me for *The Deadly Parallel*: the two books interact.

The letter which you did not get before leaving told you a little of the enterprise in writing an autobiography of Furphy. I took an extra copy of the MS on thin paper especially for you, so if you have not discarded interest in that subject you could take it as recreational reading on the voyage home.

Your domestic happiness is lovely—wife and wean—the red lantern under your coat to salt your work these days with the savour of the coming reunion.

Sincerely
[unsigned]

7.26 *To Mary Fullerton, Sussex*
Source: FP 119

Carlton
Sept 26 1940

Mary my dear

It does not seem as if there could be any joy left in the world. I hope you are safe. The family would let Em know and she would let me know if there was any cable news. It makes us sick to read the papers, but I think it is healthier to be in the midst of action—that is psychologically healthier—than to be at a distance full of grief and apprehension for one's friends.

I shall keep on writing every week in hopes that some letters get through. . . .

I enclose a few clippings.

We've had a great election here; not yet fully decided because preferences have not been counted and absentee votes have yet to come. Mr Justice Evatt of the High Court of Australia resigned his judicial position to contest the electorate in which Carlton is situated. I am interested to see how he'll pan out for Australia. He is very clever. Knows much about constitutions and international and inter-dominion and Empire law. Also he is literary having a number of books to his credit. *Rum Rebellion*, about Bligh the most noteworthy, and he has just finished a biography on Holman which has high praise by outsiders and which is utterly condemned in the sections known to the ex-premiers and such who have lived the parts. I have not read it and am not competent to judge anyhow. It is priced a guinea and got out by A and R. The luck of a Chinaman to coincide with the Election racket. It has one of A and R's windows to itself. Has a photo and cartoons of Holman and an oil painting of the judge in his wiggery to attract attention.

It reminds me I have not yet congratulated our member on his victory which is difficult I being in the position of the fly on the wheel, but not like the fly being complacent enough to think it is I who have made any dust.

I am just adding 'Jerry's Wooing' and 'Lupins and Guns' to the list of uncopied poems by my poet. I have heard nothing of my book of poems or my book of biography yet and the Govt literary subsidy has all been apportioned—So!

I sent about three weeks ago my explanatory note to the poems, and a fortnight ago T M's introduction. I hope these got through.

I have nothing to tell you personally except that I can just stay alive and that is all. I wish I had the pluck to lie down and die and be done with it.

My love to you all always
Miles

7.27 *From Katharine Susannah Prichard, Perth*
Source: FP 21

Greenmount
October 14 1940

Dear Miles

So many times I've intended to write to you—and always the things that have to be done have prevented. I meant to congratulate you on your success with *All that Swagger*—which I enjoyed so much, and which a friend of mine is always talking about. Declares she knows all the people! *Pioneers on Parade* is a fine piece of work too, and I was delighted to know you and Kate Baker are to collaborate on a biography of Furphy. Overdue, as I am in saying all this, I feel you are the sort of person who would know I was thinking it, and that my strenuous days do not give me a chance to do half the amiable things I'd like to.

Sometimes, I'm sure I work harder than any body in the world. And at so many different sorts of jobs—keeping house for my beautiful son who is grown-up now, cooking, sweeping, washing, mending etc, organisational work and lectures, and somewhere in between, I've got to find time to write and earn my living. All this, most of the time with head and heart too weary for words, and the terrible pressure of financial anxieties never growing less.

Such a wail! But by way of reply to your letter which was removed from my writing table when the police called, with a great deal of other material which has not yet been returned. It was good of you to write about applying for the grant. I thought of doing so; but the present crisis makes it unlikely that my application would be favoured. It would be heavenly to work without fretting how bills are to be paid, and having to stop and do some footling money-making article in the middle of a book. One doesn't get any younger either, and there's so much I want to do. . . .

Have you seen Hartley Grattan, I wonder? He was in the West only for two days, and I only just caught a glimpse of him at the Fellowship meeting. Usually very dull shows here, and everybody scared stiff to discuss anything political. Comical for men and women growed to be so afraid to think. I like H G's quick, critical brain, the way he sums up and yet leaves a margin for quirks and queries. Of course, some of our bourgeois liberals (?) cant 'afford to be seen in public' with me, these days. . . .

They don't affect me really. My mind is serene and undaunted. Come what may, I am content to serve my star, the well-being of humanity, in the only way, which as far as I can see, it may be served.

Love to you, my dear, and do forgive me for not having written before,

Yours sincerely
Katharine Susannah

Carlton
Nov 21 1940

My dearest Mary ... On Tuesday evening I went out to the
University, where they were holding the dinner or a dinner of
the English Association. (You can see what this is by consulting
the front leaf of *Southerly*.) Well, Bishop Pilchard (Co-adjutor
to our Sydney Archbishop) proposed the toast of the Eng Ass
and a young Dr Mitchell a member of the Uni faculty replied.
Then Neville Cardus was to have proposed the toast of
Australian Lit. and I to reply. But Neville (whom they call a
refugee) did not turn up at the last moment—probably he got
a last-minute entry to the Noel Coward celebrations which were
proceeding on a lickspittle scale in town, among all the war
profiteers and social arrivistes. So at the last minute they ran
in Inigo Jones the great Queensland weather man. I was
enchanted with the opportunity to meet him. He is 71, but young
and vigorous in manner, figure and mind, and all the charm and
simplicity of the thoughtful and meditative great. Mr H M
Green was chairman at top of top table, I on his left and the
Bishop on his right. Next to me my dear Inigo, and then a
collection of clerics of great antiquity. I am sorry that I am
delerious with fright before I have to speak so I did not get the
joy of Inigo as I should have done. He is going home to get
my books and read them aloud to his family. Said he was sure
that a person who could speak so inspiringly and movingly must
write great books. I said his family might be justified in getting
a divorce after such an infliction.

Well, ye Bishop, a nice looking man in his gaiters and shoes
&c with white soft hands and the real Oxford Haw Haw got
up and blurbed desultorily about the glories of the English
tongue—none other so beautiful and he said the Danish was
a hideous language and a Danish wife of one of the profs present
did not agree. There was a table of University people. Then this
toast was replied-to by Dr Mitchell of the English faculty. (The
sort of man who is engrossed in where the accent shd go on

43

pronouncing Priapus.) He was young and inexperienced and said all he had to say in two minutes and then went on burbling for half-an-hour, and everyone was dozing. The Bishop's talk was not meant to be condescenscious but it was just the sort of thing that has emptied the Church of England and which alienates all robust common Australians. Haw! Haw! Deah! Deah! . . .

Then dear old Mr Jones got up and spoke extempore on Australian lit—not his subject. It was a privilege to hear him no matter what he said, and what he said was very good about the glorious field for writers we had here, and said with the nice quiet mildness of the scientist: but very short, only a few minutes and I had to arise. I had prepared a 20 min. address. I said it was a great privilege to have Mr Jones with us to speak on any subject, but if we could have had him on his own we would all stay till midnight, so it was good it was literature that he so kindly came, to rescue, as I knew how tired he was after a hard day. I then said I'll give a few examples why the great masterpieces that were in Australia's scene were not yet forthcoming. I said I once went up the country with Mr Frank Clune. I said Mr Frank Clune was a very great man, and paused to note the faces. I knew what they would think of a person who thought F C great. I said he cd go into a bookshop and demand the head of the outfit and when that person came say, 'You lousy cow, do you ever give an Aussie writer a chance?' and I proceeded, 'I have chosen one of Mr Clune's milder expressions among his warmly and richly idiomatic ones out of deference to the gentility and respectability of this occasion.' There was a good round of laughter, especially from the table of profs and sub-profs. So then I sailed along very seriously and sadly. I said our period had ended as completely as that of the Elizabethans or Victorians and now awaited only the dismantling. It reminded me of an animal which I had seen running for some distance before it fell to the bullet which had taken its life. My final sentence was, 'If I have given you tonight a text instead of a toast it is because I feel that any toast to any presages or vestiges of the Australian literature that could have been should be in the form of Hail and Farewell.' And I sat down.

Then I escaped. Went across the University grounds to the slum street through which I cd get a short cut to tram homeward bound. Gate locked. A student climbing out over the top. It had barbed wire on the top and as I was in a black net evening frock I climbed out through the middle panel quite easily, glad to find that despite discommoding fluffy skirts etc and advancing years I am not yet decrepit.

Oh what I started out to tell you was that I sat next to H M Green and he said he has been asked to do a very select anthology, very exclusive for the Limited Editions society and did I know of any poems that should be in it. There was my chance. I said I had a poet that had to go in and would take it as an act of friendship to have some in. He said friendship had nothing to do with it. I said I understand that or you would be no person to make the selection, but if you don't choose some of these I'll say out loud that you were too mediocre to see their merit. He said he had seen the two articles in *Aust Natl Review* and did not like any of the poems therein. So yesterday I spent the forenoon assembling the poems and Tom's and my prefaces and sent them to him. I hope he takes two, or even one, as it will be something if the other opening keeps off too long. . . .

Then I went to the House of Parliament and was entertained in one of the rooms by Mr Mutch and some other members. Mr Mutch is a Trustee of the Mitchell library and took me through the new building of the Public Library which is joined on to it. A lovely reading hall: the building of our beautiful sand stone and all around the top frieze splendidly executed bas-reliefs but all of ancient Egyptian and such subjects winged bulls &c not one suggestion of an Australian motif. Oh my God, what crawlers. They are not fit to desecrate this unspoiled continent. The American libraries have such gorgeous murals of their pioneering deeds.

In a newsreel yesterday it said Westminster Abbey has been hit. It went through in a short glimpse but it looked to me as if half of it had gone. Has it? And where are you keeping Queen Mary that she is never mentioned at all. The king and queen are certainly keeping to their job did you see that lovely little poem to the Queen in a Chicago paper? I can't find it but it was something about London Bridge is falling down my faire ladye, but you donned your bravest smile, your gayest gown and stayed in town, my faire ladye, the London Bridge is falling down. She deserves that tribute—evidently a brave little woman, and George a decent man, doing well in a tremendous job and a crashing responsibility. And Edward with his courtesan still playing in a goldfish pond in far safety.

Now to your letter. . . . Yes, I always did resist Havelock Ellis's findings. He hadn't enough experience and give in him to make them right according to imagination as well as to scientific laboratory work. He was the delving mole trying to fly and made a squawking mess. His burblings to poor Edith about his fancies when she was mad enough to love him so were egregious. We had her in Chicago when she was undergoing that torment, poor woman—and this gentlemanly revelation explains things she said. In those days of splendid experiment in breaking bonds some women tried to stretch outside their capacity and I think Edith Ellis was one and I think she was very brave. Olive S of course was cracked to come out stark naked. I always consider that he ruined her and was the cause of her genius petering out in egotism without further performance. . . .

Yes that dead funk is a terrible thing to witness. I know what it is to feel terror through my stage fright. The torture of it is something beyond belief but I have never run away yet, but it shows me that I might, and I'd hate to act like a coward. It is bad enough to feel like one.

[unsigned]

Carlton
Feb 8 1941

Dear Mr Moir

I love your Christmas card—of all things in the way of a picture I dote on pencil drawings, and the trees in this are lovely—and all imported, of course. The native beauties are as banished and vanished as the aboriginals.

A propos of aborigines, went recently to a meeting called to get publicity for the blackfellow's struggle to get a vote and other rights, but alas, it seemed to me that each and every spouter with one exception had some axe to grind on the authentic Australians' cause.

I was going to send you a pc at Christmas but could not find your address. Then was going to write immediately but mislaid your card. Now I have found it but have not your letter so may miss some points. I think you asked me about the Furphy biography. I have let it lie since going on for a year now. K B has spoiled my joy in it. I don't know what she wants. My plan to call it 'by Miles Franklin and Kate Baker' because she gave me a lot of the best of the material resulted in her campaign of misrepresentation, and I don't want to upset her. Too much grief and agony in the world without my hurting the poor soul or disturbing her life's illusion that she invented Furphy.

Is the Hawthorne Press still continuing to publish special books? Is there any hope of your coming over to Sydney? If you do be sure you let me know. ...

Christmas wishes for next year

Sincerely
Miles Franklin

Carlton
March 11th 1941

Dear Dr Evatt

There is a vast principle involved in this Blamey impasse so I
was glad to see by yesterday's *Sun* that it was listed for
consideration. Blamey should not be allowed to get away with
it. If the Army can defy the Government we are back to the
bad old days when we were garrisoned—a poor prospect for
democracy in the new order. However, I need not stress this to
the author of *Rum Rebellion*. No one is better qualified to detect
and dissect the dangers of the situation. That such dangers are
accumulating are to be seen from the paragraph in today's
Telegraph which reports bumptious caste criticism of Mr
Fadden's manner of taking the salute.

In a time of grave national danger when all available citizens
have to take on military service in a people's army it should
be correct for our civilian prime minister, his deputy or any of
his parliamentary colleagues to take the salute in any courteous
manner natural to him.

I hope you are well and flourishing.

Kind regards from
Miles Franklin

Carlton
March 16 1941

My dear, dear Arnold and Louise

Why haven't you written to me? I wrote last. That I have been on the verge of writing to you for years is to be seen by the date on the enclosed clipping about Holland House. I meant to write on receiving it from Miss Fullerton. Do you remember my little party in Kensington when I took several of you, including my aunt and Miss Fullerton to see Holland House? Alas, it is destroyed by bombs. I had a late cutting to that effect but have mislaid it for the present. Well my aunt is still alive and living in a Sydney suburb. Miss Fullerton is in Sussex right in the track of the Luftwaffe but when I last heard was safe. . . .

I wonder if you are still able to communicate with Holland. If so I wish you would find out about my friends there—the family of the late Senator Stoffel. Simon Stoffel, I believe was in the engineering business. I knew his two sisters Lise and Hendrika Stoffel. Their address is Kapjessewell 3, Deventer, Holland. I went to the Red Cross but discovered that only near blood relatives were allowed to communicate. I saw a lot of Hendrika in London and should so much like to know if they are safe. I always dreamed of going to stay with them.

The world is in a sorry mess. To read of what Europe and Asia are suffering is enough to break one's heart.

Have you had any late news of Mab? Perhaps she is with you. If you are writing give her my love and tell her I wrote suggesting that she should come to me on her way to America, the other way about she would not be able to endure my humble inconveniences after the luxury of USA.

I am pegging along at nothing. I wish I could have a yarn with you but don't want to make too much trouble for the censor. The East Indian Dutch are sending us their best ocean liner fitted as a hospital ship. We are very fond of the Dutch

49

here and before the war were organizing to have some come as migrants.

Are your family still in Amsterdam and if so are they safe? Do write and tell me some personal news. How is Mark? Is he a big fellow like the gentlemen in the picture enclosed? or has he got thin?

I am indebted to my American friend for weeklies and other newspapers.

You can write anything you like to me. I have had only one letter opened by the censor, that was from a friend who is fiercer against Hitler than Chamberlain is so the censor must have been refreshed by such fine sentiments. We are of course not allowed to mention any military doings or to indulge in defeatism going out of the country, but outsiders can say anything in the way of opinion they like coming in. We still have the habits and manners of a free people.

I haven't any thing interesting to tell you so will wind up with my dear love as of old and every good wish

[unsigned]

7.32 *To Mary Fullerton, Sussex*
Source: FP 18

Carlton
Ap 20 1941

My dear Mary, I have not been writing as I shd. Your letter of Feb 9 arrived duly a fortnight since. . . .

I have nothing more to report re my own poet. I hope you got the copy of the letter received from Sec of Lit Fund and my reply. Not a line since another meeting next month which may be postponed to await Mr M's return. If he joins the war cabinet over there we'll have to get on without him. It must be a comfort to Mr Churchill to have a fresher younger and fat man come from the furthest extremity of the globe to support him.

I wish America would police Iceland and let loose those

80,000 Canadians to support the Greeks. They would be used to the cold—not send our poor boys tired with the desert already and still wanted in the desert.

The Japs going to pounce southward as soon as Hitler gets to Suez which he is to do in the matter of ten days now. Once before he was to get somewhere in a fortnight and is still not there. Though the latest raids on London are alarming. I have been reading Margery Spring Rice's document on the half starved women of England. One wonders as a friend of mine says how long such flesh and blood can hold out and one also wonders why people who have never had a square meal or any holidays or relief shd want to hold out. What did they get but betrayal by the Mosleys and such after the last war who went right on in their old privilege supported by plunder. We have too many of that class in fat jobs out here but they at least have pleasanter manners than our business gangsters who are rigging themselves into all the big producing monopolies as heads of munitions doing and so on.

It is a dreadful thing to feel that never anywhere again will there be safety. There will always be some conquest maniac arise and with long range air machines and mighty explosives it is a poor look out. Think what a mess Hitler's blitzkreig would have made on a city piled as high as New York and so concentrated.

We in Sydney are as wide spread as London I should think but only about an eighth of London's density so wd probably suffer about an eighth of London's casualties.

America says if England can hold out till 1942 they will be able to help her turn the tide, but it is a long way to 1942 and Hitler is making the most of it. I think the Australians would give in after one blitz here. I have been studying the ordinary common people. They have no need of free expression, don't miss any liberties in that line that are suppressed in aid of war so long as they have beer and betting they are all right. . . .

With love and good wishes to you all
Your ever loving friend
[unsigned]

Carlton
June 30, 1941

Dear Stella

Thank you so much for sending the paper. I am interested in the women of Australia, and that they think they should have the same set-up for women in the Government that we have here. I hope, however, that when they get that set-up they will not think they have done all they should do. The Bureau will then have to have help in getting an adequate appropriation, otherwise it will not be able to function properly. It is a constant fight for a larger appropriation. Even now, when we are in an unlimited emergency and our work has practically doubled, we have been unable to get any material increase in appropriation. Men will almost always weep for children, and they will do things for men, but women go sort of in between and most men never think that women can do anything but housekeeping and should not do anything else even though they (men) are calling upon them every day to enter into the defence industries; the Army and Navy are calling for the employment of women, and the office of Production Management holding back.

The outlook of the World is not very encouraging, but we are determined that dictatorship shall not be forced upon the peoples of the earth.

I wonder how you are and how you are getting along? I am eager to know of your success with your books. I am also wondering how Miss Henry is? I do hear from her now and then. Mrs Post is fine—she doesn't seem as well as she used to, but is fine both physically and mentally. She says she is now 86 years old. She has a cousin living with her.

Mrs Robins isn't so well, but still up and going. Mr Robins is walking in a walking-chair, but does not leave the place any more. However, people go to him for help in their problems and that keeps him going very well. They do the same with Mrs Robins. They have been a great help to their community. Some

weeks ago the University of Florida conferred the degree of
Doctor of Laws upon Mr Robins.

I, too, had that same honour bestowed on me a couple of
weeks ago, by Smith College.

Write me a line now and then. Much love to you.

Mary Anderson

7.34   To Desmond Fitzgerald, Dublin
Source: FP 33

Carlton
July 13 1941

Dear Desmond Fitzgerald

Your letter, posted Ap 29, reached me yesterday, so the conquest
of man by the machine is resulting in written communication
taking as long as it did in the days of sailing ships.

Your letter has the reviving quality of a congenial handclasp
from an understanding friend. It brought back those days of
delightful association with Dubliners—yes it was unbelievable
happiness compared with today, if only we had known. We
thought then we were on top of the worst. Out here we suffer
terribly from war malaise. Those at the heart of the holocaust
seem to be borne up by the exaltation of great tragedy and self-
sacrifice while our spiritual and mental vitality is enervated by
the dread spectacle of Europe and Asia and the exportation of
the flower of our young sires—from our small population.

I have referred to my files as you direct and note what was
happening as you wrote, and there was much of the same later.
I am glad the clippings reached you, I see now that Eire is on
the list of places to which we are forbidden to send newspaper
clippings. I am sorry because I have some literary fragments that
I'd like to send. . . .

I have just been re-reading Yeats's *Dramatis Personae* which
I possess. I get much from it. . . .

There was an exquisite content in so many of those books
from Ireland—Moore and Yeats, Stephens, dozens of others—

they wrote not only like men inspired by genius but as artists who took their craft seriously—it is tragic that that should be bashed and exploded out of human society.

Goodness knows to what the war situation will have advanced by the time you get this so comment is useless. You apologise for your undercurrent of depression. I have suffered despair to such an extent that had I the pluck of Virginia Woolf I wd do as she did, but also had I that pluck I would not do as she did because of that pang you mention to perhaps a few sensitive souls here and there. Because what is, is also always what it isn't, which you as a Celt will catch on the wing.

I am sending you one of my books. I hope it reaches you. Also I hope you did not go to any trouble about the rights of that literary prize.

I don't know how to address you is it Senator or what? Once a parliamentarian out here has been a minister he is Hon for the rest of his life.

With very best wishes and kind regards. I am so pleased I wrote to you and have been revived by your response.

Sincerely
[unsigned]

7.35 To Ian Mudie, Adelaide
Source: IMP

Carlton
July 20 1941

Dear Ian Mudie

Your book of poems is intoxicating to me. I think you have gone farther than any of us in capturing the spirit of Australia. It is easier for a poet of course, first admitting that real poetry is the highest product of the human intellect.

I would have to quote the whole booklet to convey my satisfaction to you. *Corroboree to the Sun* is full of urge. I'd like to take lines from it—would have to take them all. Similarly with *Earth* and *Landscape* 'Beauty and age are here and loveliness destroyed. But no one cares.' *Sheep to Kangaroo* 'Kaurna are gone: their skulls stare down from the shelves, I see where once the grass was shoulder high—'

Yes I have had the nostalgic anguish of going back to the places where I was bred and born—they are part of my being—they are my being—and there I found little tracks amid the tussocks where we had gone for geebungs and such treasures, all grown to wide gaping chasms—acres of erosion. The trees in which I had gloried, under which I had nestled snug on writing days, all dead; and a few more sheep bleating. Yes. Yes. Must it be?

There is splendid urge and challenge and anger born of worship in your poems. And ah, also there is nostalgia—gentle nostalgia. It can be a weak and debilitating element; it has been much debunked, but you might as well try to blight man into a robot by freeing him from emotion, as eliminate the power to feel keenly. Nostalgia is one of the most indelible and arresting of elements in literature—even Hitlerism couldn't purge it from us. The dying guanaco goes to his native spot to die: cattle will make back 'home' to sparse places from fat ones.

It's no use trying to write about your poems: I wish we could sit together by a fire and go over them, savoring their lines and intentions, & splendid achievement: 'Give me a land where rain is rain—patters dust on tin roofs' etc. I think galvanised iron one of the prettiest and best and wholesomest roofs in the world and I adore it because of the joy I get out of rain upon it. It was a great drop to me when I got into tall rookeries and had to look outside to see if it were raining.

July 21 I did not finish this last evening because a lovely young writer, Joan Browne by name, came in and I handed her your poems and we switched to reading them to one another. *Mental Expatriates*; *Retreat of a Pioneer*, all of them—we had a great time.

This morning I heard of a death of an acquaintance and a friend, and that finishes me for a time. . . .

The acquaintance was a young half-Chinese, who for a long time was very ill at ease with himself: clever, always rose at meetings and spoke at length, mostly against who-ever was speaking. I did not see him for some time then at a meeting where I spoke on Furphy, and incidentally lamented that the old Australian spirit stood a chance of being extirpated like the bandicoots. This young man rose and spoke at length. I had expected to be torn to shreds, but no, to my surprise, I found that he had reconciled his Chineseness with his Australianness—proud of his connection with an ancient race—and loved Australia, had vanquished his discomforts. He commended me highly and said that he disagreed about the danger of the Australian spirit going, that if all we Australians—real Australians, who understood Australia, stood together etc. Of course this was most comforting to me; just the way in which I was longing to be contradicted. Afterwards he said he and I must meet to have a full talk. Today I learn that he is three weeks gone. Gone leaving that silence that the aborigines have left so intrinsically upon this land.

The other friend was R Baker. Go to the Adelaide Library and look up his book *Australian Flora and Applied Art*. There was a pioneer, a little Englishman who came out here and gave up high remuneration in one job to take a pittance so he could do research into Australian things. He was intoxicated with Australian Flora as were the Griffins who designed Canberra. He was so charming to me, and gave me a cup with a waratah design on it which shd be in a museum. . . .

However, thank you for your poems. They are grand. Xavier Herbert gave me your address on one of the occasions long ago. I told him I was close up finish and he said I was like someone at whom a blackfellow had pointed a bone. He said 'Ian Mudie sang a bone out of me. Get him to sing the bone out of you.'

I said you might not think me worth it. At anyrate several more bones have been pointed at me since then. I have got to the stage that I don't care whether they are fatal or not.

My best greetings to you and your wife
Miles Franklin

Carlton
Sept 22 1941

My very dear Mary, Your grand letter dated Aug 1 and post-marked Aug 8 has just arrived and been devoured by me. I was writing to you this ev in any case. No, the reason you have not received my letters is because they have not been written. I've gone entirely phut. If I make a clean breast of everything we may both feel better.

One reason that has kept me from writing is that I have struck a snag with my poet's poems, when all seemed plain sailing. Mr M back, but very disturbed time, and that crowd want to postpone all publications for duration. But I am keeping on. I feel so stymied that I haven't written about it. It makes me sick not to progress. If only one of the cliques had taken up my poet all would have been plain sailing, but they didn't and I'm not important enough to do what I want. . . .

I promised to send a little parcel but it has not gone yet because I have not the strength to do much. Fares cost too much to run in often and I have not the strength when I go to an evening meeting to go in early and do my errands. I have simply been hurt over things. The Drs say nothing wrong but hyper-sensitiveness and I have always hidden that under something the direct opposite apparently. That's enough about that.

I went to two hospitals last Friday and will do the rounds again tomorrow. My aunt Lena (whom you met) in one. She is merely having some hammer toes cut away in a wizard surgeon's place on a beautiful Bay Road and is always sur-rounded with half a dozen visitors and she chatters gaily. . . . Then I went to another private hospital overlooking the Harbor in a divine spot to see Winnie Stephens. She had terrible pulmonary haemorrhages and has a great cavity in one lung—pretty bad I believe. She wanted to see me. Poor little soul, I always loved her kindness: she never said anything, not one phrase that ever grazed me in the slightest and that is a great feat where an animal is as sensitive—tho dissembled—as I am.

You asked what P R S was doing. I think I sent you some of his papers, *The Publicist*, which will answer that. *The Publicist* is owned by an eccentric old gentleman named Miles who derives his money from tailoring. He is a noted atheist and conservative in every way, read the list of points. Queer situation altogether. Nuff said. Mr Miles is very ill lingering with dropsy or some such and hardly ever sleeps and has the concomitant irascibility and P R S has his hands full at present.

Re Menzies. He had great glory abroad and came home to be repudiated. It must have been most humiliating. I believe his reports were taken without any enthusiasm. You'd have thought that there wd have been enough profiteers and warmongers and reactionaries and go-getters in his own side of Parliament to obviate such a flop as that. No wonder he refused to go back to London discredited where he had had such a reception as Prime Minister. Of course his politics are not mine but even so there is an element of pure Australianism in it. An Australian could be proved as a genius and scholar abroad and be offered a job as cashier in a restaurant on coming home as has happened in a certain case. The victim is holding brilliantly a professorship in USA now. . . .

I am astonished and delighted to hear of the play. We might be able to read it in the play circle of the Fellowship of Aust Writers. We struggle for indigenous drama but oh, the native born are still unrooted in their soil and consequently arid and barren—brave warriors but blood and iron and fire and death are not enough.

You have had a wonderful summer. You certainly have a fixation about heat. People in England live at such a low ebb with regard to warmth that they melt in mild warmth.

Haven't looked at the Furphy biography for nearly 2 years. Have lost interest. . . .

Russia looks rather precarious at present. Lately there was held in Sydney a Congress for Friendship and Aid in the USSR. I was a delegate from the fellowship. My friend Dr Burgmann was a convener. There were 2500 delegates from nearly six hundred organizations. First day was in Town Hall the second in Leichhardt Stadium. Dr Duhig nephew of Archbishop RC of Brisbane was a high light. He is so brilliant. He had been to Russia as a visiting scientist. Our old Canon Guernsey of the University said that Russia had done more in 25 years to put the teachings of Christ into practice than the churches had been able to accomplish in 2000 years. But since then Billy Hughes (a reactionary little antediluvian) has helped some minister for customs ban Joyce's *Ulysses* and the Australian Labor Party is going to expel anyone who belongs to the Friends of Russia League. The re-banning of *Ulysses* at this date is typical of our bumbles. . . .

I forgot to say that the Fellowship lecture last night was on Our Intellectual Blackout by Bartlett Adamson. I had to take the chair at short notice when I arrived. There was a black out on. We thought we had guarded against all light but it leaked out the door downstairs all the way down the stairway up which we come to our room so we had to turn out all lights and proceed in the dark. It was a strain being chair as I had no way of making myself felt. It was a lively meeting as Mr Adamson had a terrible bag of idiocies. *Ulysses*, ALP banning friend of Russia, a member of the Federal Parliament asking that Bishop Burgmann be interned because he helped to call the meeting of aid to Russia and the school magazine came out with a reproduction of a very chaste nude statue from the back with a drape put on it. It was a revel of bumble beeing really.

Bishop B's reply to the member was that the place to look for fifth columnists was not among the friends of Russia but in the groups paralleling those which had produced the Quislings in Eng and France and other places.

A fortnight earlier Mr Camden Morrisby gave a lecture on Australian literary Mystery—Brent of Bin Bin and I was in the chair. One man said that the reason Miles Franklin did not own to them were that the books were so bad anyone would be ashamed to own them. Mr B Adamson got up and said in his very humorous way that everyone knew who had written Brent's books everyone was quite sure why waste time on that what he was curious to know was who had written Miss Miles Franklin's books. . . .

The Eldershaw B partnership is doing fine—several books one on history and another on Australia. Eldershaw in Canberra in Govt Department for reconstruction for duration. B gone to

Hobart to give four lectures on Australian writers, at university.

One nice bit of news Eleanor Dark's latest novel has been chosen as a book of the month by some club in America which means there will be a big sale. She has been working on it for three years. It is called the *Timeless Land*—a nice title—and is about early days here. I am longing to read it. She has invited me to go and stay a week with her. She lives in Katoomba on the Blue Mts. Her husband is a doctor. Her Grandpa Canon O'Reilly was a bosom friend of my great aunt so it is an hereditary friendship. Her father came to see me once when I was a girl staying at Miss Scott's. Her father is Dowell O'Reilly for whom P R S claims that he invented the *monologue interieur* before it was done in Europe. . . .

I was surprised that you referred to our galvanised iron roofs as ugly. I think them the most beautiful of all roofs. They keep out the weather perfectly and are so light. If they fell in they would not be a ton weight to crush like slates or tiles and the pretty steel grey color like much of our foliage looks like a pool of water in the moonlight or when the sun is on them at the right angle and the lovely sound of rain on an iron roof. I think the idea that they are ugly is the old conservatism because they were once cheap and an innovation. Thatched roofs except for one year stacks are an outrage of poverty for the workers. They are apt to leak they are dirty and harbor all sorts of vermin and covered mean little pens for the disinherited. . . .

My nephew is still in hospital—it is bright's disease. I am very unhappy about him. My brother is nursing his duodenal and angina and is no longer with me. I am alone in this house with the ghosts. I can't struggle with it. It is exactly like Arden even to the lemon tree in the same place and same sized garden. I am going to see Em tomorrow if nothing deters. Will go to her for tea after the hospitals. I wish she lived near. . . .

[unsigned]

Carlton
8 October [1941]

Dear Eleanor

Miss Jones of Left Book Club has given me the honor of collecting you and directing you to dinner on Mon night. It is at 200 Pitt St, basement, name of Café something beginning with Dun. 6 pm.

Are you coming for week-end? Why not? Why not indulge one of my empty beds that is yawning for you? Sunday night, Norman Haire is to speak at FAW—present name of subject Sex and Censorship. Tuesday night our Committee meeting, at which you would be gobbledly welcome, alternately there is a night of Australian composers at Town Hall and St John Ervine's play at Minerva. . . .

Now I come to the hard part of the letter. I am ashamed not to have answered your lovely invitation. It wd be a life saver, but I cannot organize myself for anything. Every day I went to reply but didn't. The buckram has gone out of me. I sometimes think I am dead but still walk around. I am paralysed by desolation. X Herbert says I am like a blackfellow who has been 'boned', and that just expresses. Please forgive my bad manners, what an old retainer used to call 'Bod breedin',' (bad breeding).

Let me know what you will do. My shabby old humpy is open heartedly yours, but also if you are pressed I do not insist but would pick you up in town at near six.

Yours with love
Miles

We are all so bucked up by your success, and longing to read the book.

Oct 10th 41

Dear Miles

I have just this moment returned from Sydney & found your letter waiting for me. I can't tell you how glad I am that I am to have your company & moral support on Monday night— my secluded life in Katoomba has, I fear, quite unfitted me for 'functions'—& especially for functions where I have to talk!

Thank you so very much for your invitation to stay with you, but this two days I have just had in Sydney make it impossible for me to get away again before Monday—& two trips at such a short interval are quite unprecedented! The PEN Club asked me to a dinner too & Mr Preece very kindly arranged to have it on Tuesday next so that I could do the two in one trip, and I have one or two things I must do in town, so I shall park myself at the Women's Club which is central & convenient, and await you there at six o'clock on Monday evening. I feel less apprehensive already from knowing you will be there!

As for this 'bone' which is being pointed at you—well, one can't deny it, we are all being 'boned', and no abo ever had a more evil magic to contend with than the intellectual torpor & psychological collapse of the white race to-day. However, Heaven forbid that the corroboree-makers should be the ones to turn their faces to the wall & die! There are times when one just has to go limp & preserve a bare existence for a while, Lord knows, so I shan't bother you about week-ends until you feel ready to go into circulation again; but someday I hope you will come. . . .

Love from
Eleanor Dark

Carlton
Nov 25 41

Dear Mrs Evatt

It was so friendly of you to know that I would come if you asked me. I meant what I said about desiring a good talk with you and your husband. How are the conflicting sectional interests and beliefs to be, if not welded, directed or led for the preservation of our country? Can we seize our opportunity (provided of course that we don't all go down in defeat) or are we always to be something bobbing about like a cork because of our situation and the subservient mentality it induces? . . .

Thank you for pleasant talk and a delicious lunch.

Sincerely
[unsigned]

7.40 *To Alice Henry, Melbourne*
Source: FP 11

Carlton
Jan 29 1942

Dearest Pops

I wonder how you are getting on in these hot days. We had a shower here on Sunday but that old song 'It aint gonna rain no more', seems to be holding out.

Did you listen to Danny Delacy on the wireless. It seems to be rather sabotaged by one thing and another, but I suppose it is by fantastic chance that we still sit in peace and listen to radio.

I have a great grief to tell you. My dear and last brother Norman went suddenly on Saturday morning last and we had the funeral on anniversary day. I don't know how you faced a similar desolation. I wish I could make my peace with death

63

and pass out, but I still resent death and that I suppose is what keeps me here, for each bereavement kills me really, each loss of a friend stabs me nearly to death.

He went suddenly of heart failure at the last. He had been ailing during the week and the doctor said he wanted him in hospital. There I left him very bright with plans for the morrow—just got home and was called back but it was all over. The boy is very cut-up of course but he is working beyond his strength in military transport—taking petrol about—and his young mates rally to him. I hope he will be all right. I don't know whether he will cling to me as the last bit of the old nest or whether he will be glad to get rid of me as the last obstruction. Time will soon show.

A relative (my mother's cousin) saw the announcement in the paper and came to me just as I had returned alone after the funeral so that was a bit of comfort for the present.

I wish I cd see you. I remember how you came to me in the Passavant Hospital when the news of my last sister's death came.

No more dear at present my love as always

S M F

7.41 *From Alice Henry, Melbourne [per Isabel Newsham]*
Source: FP 11

St Ronan's Rest Home
Armadale
February 2nd, 1942

Dearest

Your letter of January 29th with its sad news has just been received.

Indeed I can sympathise with you from the bottom of my heart, for the death of my only brother was one of the heaviest griefs of my life. It is a loss that only time can heal and then imperfectly.

I have been listening to *All That Swagger* on the wireless and enjoy what I have heard very much. It is very well spoken indeed.

64

There are a great many American soldiers at present in Melbourne and some refugees from Asia and the islands. Doubtless Sydney has many of them also.

Do write and let me know what your plans are.

My fondest love and every good wish to you from

Yours affectionately
Alice Henry [per A I N]

7.42 *To the Grattan family, New York*
Source: GC

Carlton
Feb 10th 1942

Dear Hartley, Marjorie and Rosalind

Your delightful Christmas greeting to hand yesterday. Rosalind is deliciously like her daddy. Such are the vagaries of fashion and the differences of climate that we can't be sure if she is dressed for going on the street or to bed. The bow in the hair doesn't look like bed. I wish I were in that inviting American interior with the leafless tree visible through the window.

Well, since the photo was despatched Japan has decided to gamble on Asiatic conquest. If America does not decide to forgive her for her treble and double talk she will get that lesson which she nor the world will not forget, but ah, what it will cost us.

We still pass our days in a peace and comfort that is fantastic as far as the body is concerned but we simmer in an enervating atmosphere of war anxiety—naturally.

I send herewith a couple of P R S's magazines. Old Mr Miles passed away recently and P R S with two others (Hooper and Crowley) are to carry on for a further year under the terms of Miles's will, or some private guarantors.

We have had two large Australian books out lately—E Dark's *The Timeless Land*, which I am unable to judge as I stand so near to it that it is like trying to inspect a wall of pictures when jammed against them. It is to me like Australian history mixed with the prevailing fashion in sentimentality about the aborigines. No matter how shocking our treatment of them—all of which I admit as readily as I deeply deplore—the fact remains that no idealisation can do away with the facts of their primitiveness in habits. Then there is Ernestine Hill's biography of Flinders, one of my pets in our early scene. Of this I have forced myself to read only a few chaps so far because it is so lush that I mistrust its scholarship and go gingerly across its flowery marshes fearing quicksands. . . .

A fortnight ago I lost my only brother suddenly and now am so desolate that I do not know if I shall recover. You remember saying that in Australia one had to be a self-starter—that is very exhausting after a lifetime and whether I shall accumulate any motor power to begin once again I don't know and don't care. I wish I could be free of my anguished desolation.

We are asked to write short letters, for obvious reasons, and nothing of lively interest may be discussed so this is just an affectionate greeting from your Australian friend

Stella Miles Franklin

Feb 19 I didn't get this letter sent away and since it started Singapore has gone with the other victorious defeats—um.

Henrietta Drake-Brockman is here with her daughter—spent the evening with me. Julia is even more gorgeous than mama, and taller. Your name was frequently mentioned. Perhaps we shall see you here as a thoughtful war correspondent.

There is a popular radio commentator here. He was taking the chair at an Aid-Russia meeting which I attended and several people who came in asked me if you had arrived, so striking is the resemblance. Your doppel-ganger is named John Dease. . . .

Carlton
February 19 1942

My dear Mrs Robins

You don't know how often I think of you and how I long to see you and draw from your warm brave courage as in the days before World War I. I must write to you while yet I may. I lost my brother suddenly three weeks ago through heart failure. It was a terrible shock—the last of them all, I one of seven remain alone. The desolation is paralysing despite the fact that others all over Europe and Asia are suffering worse. The sheer lunacy of man is incredible. America will be the only unravaged country when this ceases and it will have been scourged with grief and loss of its young men.

I have had a young poet staying with me for four days before he goes into camp. He came to help me over a few of my days of sick desolation. We had some good hours with 'John Brown's Body', the big narrative poem by Benet which you sent me some years ago. I wish you could know how much the books you sent me have meant to me. They were sent with your rich understanding as well as your generosity. You must sometimes feel a breath from far away and that will be from here because of what you mean to me. I have not heard of how you and Mr Robins are faring physically for some time, otherwise I know that as ever you will be a centre of warm and nourishing association—a fire at which many will revive. I wish I could warm myself by it now.

Miss Henry, I hear, is very frail and a little wandery in her memory through weakness and confinement. I would go to see her but for the restrictions of all sorts that are part of life today. My garden provides little at present but bantam eggs and guavas, lemons and a few flowers. The plums and figs have lately finished.

My brother's boy is serving in the militia. We nearly lost him this winter with pneumonia and nephritis. It is a hard world for the young things. It is all brought about by man's lunacy but it seems as if the punishment for such fools is disproportionate.

I wonder have you read *The Timeless Land* by my friend Eleanor Dark. I understand it is having a success over there and I wonder how it strikes you. I am too near it to get a view. It is all so familiar to me that it is like reading an old school book. My own novel *All that Swagger* is being read as the morning serial over the Government Stations. The young are taking to it and flocking to me because the story ends on a note of hope and courage, not, as one young man says, on a stomach-ache from groping in the viscera, like most of the acclaimed novels.

We are asked not to write long letters. This is just a note to take my dear love and keep the lines of communication open. Is Lily still with you? If so remember me to her. How I should like to have a round-up of all those left of our old-time colleagues. I hear from Mrs Post and therefore of Mary Anderson, Elisabeth and others.

With a heart full of love as of yore
Stella M Franklin

7.44 *To Ian Mudie, Adelaide*
Source: FP 36

Carlton
Mar 17 1942

My dear Ian

1. Your fine letter to hand in the afternoon of the very morning I had posted a letter to you telling you some of the things you bring up. So I'll fill-in. I came to no harm on that Thurs night. I do not believe there were any avowed communists in the stoushing. They could not talk and heckle like the synthetic–dialectical–polemical reds—these toughs cd only stoush. It was the night of first raid on Darwin and feeling ran high against Adela P and the Japanese praise, and scrap iron, etc.

2. Hope Renée is by now firmly into her stride again—and dear Little Bill, no wonder he was jubilant to see you both again.

3. I wish we cd do the overland train trip in company and chronicle it. Great stuff.

4. The Form! Great. That's the idea, and the stuff; and to be able to get it down in such circumstances is to be in control of your machine of life. For it doesn't look as if there will ever again be halcyon days for poets to simmer in. I had opportunity and strength only to gulp it once so far, noticing some grand things as I gulped. Must go back to it as soon as I can. Went to a week-end where a Dr Purcell read his great poem of 4100 lines, and now he is going to add another vast canto about the present war. So don't be afraid of being too long. On you go, building on this pregnant foundation. I enclose a poem from an American paper, not as a model but only to tell you that the rhymed quatrain catches the ear like honey the tongue, or color the eye. If among the fine dingo yelps come one or two with chimes I shall love that—weakly perhaps. But a chimed chanty may last longer than Gibraltar. Old A G S said that poetry was at once the strongest and frailest of vehicles—that a fragment of words could outlast all archaeology or something to that effect.

Winnie rang me up a week ago to say tecs had come and taken Inky away. Yesterday I got a letter from some one signed Walton—do you know her?—saying that 'Mr Stevenson' had sent me a message to say he had been interned at Liverpool with fifteen others. If the detention lasts longer than ten days he will need people to take the matter up. Win asked me to say nothing so I remained quiet. But after this letter I told Hon T D Mutch, who accompanied me to one of the meetings, and he has promised to find out the rights of the case. There are two I am sorry for—that unfortunate little Winnie in her desperate state of health—and poor old Mr H who is 72 and of whom one of the people who met him said he has no brain at all and is enthused without the power of thought. He is a kind, gentlemanly, well-meaning, respectable person and I hope the adventure is not too strenuous for him.

As I was thinking about ramming I was rammed with internal

disturbances which laid me low for some days and left me weak. Things upset me.

The nephew has been in a couple of collisions—the lack of lights and the big trucks are difficult. Fortunately no one was dangerously hurt in these cases. But his captain and another lad were killed. The driver was a lad who could hardly drive a common motor, was put on a Bren and turned firmly and over went the show. Gruesome details. Jack was sick about it, said he had driven the Cap often he was a nice fellow of 38 (and a baby coming to his wife) and interested in my writings. The poor lad responsible for the accident was in a fearful state.

Well Life must go on and poetry is one of its highest manifestations or fruits.

[unsigned]

7.45 From Ian Mudie, Adelaide
Source: FP 36

Seacliff
March 19 1942

My dear Miles

Your letter arrived today, & I was already determined to write to you tonight.

Wasn't it one of the Jacobites who said 'Loyalty is a fine jewel, & those that wear it die beggars'? And now we see what happens to those who in this country attempt to put this country first—you will doubtless say they were misguided in many ways. But all the same we of Australia First did try to put Australia First—Something no other party but the old labor party has ever done. I know a fair bit of the history of the party—& I know that the pro-Jap Mrs APW was driven out because of her Anglo-Saxon slant, & if there were any out to place any other country first they left us in disgust. The only conclusion I can come to is that Maxy Falstein & his clique have got control of the govt & are out to have their political enemies put out of the way.

We can now expect to see Lawson, J T Lang and Menzies interred.

However 'The Church is founded on the blood of martyrs'. This treatment will only breed more nationalists, for the AF was, when I left Sydney, the whole movement was, moving solidly towards a pure nationalism—Australianism—with all extraneous odds & ends chopped off.

As you know by now, I got a complete copy of *The Dream*. I remembered afterwards that I'd left an incomplete copy with Browey, &, getting it back, I managed to remember the other bits. I was going to ask you to return it as soon as you'd read it, but now I will ask you to look after the copy I sent you until I send for it. For if fifteen besides P R were put in concentration camp—well, I can't think of sixteen prominent members of the movement who are less innocent of traffic with the enemy, plotting for the overthrow of law & order, acts of terrorism, storage of arms & equipment, or operating secret radios than I am—& I, as you know, am wholly innocent of such crimes. Therefore, if sixteen have already gone in, I presume I, too, will go in. So treasure *The Dream* for me, & may Australia bless you.

Yes, loyalty is a fine jewel indeed. . . . and to think that a Comm loyal to Russia First—talked from the platform of the Adelaide Town Hall last night.

We have lighted such a fire, brother Ridley.

Yes, Miss Walton wrote a magnificent 'Lyrical Letter' of nostalgia for England a year ago—it was published by *The Publicist*. I've seen her spell Inky's name correctly. She was probably under a certain amount of stress when she wrote the letter.

Miss Walton is one of the nicest women I have ever met. And, like most AF members, she is a great admirer of you.

Oh, Miles darling, when they came & fumbled through all my books, & turned through *All that Swagger* & *Pioneers* suspiciously, I just thought some silly little informer had got ideas about me—but to know now that men who have already suffered a fair bit because of their ideas, some of them probably ones who have already suffered in their businesses for them, have been chucked into concentration camp like aliens & Russia-loyal

Comms (all of whom I presume are out long ago) I at once feel angry & exultant.

Glad you liked the first bit of *The Dream*. You'll find plenty of your own ideas scattered through the whole thing. But I know you will love me for my thefts. You'll see I remembered your sheoak flowers.

Renée now much better. Sends her love.

Rotten luck about the Boy. Hope he's bucking up now.

And you, too. Look after yourself, dear Miles, & write to me again soon.

Love

Ian

7.46 To Ian Mudie, Adelaide
Source: FP 36

Carlton

Mar 23 1942

Dear Ian

The poem arrived safely. May I show it to people who are interested in poetry—say people like Mr Green or Mr Howarth of the University, whom I know? . . .

I note what you say of loyalty and agree but I did not join the AF movement for the same reason that I did not accept Mr Miles's invitation to write for him, that is because I was at variance with his views. To me the position to be accorded women in any political movement is always a sure barometer of that movement's democracy. And Mr Miles simply roared me down once at the Yabber Club when I attempted to express my point of view.

I hope you will return to Sydney when this terrible war is over and then we shall be able to discuss the matter fully. I am very sorry for poor Mr Hooper and hope the shock does not kill him. The charge seems fantastic. The crime if committed could only be committed by an insane person. Mr Salier, Mr Hooper and Mr Crowley whom I first met at the lectures on

Australian literature by Mr C Hartley Grattan under the auspices of University Extension or something like that are certainly most respectable men, rather conservative than otherwise in politics. I should have thought and poor old Harley Matthews was an Anzac. I don't know the others.

I remember during last war in the United States that feeling ran high and all sorts of people were accused of all sorts of things. These are dangerous days.

I suppose you are in camp by now. The boys here have been wet for days. I remember in 1917 being tent orderly at our camp in the Balkans and all the poles split with the weight of the wet canvas and we could not go into the bush and get a real pole that wd stand the strain. The mud used to collect on our gum boots in pancakes six inches and more wide. We were weary dragging it about—used to stand on it to pull it off and start again.

I enclose a picture of the ramming admiral whom I so much admire. Wish I had his gallant hardihood.

Excuse a dull letter I can't rise to anything better.

With love to you and Renée and Bill
[unsigned]

7.47   *To Ian Mudie, Adelaide*
Source: FP 36

April 21 42

My dear Ian

The names I know are two Crowleys, Mr Hooper, Salier, Macy, Stevenson, Rice, Harley Matthews and Bath, whom I believe is the Mayor of Manly attended one meeting and asked S to hold a meeting at Manly—has no other connection with the movement.

There is need for us to remain judicial and impersonal in our outlook (Australia's good first and foremost irrespective of persons or parties). I am with you in passionate devotion to Australia, the soil which is ours, in which we have our being.

'To Miles with love Ian Mudie' (ML)

That is as natural as fundamental as self-respect. But in the complicated progress and the interdependency of human society and relationships there are politics. Ask yourself what are your politics for this Australia. In the after-war upheaval what is your plan? Is it for that which is comprehensively called the brotherhood of man which the great masses now hope to find in Lenin's theories? Or, do you want the kind of totalitarianism promulgated by Germany and imitated by Japan? Or, do you think that we can go on with the old imperial-cum-democracy-cum-capitalism of which the USA is now the most powerful unit?

Of course it is a dreadful thing that people like Matthews, Hooper and Salier are held for babbling about Australia First. But the charge, as far as one can gather from the newspapers, is that among twenty persons arrested there are some who have used that attractive cry (which takes a poet like yourself and a homesick exile like Miss Walton) to make contact with our deadly enemy Japan and lay plans when the Japs shall arrive to supply a gauleiter to act as Laval and Quisling have done in their countries.

Ask yourself how you stand should this charge be proved. I repeat that the situation disturbs me either way. If the fantastic charge of treason is merely a bull's nest, as Danny would say, then it is a grave state of affairs that already we have so assimilated gestapo methods that 20 people can be held since Mar 10th, and that a legal Parliamentary luminary like Billy Hughes, using the privilege of Parliamentary utterance, should have called for extreme penalties for these people and be so reported in the papers while the accused are silenced. On the other hand if some of these 20 are quislings that too is a grave thing to happen in our country where, as you still find, the police are helpful friendly people like ourselves. (I like to think it is typical of our police that when I fainted in George St at the busy hour one day I came-to in a taxi with the policeman from point duty caring for me as sensitively efficiently and kindly as a nurse or a brother could have done.)

So dear heart in your passionate love of our country be sure that no stirring slogan is used to further any repressive kind of part or policy, that is all I ask.

I am told that there are sixteen interned in one place including those I have named. I am also told that there are four others, including the one woman mentioned in the papers but not named, and that Mr H S and others do not know who those four are. You see I know only so few. Among the others there may be, alas, some who have not my views of loyalty to Australia nor my belief in freedom of expression.

Believe me I am quietly doing what I can towards maintaining our best traditions as far as possible even in war time. ...

With love to you and yours
for Australia as Furphy always signed himself

7.48   To Mary Fullerton, Sussex
Source: FP 18

Carlton
May 23 1942

My dearest Mary

I am uplifted by your grand letter of Mar 23, which reached me yesterday. (You had forgotten to date it but the post mark was clear.) ...

Don't worry about us. The Japs may or may not get here: the big grief is the slaughter of youth. I expect they keep you informed from Melb of the loathsome tragedy—three women claimed now. A crime akin to that air force fellow's in London. It said of the third victim that she did not go out at night and had practically no men friends. Well I am the opposite I go out at night from one end to the other of this vastly spread Sydney and I'm cluttered up with men friends from the Bish of Goulburn to Xavier Herbert and Mr Cleary the broadcasting commissioner, to seven little lads on the street—have to lock the gate and pretend not to be home often to get respite from the latter flock but I think the charm is the lollies I get from the other gents and keep for these.

The children sound lovely. They are a great joy. One cannot be blue when children are around: they simply wouldn't understand. I wish Mabel could get a rest. She is a wonder. The able and the brave attract the other kind. I am so grateful for the *Times Lit Supp*. Here's one sample of many how they helped me. I was given a few days to prepare a talk with a man over the stations (natl) on 'Has the writer any concern in the lit development of his country?' From the *Times Lit Supp*. was able to quote Brenden Bracken and Mr Churchill about books being best export, even in war. The morning after speaking as soon as office opened at 9, Angus and R's manager rang me and asked could I give him my sources, that he wanted to print my talk, it was such a help to him. He is having trouble in being rationed paper and they (the authorities) said he was only a printer (ah, ha me boy: they deserved that because they have got out so much American stuff, but of course I was glad to help) and he is going to print all the series of talks in a pamphlet—will get you a copy if not too dear. The talks are still going on. Nettie and Vance and Katherine and Gavin Casey have to come yet. I was also cheered considerably to know that you got my silly little parcel. I wonder if the bacon and cheese were any good.

Stephensen and others languish in internment. Their case will not be considered until after the four in WA are tried in June. They were taken up at the same time. Adela Pankhurst was taken up in another crew. She appealed before the Chief Justice to be released but her plea was refused. Walsh (her husband) I hear, is dying of cancer. It is a sad case. Win Stephensen has been in bed for six months with TB. Dr Evatt is the Federal Member where I live and his brother is the State Minister so I know them both well. Glad you like Casey. He is a perfect imitation of Eden. I read in an old magazine that he said in a speech at Geelong, that given equal chances, no woman could ever equal a man. That's what he looks like.

Baylebridge, Shaw Neilson and Furnley Maurice all gone—leave a sad gap. I love Neilson's poems but had little connection with him or Furnley Maurice. Baylebridge I miss terribly. He would ring me up sometimes twice a day, and fairly often, and always comfort and cheer me. He was still in his fifties. I believe he caught cold at a bush fire and pneumonia took him at the last. The last talk I had with him over the phone I asked in a jocular way what he was doing in this second edition of the war. He said that we who had been through the last one on active service could not stand this second bout, that we could not stand it emotionally a second time.

I love to hear of Denis's hen. I too can go under my own steam in eggs from my pet bantams. I took all I could get to my aunt as she has to eat them raw and they are 2/- a doz and impossible to get them fresh enough for raw swallowing. The hens are moulting and so are lazy of laying. I am trying to get enough to make a cake for old Billy Linklater the last of the overlanders from the Gulf country who has been in Syd for some years about his eyes and is now going back, and it is hardly likely that he will return. I have five eggs already—that is plenty because my bantams lay a big egg—the yolk is as big as an ordinary egg only the whites smaller.

I was talking to Louis Esson last night. He is back in Sydney. He loves to be here. He looks very old and frail but is happy among us and that wonderful Hilda supports him here in a comfortable flat. He is going to write an introduction to the broadcast talks that I mentioned. Louis has a fine sense of humor: he was chuckling that he is obscure compared with the people he has to introduce and talked of Birrell introducing an edition of Browning.

Yes I have the pamphlet about J Furphy by Archer. He read that paper to the Hy Lawson Soc one night when K B took me there to Footscray. As he read each page he laid it down for K B to read so I expected she would correct that mistake. Everybody got up and talked, because she had 'em all organized to do so, about what a pity it was that, despite my brilliance, she had been passed over. So I got up and told the facts, that I had given her half the prize, that her name would be with mine on the book and she would have half profits, if any, but still, two years later, he comes out with his old libel. I don't think I can have told you what a campaign of misrepresentation K B carried on about me for not giving her enough credit. I found out that the poor old soul has been in an asylum long ago on acct of her mania for Furphy, and so I could not be cruel and cloud her last days. So I have to stand it. This is in confidence of course. My doing the biography with her would be a humorous yarn in itself if I had hd the strength to write it out while fresh.

You say you consider Danny the finest character in Australian fiction. I thought at first that you were saying that out of kindness and partiality, but when I come to think it over, who else is there so prominently depicted in our fiction—perhaps he is one of the best, but the clique would never admit it. ...

Rachel Field's *All this and Heaven too* bored me—it was pretentious and pedestrian, better of course than *North West Passage*, but they bellow and overpraise a lot of chaff in USA. Take for instance *Botany Bay* by Nordorff and Hall. It is the slightest most banal of novels, yet it had full first pages of the NY 'Book magazine sections'. They make that noise about Australia written by one of themselves, but will not accept *Capricornia* or *Swagger* written by us.

Well, I had Xavier H here lately had a long talk. He kept saying 'You and I Miles are the only two great Australian novelists.' I suppose when he is with others they and he are the only two great and I derided. He is a colorful personality. I enjoyed him. Told me his liaisons and all.

Well this is enough, perhaps to go to the fishes.

My dear love to you and Mabel, yours ever
[unsigned]

7.49   *To Katharine Susannah Prichard, Perth*
Source: FP 21

[nd, June 1942]

Dear Katharine Susannah

Just finished listening to you and Gavin. You have had the privilege of hearing yourself. I'm sure I'd drop dead if I heard myself. You sounded just as if you were beside me right in the machine. I was gleeful at some of the good licks Gavin made. He sounded fresh and angry and you sounded weary. Is he quite young? His disgust may be new, whereas you and I have been struggling since we were in pigtails—little female girls at that.

Your talk was very good indeed and you were most generous in your mention of your contemporaries—thanks in my case. . . .

I have not yet come across that latest novel of yours. Have just read *Botany Bay* by Nordoff and Hall. Consider it poor stuff but it is cried to the skies by American reviewers. The clique is gushing over *The Pea Pickers*. Some wonderful writing by a mature person. But under analysis the book is 'phoney'. That word just expresses it. You can't win my sympathy for two lovely young creatures, joy of life, rebellion and all that, when they would creep under cubicles and steal Italian food. And it does not ring true if they were so 'lost' that the Italians would not take sexual toll of them. I have met Italians in much more protected walks of life, and the Life Force urge in them was not so gentlemanlily or lillily controlled. Also, for two strapping young females when they went to a poor old woman's home when she was away and in Gippsland which would be reeking with firewood, to break her furniture to burn—ah, no the thing is not consistent. You can write about such 'po' white trash' if they are true to Australian life, but don't at the same time lyricise them as lovely darlings. But the descriptions in the first third of the book are unusual and charming. It will all depend on what the writer follows up with. And here's a joke, Mary Gilmore wrote to me saying that no other mind but mine could have produced it, that she felt me all through the book!!!! I dunno.

It may become the rage in USA. Abroad the readers will accept Australia only if depicted in some overseas style—for example H H R great success because she did Australia *à la* Freud. *Pageant* was chosen because it presented Australia in the genteel and accepted English style, now this book presents Australia *à la* hill billies. I wonder if ever we shall gather force to present ourselves as we seem to ourselves independently of currying favour anywhere and gain acceptance abroad as well as at home. . . .

With love
[unsigned]

7.50 *From Katharine Susannah Prichard, Perth*
Source: FP 21

Greenmount
June 9 1942

My Dear Miles

I've just been listening to myself on the air—& truly, I think my voice sounded God-damned awful! I'm supposed to have a good radio voice—but *that* sounded like a dying duck in a thunderstorm. Gavin's voice was good—just natural, as it is & as he talks. He's a fine chap. Has lots of ability. Have you seen his short stories in the *Bulletin*—though he hasn't done anything for them, for some time.

I was glad to have the script of your talk with G A. Enjoyed it immensely. But if you'd heard the damsel who read it here, you'd have had a fit. She was a very la-de-dah young English woman— or talked that way—& when I thought of your own crisp, witty, live voice, I couldn't bear it. I protested to the Talks director here. She read Jean too. Only worse. It was a damned shame. The talks have all been spoilt by other people reading them, for me at any rate. Though the man who read G A had something like his voice, & the men weren't so unlike their better-halves.

Pea Pickers? Mm. I like the imagery & use of words in the early stages—but like you got fed up with the young women. Too posey & ego-centric. Didn't feel it was Gippsland either— which I do know—& love. There's an audacity & original attack though, which ought to lead somewhere in another book, more mature & responsible.

Hate to think of you—so sad, my dear! Couldn't you take a holiday? Come & stay with me for awhile. It's quiet here, beautiful country, though cold & stormy just now. I'm the world's untidiest person too, & haven't much time to even talk. But I'd love you to come, & it might make the re-adjustment easier.

Don't rust out, Miles darling! You've got too much fire & guts for that. The big fight for a better world is on. Let's make our dying worth while. You can't be just melancholy—when there's so much to do. ...

Do think about a trip West—& I'll raise the town to do honour to M F.

Love, my dear
Katharine Susannah

PS Have met G Parry—but understand he's *not* sympathetic to people who think as I do. He was in charge of the reference room at the *West Australian* here. Thought he was of French extraction. Don't know about the university. Not the sort of person to be confidential with, I was told. K S

7.51 To Alice Henry, Melbourne
Source: FP 115

Carlton
June 18 42

Dearest Pops

I am so thankful for the two lovely rolls of papers that have reached me since I last wrote to you.

I have a book sent to me by Mary Anderson on the history of the Women's Trade Union League, by some PhD person. I wonder if it is the PhD business that makes them so dull and colorless. You are mentioned many times, and those little footnotes contain you dozens of times. It has been taken from your book largely—that early history. Goodness knows I wrote it over and over again—but always anonymously—and K Coman got credit for the [word illegible] stuff I wrote—her name was necessary as an academic. Have you a copy? I shd like to lend you mine till one comes for you, as you will be very interested to see yourself quoted so often. It is a nice little memoir to and for you, and in that part of the thing I rejoice. Mary Anderson wrote the preface. I suppose she dictated something and the typist put it into English or American. I used to write her first speeches and all sorts of things for her. I don't suppose she had any education even in Swedish, and she is an example of the rich conglomeration in American life, for side by side with all these footling PhDs is Mary in charge of a Dept with almost cabinet rank. She is a nice woman, always the same, and I always liked her—she never changed. Always stable. . . .

June 19 Those people who are interned are to be tried next week they are all pleading for me to appear on their behalf. I hate their politics, but think they have been foolishly treated. But oh, what crawlers people are—they can't get their tory friends to appear for them. It is pitiful to me to observe the way the public crawls as soon as the law steps in. No standing up bravely, or any dismay at loss of liberty—no, the nincompoops would throw away their liberties as a child throws off its hat regardless of the sun. As Editha said in the last war à propos of those who packed the sloppy plays; war is the only natural disposition of them: they are fit for nothing else. Frank Clune had some fun barging around but even he can't buck the army. . . .

Much love dearest. Let me know if you want the book.

SMF

7.52 *To Clem Christesen, Brisbane*
Source: MA

Carlton
July 28 1942

Dear Mr Christesen

Have started to write to you several times: never hatched out because I simply can't keep up with myself.

I appreciated your letter of December last enclosing receipt for *Meanjin Papers*. I am most grateful to Mr Hooper for such a valuable and congenial Christmas present. Mr Hooper has been unceasing and generous in his efforts to support Australian writers.

I shd love to write you a short statement on the importance of Australian writers at the present juncture, if that would do. I feel strongly about it. When is your deadline?

Regards and thanks for the splendid effort which *Meanjin*

Papers represents: I have found them full of nourishment.

Sincerely
Miles Franklin

Carlton
Tuesday Oct 6 42

Dymphna dear, I got home by eight o'clock off a train crowded to standing capacity—I invited two returned AIFs with their service chevrons to sit on the arms of my compartment so I had the reward of their views and news—exactly what Ian Mudie said—it takes a poet to reveal a whole thesis in one line.

I walked straight to the telephone and got your mother. I told her about the photo and gorgeous flat, and distinguished performance of *Fire on Snow* (or is it ice?) I don't think I missed any points. She is longing to go up to see you for a visit and she said the exactly right things such as I shd go often to see you and that I shd have stayed till Tuesday. I said I did not want to wear you out but that we inspired each other. All right there—kiddies well over prevalent distempers etc.

After I parted with you I ran the trams to their lairs as has been my wont in cities such as Quebec, Torino, Buffalo, Dublin, Wellington, Salonique, Rome, Rouen et al. When I got back from the first the convoy was still only 'standing out' with the corvette shepherding them like a kelpie but when I returned from Wallsend all that remained was one vessel hull down on the rim with a heavy plume of smoke. And then by great luck Mr Higgins came in and we had a beautiful yarn till Mr Bentley picked us up and I had a fine lunch enough to do me till this morning and they got me on to the train—a distinguished body guard. I was going to leave a note for Mr Higgins so it was a case of thinking of angels. I wish I cd be up there to write a novel about a successful Australian but it wd not be in the key suggested by one of the admiring critics of *All that S*. He said it was sad that I had put such a tremendous amount of work knowledge emotion and gifts in depicting a failure like old Danny. (That of course made me more bent towards Danny.) Why didn't I pick out a man like Kidman or the Anthills. Oh I would like to pick out a man like E Lew or Miss Knox, isn't she the bird that inherits the Brown millions. I think I must social crawl to meet these two just for an hour or two for a yarn would be all I'd want.

Life is so short and one is so frail and unfree and limited in power! However!

You gave me a gorgeous week-end my dear. I do hope I did not wear you out. And your pose about not being a housekeeper is just a pose—the little flat was a blissful nest where eating and sleeping were rich as well as the talk and it is rare to get them all together. Such a situation to be able to look and look and look for ever across our own mighty Pacific in all its moods.

And if that dear wall of flesh of our own so few petted men aided by the equally dear Americans of our own speech who have come so far from their mothers and own comfortable environment can't keep back the fecund hordes you are in a splendid opera box.

Thank you so much my dear love from
[unsigned]

Wd you please direct the accompanying paper to Mr Hooton. It contains something about Carl Sandburg.

7.54 From Dymphna Cusack, Newcastle, New South Wales
Source: FP 30

Monday Oct 12, 1942

Miles, my dear

Don't judge my joy in yr visit by the time I've taken to write. The Fates must have been jealous of our weekend, for on the Tues. I was laid low with a vile dose of 'flu which settled itself in my antrums & gave me an expression like a Halloween lantern. I've been in bed ever since & Dr said that I cld get out of bed to-day, but counteracted order when all the Antarctic hurled itself agst my windows. You'd love it now—like going thro' the Bight in a gale.

Everyone feels that yr visit here was something in the nature of a Royal triumph. I'm inundated by appeals to know when yr coming again. It was lovely having you—'A real nice lady'. Mrs Pearce. Train guard—Tues. morning 'Did yer Lady Friend get out Wallsend all right? Like to 've gone with her meself.'

So altogether you left yr mark in N/cle.

Later: Hig & Godfrey just dropped in for a couple of hours & we trailed the tails of discussion round my virtuous couch. They both sent their cheers & hopes to see you again. I was unfortunate that my Dog's disease prevented me from meeting Nettie.

Poor Godfrey has to face another call up to-morrow & we were all coné-ing his kidney & advising him to swill large amts of cocoa & whisky.

My joy in Nehru has grown & expanded. I've never felt so completely that another writer is my 'kind of person'. He's the person I want to meet.

Good-bye, my dear. This is just to say thank you for coming—also for ringing Mother.

Yrs
Dymphna

Did you see Currey's peurile criticism of H G's book in *Aus'n Quarterly*?

Carlton
Sunday [October 1942]

Dear Godfrey

An interesting letter!

I don't remember calling you child. Your remarking that I did is the first sign of youth I have noted in you. You struck me as being heavy with age—temperamentally—as some temperaments are prone to be in youth. I'll give you this wrinkle in the technique of living: We start with this topheaviness, but keep your decades fluid don't let them congeal into separate compartments and make a period piece of you. You'll then find out as you grow older that the oppression of age will lighten or at least mellow with progress.

We are all children. No matter how gladiatorial, how on top of the world we are, any trouble in the midriff department reduces us at once. And you must remember I have served at an advanced dressing station in the Balkans in World War I. That larned me. . . .

If you are ahead of the times instead of merely ahead of the crowd *à la* critics you will continue to find more lift in mental speculation than in mere research—in short you'll discover the superiority of wisdom over knowledge: but Mrs Palmer is a most competent literary professor: she is my candidate for the chair of Aust lit and our universities are such mere garrisons as not to possess and, a few years since, the very possibility of which they scoffed at. Go on with your college up there and get something rude and crude and intransigent and robust and brave in the mental and Australian line. . . .

How nice of your mother to remember me among so many.

This letter is too long
Miles

Carlton
October 14 1942

Dear Tom

I got the proofs of 'E's' poems and immediately rang up Peace
to find out you had caught up with my fond farewell of you
some months since in the door of the good old Metropole.

Well, I could not wait to send the proofs into the infinite,
which seems to be what happens when one tries to get to anyone
in the Army. I took the proofs to Ida Leeson to have her check
them too. She found only one little thing in yours to better.
You write 'Her feeling for the continuity of spiritual values is
all the stronger in "E" because it is' etc. The *her* at the beginning
of the sentences is obviously a slip for *the* , so it has been righted.
Nothing else wrong, so it shows that all the expense of one
university education after the other as Danny would say does
help. Many more flaws were pointed out in me.

Miss Davis also has been careful with the proofs so I hope
we have not too many flaws in punctuation.

Miss Leeson said she found the poems even better than she
had thought at first. She has not seen them for six or eight years
and of course there were new ones. So that was good.

I hope this little selection will clear the way to do a bigger
volume with more grouping and some of the poet's notes left in.

Nettie Palmer at the monthly meeting last night and also
on Sunday night when L Esson was the subject of eulogy.
Nothing left to say about Shakespeare when the clique got
through. Your *Six Poets* is getting great praise. So you will be
canonised soon.

I have had a warm response for my Lawson oration. I dunit
this year. Picture of me in *Truth* with mouth open and Bart
beside me looking like the Moderator of the boss Presbyterian
Assembly. One person wrote in and said it was pure oratory.
When you know what I have said of oratory as a male gyration
it serves me right.

Hope one of these days we'll give a talk on 'E's' poems. Do you want to read them or do the bits in between? Could we make it striped—you read the poems when I did the praise and I read the poems when you did the analysis?

Oh, who is it will do the review for *SMH*? Let me know who and if I shall send him or her the book direct. God knows you may be home and leaning on a walking stick with age and I in my dotage before the things finally appear—but I risked no delay with the proofs.

Have had praise almost from Caesar—indeed! for my review of your six poets. Wonder if you will be satisfied.

Lovely wild days here, full of grey slanting rain—and it's on the catchment area!!! Yea!!!

Love and good wishes from
[unsigned]

7.57 To Mary Anderson, Washington
Source: MAP

Mar 24, 1943

My dear Mary

Alice Henry passed away on Feb 14 and was cremated.

She had been failing for a long time, getting weaker and drowsier, and in the end just fell asleep without a struggle or pain of any kind. With her goes all the associations of my youth in USA. There is no one else within reach who shared those days with me. There seems to be little but sadness now—natural or unnatural.

I have just been reading the November Bulletin of *Life and Labor*. In it I note how the leagues have grown since 1915. I was pleased to note that Elisabeth Christman was mentioned and that Victor Olander was still on deck. I have never heard a word of John Fitzpatrick. Is he still with us?

I send you a small book with this. *Australian Writers*. It is some radio addresses made over the National Stations (Govt) over a year ago. It takes a long time for things to get into print.

I did not like the subject foisted on me. I wanted the one 'Need Australian writers write about Australia?' but of course a man had to have that. You will note I mentioned Mr MacLeish so you can shunt the book on to him for the Australian collection of his Library as all the copies were bought up at once and I can't get any more.

The booksellers are almost empty but can't get paper to print more than a minimum of books and the Government wants such vast masses of pamphlets and regulations printed that they shut out other matter. ...

Some of our boys have been in the war for three years—lads of 18 now veterans 21 or 22 or 23. The war is heavy on our men because we have so few and they are so adventurous they have been piled into the advanced lines from Jerusalem to Kokoda. It was wonderful when your boys began to be seen everywhere and to hear the American voices. To us, who were in the last war, it is very wearying to see the same old mess of lunacy over again.

My love & good wishes
Stella Miles Franklin

7.58   *To Frank Ryland [Australian Army]*
Source: FP 37

Carlton
April 21 1943

Dear Frank Ryland

Your air mail letter card of 16th inst to hand this moment. I shall reply at once. It will be great fun if they put in what you quote from me—go ahead, as you say.

Just heard from Harley M that the Magpie is held up for the moment awaiting allocation of paper. There has been another great reduction of paper allowance, but all the editing had been done and the book accepted. You will be disgusted with my story, it is merely a yarn with characterisation rather than insight displayed.

Now for your very interesting letter of 8th inst which I have been trying to answer daily but always baulked by the petty chores of existence.

I was reared on thunderstorms in the mountain country and adore thunder. However the Krupp guns on the Bulgarian frontier in last war were so much noisier than thunder that poor thunder has seemed ineffectual ever since. Perhaps it is better up where you are.

I am most interested in what you say of the Aborigines. (I always spell them and Negroes with a capital letter the same as other races.) You have a great point when you speak of the persons who wouldn't drink out of the same bucket but who would not abstain from the gins. Pursue that and you have a new contribution to literature. Most men are too cowardly to think straight there, and such doctrine as you have voiced is generally ignored because it cannot be refuted. . . .

I have not seen your wife at the Fellowship since you left but I went in to pay my friend of Russia dues, one day and found her there so we sought the privacy of the corridors and had a bit of a yarn. She was looking well, and as bright and pretty as ever. . . .

Sadie Herbert was at the Fellowship the other night and showed me the big display ads of *Capricornia* in America. They are saying it was a best seller in both Eng and Australia. There is so much ballyhoo in America that it seems splendid here, but I hope in this case that the book will really sell and bring Australia to the fore.

Theodor Dreiser was in my clique in Chicago. The last time I met him he was blurbing about how splendidly the English did things—how superior they were to the Americans. It was *à propos* the death of the American ambassador in London, Whitelaw Reid. The Eng Govt had sent the body home on a warship. That, said Dreiser, is the way to do things. I remarked, yes, but the poor are paying for it in taxes. I never could see anything in Dreiser. I disliked him personally. I have read only his *Genius*, *American Tragedy* and, of course, *Sister Carrie*. I never can see what was in *Sister Carrie*. It was so darned drab and dull. Does this disappoint you? . . .

Yes, ah me, if we could have courage! Courage is so rare.

What we crave is insensitiveness. Courage suffers the pangs or fears of hell when in a sensitive soul. My courage, if ever I had any, has clean gone. I have lost heart as the old bushmen used to say of a horse. Bullocks, dear souls, never lost heart. They would pull till they choked or their hearts literally broke and they died.

The English after Dunkirk is a sample of courage that makes me want to cheer. There they were, their small inadequate army and all the equipment gone, France gone, Belgium and Holland raped, not an ally in the world. Then up rose old Churchill like an old bull rounding up his herd when all the others had stampeded and saying 'We now have good and reasonable hopes of victory!' Had that courage something of insensitiveness, or over self-confidence or lack of imagination, or was it just plain courage?

Now to the important part of your letter. If you feel you have a novel in you let it grow with enthusiasm in the attempt, don't worry unduly. There will be times when you will think, I can do better than that or this one. There will be others when you'll feel that Thwaites and Zane Grey are geniuses compared with yourself but that can't be helped. Only yourself can tell whether you can do it or not. The time, place and waiting readers are ripe. At anyrate a first novel is a grand adventure. You are young enough, you are mature enough and you are poised in a marvellous moment of history and of time and your material is gorgeously new and vivid. There was never a better time to bring to birth a good sound full-dress novel on Australia.

So go to! Good luck
[unsigned]

F D Davison is going to edit *Coast to Coast* this year. That book is not out yet, nor *Southerly*. Isn't it the irony of fate that we have no paper to seize this chance to get ahead of syndicated oversea slush. What a pity those Russian ships used to come down in ballast because of the paper ring's machinations, as stated by Forsyth.

Carlton
July 4 1943

My dearest Mary, I have had no letter from you since last I wrote
but will send you a line. I'm sorry about your sister Annie. She
seems to be very frail. It is wonderful that you are still all in
this world where you can communicate with each other.

Well, on Friday, I took three typed volumes of my special
poet—450 pieces in all—and plonked 'em on Douglas Stewart's
desk. I can't find the *Bulletin* clipping in which he reviewed
'Moles'. I forget if he said that there was no real poetry in my
bird or not—doesn't matter if he did, but I remember that he
wound up by saying that no one wd know whether E was a
poet or not till the mass of pieces Miles Franklin had could be
seen. That was what gave me my little leverage. I gave him a
chance of seeing them. He said it was very impressive to see such
a mass of work as he turned over the pages. That's not all, said
I. I have over a hundred more pieces but as they have been under
other eyes than mine they can't be produced at present. Dear
me! said he. I said I don't know whether I'm an ass or not, I
don't pretend to be a judge of poetry, but this is either a poet,
or either she is not. If she is not, well and good, but if she is,
it is a terrible thing that her stuff shd be mouldering here and
we not to recognise it till we are dead. He eagerly said he was
sure that there was great merit. ... Then he said in this matter
of the poet when the time came to divulge her name would I
consider the *Bulletin* and give the story to the Red Page, that
I cd tell it any way I liked. That wd be most exciting I felt,
and a good thing for my poet to have a real place like that for
her story. I told him I wd certainly consider the *Bulletin* and
that he could be sure that the identity would not leak out from
me that I cannot be smoked out in these things—I've had much
guerrilla warfare practised on me without success to the
guerrillas in making me divulge literary secrets. You see, in
keeping such secrets you not only have to be staunch and keep
the secret, but you have to have more intelligence than the

detectives or they can arrive at things by inference and deduction. He is to let me know some time. But he says he is swamped now with poetry especially AIF stuff, and that has to have his consideration. He is a frail looking chap and only 29.

Then I went to call on B Davis, who is editor of the Angus and R publications. I asked her casually how Eve Langley was getting on, the author of *Pea Pickers*, which I abominate, and over which B D and I had a stiff difference of opinion. She told me (this is confidential) that poor Eve is in a lunatic asylum and all communications about her royalties have to be directed to the Master in Lunacy. I was shocked. Though I considered her stuff sheerly phoney and her a poseuse I did not go as far as this—we are frail mortals—all sorts of devils lurk to defeat and devour us.

I'm going out to the University to hear Green lecture on Bin Bin. . . .

My love to you and Mabel

[unsigned]

7.60 To E J Brady [Melbourne]
Source: FP 37

Carlton
Aug 10, 1943

Dear Mr Brady

It is very nice to have a letter from you for any reason though I cannot help you about J F Archibald as I never saw him nor had any communication with him. I was not in the *Bulletin* galaxy. Never had any association with the *Bulletin* till I won the Prior Memorial Prize in 1936 with *All That Swagger*. This would be the Irish family which I'm glad you enjoyed.

I nearly wrote to you last month but it was one of those impulses that died. The subject of my communication would have been Nancy Consett-Stephen whose death was announced recently. You will have forgotten, but I remember clearly. Miss Scott's drawing-room was full of people who came to call on

me, but who of course did not linger long with an unsophisticated girl from the bush in a sailor suit, but had great re-unions
among themselves.

You had a long talk with Miss Stephens and a few bantering
words aside for the sailor collar—but I have never forgotten
them. Never before nor since perhaps have so few words had
such powerful effect on an Australian writer. Under the
mournful influence of my dear, dear Hy Lawson I was in the
sad heart breaking sunset aura. You said that was nonsense—
sheer nonsense. There was no tragedy in Australia except what
people made for themselves. Here was a great warm continent
where even swaggies without a copper could be comfortable in
the friendly bush. You struck for me the key note of my natural
outlook. . . .

> With kind remembrance
> [unsigned]

7.61   From Vida Goldstein, Melbourne
Source: FP 10

> South Yarra
> August 18 1943

My dearest Stella

We were glad to hear from you, & glad too to have John with
us on Sunday afternoon. Still more glad to hear from him that
you are coming over so soon. Give us a choice of evenings when
you can first come to see us. Wednesday, you may remember,
is our Testimony Meeting, but usually we are free other evenings,
& on Saturday and Sunday afternoons.

We liked John immensely. At first he was shy & quiet, not
being quite sure of his ground with three old ladies! But when
he saw we were not so unapproachable as our age might suggest,
he became perfectly natural and at ease. We were much interested
in his description of Air Force life, planes, flying etc.

Try, my dear, to put him in God's care. This will help you
to overcome your fear about him. . . .

Miles Franklin with her nephew, Norman John Franklin, who qualified as a pilot 22 September 1943 (ML)

The elections! What do you think of them. In all my 40 years knowledge of Federal politics, I have never known them at such a low moral ebb. In a time of national and international crisis, it is deplorable that there should be such mud slinging.

Lovingly
Vida

7.62   To Clem Christesen, Brisbane
Source: MA

Carlton
Sept 2 1943

Dear Clem Christesen

I'm so glad *Meanjin* is going to give space to Tom Collins. Indeed we wd honor ourselves and take up a little of the slack of the disgrace of our neglect if one number at this time were all his. I have done one article on him over the air, one for the Comm Review and another is asked for: and the literary difficulty is this. Were *Such is Life* widely known I could do half a dozen different articles on T C. But *S is L* is not yet available and there is need of a basic outline of T C himself; and that material is limited and cannot be varied. This need was brought home to me the other day when an educated and informed Furphyite told me she had hung on the radio dial like a man awaiting a race meeting announcement lest she shd miss what I'd say of Furphy because she could find no one who cd tell her who and what he was. Such people have to be catered for at present.

I have a number of letters from Furphy from which I used but limited extracts in the Furphy biography (in MSS) firstly because they wd take up too much space and secondly because I did not want to insert too much of myself in the book. He exhorted me on democracy, on writing and on marriage etc. Some extracts might be good meat now, as I don't suppose there will be a printing of his letters in full for a long time, and he is well ahead of the most advanced of our reformers, democrats and revolutionists on the question of the 'new order'.

I have been tempted often to write a letter to T C but it will have to wait till I have more time for thought: the airing of any trivial issue hurriedly makes a shoddy showing before his magnanimity and calm sense of purpose.

Let me know about the extracts.

Sincerely in haste
Miles Franklin

7.63 *To Kate Baker, Melbourne*
Source: VKP

Carlton
September 28, 1943

Dear Miss Baker

According to promise I send herewith (two copies) my message for the Furphy ceremony on Oct. 2. It is 125 words and takes one minute to repeat slowly. Mrs Palmer read my message in 1934. I should like her to do so again, provided, of course, that she would feel inclined to do so and well enough.

Sincerely
Miles Franklin

JOSEPH FURPHY'S CENTENARY

We are here today, in spirit or in person, to mark the centenary of a distinguished Australian. His own fraternity—the writers of this Commonwealth—reverence Joseph Furphy as one of our ablest interpreters, one of the first, as A G Stephens would have said, who wrote in the Australian idiom untinctured by alien notions. By his great gifts of artistry—self-tutored and self-disciplined—Joseph Furphy gave us *Such is Life*, that grandest of works produced entirely *in* Australia, *about* Australia, *by* an Australian, *for* Australians. Because of his nobility and surety of purpose, this man and his book, inseparable in legend, are a beacon of faith, courage, and integrity in our developing national and world consciousness. We hold in grateful memory—JOSEPH FURPHY!

6 October 1943

Dear Miles

Last Saturday at the Furphy tree-planting I read your message, as you wished. I haven't your good, rich voice, but there was a mike and at least I made it clear. It was very welcome. I think the ceremony was a success—a perfect afternoon, plenty of interested outsiders & a solid core of devotees. I was very glad indeed to met Sam Furphy. He told me a good deal about his father, & must have been a great help to you, in places. Miss Baker managed marvellously, but I wondered if her strength would give way afterwards.

The day before that, I went to see Mr Catomore, of the Equity Trustees, to find if it would be legally correct for me to invite you to do part of the work on Alice Henry's MS. Miss Newsham had told you all about her forthcoming move to Sydney.

May I put it to you quite simply as I see it? In the first place, Miss Henry hoped you would be her literary executor, but this was impossible as you were not in Melbourne. So I was appointed, and this year I have been through her papers up to the end of her autobiographical MS & others; with Miss Newsham, obtained answers & advice from some of her American friends, & then had to pause through sudden illness that hung over a good while.

Now that Miss Newsham is going to Sydney, taking all her papers, it is easy for you to get access to them. The MS tails off at the year 1924. Would you be willing to write in your own [word illegible] a short resumé of her later years, with retrospect on your experience with her at work in America? Would a fee of £10 be reasonable for this? Mr Catomore said it was legally my job to ask anything.

The idea was—*I'd like your opinion on this*—not to attempt to get a printed book done, as it was never finished off. We thought of a roneo MS bound securely & produced in, say, a hundred copies for presentation to selected libraries, here & in

America, for use by students. Mrs Mary Beard approved of this & said she could place a dozen copies in libraries where they would definitely be used. I'm enquiring here at the National Library about such copies, which are usual enough in American libraries. They are going to show me some, received from America, & I need to get an idea of the cost. Also it may be difficult to get even so simple a job done efficiently in war-time.

All this is just business—I'd like to say how glad I am to have worked in any way on Alice Henry's heroic & enterprising record. First & last, she was a wonderful woman. Have you ever thought of writing, independently, about those years with her in America? . . .

With my good wishes
Sincerely
Nettie Palmer

7.65 To Dymphna Cusack, Newcastle, New South Wales
Source: DCP

Carlton
Oct 13 1943

Dymphana m'dear

You flatteringly ask how I reconciled the claims of job, personal and literary life, etc. Well, *I didn't*. I have never written except rough fragments which are merely a sample of all that was once dammed-up in me, and which is now atrophying.

As to biographies: were I a czar or a god, and could I issue a decree it would be that I should be cremated and pass without even the small notice in the *SMH*'s expensive mortuary cols and no memorial meetings or pilgrimages. That is why when called upon to do the Lawson and Furphy orations—I made them wholly affectionate and a flourish—a humble tribute. I think there is nothing so pathetic as some little mediocrity patronising his dead superior, or as Sam Furphy said of Kate Baker, 'having a career on the shoulders of dear old Dads'.

I too have ensured that there will be no data on my love life.

I recently went into a great trunk and destroyed scores of letters. One dear old friend went around telling everyone how I had refused him. I used to argue that he had never really proposed. Had entirely forgotten; but there among the letters were his very definite proposals; not only from him but from others I had similarly forgotten. A Senator from another state called me up some months ago and asked me had I forgotten his proposal to me on board the ship when I first left Australia. I'm sure he never proposed, but he swore he had done so. So I said flippantly, 'Are you proposing again now?' He said, 'Yes, if you are the same radiant creature that I knew.' 'Don't be an ass,' I replied; 'how radiant would you be after thirty years?' I'm sure this man never proposed to me, but I think he imagines he did. I think that when a girl is the rage lots of men who have never said a love word to her imagine they have had great sentimental sessions. . . .

Now to business. I think the poem of Ian's I read you was about Ned Kelly. It is not yet printed. I enclose my only copy as I have not time to copy it. Will you please treat it like a sacred relic and return. . . .

Ian has just won fifty pounds as a prize for a long Australian poem. Crowley and others gave the prize in memory of W J Miles, which mightn't seem propitious, but the judge was Louis Lavater, who is one of the elders, orthodox poetically, with a great admiration and knowledge of the sonnet form; and there were 152 entries. As Ian is so unorthodox metrically his winning under Louis from such a large field has exhilarated me, and you will be right up to date in the poets coming home. The conditions for this long poem contained the proviso that they or it had to have love of Australia. . . .

My nephew—oh, you know him, so I can say John—has gone north on transporting troops to the islands—three months as second pilot to harden his training: but troop planes without guns are a fat and desirable target. How is your John?

No time for more, love from Miles

Carlton
Oct 19 43

Dear Nettie

Thank you for reading my message. I know you did it better
than I cd have done. Also thanks for news of Furphy event. I
hope Miss Baker still thinks there is more to do as it is her very
life and it is nice to see a person of her age so harmonious and
absorbed.

Now as to the Alice Henry memoirs. I have no idea whether
ten pounds or a hundred would be too much or too little. It
is not that I wd want a lot of money for doing them but that
I cannot afford to be out of time and pocket. I don't seem to
be able to rise to the job emotionally. If you and Isabel were
here or I there and we three cd consult surely we could finish
the thing pronto.

I left Miss Henry in 1915. I saw her again in Chicago in 1923
and stirred up the powers to do something for her instead of
just turning her out to grass (that is Aust) when they had done
with her and she was getting 'quite senile' as they said. So she
was given a year in London and I saw her there. She returned
to Australia permanently and then came and stayed a month
in the house with us and again was in Sydney at the YWCA.
Her life when she was dumped back to Australia to be with
her bro and then his loss was a sad tragedy. She told me in '34
when I spent some weeks with her in Melb that she was dying
of inanition for want of being with people who mattered and
using her special faculties and knowledge. So I suggested the
memoirs. I knew she was incapable of focussing them to a
conclusion but all I wanted was something to engage her
attention. By her letters to me I am sure the memoirs served
this purpose. She took the task with monumental seriousness.
I started her on her other two books and the task of extracting
them from her was monumental. It wd increase my desolation
and enervation to have the memoirs dumped on me and would

be the irony of fate. With you and Isabel (I mean the three of us) it wd be a tolerable adventure.

This is private of course.

She was enchanted to have you as her literary executor. She thought that out of dutifulness she shd mention me but I knew her satisfaction when I agreed that you would be at hand and also so much more suited to the job. I know she would love to have these memoirs completed and distributed as you suggest (that alone shows you are the right person on the job) and I think she is entitled to spend some of her income on it provided that it is not impoverishing her sister-in-law in her frailty and old age. So don't have sweated labor ideas in asking for any allotments for the work. . . .

Sincerely
[unsigned]

7.67 *From Hilda Esson, Melbourne*
Source: FP 38

Parkville
15 Dec 1943

Dearest Miles

It hasn't been easy to write to you, though I have thought of you so much during the last weeks. You have had so much personal sorrow, that I can't bear to think of your suffering for other people; but your wisdom and sympathy are a great support to me—

Louis, of course, had the highest opinion of you, and real affection, and he appreciated your rare and pungent wit; as he always did love a good phrase and a well-turned epigram. I find scattered through his letters and notes many quotations that took his fancy.

It has been very hard to re-adjust. I'm going through his work as objectively as possible, trying to decide what he might wish to be remembered by; but my memories of all our years are so vivid and I was so close to it all, it is very difficult. He was such a unique & rare mind & spirit, and had such a heart-breaking time, that perhaps he never quite expressed his real genius. My greatest regret is that in his last years, he was too ill to have the will and energy to do himself anything like justice.

I hope you are feeling better—Don't let yourself be overcome by grief and anxieties. You are too valuable a person yourself to allow anything to prevent your giving all you have to your own work—

I hope I'll be able to go to Sydney next year. I'm most anxious to see you & have a long talk again.

Yours lovingly
Hilda

7.68 To Mary Anderson, Washington
Source: MAP

[page 1 missing]   [received 15 December 1943]

... Two Alabamans wandered into our Fellowship of Writers' Sunday evening lecture lately. It was a play night with a sketch about our drovers taking cattle in the dry centre ninety mile stretches without water. They could not understand that. They said there was water everywhere in Alabama, yes ma'am! I said there also was water everywhere in my part of the country, which is the SE corner of the continent. By the way it has lately been made into a great national reserve like Yosemite Park. I was very proud because in the papers it referred to it as the Miles Franklin country. It is the country mentioned in *All That Swagger.*

The visit from Mrs Roosevelt cheered us all up. My nephew is flying in the Pacific area. Anxious days. He was expecting to be put with the Americans. That would delight me, of course. God send he comes back safely. ...

Now I'm going to listen to Camilla Wedgwood talking on Is Chastity a good thing? She is the daughter of Lord Wedgwood the China man. She came out here once as delegate to a scientific conference and was so taken with Australia that she never rested till she got a job here. She is head of the Women's College at the University and says she would live nowhere else but here. She is capable and learned—the sort of person we need from overseas.

I am so homesick for you all over there—what's the good? There will never be a new order that will give me a chance to see you again I fear. The new order will be like the old with the haybags and gangsters enjoying all the loot and the rest of us struggling to pay the taxes and scrimping to keep body and soul together.

Your loving friend
S M Franklin

The Hon Camilla Wedgwood was very good. Forthright and clear. She is an anthropologist. She evidently believes in chastity same as I do, but the fashion has been so much otherwise for a generation that one has had to let the non-chaste rattle about their exploits and keep quiet—keep one's wowserism as a dark horse. The funny thing is I am at work on a play with Camilla's thesis but it is very difficult to do. The play was too advanced even for New York ten years ago. I was afraid it might now be too behind the times, but Camilla's talk was the same thing in another form of literature—the radio short talk.

7.69   *From Harold Ickes, Washington*
Source: FP 12

The Secretary of the Interior
January 27, 1944

My dear Miss Franklin

Your letter of December 14 has just reached me. I am glad that my voice carried on the air well as you describe. What I had to say touched on matters that are of vital interest in this country and in England as well. I suppose that you have your own problems on account of the war.

Your pronunciation of my name is not as it has been pronounced in the family for as long as I can remember. It is the second syllable that seems to cause the trouble, but the correct pronunciation is not, as you put it, Ick'ees'. The 'e' is a short 'e'. The pronunciation of the final syllable is almost that of a short 'i'. Literally, I suppose that the pronunciation is between that of a short 'i' and a short 'e'.

Astonishingly enough, your letter was not opened by the censor. This would seem to indicate that the officials in Australia have a greater respect for a member of the United States Cabinet than our own censorship office, which has no hesitation in opening letters plainly addressed to me by official name. It might almost be assumed that anyone writing from anywhere to a member of the Cabinet would not be transmitting military secrets in the expectation that they would be forwarded to the Nazis.

The war seems to go well but I am confident that the worst is ahead of us. It is a long, costly and frightful affair from any point of view.

Margaret Robins has been having a bad time with her heart recently but Raymond seems to be holding his own.

Sincerely yours
Harold L. Ickes

7.70   *To Mary Fullerton, Sussex*
Source: FP 18

Carlton
Mar 24 44

My dear precious Mary, How could I live without you! I have been away three weeks in my native fastnesses beyond Canberra and find your wonderful letter of 28 Jan, which arrived probably about Mar 17—or earlier. Containing three poems *Chart*, *Choice* and *Gold Fish*. Also among my mail was a request from Elisabeth Lambert, who says she is editing an Australian edition of the US verse journal *Voices* to appear in summer and she wanted some of 'E's' to choose from. The letter has been re-addressed and astray because NSW was omitted—had been to Melb, St Kilda etc—I hope the delay hasn't excluded 'E'. . . .

I went back to Brindabella fifty miles beyond Queanbeyan and Canberra to my mother's first married home. The trees remain and the outlines of her garden beds and also the furrows on the flat which were there before our advent. I had not been back for 44 years. There was much sadness in return and much bliss too. My cousin—the one of my decade, is still there. I separated from him when 8 and found a new man. He was like his mother and like my father and also had touches of my brother—it was like balm to find him there welcoming me, so gentle, with the family wit and hospitality. A healing gift on my desolation. He and I went riding the very first day on a pilgrimage. But he is so frail. About like you in physique and it is so hard in the country now—no man power at all. No one to do anything. His son Lindsay was released from the army after two years and went home the same day as I. They wondered how he wd shape. He is 23 and a beauty. Six feet or over and perfect in face and body—I have never seen a film star more beautiful. He chored around the house for two days and then took his bit of bread and beef and some apples and went out six or eight miles on the run to ring-bark as the scrub is getting away from them. Rabbits galore eating everything and parrots also swallowing the orchard harvest and the cockatoos come to eat the maize. I don't think they'll get a bite as they have no ammunition. There that boy slogs all day, gets home at dark to kill a sheep, and then, there being a terrible drought on and the bath full of precious carried water he goes off in the dark half a mile to swim in the river. Worked all the week, even Sat, till dark and on Sunday spent his time constructing a case to fill with apples for me to bring home. He really is a darling. The town parasites show up very badly beside that kind of boy. His sister is a living wonder. Ran the mail, ran the house, ran the post office, breaks in horses, oodles of fowls, knits her jumpers, mends, and when crowds of unexpected guests arrive at the oddest moments never fails to rise to the occasion like a trout. There is a fearful drought on. Even the creek that supplies the water system is dry, and water to be carried up a fearsome hill. It means too, stock have to be shifted out every day to get water. Terrible to see the winter coming and they already hand-feeding. Willows cut down for the cows, even. You hear a lot

*Miles Franklin and horse, near Brindabella. As late as 1944 she
relished the chance of a ride (ML)*

about the land-grabbers but I'd like to know what such people get out of it. After a hundred years that boy begins all over again on those hills with his own strength.

Even the drought and lack of workers couldn't quite destroy the loveliness. Orchard full of most glorious apples, plums, pears, almonds—and quinces coming on. I don't know which I like best—damsons, egg plums, greengages or prunes. They had gravensteins and twenty-ounce apples, and the old two-pounder pears. . . .

Well, this is a terrible long letter. You need not read it all. I enclose two clippings—one mentions E. I'm taking *Meanjin Papers* for this year and will send on to you as it comes along.

All my love and praying that the pain will ease.

Your devoted
Miles

7.71   From R G Howarth, Sydney
Source: FP 33

University of Sydney
20 V 1944

Dear Miles Franklin

I should have answered your letter before, but have been struggling with (at the same time) lectures and a cold. I hope you'll forgive me.

Unfortunately, the rest of what I had to say about you in that article was cut (with other matters) to fit it into a certain space. I thought that 'one of the three books that patently compose *All That Swagger*' might have been a better choice. Of all your books (all of which I've read, some more than once, ever since my delighted discovery of *My Brilliant Career* when I was an undergraduate), I like *Old Blastus* least. 'Old Blastus' is the 'true character' I referred to, and I feel that he is weak and does not altogether live up to his name: that is 'imperfectly realised', does not become real, take life. Mabel is not a 'character' in that sense, and I think she is better done. Dora, on the other hand (since you invite my views) fails to convince me. Would a girl of her time and situation really regard her sister as 'a bad woman' because of something that had happened to her when she was young? Would Old Barny, for that matter, act as he did in the whole business?

The trouble for me is, I suppose, that the story belongs to a time before mine (and in a way too to the conventions of that time), and so I am quite out of sympathy. But even on its own canvas I feel that it is only a near-success: that there was good material ('Old Blastus' especially), but it is insufficiently organised and vitalised. You, I know, will want me to speak plainly.

In *All That Swagger*, however, I feel that, but for a rather staccato style, you control your theme. I think you've packed too much in—you had material for a whole saga—but you record life and make real a succession of lives. In *Pioneers on Parade* (with the exception of the Ned Kelly business, which I think misses badly), you and Dymphna Cusack have done something extremely clever. And let me add that I enjoyed *Bring the Monkey*!

But now, I want *My Brilliant Career* in the Australian Pocket Library. I can't help feeling it is still, after all, your best (whether you are Brent of Bin Bin I leave out of consideration). There you wrote a most brilliant book for your age and your time—perfectly within the time and all the better for it. It has all the dash and fire of your later work with (may I say?) more discipline. Why not *My Brilliant Career*? Can't copyright difficulties be overcome? Surely it cries aloud for the attention of the Commonwealth Literary Fund. It has never been reprinted has it? (By the way, I came across a reference to what is apparently the American edition, in— of all places—a treatise on *The Rhetoric of Donne's Verse* published in 1909.) If we are to have 'classics' revived, let us have *My Brilliant Career*.

I too think some of the other selections peculiar—more peculiar than I was able to say or suggest. Again there were cuts, of course. I should like to query *We of the Never Never*, *Haxby's Circus*, *Tiberon*, even *Man Shy* and *The Passage*, both of which would well be revised and also, in parts, rewritten. The *Glass-*

House I did query, and could say more. The *House is Built* is still, I believe, M B E's best.

There seems to be a wholesale confusion and clash between 'quality' and personal interest or convenience. I am sorry to see it. There's going to be continued criticism.

You refer to 'Furnley Maurice' as 'academic'. But isn't it the fact that he began as a bookstore boy, had no particular education, and was put in charge of the Melbourne University Press largely because of his experience and his own independent literary work? I deprecate any depreciation of 'academicism' (there's more, in the worse sense, in Australia, surely), because only among university-trained people, I believe, can there be found unbiased, disinterested criticism. Perhaps they take too wide (not too narrow) a view. But they usually know what they are talking about. You will allow me to make this defence. See, for example, *Southerly* criticism. I must stop. I'm very interested in what you say about those words.

> Believe me, Your sincere friend
> Guy Howarth

7.72 *To R G Howarth, Sydney*
Source: FP 33

> Carlton
> May 22 44

Dear Mr Howarth

I was sorry immediately I had dropped my note in the letter box, feeling it an imposition on your good nature, as I'm sure you too suffer from endless calls upon you, and I had heard that you had been suffering from overwork. Your good nature in response calls for rejoinder without delay.

First of all, a small point; do you mean that there is a reference to *M B C*—an American edition? I shd like to be sure about this. It wd be pirating, and I shd be horrified. I clearly stipulated that no copies were to go to USA. There are no copyright difficulties with that book. It belongs to me. I withdrew it after it had run to a number of editions because the way it was acclaimed was such a disillusionment. The signs are that it would have sold more copies than *We of the NN* if left in circulation. Horrors! I have never looked in it since the year it came out, and have forgotten it.

I see that in *Blastus* I have not failed as much as you think. It is inconceivable that people shd be so incapable of realising past attitudes, even when that past is only a decade or two before their own time. I know of two mothers of Mabels who never left their homes again to visit so keenly did they feel the disgrace. . . .

On my first return after absence the old Australian way of life I had left was still hanging there, surprisingly, like a ripe plum. I had become a different mentality, but not my neighbors. The old pioneers plagued me for a book about the country so, tho in the midst of a holocaust at the time, I tossed off *Old Blastus*. I meant it to be a simple thing set exactly in its time. Novels of its time had chapter mottoes so I wrote my own instead of orthodoxly choosing high flown quotations. Do you mean to say that you don't realise what it was for a girl to make a slip in those days; right up to 1911 and perhaps later? I know of a feminine Arthur—a bright splendid girl ahead in studies—and sports—who, when she found out her aunt was her mother, turned sour and never went out. I know of a father who was a fiend to his sensitive shrinking daughter. He made her lie on the bed she had made by dragging her to court every now and again to sue for maintenance, tho she never got anything from the man involved. She would never have appeared outside again, but the child died and the father—hero—hunted her to church. That girl was a few years older than *myself*. I was about thirteen. On arriving at the church I was met by the other girls of the congregation with the great news that so-and-so was hiding in the porch! 'Don't go there!' I'm glad to remember that my sympathy was all for the girl. I marched straight in, kissed her effusively and took her into church with me. The remarks that went round were full of surprise that I shd act so, I, whom everyone had thought to be the 'purest and cleanest girl in the district'. Mark the silly adjective *purest*. Contraceptives must have resulted in an even greater revolution than I had realised in the attitude towards technical chastity. You can be sure that the material in *Blastus* is as sound as something a doctor might assemble on the basis of his case book. *Old Blastus* and his rages are composed and compiled from echoes that dropped from old men's beards when yarning.

I must have another shot at another case in which the girl committed suicide rather than face her disgrace.

I don't mind criticism at all. I'm always astonished when commended, the thing that gravels me is to be denigrated up one stump when I'm barking up another. For example, I don't mind people classifying *Pioneers on P* as trash, but what saddened me was the reaction of a number of pretentious people—people who can gibber about English stuff very creditably and think themselves sophisticated—and then to show themselves pitifully suffering our isolation and segregation in its restricting consequences—the reverse of the effect it had on a vast talent such as Furphy's.

I'm surprised you enjoyed the monkey. I wrote it as a lark. I have read no more than three detective novels in my life, but you'd be surprised by the amount of reading on criminology I did for that short effort. The cop on the beat came to my hostess's on business and I thought him a wonderful windfall, to get some information from the horse's mouth, but he was distant and respectful, and he didn't like to say, etc. The upshot was that he told his superior and an Inspector called and spent ever so much time going over points professionally—seemed to think it a great occasion. That's London for you. I had one triumph with the monkey: John Hobson, the economist, who, like many intellectuals, took recreation in detective fiction said the book hadn't a dull page in it and that he detected the murderer surprisingly late. His wife insisted that he didn't guess at all till the last.

As to *Blastus* getting into the pocket library—I can envisage the difficulties of the choosing committee—but time will sort out the chaff and include the best works of our best writers. It is a good move I think. *Swagger* is not yet free for a cheap edition. ...

I don't like either *Blastus* or the *Monkey*. In fact I don't like anything I've done wholly, except perhaps the unpublished sequel to *M B C* and that in print might be as. ...

[end of letter missing]

7.73 *To E H Burgmann, Goulburn, New South Wales*
Source: FP 27

Carlton
July 6, 1944

Dear Dr Burgmann

I've had an envelope addressed these many weeks but something always defers its despatch. I had hoped to have a book in return for your letters in the *SC* but delay in publication and the small editions are disheartening, when even despised Australian authors could sell in tens of thousands. One wd not complain of one's books being kept out of print (despite that it means no income) in face of the horror that puts millions of young men out of life or health only that there seems to be plenty of paper for trash and the 'nasties' and 'gigglies'. So in lieu of a book I enclose five shillings in stamps for a subscription. The paper, after I have read it has gone to the Middle East or to NG to boys of the Southern Districts who know the towns of your diocese.

I draw inspiration and comfort from your messages and am glad you are alive and in Australia. I wish you were within reach that even once a year I cd have the privilege of a confabulation with you. As it is, I faint in desolation, spiritual and physical. If only the silly slaughter would cease! What is to be done to bring under sane control the belligerent instinct of men combined with proneness to sexual intoxication—two drunkennesses which leave him continually the victims of the silly exploiters, the spurious patrioteers and others of that ilk. And whither Australia in the vortex?—Australia like a small child with a big prize in her hand. At anyrate I cling to personal and individual decency come what may—belief in goodness for its own sake

114

and the bedrock of all. And I'm against—definitely agin—any theory of filling up this beautiful globe with human beings just for the purpose of having one population big enough to counteract another.

Were I an absolute world dictator I'd give India over to a Committee of the Gandhis, Nehrus and all who crave national independence with the proviso that such Committee was to be doubled by the addition of the same number of American school teachers and physicians from New England and the Middle East—all women, and as many as practicable of them over 45 and unmarried. Japan I'd hand over to the Soviets to be taught to be comrades even under barrage. A dictatorship that has taken the women of Uzbekistan and such people off the dung hill and put them as members in the boss parliament of the USSR should be able to give Japanese a strong 'directive' about women that would cheer me. England could have China for a twin soul and they could paddle along together no doubt with interesting results. Australia I would give over to you provided you did not allow it to be too thickly overrun with human epizoa and that I shd have every facility to roman about the land which I love so much and attempt to communicate my ecstasy. North America and (Russian) USSR I leave to their own experiments for the present. South America could be forgotten for a time. This leaves all of non-Russian Europe unprovided for. But I think that the small Scandinavian countries, Switzerland and England have a right to express themselves. Have you any ideas.

Greetings and special regards to you and Mrs Burgman
[unsigned]

Diocesan Church House
10/7/44

Dear Miss Franklin

It is good to hear from you again. Many thanks for SC sub. I know what it feels like to have a MS in the hands of the publisher. Angus & R have had one of mine for months. They say they want to publish etc etc. but I wanted to get a word in on 'Education' while it is in the air. However I hope your next soon appears.

I approve your general disposition of world affairs, except my own allotment. Perhaps we shall meet sometime and make more precise allocations. Africa is a bit of a problem. 'Flying Bombs from Dakar land on New York'—a next war headline. So you see how important Africa has become. I have a feeling that the flying bomb does change things radically.

All the best always

Yours ever
Ernest Goulburn

7.75   *To Ian Mudie [Australian Army]*
Source: IMP

Carlton
Aug 31 44

My dearest Ian

I have not been able to get my head above water for a long time. I have three different vocations and they are too much for me: 1. charing and running this house and garden—all in a mess. 2. then I should like to write—no time, nothing but constant interruptions. 3. then there is life in general with all the calls you can think of, each one of the three would fully occupy and take all my time and strength—result is can follow none of them and so it's chaos.

I have your lovely *Dream* and congratulate you on M Preston's cooperation in the cover. Her drawings are just right for your work. Glad to see it is in second edition. Thanks for the copy you sent me. I heard you on the wireless one night but your voice sounded lighter over the air than when you were reading to me. Also saw your article in the *SMH*, and hooray for your paragraph in Autumn 44 *Meanjin*. I note that the *Dream* was adapted for radio—sorry I missed that.

Well Hope went for Max H in [the] before-mentioned *Meanjin*. I find that he (Max) is a young creature . . . [page damaged] will develop into an ordinary nonentity or a tiresome filibuster with age unless he had a spark of genius or any big talent. At present he is merely noisy. But it is wonderful how self-praise gets over, here, in our sparse population.

Have you completed your anthology? I hate to ask if it will soon appear as I know how things drag and drag, till it is an irritation continually to be interrogated about them.

Harley has been out to see me. There's no doubt he was hurt by that A First mess more than he will acknowledge. Also have seen Godfrey Bentley, who is going to join the noble army of the married sometime next year.

Oh, I nearly forgot. Last Sunday evening at the F of A Writers we had a trial of The Angry Penguins. There was a mixed jury and James Meagher was counsel for Def and I forget the name of the man who was prosecuting. Tom Moore was run-in as judge ten minutes before. Geo Farwell and Thompson were witnesses against and D Ingram Smith and some young fellow named Dane (?) witnesses for. For an impromptu affair it had some good things in it. Geo Farwell and Thompson were very good in defence of poetry, Tom was most humorous as the judge, giving ponderous ass rulings and defining poetry in the same strain. The jury kept asking questions such as the definition of poetry and if they could have the concise *Ox Dictionary*. The prosecuting man was good in the flat way he read poetry just as lawyers reduce everything to sawdust. Meagher was brilliant and put up a really good case for hoaxing—quoted culturedly in poetry. The verdict was guilty but recommendation to mercy.

I forget why. Then A Halloran (another lawyer) gave the vote of thanks and gave another decision in favour of Penguins. It was an amusing, if slight, affair, and a great ad for the Penguins of course. If you have a horn and keep on blowing it at least attention is drawn to the fact you have a horn and eventually the unthinking accept the noise that issues from the horn on the value the tooter puts on it.

All good luck always. If you don't hear from me you'll know it is not through lack of affection but because of other limitations. . . .

Much love to you [words illegible] and Bill

Miles

7.76   *From Frank Ryland [Australian Army]*
Source: FP 37

Sunday morning
[nd, 11/10/44]

Dear Miles

Just a line to let you know how things go down South of the border. I spent a most interesting afternoon with Nettie Palmer quite recently, and she asked me along to the Melb Fellowship, where I had a pleasant evening listening to Max Dunn criticise three recent books of verse, and later, Alan Marshall relate his experiences caravanning around the soldiery up North, and with the Airforce boys too. There I met Russell Oakes who took me along to the Bread and Cheese Club. . . . I got into a discussion again with Max Brand on poetry, and so he made an appointment to take me along on the Saturday week to meet Bernard O'Dowd, which I considered of course, a singular honor. At the Bread & Cheese Club (men only) a poet read the introduction by Mary Gilmore to a new Melbourne publication called *The Corroboree Tree*. A wonderful afternoon it was, and on the wall I noticed, among many other interesting pictures, one of Miles Franklin standing smiling across the border of one Aussie state, while Frank Clune smiled back at her from the Southern side. . . .

It was yesterday afternoon that I met Bernard O'Dowd a stately 77-year-old man, upright and forthright, a real personality, Miles. He introduced me to Marie E J Pitt, who inquired kindly after Sydney and its writers. O'Dowd gave an hour's talk on his friend Sydney Jephcott, and in a most beautiful voice and with just the right emphasis read (or rather 'sang') his friend's songs in a way I have never heard it done before. Bart Adamson and Roderic Quinn have that singing style, but O'Dowd read them better than anyone could, I'm sure. Let's hope the CLF publish his two out of print books with the addition of new ones yet unpublished because Jephcott of the cattle ranges and the Kosiusckan torrents, is truly Australian in spirit and a really great poet. O'Dowd has no time for the socalled modern poets who take obscurity as a special brand of profundity, but believes that one must make oneself understandable. Simplicity is his keynote. . . .

The Bread and Cheese Club specialises in real mateship and has but one shortcoming: its exclusion of women (except the woman-founder!).

The Fellowship here is more literary than ours. They think our executive rather too red, for they are Victorian which seems to be synonymous with conservatism. And Associate members seemed to be frowned upon. But all in all I have found Melbourne people most kind and warm hearted when you get to know them. They have their funny little ways like we have, but made a stranger very much at home.

Cheerio Miles for now. . . .

Yours sincerely
Frank Ryland

Carlton
Nov 22 1944

Dear Mr Roderick

I do not think that such a vol as you plan needs a foreword by anyone but the compiler, but you may disagree. As you expect to gain a Litt D through it, this automatically rules out any prefatory note whatever by me. I would not do you a disservice.

A more serious matter. You came to me in a friendly manner, so I am impelled to advise you out of my uncompromising stand as to what is owed to Australian creative writing.

You tell me you have obtained permission to use certain definitely specified extracts from numerous novels. I note that the Australians have given theirs whereas the English publishers have at least claimed some payment for their property, if they have not protected the geese that laid it.

Excuse my drawing your attention to the facts: you have been presented with over-generous excerpts, but you also make resumés and add connecting passages. In some cases you have done this with more than one novel of an author in your projected compendium. This makes of it not an anthology but an abridgment of these novels so that there will be no need for ordinary readers, and certainly none for those students who are only examination-passers, ever to look at the whole novels. It is an unwritten law that commentators and reviewers must not tell the story of a novel.

As to your claim that you are advertising Australian authors: a lady decried Mr Idriess to another Australian writer, because Mr Idriess had resorted to law to restrain a rich draper from appropriating one of his stories, and said she would have thought that Mr Idriess would be grateful to have his work advertised. The writer retorted that if Mr Idriess were to lift the draper's goods, the draper would demand payment as well as the incidental advertisement involved in the loss and/or use of his property. Self-respecting and aware writers would agree with this.

I consulted a poet with experience of compiling anthologies and he emphatically condemns the making of a précis of the novels. I also consulted Miss Prichard, whose judgment and experience are respected. She considers it a great disservice to Australian writers for any commentator to tell the story of a book and that this sort of confidence trick should not be permitted.

For years Australian works, which would have presented Australia authentically and adequately, have been out of print while spurious stuff, lacking all quality of genuine Australianism has been reaping a war harvest. Now, many distinguished writers are in danger of being swamped anew by the trade machinations and wares of English and American publishers.

I am sure that in your ambition to procure a doctorate of letters, and thus to reap emoluments from Australian literature not enjoyed by those who create it, you do not wish to be yet another obstruction between writers and their just rewards. I have given to this matter more time than I can afford simply out of devotion to the cause of Australian imaginative literature and in goodwill to you, who are acting perhaps merely out of inexperience.

[unsigned]

Carlton
Nov 24 1944

Dear K B, OBE

Thanks for your letter of Nov 19th. I telephoned the Manager
of A and R and was promised the bibliography page within a
day or two, so hold on. After all the waiting this further hitch
at the last is disappointing, but every author is in the same boat.
It is, after all, a lesser matter when one thinks of the boys and
what they are facing.

About presentation copies: A and R sent one to Sam. Mr
Pescott and Mr McCartney will also be taken care of. I tell you
so we shan't lose our precious complimentary copies in dupli-
cation, and can keep them for other friends.

Of course half the royalties belong to you. The adventure was
a full partnership. As things went at the last (not through my
wish) I term it association instead of collaboration so that I can
take all the blame and brickbats, but due acknowledgment is
made of the fact that the work would never have been attempted
without you and your valuable original matter plus your
wonderful knowledge and clarity among the documents. I shall
tell Mr Cousins once again to divide the royalties between us.
Furphy would not have it otherwise, I'm sure.

I feel sure too that he would be kind to the book and forgive
its faults and omissions. If consciousness could be carried beyond
I think further that his great sense of humor would be tickled
by Helenar going modern in her behaviour. She will perhaps be
all the more satisfied to get back to Sollicker in the second
edition. So you note carefully the errors in hopes there will be
another edition in which they can be rectified.

With all good wishes
Sincerely
Miles Franklin

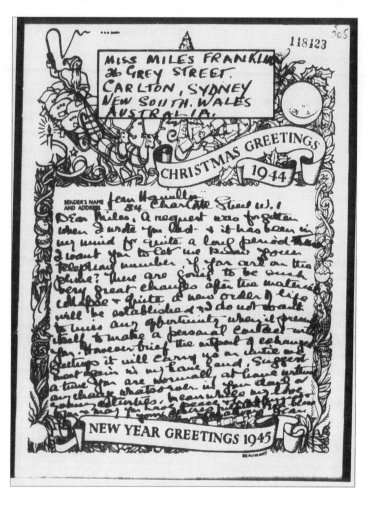

'May you have peace & happiness & your desires fulfilled': a war-weary lettercard from Jean Hamilton, London, 1944

Carlton
Feb 22 1945

My dear Catherine

How generous of you to write so about the Furphy effort—
life-saving just when I need it. The book wd have been more
interesting with more photographs larger, but we were limited
in art paper. It will have served its humble purpose in recording
a few facts if it inspires others to do better. As you say the
field is vast and exciting. Tackling it one feels like a puppy
when he tries to run off with a green bullock's hide laid out
for pegging.

As for the White Australia policy it was the religion of all
decent men in those days. Democrats didn't want indentured
or submerged classes. Also miscegenation was looked upon with
horror by those unfamiliar with it and practised with the usual
abandon by those who had the opportunity.

I doubt if miscegenation as a sin or if such a thing as
miscegenation will exist much longer. If the world becomes one
unit and all receive education tribes will not be able to look
down on one another because of complexion. They will
intermingle wholesale and become shaded down. In the light
of new studies it appears that all brains are much the same, that
men when reared in similar environments with similar chances
of development are much alike. The necessity for an unborn soul
is to procure a body, some body, any body black white or yellow,
a body being indispensable for our functioning on this plane,
without one a fellow is handicapped and relegated to the
frustrated antics of ghosts.

I'm so glad to hear about your play. It is grand to think of
you and Hilda in cahoots about it. It is desperate that we have
no working theatre here. Without that we can have no national
drama no matter how many subsidised buildings we may get.
I wish you and Hilda were over here. It is a big country and
we are so scattered. We'll be getting somewhere with native

drama when it will be usual for critics and others to go from one capital to another to see a new play by C D or some other Australian put on and when Melb wd have notice of such when put on in Syd and vice versa. . . .

Keep me informed about your play. Miracles sometimes happen unexpectedly, and I might see it there or here.

For the present my love and thanks for your cheer
[unsigned]

7.81 To Lucy Spence Morice, Adelaide
Source: FP 22

Carlton
Ap 18 45

Dear Friend

Yes, thank you, I have a copy of *An Agnostic's Progress*. It is the copy which your dear Aunt sent to Alice Henry in 1901. At the last dear Alice Henry sent me various of her treasures. She also gave me a copy of *State Children* and when I was in Adelaide I found a copy of *The Laws We Live Under* in a second hand book shop. So anything you have had better go to the Archives as every scrap will be sought in later years.

Now to business. I am on the Board of the Fellowship's embryo Co-operative Publishing Society and have been asked to proceed with my ambition of getting *Clara Morison* in to the Australian Pocket Library, which is sponsored by The Commonwealth Literary Fund. There were 25 books chosen by the Committee of the Literary Fund for this library, as you may have noticed in the Press. Twenty-five-thousand copies of each book are printed in cheap form so that the general public can have an opportunity to buy some genuine Australian works— old classics and new. I want to get *Clara Morison* into the second list. You know what I think of it and I would be willing to write a preface saying so.

Your Aunt died in 1910, so there will be some years of the copyright of the book still to run.

1. You are your aunt's nearest living relative, are you not? or has she other nieces or nephews still living?

2. Did your aunt will the copyright to any special person either directly or as part of the residue of her estate?

It is likely that the book is yours. In that case will you please write me a letter giving me power to act as your honorary agent.

3. Do you know of a copy of *Clara Morison* anywhere that I could use to get it printed?

There is one copy in the Mitchell Library and it would be necessary to go there and copy it out unless some private copy is available.

In the event of the book being printed, ten per cent is the royalty paid on the retail prices of these books, and it would go to you.

It has long been my dream to have this book in circulation. You don't know how I regret that I knew of your aunt only as a reformer. If I had only known of this book what communion we might have had. When I came home and read it she had gone, and the fact that I missed knowing her as an author has filled me with irritation for her great admirers ever since and so I want the book to be got out.

I am glad you are comfortably fixed again domestically in your lovely cottage and with a congenial daughter-in-law at hand.

> With love and hoping to hear from you
> Stella Franklin

7.82 *To Elisabeth Christman, Washington*
Source: FP 24

> Carlton
> April 20 1945

Dear Elisabeth Christman

It is your turn for a letter and yesterday I heard the sad news of Mrs Robins' death and am so saddened that I have forgotten what I wanted to write about. She was the pivot on which we revolved during the years I was there with you all. It is so lonely to be so far from you all when these gaps occur. How I wish I could see you all once again.

Mrs Robins with her warm vivid personality, her courage and resourcefulness was never dismayed but always full of energy and plans to transcend difficulties and banish melancholy. She was particularly near and dear to me as she supplied the loss of relatives (so far away) and had me with her so much at her home and when travelling, even to sharing her sleeper on those sorties when we went two in a berth to save funds. Thus, not only in a public way did she take me into a new life so different from my early days but she filled it with affection and care as well. She was certainly one of the great personalities during her public decades.

This morning in my mail box were the February Bulletin and the green covered brochure about post war jobs for women. Don't fear that these are ever wasted. I give them to Muriel Heagney, who was over in a labor delegation just before Pearl Harbor, or to the editor of our little *Women's Digest*. This was started a few months ago by Jessie Street, our woman delegate to San Francisco Conf. I am on the board of advisers. Of course we have a struggle to get paper and money and so on. Reminds me of when we started *Life and L.* I send you a couple of copies. One has an article about Mary Anderson.

I send you also a copy of my latest book *Joseph Furphy*. It can be of no interest to you as it is about an unknown Australian but you can take a squint at it for old sake's sake and pass it on to the Library of Congress. . . .

Dear Elisabeth, do tell me about yourself, personally. How do you live? And I am so eager to hear from Mary now that she has retired. Tell her to write me a long letter. She will have time now. There's a great drop in going out of office. I turned to my literary campaign, of course, and there will be plenty of use for me there as long as my mind is agile. If you stagger through the introductory chapter of Furphy it will give you a light on some things here. We are at the stage USA was in 20 or more years ago when Mencken and others began to filibuster for real American literature. Our Universities are English garrisons of thought and most of our writers are imitators of English just as they were with you once upon a time.

Dear President Roosevelt, we were all broken hearted by his sudden going. I saw it on a headline a man was reading when I went into town and it made me sick. He was at the height of his power like Lincoln. Thus he will be perpetuated forever without any tedious decline. His personality penetrated to every corner of the globe. . . .

Mrs Roosevelt certainly made hay while the sun shone and took life during the opportunity afforded her as a grand spree. I hope the new first lady won't be such a poor little rag as Mrs Wilson number 2.

We were almost safe from the war here except when it reached out and took our young men and boys. Nevertheless we are very tired. We tried to do too much with too few people in a big continent. . . .

My dear love to you as ever, your old colleague

[unsigned]

7.83 *From Elisabeth Christman, Washington*
Source: FP 24

National Women's Trade Union League of America
July 20 1945

Dear Stella

What a joy to have your long letter. Hail to my illustrious predecessor! How I do treasure your warm and straight from the heart tribute to dear Mrs Robins. I shall send a copy of it to Col Robins, who as you know has never quite recovered from the fall which caused paralysis from the waist down. He gets about some with the aid of various contrivances—but now with Mrs Robins gone he is very lonely—and Chinsegut has lost its sparkle. I miss Mrs Robins terribly—her letters were always an inspiration and never missed giving expression to a new thought or a forward seeing suggestion. The last time I saw her was more than two years ago when she spent a week in Washington on her return from Maine and on her way to her home in Florida. We had a high tea for her at the Women's University Club. Many old friends came and some new ones. Mrs Robins was gay and in high spirits. She made a speech—for the League—with all her old fire and conviction. She was ill then and looked frail. (She would not admit this.) During the last year her heart behaved badly at intervals. Dear Mary Dreier went down there often and was with her when she died—peacefully and without further struggle. And so a great light went out of our lives— a light which illuminated our League for many years. The women workers—and especially the trade union women owe much to her efforts, so that they too would glimpse the mountain top. By now I hope you have the June issue of *Life and Labor Bulletin* with our tribute. Australia seems so far away, despite the fact that the world has grown smaller because the airplane has conquered distance. . . .

I am almost a Washingtonian—having lived here for 15 years. . . . The National League is getting on—perhaps as its Executive I should not boast and say more. I raise the National budget etc etc and when occasion requires I am the Secretary–Treasurer! And we are financially solvent! I had to get in that plug. I have a comfortable small apartment and enjoy it. I am well and am sprouting some grey hair—not too many—but I can see 'em. My job is a hectic one but I like it. I was released for two six month periods with the US Women's Bureau to work for equal pay in war production industries. It was an exciting assignment and I learned a lot. Besides it took me close to the war jobs done by women. I was in the field part of the time—but always kept my hand on the League—because no one was appointed in my place. It was not an easy year—but I loved it. I was asked to remain for the duration—but the Board said no. And so I returned to my league desk. The contacts I made are helpful to the League.

Thanks for your book. I shall read it with more than ordinary interest. Then pass it on to the Congressional Library. Mary Anderson wants to read it too. Thanks too for the *Women's Digest* which I am glad to have. Is there a biography of Alice Henry? Someone asked me about it not so long ago and said that a friend in New York had a copy. I read the piece about A H in the *Digest*. . . .

My nephew—now in the Philipines—was in Australia for

close on two years—I never knew where until he had left it—but I did write and suggest that he look you up if anywhere near where you are. (He was in Brisbane and other points.) Margaret Bondfield has paid us several visits—she is wonderful and as dynamic as ever. Put me on your list for a letter now and then—it's grand hearing from you.

Lots of love to you—

Affectionately
Elisabeth

7.84 To Clem Christesen, Melbourne
Source: MA

Carlton
July 22, 1945

Dear Clem Christesen

Will you act as one of a team of five to select the first book of the month for the new Australian Book Society? I have been deputed by the working committee to write to those named. Mrs Palmer has consented to act, also Mr Howarth, editor of *Southerly*. I am another, and I wanted Marjorie Barnard but she finds it utterly impossible this month or next. You were my choice, and Mrs Palmer has also asked for you—being in Melbourne you and she will be able to confer. The plan is a roster of all ranking writers to be drawn upon, the theory being that people like yourself, Vance Palmer, Guy Howarth and others already are acquainted with most books, and can serve on this team without so much extra wear and tear on your time and eyes. Plans have to be worked out: the Hon Sec of the Soc, Mrs Hanford, is to send a circular letter. All is still nebulous for the judges: they will have to work out procedure. The suggestion to date is that the books (eligible) will be sent to the judges, they will each send in a report ranking them as one, two, three, etc. and saying why, and the book that gets most *one* votes is *it*. Australian books mean those dealing with Australia no matter where published or what the nationality of the writer, and I think, could include anything from poetry to travel, if it has quality. . . .

Yours in haste
Miles Franklin

7.85 To Dymphna Cusack, Hazelbrook, New South Wales
Source: FP 30

Aug 9, '45. Didn't have time to post the other part yesterday so will add a note. Yesterday dreary day. Had to go to a tea party—a family gathering—but not my own relatives. Am dragged in because the head woman comes from my native town. I knew no one, so was unable to retreat upon who married who, and is Mr G still alive, and what became of Dot's husband. Nothing but knitting recipes, and I can't knit. One woman kept shrieking at me across the table, what are you writing now? Are you still writing? 'Haven't time,' said I. 'Why haven't you time. What do you do? War work?' I felt like saying 'You're not the only band of banalities that is for ever making criminal demands upon my time.' Then there was a pianist—Bessie Carter from Gundagai. Bessie was a well-set up woman and went to the piano gladly. My heavens, how can some people get such a volume of noise from that most motherly, most benign of musical instruments, the piano. . . . From this ordeal I went for the hat and that was such a topping-off that I came home to bed so depressed that the atomic bomb seemed the logical conclusion of all. I was reminded of my lovely Editha Phelps at outbreak of last war who said of the people who went to popular plays. 'I tell you what, little Franklin; it is a great relief to me. I feel after such a night, that it does not matter what becomes of such people—war is good enough for them.'

Dear me, have you seen the spread in the *DT* to celebrate Dame Mary's 80th birthday. 'First Lady of Labor.' But that isn't a labor paper. And the *Sydney M Herald*—'Our literary matriarch.' Damed for her great services to literature. Her greatest literary feat is the way she has advertised herself. If you've only got the pluck to keep on blowing your horn, it at least draws attention to the fact that you have a horn, as a member of my office force once said of a blowhard who afflicted us, in search of a job. ...

Oh, you remember that advertising firm. They have got Nuri Maas to approach me now. They want writers to write something on a page of advt of Peak F's biscuits—about 200 words—for which they will pay five guineas. Some of the other distinguished writers have already come in. I asked who. Idriess and Will Lawson; and Miss Prichard said she was too busy now, but wd think of it later. I said I had no time now for them, to go ahead with the distinguished writers—Miss Marjory Barnard. What a blessing that woman brought herself to my attention. I always mention her in such impasses. ... They think Australians wd jump at 5 pounds for their name to be spluttered in perpetuity around some biscuits which may be poisonous. I must go and call K S P and warn her. I have always to be fighting these things, and those fools ask me what I'm doing.

Love to you all
[unsigned]

7.86 Telegram from Hilda Esson, Melbourne
Source: FP 38

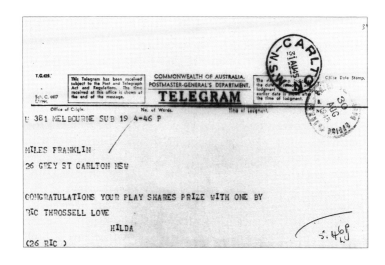

132

Carlton
Sat [? September 1945]

My dear Hilda

What a darling you were to send that telegram. It always comes
ping with more effect than a letter, and when it's something
jolly it's grand.

I'm staggered to think our little effort was acceptable. We
thought it's only place wd be in the Monty Grover satire
competition but we were too late for that and sent it to the
lure of you and Nettie as Judges, hoping you wd at least be
amused. It is merely hilarious propaganda. Do you know the
other night at Fellowship a lady who has been abroad got up
and said where was all this demand for Aus Lit that was being
talked about. She had gone to the leading book shop and was
told by a woman there (D and I both know that woman and
that shop) that the sophisticated Australians read only overseas
good stuff and the unsophisticated wanted only detective stories
and no one wanted Australian stuff. . . .

SO!!! I think that if our *Ghosts* is put on soon with great
vim and with every line plainly declaimed it will be useful. I
know several book store men I'll invite lovingly to a performance
of it.

I'm so glad Ric got a prize too. I hope his effort will be
something more timeless and therefore ageless. The sooner ours
becomes 'dated' the better for our progress in Australian books.

Thank you so much for that telegram, you were a dear to
send it.

Love from Miles

Prime Minister
10th September, 1945

Dear M/s Franklin

Mrs Chifley has forwarded me your letter of the 29th August.

Thanks for your kindly thought in providing a detective story for my leisure hours, which are indeed very few.

Best wishes.

Yours sincerely
J B Chifley

7.89 To Mary Fullerton, Sussex
Source: FP 19

Carlton
Sept 16 1945

My dearest Mary

I sent or rather wrote you an airmailer yesterday which will be posted with this. You can connote the exact difference in time of passage, as the man from next door (not Porlock) will take them as he goes to work tonight.

Your letters are wonderful to me. I am sorry the response will be inadequate, gappy and scattered as I send them on to Em before I have answered and my memory is no good now—you must forgive me. No, your photo in bed did not shock me between the lines or above board. I thought it was wonderful, seeing the length of time since we parted and all the suffering you have been through. You were always a physical wraith. I remember my aunt on beholding you took me aside to observe that your legs were as thin as hers and she said, 'You think she's all right. And I wonder if *her* family is always fussing about her skinniness and tormenting her.' And you should have seen my father, on the other side of the house, so now I have honestly, on two counts, ascended to being a competent and irretrievable scrag.

I have been coming across Dr J D Unwin's theories on sex. Same as mine. He thinks that physical and mental power all come from sexual continence. He says without chastity societies lack energy and individuals are compelled to perpetual unawareness etc. But he says puritanism can be diabolical if not directed ethically. The book is called *Sex and Culture*. I wish I had it. I got this only from a work by Aldous Huxley, who extols him. ...

I enclose clipping about the Australia-first internees. I'm glad my nice friend Harley Matthews got a few pounds but it's only *pour-boire* compared with the total loss of his vineyard etc. And they never cd undo the fact that his mother died without seeing him vindicated: and she was of the old stiff school: and when it came out in the paper she said if he was such a traitor he shd be shot though he was her son. I wrote a letter to her saying how grotesque such a charge was against Harley and that it wd be hilarious if not so tragic. That was the first intimation she had of the other side of the question. I have a letter from her saying that of all the people who came to drink Harley's wine and burden her with endless hospitality (giving it without notice like an old time country house) I was the only one who had the pluck and honesty to write such a letter. I wonder what P R S will do next. Winnie says he has shaken the dust of Sydney off his feet and will live in Melbourne. He talks of going farming, but I can't see him sticking to the earth—too hard and not enough money in it. ...

I note that MacArthur is much more careful of giving or leaving liberty to the big industrialists in Japan than to women. The geishas are to stay and operate. Of course the two things go together, business licence and woman suppression. A lovely little friend phoned me yesterday, she is young beautiful and married, and she is going to organize the single women to take care of their rights. I said it was time a new crop of girls arose and tried to burst a few more bonds. They have lived for nearly two crops on what the suffragettes won, and have misinterpreted most of it to mean the right to sexual lust equalling men's. ...

Such is life
[unsigned]

Carlton
Sept 28 45

Dear Frank

Thanks for your tremendously interesting notes. You have a
great chance for memoirs—reportage—of the moment and for
more permanent things through your short story gift. . . .

I was reared on both sides of my family to like Chinese. My
dear old uncle on my mother's side—dead last week—thought
they were perfect. And Peter in *Swagger* was a real person. I
can remember him when very small. And these were only the
lowest class. They were liked for their honesty and gratitude—
good qualities on which to build. But I demand more of a
boasted civilization. How does it treat its lowliest workers? How
do the women who are still more lowly in situation fare?
Nothing else satisfies me now. I should prefer the civilizations
and cultures of America, England and France with all their
inequality, poverty and snobbery and backwardness—being a
woman. That is why Stalin's régime interests me—bravest
attempt to give women a square deal. A man who can take
women off the midden and put them into parliament commands
my interest before all other warriors, politicians and Victoria-
cross-winners in the world.

Your sergeant who thinks they are going back to old ways
in the East is like a woman refugee here who thinks the British
will have things back at par in no time—'they always do you
know'.

I suppose the Cathay hotel is like one of the smaller hotels
of Chicago or New York.

The Chinese outbreed and outtrade every other race where
they go, in a generation. What is to be the end of us few
Australians with our big territory? It is a bewildering speculation. A statesman as great as God himself might well be baffled
by the tasks ahead. But life goes on as a great blind force, finding
its level regardless of prosperity, despair or ethics.

I hear Jean is home and K S P is going to Tasmania to give the C Lit Fund Lectures at Hobart. I wonder what you'd think of the two Lindsay novels—Jane's and Norman's. They stagger me by their soullessness.

D's and my little play is being produced in Melb. I think the New Theatre League is going to read a little Furphy play on first Sunday in Oct at Fellowship. It was to have celebrated Furphy's birth month (Sept) but they did not get it ready in time.

Next time you come to a meal you must tell me lots.

For the present we home birds will try and keep societies and things from dying right out till the boys come home to jump into them and give them a new start.

All the best
[unsigned]

7.91   To J B Chifley, Canberra
Source: FP 39

Carlton
October 14 1945

The Rt Hon J B Chifley
Dear Mr Prime Minister

As you no doubt know, the writers of Australia are troubled by the conditions which confront them. This is not alone because of their livelihood being involved, but also because of what Australian literature means to us all as a people.

We are peculiarly placed. For example: a student of literature in big populations like those of Great Britain and the USA could become outstanding as a professor of literature in English and ignore the literature of a small group of English-language writers such as ourselves. On the other hand, Australians would have to know and have access to the books of Great Britain and the USA or be limited and blighted by mental isolation.

The problem, therefore, is how best to prevent the swamping

of Australian literature by imported literature whether admirable or deleterious.

Without a literature of our own we are dumb. In the disturbed world of to-day, more than ever we need that interpretation of ourselves, both to the outside world and to ourselves, which is the special function of imaginative writers.

Various expedients have been considered but we need a survey of the whole situation by people qualified for the task.

I feel, therefore, that it is a matter for you and the members of the Government to take in hand, by a Parliamentary Select Committee, if that is the best way. It concerns us all, not only writers.

With all good wishes
I am, Mr President
Yours sincerely
[unsigned]

7.92 *From Arnold Dresden, Swarthmore, Pennsylvania*
Source: FP 35

Swarthmore College
5 November 1945

Dear Stella

A copy of Alice Henry's autobiographical notes came into my hands recently—Hartley Grattan had presented a copy to the Sw Coll library. The reading revived many old memories. You will not be surprised therefore that I am impelled to write you, in the hope that we may hear from you. Another war has come and gone (!) since I saw you last. . . . Will the next generation respect the mistakes of the past and the present? The control of atomic energy should concern even the most stupid of our 'statesmen' that their procedures in international relations have been reduced to absurdity. The scientists, who were called in to help during the war, have proved to be the dwellers in a Trojan horse. Are they going to allow the Trojans to subdue them, to drag them down to the level of "practical statesmanship", or will they succeed in making the scientific spirit effective in international relations?

No don't worry, this is not going to be a long winded disquisition on philosophical vacuities. I want to hear from you, how you are, what you are doing, planning, hoping, thinking. ... I am still spending most of my time teaching mathematics to [word illegible] interesting students, and I accomplish very little else. My family in Holland have suffered greatly during the occupation years. Twelve have become victims of the *furor teutonicus*, my youngest brother among them. The survivors have been carrying on bravely. ...

Now tell us all you can about yourself.

Best wishes and a good hug
Arnold Dresden

7.93 To Mabel Singleton, Sussex
Source: FP 25

Nov 16 45

My very dear Mabel, your airmailer of 3.11.45 to hand about an hour ago—it was posted on 4th so that is 12 days. I wrote to Mary on Oct 29 so she will have had that and know how I am chored to the eyebrows. I am so disturbed to know in yr letter Mary was suffering again—a great strain on you both. ... The one bright spot in your letter was that Mary had the proofs. I had forgotten they went. No further move since—printers still on strike, part of the general mess but we are otherwise saved from so much horror here that it wd seem petty to fulminate, even tho our lives and livelihoods are going. John still hanging around—machine not fixed and squadron breaking up—aunt on the job as laundress and trying to scrape meals, as he has no coupons having landed outside the regulations and our meat has gone to very little, and sugar cut in half because of coal strike. I am sad for him of course. He rackets and goes dancing and seems to have no plans for the future. Perhaps I'm the fool to be so worried. ...

We have been having showery weather for some time now. Before that it was dangerously droughty. I hope there are great harvests everywhere and that we'll have sense enough to send it where it is wanted. If there had been shipping we would have been so happy to take butterless and sugarless and meatless days in addition to what we already have to send shiploads to England. Potatoes are in again and I have plenty of eggs. John says they were lately allowed two eggs a week at Moratai— a great treat. My little bantams give me plenty and some over for neighbors. There has been trouble to get food. I got a bit of wheat and the neighbors saved their stale bread. One woman gives me half loaves—so much that I have to bury it for manure. Sometimes my hens are eating cake like Marie Antoinette. I have a carraway seed cake there now. Perhaps the hens will like it. I loathe the seeds, did not know they were still in existence. One woman also never eats fat—so my hens get that, and often a good meat stew. I think how Asiatic children would like the food. No fruit in my backyard now but lemons. Guavas and loquats gone: peaches and plums half grown. No fruit on the market except that too dear for me. No canned fruit, no dried fruit, but we have sultanas and currants, and all the jam we can buy. I still have the same three coats and skirts I had in London and they look all right. Price of hats sailed to glory, also the doing-up: what used to cost 7/6 and 12/6 in that line now 25/6. That's what I gave to have an old hat done up that came to me from my aunt four years ago. The hat woman said she would charge me four guineas for it to-day. My figs are ripening too and their jam is the delight of all who eat it. I wonder if sugar will be procurable in time.

Well, my dear, shall we ever see each other again? I sent a story by Jane Lindsay, not that I admire it but I happened to have it and Mary will like to see what the youngsters are doing.

Much, much love to you both for ever

[unsigned]

Carlton
Dec 17 1945

Dearest Phil and May

I was so glad to get Phil's letter a day or two since. I am sorry
about the nervous breakdown and the asthma. It is sad to think
of you and May being such an age. You seemed such girls
compared with myself when I met you at Deptford, but that
was partly the English complexion, and when one is young a
few years seem a lot, but as you get up in years people who
once seemed to be so much younger or older don't turn out to
be so far apart.

I too am getting high in years and have not the strength I
once had and I am feeling very desolate since my brother died.
John my nephew who homes with me till he went into the forces
is still away flying in the Pacific. I have an old wooden cottage
in the outer and common suburbs of Sydney, everything in it
worn out but still I have everything and it is comfortable and
healthy. My mother left me an income of three pounds a week
which since the war has come down to two. It is drawn from
the rent of a little old shop, and if there was another financial
slump, the shop would be empty I'm sure, but it may be all
right for a few years while there is a shortage of houses. Then
I was able to make a little from my books but with the shortage
of paper that was curtailed and Australian authors are now in
a sad position with the English and American publishers
struggling over us like a bone and swamping us with throw-
outs from overseas which can be produced cheaply. However,
we are putting up a fight on that. . . .

Now here is a suggestion. We are still young enough to get
something out of life: we can't just sit down like dummies till
we are buried or cremated. Why not each of you take a year out
here? I have oodles of spare rooms and beds and linen and you
are welcome to one and to share my humble grub the same as you
were sisters. It wouldn't be stylish, but is very respectable. Clothes

last a long time. I still have the suit I was wearing when last I met Phyl and some one the other day said I must have got it on the black market—it looked so smart. I can give you board and lodging and delighted to have your company—it wd be heaven to see you again. Could Phyl get a year's exchange with some teacher out here—then she would be set. Why not make enquiries at Australia House or Depts of Education or however that sort of thing is arranged. There was a woman at the Minerva Club when I was there who had just returned from a year in country schools here. She loved it. If you arranged it that way it would be leave of absence and you would not be risking your pension.

Now for May. Perhaps the climate here would relieve her asthma. I had an old school companion with me over the weekend who is a trained nurse—has been matron and during the war had to nurse till it got too much for her—she is big and heavy. She says to be registered here you'd have to go through the exams and that at our time of life is a bugbear, but she says I cd introduce you to her and she is in with doctors and you could take a case now and again and perhaps get about the country. That would give you a little more money and you could always kite home to me. I am not promising any money as I don't know how things are going—I may not be able to sell any books—but there is a chance I could and then we'd have that too. What's the use of sitting apart and being independent and that sort of bosh and dying of desolation.

So turn it over in your minds.

Fares used to be cheap. I went around the world last time and stayed away for 22 months on very little. Of course I travelled steerage on the ships. In 1923 I went around the world and was away from London six months (leave without pay) and did it on 250 pounds and travelled second class on ships and first class on trains across America. I suppose today the cheapest would be twice that but even so the English pound is worth 25/- or more out here. That is why I can't think of going to London ever. We would get so little for our pound. If May came out on a holiday—have it stated whatever way is official then she would not lose her old age pension. . . .

And you wouldn't be tied to me by any obligation if you could see some good chance to see the country. I'd be just a base.

Think it over—make inquiries.

We are in the midst of lots of strikes. The people in the conquering countries—if you notice—are all in rebellion against their exploiters. The defeated countries are kept down by force of arms or else poor things are too weak and hungry and dejected to rebel. We are having great drives here for food—the ships are taking tons of things. At present all electric lights have to go out after 9 pm and only one 60 watt light allowed till then. Radio one hour a day for the news. Lots of newspapers stopped, no electrical appliances. I believe we are to be allowed to iron for Christmas. I have an old copper and plenty of debris in my neglected garden so I can do laundry and have all the baths I like in old fashioned style. . . .

I boiled a lot of Christmas puddings the day before the strike restrictions came in and baked a big cake. I give my friends who are living in rooms little puddings and they can boil them, in a pot. The miners are going back to work but the restrictions can't be lifted in January because stocks are exhausted. There were no trams in Sydney for the week-end. I believe Adelaide is worse. Trains cut down in numbers and length. People will have to stay at home.

For my lunch I am having cold lamb cooked yesterday, some of the Christmas pudding, beans from the garden, stewed peaches, also home grown potatoes. Wish you were sharing it.

With love and good wishes from your old pal
[unsigned]

'Frayles Farm'
17th December 1945

Dear Miles

Perhaps you will excuse this belated reply, to yours of 17th October, when I tell you that I have retired completely from politics and fine literature, and have become a farmer! This means dawn-to-dark hand-toil, as you know, with no leisure for thoughts. All my interests now are in the 55 acres of mountainside surrounding this house. What is happening in the doomed Australian community outside my farm is of very slight interest to me. I love Australia, the land, but on the whole I despise and dislike the British colonials who at present live here, but are rapidly becoming extinct. In effect, I have 'gone bush', become a hatter and a recluse, and I gladly leave the culture-struggle, which for ten years prior to 1942 engaged my whole energies, to you and to the other Leftists, proletarian sentimen-talists, Muscovite internationalists, and Grattanic dollar-imperialists. 'Long live internationalism, and down with all Nations!' It's a well-worn Jewish idea, the same old Christianity in new jargon-guise, with a new hierarchy of Trade Union secretaries substituted for old-style bishops and priests, fooling the people still with promise of 'Heaven', and bitterly perse-cuting opponents.

I spent 3 years 5 months 7 days as a prisoner—without trial, in 'Democratic' Australia, under a 'Labor' Government, with a Rooseveltian humanitarian, Evatt, chief wangler of this revival of the oubliette as a political weapon. You did not protest, and apparently nobody protested. You thought it quite all right. I don't. It's so utterly bad that I would not now even protest against what was done to me. Nor would I ever write another line, or lift a finger, to help Australia now—unless perchance the community belatedly redeems itself from utter disgrace by spontaneously making some amends to me for what has been done. I shall wait perhaps ten years, just to see whether a younger generation will become national-minded; but it's only a faint hope. I am silenced, and effectively; but a time will come when my outstandingly unselfish and far-sighted work, from 1932–1942, will be seen as true pioneering, and credit will then be given to me for it, perhaps after I am safely dead.

Tom Collins and Nellie Melba were born near here. I am in the Baw Baw ranges, on the 'Braes o' Yarra'. Timber is mostly messmate and mountain ash. Lyrebirds and wombats are near. I milk my own cows, ride my mare daily to the post office. Merry Xmas!

Farewell
Yrs P R Stephensen

7.96 *From Dymphna Cusack, Hazelbrook, New South Wales*
Source: FP 30

'Pinegrove'
20/12/45

Miles, dearest

Life is moving in such a whirl of Christmas Trees, parcels, mail, kids, cats, Siltams (cross between Silky and Bantam) that I have hardly time to get my own life organised. Little Dymphna is up here and between making a billy-cart, rehearsing a play and general excitement, we scarcely know what we are doing. We have our hall-way blocked by a small pine-tree which fills the house with the smell of resin. It has magically sprouted silver pine cones, gum-nuts, drumsticks & mountain devils, and the young, too, are silver-speckled from painting the Fairy Flora.

At the moment there are tears & sorrow. 'Horatio'—our last kitten—has just been collected by his proud new owners and has gone off in a box marked 'Fragile' amid much lamenting.

To-morrow the little Dutch cousins and sister-in-law arrive & we celebrate Xmas—anti-clockwise on Sunday.

So here am I saying my Christmas greetings to you: we'd love to be able to say them in person—not that Xmas *qua* Xmas means anything except for the kids—but I am always sufficiently caught by the convention to feel the desire to make explicit what I take for granted the rest of the year.

This year of rural retreat has enabled me to get a lot of things sorted out—rather as rocks come up on a beach as the tide recedes. And one of the permanent guide-posts left on my beach is my friendship with you. It has not only brought me great joy personally to know you so intimately and enjoy so rich hours with you—alas, too few—but I feel that my meeting with you and our relationship has been of the greatest value in re-orientating me in my own country. All the corrupting influences of academicism and expatriatism had left their mark on me and meeting you swung me to my own pole again. That is something for which I can never be sufficiently grateful. All the richness of my own country was revealed afresh for me. All the knowledge I had of it transmuted into something imaginatively richer. You have been a touch-stone of essentials for me and the rest of the work I do—I should say perhaps—the *real* work I hope to be able to do in the future will be in some subtle way yours too. Without your influence I should never have projected the work I hope to do after 'the women' is finished—a great secret: a book on Newcastle and one on Broken Hill—

For everything, my dearest friend, thank you.

Love
Dymphna Cusack

8 THE WARATAH CUP: 1946 – 52

'I was wishing you were here last night. I had a lovely fire and a kettle of tea and cakes and orange rings and five guests among them Rex Ingamells, Nancy Keesing, who is doing something with D Stewart (that maybe private but she did not say so) and Roland Robinson and new wife. Harley Matthews was not able to come. The arguments were good and entirely on literary points. I nearly forgot Ray Mathews who made mud pies of Australia and was the runner up for the Grace Leven Prize that Rex I got. He had the waratah cup.'

MILES FRANKLIN TO HENRIETTA DRAKE-BROCKMAN, 22 JULY 1952 (FP)

The later years of Miles Franklin's life encompassed the post World War II settlement and the coming of the Cold War to Australia. Miles did not much like the way things were going; and inflation made things hard for those on small fixed incomes. But, she once said, too much attention to periodisation is ageing; and, as far as possible with so much paper about, she kept to her mother's standards. There is a pleasing patina of suburban domesticity, of bantams and jam and children in the street, to these later years. And with only her nephew to consider, she was freer to dispense hospitality. These were the years of the waratah cup, and the waratah book: when favoured guests took tea from the delicate cup and saucer set with the waratah design given her by Richard Baker in 1940, and wrote in a red-covered album with its historic inscription, dated 26 August 1902: 'To Stella Franklin with love and admiration from her friend Rose Scott'. (Both set and album are preserved in the relics collection of the Mitchell Library.)

When Mary Fullerton's death finally came on 23 February 1946, Miles kept an even keel. The positive event of the year was the publication of *My Career Goes Bung*, written in 1902, rediscovered in 1936. Her children's romance of the Easter Show, *Sydney Royal*, went to press. The Franklin/Cusack bookshops play *Call Up Your Ghosts* was performed in Adelaide; and Miles cheered as Dymphna Cusack and Florence James worked on what became *Come in Spinner*. 'Brent' stirred, P R Stephensen calmed down somewhat, and 'the battle of the books' ended, in favour of British publishers as usual. Meanwhile, Miles had gladly relinquished the Book Society to Marjorie Barnard. And as the political temperature rose, her low expectation of the postwar world seemed to be justified by instant ideological conflict and shortages. In 1946 she was smeared as a 'red'; she supported the radical Jessie Street, Australian woman's delegate to the United Nations; and she sent her first food parcels to Britain.

By 1947 Miles Franklin's American links were weakening. English friends were often found to be living lonely lives in seaside towns. With limited means herself, Miles sent more food parcels. She still suffered insomnia and now felt the cold badly. The world seemed to be a mess and the red scare worsened. In 'the age of austerity' she was glad to have a roof over her head. Had she reached 'the contemplative stage'? Not really. It was just that 1947 was comparatively uneventful. Miles remained a friend of Russia; she made merry with the likes of leading anticommunist W C Wentworth; she edited the Fellowship of Australian Writers' bulletin *Fellowship*, aided by a lively young Melburnian Glen Mills Fox, an associate of Aileen Palmer's; and she still got a lot of fun out of literary dinners. *Sydney Royal* appeared; and while other writers anxiously awaited the results of newspaper competitions she had a minor windfall when the *Newcastle Morning Herald* published 'The Thorny Rose' as a serial.

Theatre and plays seem to have been the liveliest aspect of 1948, when Miles declined all executive positions in the Sydney Fellowship of Australian Writers, an increasingly ideological body. To her great satisfaction, the long-awaited *Daily Telegraph* prize went (unannounced) to *Come in Spinner*; and she welcomed new works by Eleanor Dark and Sumner Locke Elliott, encouraging also other younger Australian writers; for example, poets Roland Robinson and Laurie Collinson. As with Frank Ryland, and later Tom Ronan, her enthusiasm often had a supervisory quality, hardly surprising given her age, experience and vigorous views. (By 1948 she had definitely taken against the biggest book of the previous year, M Barnard Eldershaw's *Tomorrow and Tomorrow*.) Her reading in 1948 strengthened her already strong views on sex and alcohol, views which are more respectable among the thinking classes today than any time in the intervening years. She suffered a bad shoulder, and tentative plans to visit Western Australia had to be abandoned. Perhaps it was the cold she caught at Angus & Robertson's first staff ball since the war in June. Perhaps it was the rationing.

In 1949, the year of the great coal strike, when a Labor government sent troops to the mines, Miles grumbled and got on with her work, which meant encouraging other writers and getting more of her own published. (In fact she approved the intervention, just as she deplored Cold War polarisation, an aspect of sectarianism in her view.) Free speech was now the rock of her politics; and she at first stood aloof from a reviving peace movement. Having remained a member of the Sydney FAW, despite its betrayal of her notion of a strong writers' union, she was rewarded by a new, true congenial, the recently arrived David Martin. In May Dymphna Cusack followed Florence James to London with the *Spinner* manuscript. In September Miles visited Newcastle again, an hilarious event. Her penchant for secrecy, now legendary, seemed to be justified when it looked as if Angus & Robertson might be publishing all the 'Brent' books. During the year she mourned the deaths of Ada Holman, Vida Goldstein and Lute Drummond.

The year 1950 began with rumblings from congenial Jindyworobak Rex Ingamells and others about a Nobel Prize. (The first Australian writer to win the prize was Patrick White, in 1973.) It was marked by poor health, a throat infection at the beginning and heart problems at the end. However, thanks to Henrietta Drake-Brockman, in 1950 Miles Franklin was presented with a great opportunity. In July she delivered the annual Commonwealth Literary Fund lectures at the University of Western Australia, a partial success only due to a weak throat. She was thrilled to be looked after by Joseph Furphy's only daughter, Sylvia Pallot.

Sydney seemed grubby on return. A paranoid political climate prevailed, with the Communist Party Dissolution Bill threatening, and Melbourne writer Frank Hardy charged with libel in *Power without Glory*. In 1950 her nephew John Franklin collapsed into alcoholism; South Australian writer Myrtle Rose White, author of *No Roads Go By* (1932), proved a sympathetic friend from afar during this trial. Not surprisingly Miles could hardly contemplate the insanity of another war, this time in Asia. She now joined the peace movement, and drew a bleak conclusion about the position of women in the century of total war. In November Angus & Robertson published the first 'Brent' volume *Prelude to Waking*, originally titled *Not the Tale Begun*, written way back in 1925. Preparations began to celebrate fifty years of Australian federation in 1951.

In that year Miles lay low. The attempt to suppress the communist party was defeated by referendum. Otherwise she seems to have had three main concerns: her health, the Jubilee literary competitions, and her reputation (now aged 71, she feared she had 'not become part of the literature of this country'). Macquarie Street doctors failed to find what ailed her. The Jubilee failed to unearth new talent. And Miles worked on her CLF manuscript, fending off a fresh spate of inquiries about 'Brent' caused by the publication of *Prelude* the previous year. *Spinner* finally appeared, with its dedication to Miles. Rex Ingamells dedicated his prize-winning poem 'The Great South Land' to her too. She took to the newly arrived young American literary scholar, Bruce Sutherland; and hoped for help with plays from the young Eleanor Witcombe (who later wrote the script for the film of *My Brilliant Career*). In 1951 Sam Furphy died, and David Martin went to Melbourne.

February 1952 found Miles in Melbourne for a break. She had been working on an antiwar play *The Dead Must Not Return*, a testimony approved by David Martin. She stayed with bibliophile J K Moir. Alas it was too much for her, due to the 'bent heart' problem, but not serious. On the way home, she spent three days with P R and Winnie Stephensen at Bethanga Lower, near Albury, a rejuvenating experience. Bruce Sutherland's fellowship ran out in June. By July she had finished a draft of her 'little essay' on the novel, delighting to add a quote from Ian Mudie's marvellous new poem 'They'll Tell You About Me'. (J K Moir was a great help with the protracted checking, and many of the congenials were called upon to give opinions.) An English edition of *All That Swagger* appeared, so she could no longer say that after fifty years' work none of her books were in print. Dymphna Cusack was still away, doing well, editing the story of Sydney barmaid Caddie, who later visited Miles. (A wonderful letter describing the visit is to be found in Chapter 9.) Beatrice Davis was also in Europe in 1952. In September 1952, W C Wentworth went too far with his red-baiting and Katharine Susannah Prichard sued him and the *Sydney Morning Herald* for £10,000. Miles was all for slapping his face. She was still spirited, if no longer strong.

The waratah cup and saucer, design by Doulton (ML)

8.1   To Kathleen Monypenny, London
Source: FP 22

26 Grey Street
Carlton NSW
Feb 5 1946

Dear Kathleen Monypenny

All your friends will be sending you the enclosed so I had better
join the throng. Glad to hear of you safe now the blitz and
doodles have ceased for a time, and also congratulate you on
such a nice job. You will meet many interesting English there
and all the worthwhile Australians who go to London: and
Australia—any country of small importance in fact—is much
more important to the representative socially and financially
to represent abroad than to support at home.

  We are sinking back into normality after the big debauch.

What awaits us I dunno. The profiteers are coming out of their hideouts again everywhere—at St Moritz and in NY and London and here. The rest of us find ourselves poorer and older and sadder.

I went into the Mitchell the other day and Mr Mutch met me with the sad comment that Miss Willis was a great loss. I nearly fainted. She had gone on Jan 10—appendicitis, after a record of over twenty years with no sick leave. Her dear kindness was like a benediction always. Very few originals left now—Misses Cox, Armstrong and Ross. Miss Leeson departed to the Army in Melb some years since now. Is a Major I understand, and will not return to the Mitchell. Complaints are that she did not know how to train any to replace her, which is sad for the Australiana. Some Miss Mander Jones has been recently appointed in Miss Leeson's place. ... Little Miss Small, more like a fat pillow than ever, is running a real estate agency and two little fiction libraries near me. She lets us meet in her library once a month—that is the Propeller League of writers for this district, of which I am patron and Camden Morrisby President. A harmless little group—all the might-be writers dispersed by war. We try to keep these things alive for the people coming back, as it is deadly to come back to nothing—no refuge—no point of starting. ...

[unsigned]

8.2 To Winifred Stephensen, Warburton East, Victoria
Source: FP 39

Carlton
Feb 11 46

My dear Winnie

Alas, I have few recipes for jam as in all my family households the women came out of the Ark knowing all there was to know by constant practice and experiment and I took to it like a duckling on the home pond and it was in our heads—now all the heads but mine are dead and I'm forgetting.

We never made crab apple jelly because crab apples were fish I never saw till I went to USA. Of course you can't risk sugar in experiments these days but I shd think crab apple wd jell well being a barbarian fruit.

Normal jam-jellies are made by choosing fruit not too ripe and fresh off the tree. Boil till soft enough to strain first through a collander and then through cheesecloth.

Guava might be a model. For that we used to crush the fruit and to every four quarts of fruit add one pint of water, boil till soft, strain as above then add one pound of sugar to every pint of juice and it took only about 45 mins to jell when boiled.

For gooseberry jelly you do the same and put a cup of sugar to a cup of juice and it takes a long time to boil. You have to keep trying it with a bit of stuff on a plate in the wind to see when it is just right.

You would use all the fruit of crabapples—core and pith— as that helps to jell, but of course cleaned of whiskers or grubs or dust etc. You may need a little extra sugar for crabs and a lemon carefully skinned and cleaned of every particle of that bitter white pith but the pips left in will help with jelling.

Once upon a time there had to be brewer's crystals or pure cane sugar we thought beet sugar was no caste but living abroad I found out whole nations doing very well with the beet article who had never heard of cane sugar's superiority.

I so love making jam that I'd boil some in a top hat if I had no other way. I've just finished about 40 pots of fig. Friends who don't drink sugar in tea contributed sugar. I had to use some 'raw' sugar which gives a coarser flavor and makes my aristocratic Portugese figs taste like the common colored figs which are found in some of the bought preserve. Wish you were here and I'd give you some.

I had forgotten all about the MS at Mrs Lang's. Will go for it and answer your letter etc when I get it.

The crabapples won't wait so I get this off.

Love
[unsigned]

Carlton
Feb 25 1946

Mary, my precious, my dear, have you gone beyond our voices
to something splendidly different or to blessed sleep and relief
from pain? I got your beautiful message about my nephew and
have kept it for him. It will be a precious heirloom.

Have just been rung-up by a friend to tell me 'Yellow-box Tree'
is in this week's *Bulletin.* Also last night K S Prichard gave a lovely
exposition of Furnley Maurice's poems at the Sunday night
lecture (public) of the Fellowship of Australian writers. She was
helped by Muir Holborn and Marj Pizer, the two young uni
people who are doing an anthology (held up by printing troubles)
of poems of protest and for which they requested some of 'E's'.

There was a big house, whether for poetry or K S P I don't
know. I have therefore been asked to start the first programme
when the new Bd is elected next week, with an evening by 'E'
or on 'E'. This will coincide with the second vol, which is
imminent each day now, like waiting for a baby. If T I M can
be here, of course, he will be my coadjutor or I his. I wonder
if I can woo B S to recite or read too in view of the second Vol
being under his editorship. I'll see, but it is a great chance. If
Dymphna were down from her mountain retreat, she reads
beautifully, and Ian Mudie might be here. It depends on the
team I can seize.

I have had a wild week-end. John been in and out. This morning got up at six to get him off again. He said to watch him
go over in his four-engined Liberator. I've been running in and
out like a puppy dog. Many calls this morning. As samples:
Dame Mary Gilmore says she has a terrific character and story
just come her way, will I take it on? No time. She must seek
another exponent. Then one of John's best girls, and one of his
flight colleagues, who missed the bus. Then long call from Mrs
Ian Mudie, who has been over. Another long one from Musette,
who wants to come over for that night of 'E' together. She is
writing you a letter by air. I could not tell her, dear, that you

may not be there to read it. I will not be able to accept your absence for some time.

We have had a great night at Fellowship with Harrap from London in the battle of the books. Eng is struggling against American invasion of this, their closed preserve for so long, and poor Australian writers are in between and getting a bad deal from both angles. It was all on the huckstering level. No amount of technology or salesmanship nor big business or even taxpayers' subsidy can create literature. That is a gift of God and perhaps till man blows himself into some other era will have to come from the souls of the few—a gift and at sacrifice. As for example Furphy's great book, poor Lawson's stories and the poems of 'E'.

My novel entitled *My Career Goes Bung*, written in the early years of this century, has got as far as galley proofs and should be out in a month or two. Georgian House the new Melb firm is bringing it out. I wonder how I will be annihilated for it. I don't care, really. I'm getting too near the end for it to matter now—no one left to do things for or to whom I meant anything, if ever I did mean anything to anyone.

Well dear, I must not weary you, or dear Mabel, if you have shut your blue eyes, as my brother did his, for the last time on earth—on this beautiful world if only—ah, it is always if only. Mirage. Mirage. Dreams and illusions. When we lose our dreams we die.

Your ever loving friend
[unsigned]

8.4 *To Mabel Singleton [London]*
Source: FP 25

Carlton
Feb 27 1946

My very dear Mabel

Em telephoned me on Tuesday morning to say the expected news had come and I went out to her at Bondi. Mary's heroic suffering and your noble vigil have ended. You will be exhausted and must have rest.

By the irony of fate I received 12/6 to-day from the *Bulletin* for a poem. The first they have taken for a long time. They dumped back her story 'Mangy Lion' the next day without comment. The difficulty of getting anything accepted has blighted me. It has stopped me from writing to Mary every week because I had only refusals to report. I have also refrained from sending books because I feared she wd think it the long-delayed vol and be disappointed. Did the story in *New Writing* appear in time for her to see it? I hope so.

I was such a feeble coney in trying to help her, and accomplished practically nothing. Now my task is done. I have the wonderful poems safely kept. Someone better equipped than I to deal with them will be found with time. A big task still awaits you, my dear, and I hope, when you are rested, that you will have the strength to do it and yourself justice.

Mary's contemporaries in Australia were too conventional and mediocre to discern her worth; she was too retiring to push her own case. The younger ones at present are too depolarised by the war, the present disorganization and what looms. But, if we are not too dispersed by the atomic bomb a time may come when people will be as avid to know something about Mary as they are to-day to know about Emily Dickinson, and you have the power to supply that information in a memoir that can be kept till the right time. You must tell about your meeting with her, all that she meant to you then, and the last heroic years when you were more than a mother and sister in one to her. It is a glorious and rare friendship, knowledge of which must not be lost to the world.

If you try to be literary it will be stodgy and ruined. If you write it down as you write your letters without premeditation or straining for effect it will be valuable, and could be rare. I wish I were near to help you with my experience. Get exercise books—they are the best as separate leaves get astray. Write on one side of the page only with plenty of margin, put things down just as they come to your heart and memory—just as they come—they can be set in proper chronology later. A first draft contains much that can be rearranged or dropped. This will be a big and important and wonderful thing. It is your responsibility, and will be your reward, I know.

I kept on writing till the very last, I could not bury Mary till she was dead. I knew the letters were equally for you and that it is you who had to act upon them for so long.

Her last letter, a very lovely one written on Jan 15, came on Monday Feb 23. In it were some lovely poems. I am keeping silent about 'E' for the present as in her last letters she said she was more than ever desirous of remaining anonymous for the present. There is enough for the curious at present in the works signed Mary Fullerton. There are novels with her name as well as the one she gained the half-prize with (she never could find that one for me, I hope it remained safe through the blitz). There is her 'Crab Apple Farm'. I think we'll leave 'Rufus Stern' for the present to come out with the 'E' things. She also had a good novel in MS about the Settlers. It had wonderful possibilities, but Mary never had the strength to work sufficiently on those big things, and I had not time to undertake it with her before my money ran out and I came home. Yes, there's plenty about Mary Fullerton for the present. Also her book about the Bush (Dent's) and her little classic *Bark House Days*.

Re Brent. If any more letters reach you, just put them in a plain envelope and readdress it to me please, and *silence*. Don't be smoked-out as to how much I may or may not be concerned.

I suppose I shd write something to go in with your memoir about the heavenly time I had in London with you and Mary and Jean. Oh, my dear, I wish I could see you again. They can prate about new orders and that the world is small because we can get from London to Sydney in a few days, but it is still as big as ever to those without money and pull and privilege.

We hear such conflicting things about the food situation over there. What things are you actually short of? Do you want me to send you anything special if I can get hold of it or get it packed. . . .

Don't let anyone see my letters to Mary, please.

[unsigned]

8.5 To P R Stephensen, Warburton East, Victoria
Source: FP 28

Carlton
Mar 4th 1946

Dear P R S

Thanks for your note of farewell. You are lucky to own so rich a spot and still have the youth and strength to work it or to sit and write if you like. Luckier still to have time to withdraw for ten years and still be young enough to re-emerge to whatever part of the fray attracts you.

You say I thought the incarceration of the Australia First group all right. You have been misinformed. I protested as well as I was able to on the grounds—which I still hold—that whether the internees were right or wrong they should not have been held and vilified without public trial. Outside of the bigoted partisans, for and against, it was dismaying to note (1) the total indifference and ignorance on the part of the public as to what was being done with hard-won human liberties, and (2) the way the newspaper reports of the affair were accepted without question, in fact were brandished in one's face as ultimate.

No one can take up your case now but yourself. I understand that Harley Matthews was unsatisfied with his vindication and is proceeding further. You are better equipped than Mr Matthews to have your case similarly ventilated. Those who believe in you will be surprised if you don't.

You say you have no interest in the community outside your farm: how do you purpose to keep your retreat safe, select, comfortable and apart?

A new world will come out of the present disorganization but I am too feeble a coney to have any part in it, so my farewell will not be merely rhetorical as yours is or I am mistaken.

With best wishes
Sincerely
M F

Carlton
Mar 31 46

Dear Tom

Always a pleasure to hear from you.

How nice of poor old Scullin, but I fear it is rather late to elevate my state by the accusation of a 'sexual wallow'. There are others of equally scullion blimpishness suggesting that it may be necessary to boycott my books because I'm a communist.

There is, I hear, a bright little fellow named Wentworth, apparently with a semi-detached intellect, who runs some bureau for detecting anything ever so slightly off the beam of *S M Herald* approval who has dossiered me as a red.

I am a small speck easily removed but that business men— those modern giants of energy, enterprise and progress—should lean on such trivial and false informers is sad. Folks so naive will not be able to hold their Australian own against the world—or perhaps all business men are similarly restricted in mental range.

What did you say to Scullin *à propos* his fears of me that wd be interesting to me. You are really worser because do you remember complimenting me on the handling of the Molly McCarthy embroglio? You said that you could not have believed a woman could do it so actually and humorously.

I have a novel coming soon which I think will be even more depraved. It was written 40 years ago when I was a girl in the bush with my own way to find in sexology and sociology, sophistication and other wonders. Beware if you patronise me about not going deep enough and all that stomachy bilge which the war has knocked sky high for I have not *retreated* from the demure imp I was in my unadulterated teens.

Your premises about Australian earth-vigor, realism, drought-shadow, understatement and radical democracy sound juicy. I cd write a good thesis on any or all of them but am so placed that I have no outlet for that sort of thing. I agree about earth vigor. Back to the earth even if the atomic bomb destroys our whole civilization, reduces it to rubble and lava, it will start somewhere somehow again out of the earth and only out of the earth. All else is superstructure and gets so high after a while that it topples for lack of balance or fades out in anaemia. I'd like to hear your series. Perhaps you will pass through Sydney and could give us a gisty and gusty section some Sunday night at Fellowship. Les Haylen President this year.

What a delightful collaboration with Pacita. Hope you manage something unique and special.

I am run to death with futile chores. I have no leisure at all, that is no uninterrupted moments or any free from the fear of interruption. So please excuse hasty confused screed.

Hope Peace is rested and entertained by life in Canberra. My love and good wishes to you both

[unsigned]

8.7   *From P R Stephensen, Warburton East, Victoria*
Source: FP 28

'Frayles'
24th April, 1946

Dearest Miles

Yrs of 4th March, enclosed with one to Winifred, has been staring me in the face all that time. I've been hoping to understand what you mean by saying that no one can take up my case now but myself. It seems to me that the disgrace of my having been locked up for 3½ years without trial is not on me, but on those who did it, and, more generally, on all who didn't sufficiently protest. It's a disgrace to Australia, and specifically to men of the Evatt-Haylen-Grattan-Rooseveldtian type of mind—bogus 'Democrats', power-mad warmongers and mouthpieces of the British-American-Russian type of big-nation imperialism. I've drifted and swum away from all that category of thought, and I'm striving to reach the mental place where men such as Gandhi and De Valera have their thoughts.

Ideas are coming to me, but I can't write them, yet. If ever

I write another book, it will be as basic—and as truly influential—as was *The Foundations of Culture in Australia.* It will probably be as much plagiarised and unacknowledged as was that other memorable effort. In the meantime, please take my word for it that I am properly in abeyance. Let the Evatt-Haylen-Devanny type have their fling. They're making a proper mess of things. Conditions in Australia will get a lot worse before they get better. It is quite possible that the British branch-community in Australia will die and wither of its parent tree's diseases, and that we'll see the pathetic truth of Forde's dictum—'If Britain goes down, Australia will go down too.'

Am returning the Pentonian piffle about H H R herewith. Poor little fellow, like many others who are runts in stature he adores 'greatness' and gets reflected glory from it. Yes, I published her story, 'The Bath', in Sydney, 1933. What a lot I did, really—and what a reward I got! She was the ideal expatriate, and will ultimately be seen as of little value.

Chores take up all my time. Winifred is much better in health than formerly. She made nice crab-apple jelly. Perhaps you will come and stay with us sometime. We have a comfortable house, with a spare room, and milk from our own cow.

> Bless you! Yours affectionately
> P R Stephensen

8.8   To Dymphna Cusack, Hazelbrook, New South Wales
Source: DCP

> Carlton
> June 14 46

My dear Dymphna

Yes, I would like to talk to you someday about Mary Fullerton, but it can wait till you come again; now that she has gone, and I was able to do so little for her, though I struggled hard enough. . . .

Such a pity that the *Rats* has been declared obscene. It is not worthy of the publicity it has attracted. I have forgotten entirely what in it could be considered obscene. The judge shows himself ignorant of literary values when he says it rises at time to great heights—its heights are never heights, and its depths are shallow.

I am very much interested in a review of *Figi*, Margaret Trist, and one of Kylie's novels in the NY *Times* by Christina Stead. If ever there was an expatriate it was she, born so, yet now I think I can soon embrace her as having come home, the way she says 'the capital cities of the Commonwealth and its vast pastures and wheatfields were not made by such amiable riff raff' (as contained in these novels). I think she is generous to call them amiable. I shd have used other adjectives. She concludes that certainly 'other books are written by other Australians about other types of *my countrymen*'. Underlining mine. So! Salutations to Christina. By the way, I sent E *Kurrajong* and in one of her last letters she reared herself to a splendid philippic of distaste.

I have no news. It was comforting to have your letter, my dear. Thank you.

> My love to the family as well as yourself
> Miles

8.9 To Dymphna Cusack, Hazelbrook, New South Wales
Source: DCP

[nd] Friday night [1946]

Dearest D

About the children's book week, better write to J E Tickell, Sec of Book Soc, Box 41, GPO. I believe there is some time yet till the entries close. At Book Soc lunch on Monday K Slessor spoke and I believe he went for Prof Murdoch like everything because of the *Oxford Book of Aus Verse*. Glad someone as well as myself sees that Murdoch is an obstruction of Aus culture.

Dropped into Jessie Street's conference to make a women's charter. Lucy Woodcock was on the platform. I do admire her. She arose and roared scornfully as one who knows the hopelessness of the prevalent idiocy but who nevertheless keeps on.

And her hat! Evidently one of those idiots who know nothing but to be fashionable had bashed her head about like the one who tried to subjugate me, but Lucy is a greater soul than I, she let the hatter get on with it and took no notice. She had a very smart doll's hat that wd have been a cheeky conceit a- top a lot of girlish curls. But Lucy wore it like an eye shade and it was laughable, bless her! Have you got anything against her?

There was something very game in those women trying to make a charter in teeth of priorities, transport difficulties, atomic bombs, etc, in a debauched world. Reminded me of an American gentleman who nearly wrecked his party when the women were struggling for franchise, because he said they shd have it to help them in trying to save, despite the lust, brutality, belligerence and paranoia of men, a few children out of each generation's crop with which to carry on the human race. An Indian barrister was very good and clear, and you may have noted in the papers the visit of those three women who have lived in the Gobi desert. Staying with Archbishop Mowll—best thing I've ever heard of that gent. One of them spoke to the conference, real good old implacable English type. She said she came from where there was nothing ever done for the alleviation of women, gave horrible examples and cheered the conference on in a good forceful roar as uncompromising as L W's.

Love in haste from
Miles

8.10 *From Pixie O'Harris, Sydney*
Source: FP 35

Vaucluse
July 29th 1946

Dear Miles

It has been in my mind since our small talk to write to you, why I don't know, except that often one cannot express one's admiration and affection in words or looks always, sometimes one can write them.

'A Farmer Rabbit's Wife' by Sydney children's author and artist Pixie O'Harris. Another small drawing from the letters of Pixie O'Harris to Miles Franklin late 1940s-early 1950s is reproduced in chapter 9 (Courtesy Pixie O'Harris estate, ML)

You certainly have mine from the first time I met you, not through your writing because truth to tell I do not know it as well as I should, but for you, the personality, Miles, the soul, the staunch heart, the mixture of courage and timidity, the mixture of all that you are, we are, each one of us, only you more so than most people.

There is a greatness in you Miles. Where? I have not discovered. But I know it is there. I have a feeling that you as a personality are more personally loved in our circles than most. And you think you are lonely. You are afraid of death, so am I, but there are so many ways of looking at it. Milton says

> Oh let my lamp at *midnight hour*
> Be seen in some *high lonely* tower
> Where I may oft out-watch the Bear
> With thrice-great Hermes, or unsphere
> The world of Plato, to unfold.
> What worlds or what vast regions hold
> The immortal mind, that hath forsook
> Her mansion in this fleshy nook.

. . . Love
Pixie

8.11 From Dymphna Cusack, Hazelbrook, New South Wales
Source: FP 30

'Pinegrove'
14/8/46

Miles, my dearest

. . . I've not been reading these last few days but have now started and am just reading Sydney with Sybylla. Those early chapters are so painfully vivid & so extraordinarily rich in characterisation that one almost *lives* them. 'Ma' is superbly drawn. . . .

I'm so glad I was born a generation later! It's amazing the way you can re-create background—not only the physical aspects of Possum Gully—but the mental aridity, typical of such a place even today. The clash between the mother & daughter is superb—Sybylla couldn't have chosen a worse mother for her temperament. It's painful too to see the appalling similarity between publishing attitudes then and pre-war II—and even post-war II! Once more thank you for a precious gift.

Have you done anything with 'SR'? We are having a brawl vulgar & quite colonial, with Consolidated. Not publishing us before next March: we've written to have MSS returned will tell you next step—

Goodbye & love—

Yours
Dymphna

8.12 *From Beatrice Davis, Sydney*
Source: FP 38

A & Rs
21.8.46

My very dear Miles

You are wonderful and *My Career Goes Bung* is a delicious book. How dared you decry it and keep it dark so long? (But from what you've told me I should blush with shame for A & R's responsibility for that.) I love the book's generosity & integrity *and* wit, and its enormous verve; and so much of it (apart, perhaps from concerns for women) is [word illegible] now still.

I just wanted to tell you how proud I am to know you, and to send you my love.

Beatrice

11 Malcolm St
Sept 2nd 46

My dear Miles

What a blessing for us and later generations that your career went bung. That's an enchanting book, Miles. Much laughter with the sigh and glint of tears behind that is always life. I haven't really so *enjoyed* anything for ages and ages; and after all, say what you like, the real purpose of art and life, or if you like it that way, Life and Art, is the enjoyment of being a human creature . . . and you added very much to my enjoyment of same situation, for several happy hours; and without doubt will frequently again . . . like Jane Austen, you will be kept close at hand.

It's better than the first, as it should be, if you speak true in the preface; but since you are such an adept at the Great Australian Leg-Pull, I never know when to believe you, or not . . . when you aren't under my eye . . . I'll admit I did suspect Sybylla on page 161, par 3, when she thought a thought 'in the years that have gone'—the thought is somewhat more mature than the twenty she achieves at the end, or so it seemed to me . . . also the analysis of egotism, and its division onto two species, one (don't we know it) with that detached analysis of self as part of a universal complex force . . . These are surprisingly mature thoughts expressed with surprisingly mature economy of words; but then of course, Sybylla was nothing if not surprising. And yet—the little minx is the universal prototype of all girls of wit and spirit who, even to date, have grown up in Australia . . . her fan mail told her once, it will tell her again . . . She may have been Miles, she was Henrietta, when Julia reads about her, she will also be Julia . . . *eh bien chérie*, Sybylla stands on a very high peak, she is nobody but herself—yet she is something of all women, even the Edmées. . . .

I find I have also a letter of yours dated June 6th to answer . . . Yes, I too stick in the living when I get the chance—in my CLF lectures, and articles etc. I can't see why the writers of Australia are so mean, because lots of them are. If we put our shoulders to the national literary barrow, the whole load goes forward quicker—its so obvious. Apropos, and allowing myself the naughty wit that is sometimes yours: what price the canonisation of St Louis Esson? He was the nicest and kindest (and grubbiest) little man, when I met him. In great confidence, I have also thought he must also have been the laziest. And what you said re Haylen's *Blood on the Wattle*, surely goes for his *Southern Cross*? One must always dip one's lid to his early one acts, and I shall read this new collection with the greatest of care, but I have a sort of feeling that he must be an Australian Johnson, really, lacking a Boswell and even anything so solid as a *Dictionary* . . . Would he really have even been what he was, without a devoted wife who was determined that he should? And he certainly didn't get much encouragement from some quarters now largest in praise, Hilda herself told me . . . Hilda Esson and Nettie Palmer: two brilliant women, especially the latter, determined that their spouses, dead or alive, shall be Great Australian Classics. Nice matter for a play itself; stuff for naughty Sybylla: how about it? Dear Miles, please burn this letter, you are the only person in Australia to whom I could so unburden myself of thoughts that may, or may not, be just . . .

K S P is very frail, after the terrific knock of her daughter-in-law's tragic death. But I have known her in worse shape; she has great heart; and she is coming through as every time she does. She is getting horrible knocks re her new book: Ian Mair, of the *Argus*, said over the air, that a typist could have done it, or some such—such a method of criticism; one can think of many retorts to that! We find it extraordinarily interesting and graphic, it is so valuable for its background alone, though I personally will not class it above *Coonardoo*, which was for all its slighter appearance, in fact harder to present: the history and tragedy of a race, a perfect background, and fully rounded characters. In comparison *The Nineties* is only an epoch and glossary of types . . .

My dear I must fly . . . here is this letter full of dynamite. . . . *Must* go,

love (and silence *please*)
Henrietta

Carlton
Sep 4 1946

Dear Mr Robins

It was good to have another letter from you. It was an incredible
time on the way. The shipping services have not been restored
and I think mails often hatch for six or eight weeks before setting
forth. However, what matter when no rush for profits, politics,
or the even more popular pornography is involved.

I sent you a book with a picture of spoonbills: I don't know
if you have them in Florida. The spoonbills have aigrettes and
a boy once sent me a bunch of them from N Queensland. In
those days so ignorant were we—such an unlimited fairyland
had we to despoil that if we fancied a tail of the incomparable
lyrebird we just took it. I had these white aigrettes in a toque
and once when running around the corner of Dearborn St into
State I met dear old Uncle Jenkin Lloyd Jones. . . . Well, Mr
Jones addressed me: 'Daughter, what do I see in your hat—the
feather of the white heron, and I the Pre(?) of the Audubon
Society.' I flippantly (he once said that young and ignorant
nations were noted for their irreverence) said, 'No, you're
mistaken, that's the tail of a mere rooster that didn't believe
in woman suffrage.' Mr Jones said, 'Your wit has preserved you
from wrath this time, but go and sin no more.' As a matter
of fact, I did not know, till he insisted, that such feathers could
be from female nesting birds, so used were we to bird males
having all the grandest feathers and to human females appropriating them.

I shall be most grateful for the book by Mr Harry Ward. When
I am lonely for the old days that were so full of life and friends
and colleagues in USA I go back again to the books you and
Mrs Robins gave me. You gave me Theodore Roosevelt's
biography and I have Sandburg's *Lincoln's Prairie Years*, and
Two Vols of Mark Sullivan's *Times*.

I shall send you a little novel that I wrote some years before

I met you and which is just now published for the first time. It is being hailed here as the most interesting thing that has happened in the Australian book world for years. I think that you will perhaps understand it better than most people.

I wish I could have a serious talk with you about the end of this life. It takes courage. I wish I could have been with Mrs Robins again. I'm sure she was brave and generous and warm-hearted till the end. And I wonder what she thought.

Well the USSR and the USA now have the big political sticks of the world and England moves down one in imperialism. I can't see why England doesn't give the Arab-Jew question over to the USA completely to manage. I suppose British Big Business wants the oil there. If ever a country did *not* discriminate against the Jews it was England—half the peerage are Jews—when they're not brewers—they have been made into Marquesses and Earls and all sorts of big wigs yet now the Jews turn on their staunchest pal.

The world nevertheless is enchanting, the biggest tragedy is that we are such ephemeral moths.

With very kindest regards
[unsigned]

8.15 To Henrietta Drake-Brockman, Perth
Source: FP 33

Carlton
Sep 9 46

Dear Henrietta

Such a letter as yours of Sep 2 entices an immediate response. Written, as you observe, between business calls and domestic chores, it takes me back to my struggle with *All that Swagger*. I had to do it between answering the door and telephone, thinking up a pudding, getting tea for endless, inane—no, not inane—prosaic callers, real house-cleaning and laundry when the women who 'obliged' failed, and so on, and so on. I couldn't get a day for weeks on end to do the final pagination of the odd bits and pieces. Do you think we are so much frustrated as obstructed, and is the difference too subtle to bother about? If only we could have a real one-night sitting to yarn, as you say, for letters enervate me—I'm smothered by unanswered ones. . . .

The canonisation of Louis E, about which you inquire and so penetratingly sum up: I'll confess in confidence that I—harassed on every hand for a spare moment and seeing him sitting at repose in a flat provided by his wonderful wife—used to be impatient at first, but finally came to the conclusion that he was too ill for the supreme effort of literary creation. He had that terrible operation about two years before he went and the cause of it must have been hatching and sapping his vigor. . . . Louis was near the end when I knew him. He grew frailer and gentler but in our unfurnished mental spaces he was always an inspiration and a support. Now that awful silence enshrouds him, and I was glad to be asked to pay him a tribute tho I had seen him so little compared with the others who spoke. I agree about the clever wives. Hilda has fire, Nettie persistence. Had some of the rest of us similar or comparable promulgation and protection perhaps we shd not be so bilked and flattened, perhaps rather more tattered than flattened. You can be sure your observations are safe with me, I trust mine are with you.

And now for your kind words about Sybylla Penelope, from which I have been shying till the last as I have been shying for forty years. I can look at the book almost as impersonally as you can at this distance of time. In fact I'm sure you can now get more out of it than I can. I can assure you it was written at the time. I did not meddle with it for reasons mentioned in the preface. I'll add for you that I thought at first of re-writing it under the cover of 'editing'; but quickly realised that I could not alter it without making grave mistakes whereas I could trust my indelible powers of observation and transcription to know that at the time it would be ping on the nail. For example she says that the *Bulletin* was a mine of fascination but not considered nice for clergymen and young girls. That is so artlessly jolly like *The Young Visiter* or Marjory Fleming, and also so deadly on the target. I remember a visitor saying he had travelled with a parson who was an old hypocrite, for there he was reading the *Bulletin* as bold as brass. That's how I got that.

You remark on par 3 p 161—I can trace the genesis of that thought at the time. There used to be great yabber about the feminine side of H Lawson, to which his sympathy was attributed—that a man inherits from his mother as well as his father, which was great new psychology to me at the time. I can trace nearly everything in it back to what set it off.

You say it is a study of feminine adolescence, yes, but I was too young to be wholly conscious of that; it is, I see now, partly reckless confession of actuality. I think much the same still but with tremendous enlargement and development but haven't the pep to say it. An I don't-care-which-horse-wins-the-boat-race lethargy is silting me up. The want of opportunity to exchange fruitful sparks of ideas among 'aquils' or congenials is atrophying.

Sybylla Penelope had the same sharp resistence to being exploited, the same disregard of consequences in saying so as a child has to authority. You know how an infant naked across your lap will suddenly take a notion it's had enough and will stiffen its spine and rebel with a splendid fire, quite ridiculous and wholly endearing in such a soft helpless blob.

At anyrate I'm profoundly grateful to Geo Robertson that he wd not do me the disservice (his own word) of publishing it when it was written. I could not have lived through it on top of the first book—and pity my poor parents, who were so splendid. It must have been a tremendous annoyance to them. I wish I cd have got it out before Mother died, but the old dear was getting frail before I resurrected it and may have been more upset than entertained by it.

I'm glad you think *Bung* better than *Brilliant*. I haven't the nerve to re-read *Brilliant*. It must have been terrible. I had had a scorching mass of experience to tune me up in the second attempt and was careful to expose only one narrow facet.

Well, many thanks for a hand under my chin to float me off the mud in which I'm chronically shoaled.

Yours with love
[unsigned]

174

[nd, Sept/Oct 1946]

Dear Girls

. . . Have gulped the MSS at a sitting, just ran along because
of my interest in you and in the material. What you would want
to know is what I feel from this sample about it as one craftsman
(or one without craftsmanship but the temerity to print books)
to another. Well, you've got a whole paddockful of horses in
the [word illegible] of a rolling season kicking up their heels
and galloping wild. One of you is galloping on the tail and the
other must take the wing to get them yarded—I shall be
breathlessly interested to watch you do it—from the roof of the
cowyard. You have here about 90,000 words and you've not
begun to swing the mob towards the yards yet, I shd think you'd
need another 50,000 lay-out and then it would take yet another
100,000 words to draw-in the strings of the net. I'm not quite
satisfied with the trapping of Eily so far. (Please remember I've
been on a vice commission in Chicago.) Would a girl today be
quite as simple as Eily—a Sydney girl—and why did her mates
lock her in—because they had no other key or what? Perhaps
this will be cleared-up as the story ripens. You'll have to be very
authentic about this as every male in the universe and the 90%
of men-debauched women just dote on brothelism in men—
think it is their nature. If you are writing from exact facts
nevertheless you'll still have to be careful of the other kind of
verisimilitude, like Sybylla when she wrote of love affairs—they
did not catch on tho taken from life. This part will have to
be more than real to be irrefutable.

Love and goodluck
[unsigned]

Carlton
Nov 4 1946

Dear Lisa

Such a lovely letter from you today and I still have your other one reproaching me, but it's no use, I cannot keep up. You will always understand, won't you, that it's just a matter of lack of strength.

I managed to get off a few theatre pars from London to you today which you may not see in papers here. I posted it on my way to town, and your letter was here when I returned. I went in to broadcast over a country network—someone had requested that I be interviewed and give a greeting.

It all sounds wonderful about *Ghosts*. I do hope it repays your trouble—the trouble of all concerned. It sounds as if much thought had been put in it. I wish I cd see it. I'll send your letter on to Dymphna. . . .

I'd love to see you dancing in your part. Dear me we are so scattered and scarce that we are like a jigsaw puzzle of which the parts are never all assembled. The music all sounds good too; everything. Nov 9 is one of my favorite days in the year so I know it will go well. . . .

I've just had a nice letter from dear old Mrs Morice. I fear she will not be vigorous enough to go out at night. I shall love to have the article when you re-find it.

I don't know if I thanked you for your cheer about my little book. I believe that Norman Lindsay wrote me a charming open letter in the *Bulletin*, which I did not see. One of the men at the ABC rang me up about it.

I hope the American Consul will be amused. . . .

Yours with love
[unsigned]

Carlton
November 16 1946

My dear Rika

It was a great joy to hear from you again after the years of horror, and to know that you are alive. It is, however, sad to hear that your dear sister suffered so, though she escaped the horrors of invasion. I have the book she gave me in London inscribed with her name and mine: one of Duhamel's. You will miss your sister terribly. I know how I missed mine, but I am glad they went young and do not know the desolation and sadness of the world as one grows older and weathers two mad wars.

It is sad to hear of your brother's grandchildren dying of want and hunger in a country like Holland—the whole thing is so mad there is no use in trying to discuss it. I never had any hopes of a new world after the war, not for two generations. The old will go, the middleaged will be saddened beyond recovery and the young debauched and tried beyond repair, only the very young will come up renewed, if there is cessation from men's belligerence for a space.

You, like us in Australia, are a member of a small population, and there is no more neutrality for small countries. With whom do we align ourselves to make a safer position? England's world power has waned. It now lies between America and Russia and the sleeping Asia. Asia is so backward, so clogged with benighted impoverished millions that she will not come to full industrial or military force in our time. Russia is for totalitarian brotherhood and raising of the masses, America is for the old gangster free enterprise of great riches and great poverty, and will England's liberalism be of any influence? Life will go on and the supreme tragedy is that we each have such a short flickering share in it.

I'll send you a little book of mine just published: the preface will explain it. It is causing much laughter and praise here but it may be too remote from Holland and your hearts be too sad after such destruction and death. . . .

[unsigned]

8.19 To C Hartley Grattan and Marjorie Grattan, New York
Source: FP 23

Carlton
Dec 19 1946

Dear Friends

It is time we took up the thread of our conversation again, if it is not permanently broken. I dislike being broken into by censors, no matter how harmless my discourse nor what the censors' qualifications for nosing may be, and that was one reason why I went mute. *A propos*: all bigots—military, religious, political, moral and what not—know their onions in meddling, because one can form the habit of shutting-up without even contemptuous comment. Easier that way. Another reason for silence was that you meet many of our people in authority and know from them more than I do of what is going on in major affairs here; also you must have more letters than you can cope with.

As you subscribe to the little dominie magazines you will ·know what is going on in that line, but I enclose a copy of *Fellowship* which you may not see. Dymphna and I have had fun with a little satirical play on the attitude of book vendors toward native books. The main character is a GI Joe, and in Adelaide the American Consul supplied a uniform for him.

Great rush of children's books; even I am trying a tale for teenagers. It is being published by Shakespeare Head, the firm which is now the book dept of Consolidated Press (*Daily Telegraph*, etc). Head of it, imported by Mr Packer, is a Mr Ward, owner of *Burke's Peerage*—from Burke's Peers to Bunyips—what a pity the name was not the 'Boogong Head' to make the incongruity more pleasing—to me.

Ernest Moll is back to do a long poem in sonnets—subject

Australia. F T Macartney is also doing 500 lines on same theme. ... Moll replied to the toast of Aust Lit at the dinner of the Eng Ass at University this year. He sat on one side of me. On the other I had a professor man with eyes like a poodle Peke, who asked me superciliously of Aust Lit 'Is there any?' So I inquired what he was to speak on, see—the subject. He said, 'Greek vases'. I said 'Why *Greek* vases: Why not Phoenician or Etruscan?' It wd be more natural for vases to attain the international and universal category from the jump, free from any taint of origin, than for imaginative literature to do so. However!

I never heard if you got the copy of the Furphy Biog that I sent. The book or your acknowledgement may have gone to the fishes. Poor old Furphy is now really dead as evidenced by the dominies beginning to rummage in his dust. *Rigby* is in page proof and I have to do a review in 600 words (difficult) for *Book News*, edited by Geo Farwell.

I'm a bit late for Christmas but wish you all the good of the New Year before its whiskers are too long. Rosalind and the twins will now be real girls ready for their debut, in the kindergarten, if not in sassiety.

If you have not forgotten who this is I am still with warm regards as of yore.

[unsigned]

8.20 From Marjorie Pizer, Sydney
Source: FP 39

201 Macquarie St
Thurs 17th [1946]

Dear Miss Franklin

I would like to thank you very much for the exciting & stimulating evening Muir & I spent with you. To go to all that trouble to regale us with delicious food, & to spend the evening regaling us with delicious & penetrating notes, & to encourage us in our work, was wide hearted & we loved it. ...

If we continue our work & make some small contribution to Australian literature, it will be due, in large measure, to encouragement from such persons as yourself, Katharine Prichard & E J Brady.

Again thanking you,

Yours sincerely
Marjorie Pizer

8.21 To Emmy Lawson, Southport, United Kingdom
Source: FP 39

Carlton
Jan 13 1947

My dear Friend. A neighbor took me for a little respite up our Blue Mountains as she said it was disgusting that I had never been there and when I got back your letter was here. It was so nice to hear from you in such short space of time. So on Dec 2 I went to town and sent you what they call a hamper. It contained 16 oz honey: 24 oz marmalade: 16 oz dripping: 12 cheese: 4 oz meat treat: 16 oz pudding: 12 oz Cheese/macaroni three 4 oz cakes of soap.

It doesn't sound very nice or very much but there is little choice. Some people pack their own parcels but that entails getting tins soldered and parcels carried to post office and I am not strong enough for it. The groceries don't cost more than half—all the rest of the pound goes in insurance and postage. So let me know if it does not arrive and I can claim insurance and try again. Also let me know if you hear that Mrs Atkinson and Miss Reeves got theirs. Have just had a letter from Miss Hodgson joyful about hers. Anything you don't like I'm sure someone else will. I did not write on Dec 2 as the parcel takes so much longer and this may arrive ahead of it. On Christmas my sole surviving aunt and a cousin and I had dinner at one of the big hotels here. The Prices Control limited them to three courses and 7/- price without wines. It was very simple. Choice of two soups; choice of baked lamb, roast beef and turkey with

York ham and then plum pudding and ice cream and bananas, cherries and raisins. Coffee served in lounge after. The cafes and hotels run by European hoteliers got round the regulations by charging 30 shillings for coverage and in some places the people were so disgusted they walked out. My English friends wrote me five days after the hail storm on Jan 1 wondering was I safe. I was tho we were in the track of it. It was like a rain of blue metal on the roof. I thought it wd go. Cottages with tiles were wrecked. I had the leaves of some sun flowers tattered a little that is all. The hail here was as big as golf balls. In other places it was as big as cricket balls and in chunks as big as a cup. One face of our big railway clock was broken and the glass sheds over the train tracks were smashed dangerously. . . .

Where is Southport, exactly? I have forgotten. How do you get to London and how far are you from there?

A man recently returned from Germany was speaking over our broadcasting network last night. His tale of the poverty and destruction in Europe is awful. Also coming as news was the tale of the German children's feet being amputated due to freezing. I wish we could have butterless weeks and meatless weeks here and go on short rations to send food. But where are the ships and not enough people to do the work. A friend just back had to leave his father and mother awaiting priorities and yet the ship he came on was empty of freight and half empty of passengers. Muddle somewhere. . . . How is the Mosley crowd bearing itself these days? Miss Hodgson sent me a paper with an article on Mr Aldridge and the work he was doing advising people about reparations for their war losses. The thing was take over by the Govt last Oct or his part made obsolete by a law or regulation. He was described as a tall affable man with a fringe of grey hair. He was interviewing people on the old Kent Rd in this acct. Ever your loving friend

[unsigned]

South Yarra
23.2.47

Well Stella dear, I have read *My Career Goes Bung* & I find it very difficult to know just what to say about it. Of course it interested me, but I cannot say I enjoyed it: because sexy things never attract me. Perhaps, compared with many books of the day, you may think this does not loom very largely in yours but then I avoid the books in which it does. Do you think me very old fashioned & prudish? I consider those books that have been so very outspoken have done much harm to the young people of the day. They have aroused the passionate side of their natures & glorified it.

I'm so sorry if I hurt you, but you would not have me other than honest.

Of course the book is clever & amusing—but where do you get some of your words from?

I certainly hope your ideas of God have undergone a change since you wrote the book. Nothing could be more hopelessly unlike the truth. No wonder you did not find comfort from such a belief.

Vida & I went to hear William Winter last night. We liked him very much. He spoke for an hour & then answered questions put to him. He certainly is a world citizen. I agree with him that we must overcome this nationalism. As long as we each feel that our nation is the best on earth, the result must be conflict of some kind.

I am reading *Hiroshima* by John Hersey (a Penguin). Stella, how can men be such savages: how can they make innocent people suffer so terribly? What a blot on the escutcheon of the Allies that it is that the atomic bomb was used by them. What would we have said of the Germans if they had used it?

What did you think of McKell voting for his successor? I wonder how he will get on as GG. I do not think people will be enthusiastic about attending his functions. A very trying position to be in.

Please excuse this very untidy letter. My pen & I do not get on well together.

Much love
From Aileen

8.23 From Rex Ingamells, Melbourne
Source: FP 40

The Jindyworobak Club
18th March 1947

Dear Miles Franklin

Many thanks for the bonzer corroboree and champion tuck-in of the other night. I'm sorry that perhaps I did not appear to appreciate it as much as I really did. Fact was (as I didn't explain) that I arose from my couch in Auckland at 6.00 pm (Auckland time), after a late night out, and, as Sydney time is 2 hours behind that of Enzed, I'd been up and about quite a while by the time I arrived at Grey Street (consid'rin' as how I'd had but a few winks the night before). Consequently, you will understand that I was quite blissfully happy to sit back and, while making as little effort as possible, drink in the glories of the company I found myself in. I'm grateful, indeed, for your arranging for me to meet Harley Matthews and Les Cahill, both of whom I had long wanted to meet, and also for the opportunity of meeting Mrs Mills and Miss Dutch-worker (I'm afraid I do forget her name). The others present are all old friends of mine. With you presiding as hostess, I felt happy and honoured, although I must have appeared dull. After catching up lost sleep, I was, I believe, much brighter when I visited Margaret Preston for a brief while on Saturday afternoon before catching my train. Those lucky people, the Prestons, as you no doubt know, are about to truckabout in the outback. MP, by the way, is doing an article for *Jindyworobak Review*, containing some of her thoughts on Aboriginal Art and the Museums, and this links up very well with the Jindy outlook. I'm greedily and proudly

Esteemed literary editor Beatrice Davis, a good friend to Miles Franklin and her work (Photo by Quinton F. Davis, courtesy Anthony Barker)

looking forward to the article from M F when you have it ready. So long, Cobber. Love and all that.

Sincerely
Rex

A & R Castlereagh St
3/5/47

Dear Miles

I loved the gaiety and fairytale quality of *Sydney Royal*. Read it last night with great pleasure, & revelled in having my own copy given & inscribed by M F. Poor Grannie. I didn't quite work out the mystery of her birth, and hoped she didn't kill herself as you threatened. The benevolent uncle was a darling.

Do want to see you soon

Love
Beatrice

Carlton
May 6 1947

My dearest Emma

It is always so good to hear from you. Also came the book about the indivisibility of peace. I am so glad to have it and am reading it carefully, but find it heavy going. There is so much repetition, typical of the learned folk, especially PhDs, who have a mistaken idea that university knowledge can make a writer of people. So much for the heavy style: as to his premises: he depends upon *law* greatly, and extending it internationally. But do you remember that Brailsford and Glasier in our war, also Mrs Swanwick and others, pointed out the dangers of an international police force that perhaps could maintain order but could not ensure liberty of thought. The real trouble is that science has outgrown ethics, and men are going more sex mad than ever. All the world is taking to oriental indulgence—phallic worship, unrestricted and continual preoccupation with lust. Look at the orient compared with the occident for human energy, and think out the plausible reason. Dr Unwin says you can't have both sexual indulgence and great energy for more than one generation. We are at present using up the bank of energy gained by continence. At least half the human race had continence forced upon them by manners and some of the men too had to conform because there were not enough nymphomaniacs to supply the demand in our generation.

Emma darling, you are very naive about my newspaper photo. Don't you know how photographers take out all the wrinkles? and I still can raise a grin. I look about a thousand really. As for life not having treated me badly it is I that have struggled unavailingly to be good, or worth something to life. I'll get some copies of the photo now perhaps. But everything is in such short supply, you have to wait months and the price is frightening to those of a tiny fixed income, and not even fixed so that it mightn't melt altogether at any moment.

As to the nephew. He has been here for a weekend and today is off to Tokyo. He says cheeringly that I'm not to worry that only 40 per cent are killed nowadays. I'm always apprehensive. . . .

I loved the kodak of you with your young relatives. I suppose Dart is a staid family man now. He was such an entertaining young sapling that time in London. I think we always dote on the ones we have known as young things. They get their tentacles around our hearts as little creatures and no matter what superstructure of he-mannishness they build on that, we are still soft about them at the core, as babies. A pity we didn't know that of our own elders, tho I can't complain I always was very, very happy with my elders, and the elders always had great patience and friendship with me.

You ask me about living alone. What is a duplex—it is a

term new since my day? I think one of those adorable American flats near your relatives wd be the nearest approach to heaven we cd get in this world. If you were only near it wd relieve the increasing desolation. People are always against my staying in this old humpy in this uninteresting locality but to have a roof of any sort today is magnificent, and I'm afflicted so that I cling to it. I have been in some of my friends' swanky flats, and I'd go mad with the radios. I have to stick here because I can sleep here. If there is a noise at one side of the house I can move to the other. But I can't do the work now. . . .

Yes, growing old is sad because so many of our generation drop out and leave us desolate, and because of the physical inability to do for oneself. But I had old friends in England who said the last years *were* the sweetest. But they had someone to care for them like acolytes, and the English—as someone pointed out, through long usage of a lower order—can be happy being waited on, and others are content to do the waiting. It is not so with Australians. We have had to care for ourselves largely, as the underdogs have been very scarce and always on the rise to become top dogs themselves, which is democracy, but has its drawbacks for those who need help. . . .

All the world is afraid of USA and Russia now, some think one is the greater menace, others think the other, depending upon their political outlook. USA wd seem to be cosetting Japan as a prize for big business and as a bulwark against communism, but I'm hoping the women will absorb American notions and get out of hand.

India is a nice mess. I wonder what they'll do when they haven't got England to blame. I see the English are marrying the Germans in shoals. My cousin writes that one of his nephews is marrying an English major and he's so glad that he has a coat of arms as the crests of the two families will look so nice on the invitation cards. My cousin himself is furbishing up his English with Lord someone, he says he is so glad to have an educated man, as he is very particular about the kind of English he speaks. Also he speaks of the thoroughbred that he has to ride, lent to him by the Princess, so I can't make out what the conditions must be. One thing I'm sure of is the madness of men. Why set two young armies in opposition to slaughter each other? Why not dress them up in uniforms and exchange Germans for English, Russians for French, Americans for Japs or Italians, without fighting? The novelty wd please everyone.

Well my dear, this is a long screed. I'm sending you another little book, of a different type from the last, which may entertain you. I have an amusing letter from St John Ervine about *Career Goes Bung*. He says it bewilders him, and that I shd not write a book like that, but winds up that it shd be at least twice as long, so it cd not have bored him. I'm telling him I bewilder myself, I'm so complex, so how cd he who knows me not, be able to unravel me?

Ever your loving, loving friend,

[unsigned]

8.26   *To Aileen Goldstein, Melbourne*
Source: FP 10

Sunday [22 June 1947]

Dearest Aileen

This will go in Vida's envelope: I wrote her a note on Friday night, and on Sat morning the post brought a packet with her name inside the wrapping but your writing like the voice of Jacob on the outside. Such a fragrant cake of soap, such a generous packet of rinso! Did you send it to wash my sins away, or have I mentioned that soaps are scarce here? tho never so scarce that I have wanted for them, because I use so little. One piece of toilet soap does me at least six months, as my skin is so dry. In any case it was most kind and generous of you, and I thank you. . . .

Did you hear Geo Farwell's play *Sons of the South* when put on in Melb? I went to the first night here last night. Capable proletarian document but lacks magic. A novel or a drama must include an element of magic, as a personality must be endowed with charm before it can enchant.

I remember something in your last letter about *Career Goes Bung*. It doesn't matter at all that you don't like it, but to accuse me of sexiness because of it shows how the walls of a nunnery, though not concrete, have shut you off from knowledge of the worsening or loosening, or whatever you like to call it, of behaviour. Your accusation is humorous because men who approached me in my nubile decades always, when defeated, accused me of being sexless, of being not a woman but a mind. . . .

In another way *Career Goes Bung* is a most useful tome to me. It reminds me of Rachmaninoff and his popular prelude— the one that everyone knows. He said that his audiences would encore and encore him till he played that prelude when they would desist and go home. It was as efficacious as 'God Save'. A splendid thing to save him from exhaustion. So with *Career goes Bung*. People of the Blimp school of thought every now and then try to get up an argument with me. Heaven knows I haven't strength to bother with their outworn ideas so I send them a copy of *Career Bung* and, like Rachmaninoff, I am then let alone. The book has thrown a cynical light on what is called human nature. We haven't advanced any in really freeing women since Miss Scott and Vida were on the job. Women are more freed to ape men's vices and *amours*, but not to let out the devils or angels which may be confined in them as men are freed to strut and bellow on the motive power of their ego, no matter what its quality or character.

I have no news whatever so will not continue this screed. It is always nice to hear from you.

Ever affectionately
[unsigned]

Carlton
Aug 1 47

My dear Anne

I glanced at your letter and put it aside till I cd give it full reading, since then I have not been able to lay my hand on it so must reply without full knowledge of what you put forward.

I am, of course, in favor of the Indonesians gaining their freedom from European overlords and hope if you have a committee to study the situation and if it is in communication with any Indonesians of authority that you are throwing all your weight against this threatened scorched earth policy, no matter what the 'whodunit' excuse. Such an exhibition from the Indonesians in face of world famine and shortage would suggest a filibustering hysterical policy. If they have the requisite political sagacity to win and use freedom they will realise that world opinion and time are on their side. With England relinquishing India and other communities the Dutch must follow in the same way.

There has been too much destruction and death—man-made and unnecessary—for any community to add to that unforgivable score now would be madness.

I feel deeply about Australia's position in the holocaust. How are we to give power to our ideas or methods whether blimpish, imperial ideal or merely impish? What about our own Aborigines? What about our own men who will not give women equal pay for equal work with men? What about the imprisonment of women in brothels—regulated in two states? I wd like to discuss the whole question with you some time but there is no time. I had to lie down for a day this week I was so overdone with chores and requests, and now all sorts of picayune engagements await me and nag me.

No time for more
[unsigned]

7th October 47

Miles Darling

You must be thinking we're all dead. Well, I am, more or less, with rheumatism. That's a nice way to begin a letter from England where we've had the summer and are now busy having the record dry autumn of the century. But the fact remains that I haven't had a twinge of rheumatism in Australia, but the minute I hit this country I reverted and I've had a fierce stiff neck for a month and have been laid low on my bed for several days with rheumatism down the big muscle on the right side of my back. It was so acute I thought it pleurisy at first. Then add to that, that I nearly sliced the top off my left little finger a while back and am still typing laboriously, and you'll know what my arrears of correspondence are like.

'Nuff of the gloom! Yours was the very first letter that I got after my arrival. And it was like a breath of home. Please dearest-darling, go on writing me bits and pieces of local gossip about our literary friends and enemies, and keep me alive. I don't belong here Miles, not a bit of it. I'm enjoying being here, it's not that. It's that every now and then, in the middle of good conversation, at the theatre . . . it suddenly sweeps over me that I'm not at home. My terms of reference are different, my southern eye has a different focus, and my irreverent southern tongue has to be sternly checked. I like the English people so much, and I'm proud to be sprung from them (that is the half that isn't Scottish and Welsh), and I could weep for the fate that has overtaken them and the courage with which they're facing their recurrent crises. But I could shake them too. There's a general air of clinging to their departed glories that puts the whole nation in the genteel poverty class. And as for the publishing world, after the glorious publishing days of the thirties, I can't recognise this shrunken trade that has to reprint the classics for a living and dare foster only the likely best seller among the younger writers. It will take only a few more years of the present control of paper, to kill off a whole generation of writers—but the gov seems to think it's worth it to keep up a plentiful supply of toilet paper. ...

I just can't bear the thought of not coming back Miles and the children, happy as they are in their school here, are little Aussies at heart. ... How about you my dear? I can see you in my mind's eye tapping away at terrific speed on your typewriter in the sunshine, with Ginger's and Greedy's friends and relations conversing at the far end of the garden—and perhaps one of them broody in an old saucepan in the laundry, or on the floor in a cosy corner beside the WC. How I'd love to stretch out on the floor in your front room and have you read poetry to me—how I'd love to be with you all again. So much, that I'm coming back. Maybe *Spinner* will bring me. Maybe, of course, it won't. But there's nothing like building a few castles in Australia. Our love to you Darling-Dearest and letters please with lots of news of home.

Florence

8.29 *To Florence James, London*
Source: FP 30

Carlton
Nov 16 1947

My dearest Florence, It was gorgeous to have your letter of Oct 7 and I've been honing to reply ever since. Held back by the constipation of the Telly's competition. After D wrote that she had been called to the presence we were expecting a win and I did not wish to crash into your expectations with mere banalities. ...

I note that you haven't taken root yet, but you will, that is natural. Life over there will begin to absorb you. Dymphna was sending you dripping and I wanted to drop bantams' eggs in it but she said you have many friends to send the children jam etc and so I sent parcels to others who have no one outside England but me to help them. Conditions seem to be hard but lots of immigrants stay only a few weeks or months here and turn tail for England again where conditions are better and houses procurable. Mrs Fogden is as anxious to get home as she was to get abroad tho by all accounts her people are better supplied with many things than we are here. What do the people think of the royal wedding? Philip has done well for himself. And the papers divulge accounts of plenty of people who are still rich as of yore and as full of airs, I'll swan. Glen Mills Fox has gone to Melb for an indefinite stay: she and Nettie shared the same compartment on train and Glen reports that Nettie probed industriously about 'this famous hospitality at Miles's'. I had no idea that it was ever mentioned or had any claims to fame. Had a big party while Glen was in hosp and had her husband as I seem to neglect him, that night had also the expert on coal brought out by the Govt, one Webb. Dymphna, Jim Gaby and Harley Matthew were here one evening not so long since. The yarns were ripe and rich! Harley and D remained all night, J went after midnight. Harley is a tremendous original: am glad he was up to my claims for him with Dymphna. I don't believe you ever had your tea out of the waratah cup after all— you'll have to come back specially for that. If you are passing Aust House will you please toddle in and find out how this British Bd of Trade regulation against Aust books really works. For instance inspect the book shop at A House, if any. Find out if any of our books are there: please ask about *Sydney Royal* too and *Swagger*, which Harrap prevented from being published in England. Cousins said when books had dried up here he had been sending thousands to London but this regulation wd stop that if it cd not be circumvented. I try to get time but the calls are continuous. For example today have to go to see Ada Holman. She has been at death's door again with heart and pneumonia and I can't neglect my elders as they are thinning out so fast. ... I don't think I told you I put a light story in the Telly comp as I had the mistaken notion that they would take a number for serials *a la SMH* and it was quite good enough for that. Of course it was thrown out by the office boy. Then *Newcastle Morning Herald* started serials by Australians beginning with Glassop's, he being a native boy. They asked me to let them have something so as to encourage other leading writers

'To Miles with Love, Dymphna Cusack 1947.' (ML)

to do likewise, sent my serial. Gave me 50 pounds and very pleasant attention, such a lot of people wrote to me. I was lucky as it was the last of the venture as paper restrictions came down then but I have fifty pounds neat as they even added the bob for the exchange—nice touch. Dymphna is off to the Mtns again this week she hopes. She is plucky to start off again without melancholy after Pinegrove—that was perfect—only once—ah, and never again such a combination as that of friends and the dear little girls and the animals and birds and real good Australian small town half bush freedom. . . . No more space except for love to you all from

[unsigned]

8.30 To Katharine Susannah Prichard, Canberra
Source: FP 21

Carlton
Nov 20 1947

My dearest Katharine, I'm in need of a little dissipation such as writing to you. I hope you are keeping up your strength and the kind of fizz necessary for literary work.

We are having quite a bit of fun with *Tomorrow and Tomorrow*. It went to J B Miles from me with all my ribaldries thick upon it and he added to them with deeper and more political if less scintillatory observations. It became a game to me to find out the word *pattern*. J B Miles found a good many and marked them missed by M F. Then the book went to Marjory Pizer and she is very cocky because she found several *patterns* which she marked missed by both J B M and M F. In one spot I noticed J B M had put M B E = M F. I must investigate whether that is an insult or a compliment. I made an additional entry that I had missed the *patterns* through kangarooing. I shd read the book properly to be sure I'm not doing it an injustice but my snap judgment is that it is a great piece of composition but no creation. . . .

I've met that Billy Wentworth since you left at a wedding of my young cousin. The bride was given all the linen etc by

Packer or Theodore who were both at the church with some ladies I don't know if they were all wives. They were too busy for the reception. Wentworth hailed me and we began to talk and then I remembered and said, Ha, ha, me boy, I've been meaning to go for you for a long time and now's my chance. I told him : A member of *my gestapo* informed me that *your Ogpu* takes the form of a black list of certain people, and that my name is on it and a certain publisher said it might be necessary to ban my books because I'm a communist. I said, 'I am not a communist.' 'I shd hope not,' said he. Then he said, 'I never said you were a communist, tho I have lots of others on my list, I said you were a stooge for communists.' I said I accepted that as quite fair because communists were sure to quote advanced thinkers, such as I hoped I was, whereas the blimps would fly to him for backing. I told him I had said something pretty stiff about him. Pretty blasting I expect, said he. No, brilliant, said I—you know I *can* be brilliant if I bestir myself. I said my remark was that *I* did not matter, I was frail and obscure and of no account, it wd be easy to obliterate me, but my one axe to grind, my great love, was Australia, and what alarmed me was that our business men who would have to meet the business men of other countries, for Australia's sake shd depend for information upon any informer who cd be guilty of such misinformation.

I think he's cracked. I put up with him to have straight from the ass's mouth the wisdom of a blimp but he was such a bore that I soon tried to escape him. In vain! He pursued me. So I gave him my favorite who dun it Joe Stalin because in one slap he had taken women off the midden and put them into parliament. Wentworth said blandly that that was not true. I said one must believe the Dean of Westminster. He said the need to free women is all hooey they have always been free. You can guess how he endeared himself to me. He's such a bore in his halfwittedness, is the trouble. Says he's going into Parliament or to try to get there again. The most hrrumphing moustached barnacled Anglo-Indian of yesterday would be a bolshevist compared with this museum specimen. I like his little wife and am sorry she has such material to labor with. It wound up by them asking me to dine with them at Prince's. I came home to Glen, whom I had here then and Marg too to work on *Fellowship*. Oh why was I such a fool as to miss my chance of sitting between Mrs and Mr Bill W at Prince's when they had photographers laid on. It might have saved my life when I'm to be hanged for associating with communists. I must try to make up for such a miss by going to Canberra and being clasped to the bosom of R G M on the steps of Parliament house. . . .

Well royalty is now on its way to the Abbey. I wonder why they didn't wait for summer weather. Philip of Spain tried to take the great Elizabeth of England and lost his Armada. Philip of Greece had better luck with a lesser Elizabeth—has made a great match. I wonder what is his private fortune or is he a comparative pauper like Marina. The people have to have someone to worship—silly mugs. One grows cynical about the whole silly gallimaufry. Did you hear Hartley Grattan in the international quiz for the latest loan? I have no news so will end this screed with much love dear

[unsigned]

8.31   *To Glen Mills Fox, Melbourne*
Source: FP 40

Carlton
Nov 28 47

Glen me dear, It's a good day when I get a letter from you, a desolate one when I don't. Let that suffice, while I get on with the washing. Immensely glad you sent that clip about Mrs Holman as she is ringing me daily about the distribution of the book, as if I were the publisher. Wonder who C C Eager the reviewer is. What a funny little old bald head F D D looks in the picture. That moustache! It's truly a mo, a mere mo.

You can write up from your article if you like how I am mistaken for others. Had a new mistake since you left. Was introduced with a great flourish to that sister of Eng Min for Food who is here, oh, as a wonder, how everyone was going

197

to say this and that to Miles Franklin when they met *him* and then to find *he* was a woman because Miss Franklin wrote all her life under the name of Tom Collins!!!! Tom Collins was older than my father so no wonder I'm a legend—all that time.

We certainly can't run two reviews there won't be space for the usual length of one. There's Mrs Holman's book, trash or not, there's *Flynn of the Inland* and one or two others that slip my mind now. Last night I went to the Eng Ass dinner at Uni and sat between Prof McDonald and Dr Mitchell. I got Mitchell on to his glowing review of *Cyclone* over the air and accused him of liking it because of his interest in words apparently and because Vance hadn't used any in wrong places, because he had reviewed from that angle instead of from a literary one. He combated that and said didn't I think that the book had a pattern. That word was a red rag to a bull so I dressed him on that so that two university adorers on the other side gave up their worship and craned to hear. After some discussion he wound up that he thought V P had style that he was a good competent writer but no fire—the *Cyclone* was *The Passage* boiled down. 'Mind you,' he concluded—for reading I'd rank Palmer in a very low priority.' And yet you see he wd boost him over the air. A reader at the Hornsby library, friend of M M's said you couldn't read *T and T* you could only plough through it. Mitchell also asked me didn't I think *Wash Dirt* was awful trash. I said yes, just what I'd expect with that subject and the only readable book on it was Carboni's and the great literate genius had never heard of Carboni!!!

Betty Roland replied to the toast of Aus Lit, put there as Beatrice D (chairman) said because she'd look nice and the men would like her. She was got up like a prima donna and said she was invited to speak because the Ch had said she'd look nice (coyly) and I've tried to dress myself nicely for that. The men did sit up and lick their chops but poor Betty was so flash and phony that all admiration died after a bit and she looked like one declining into the double chins and appearance of a publican's widow. No good of presuming on your looks once youth has gone. Every utterance she made was ancient stuff and off the key and thin and after S Tomholt among others swarmed me to make complaints, as if I owned her or had been chairman or anything. Oh by the way Tomholt says he's starting a lit agency for London firms. . . .

If you can dig into anything, dig in, foot first and then you can arrange for other personal affairs later. I didn't quite mean what I seem to have written about the flat and odd jobs. I mean that you don't show any tendency to stay put long enough to nurse a business and that some roving commission life correspondent

[remainder of letter missing]

8.32   From Vida Goldstein, Melbourne
Source: FP 10

South Yarra
22/12/47

My very dear Stella—Here I am bobbing up at the last lap, as usual, to send you the season's greetings, & what I find most useful in the kitchen. White dishcloths always get such an abominable colour, so I make them of coloured cotton; they are satisfactory and durable. I would draw your attention to the stamp on the envelope that carries this letter, the twopenny one I mean, with the head of George V. It was to have taken one of the many letters I have *intended* writing you through the years. I am sorry my friends have to take my love for granted; they get mighty little proof of it. Well what do you think of our postwar world? Doesn't Hitler seem to have won the war? He said something to the effect that if he didn't win it, he would bring civilisation down with him. As you know I have not a fraction of sex antagonism in me, but one is almost driven to think that men are absolutely unfit to govern. They seem incapable of thinking & acting on other than belligerent lines. War, war, war—either fighting wars or trade wars. Humanity their last consideration. The Atomic Bomb doesn't kill off enough human beings quickly enough, so now they turn their attention to bacteria to accomplish their devilish ends.

But what about women also? I feel they, too, have failed humanity in 2 world wars. They proved their ability to help their country in a time of national crisis, but have done nothing to help prevent crises recurring. Where are the women's demands & organisations for a practical humanitarian programme, a 'fighting' programme, to make the world a fit place to live in? I marvel at the silence & inaction of women. Why don't they rise & war against war, call it by its right name, *mass murder*, strip it of its 'glory', expose the vice, the political & economic & financial corruption that go with it; and above all the trade policies which make war inevitable? Sometimes I wish I were 30 years younger, & could have a say & do again on behalf of the common people!

Lots of love from
Vida

8.33 To Jean Hamilton, London
Source: FP 26

Carlton
Jan 11 1948

Jean Darling, How are you and where and why and when? I note among some old papers that you sent me a cable for 1946 and I believe that is the last whisper I have had of you. When I sadly had to leave you I said I expected a few letters because you were always so engaged, charming and being charmed, that you did not go into dull corners and write as the natural born correspondents do. Many people are a pest because they always have their noses on letter writing, and I said you can't have it both ways. For a time you astonished me by sending grand letters. And I had those photographic ones during the war but now when the holocaust has swept past leaving you safe and sound—not a word from you. I spent all my energy in trying to do something for Mary and she was my thread of communication and that seems to have broken since her death.

I suppose you never think of coming back to Australia. You who stood London in the dreadful years are not likely to forsake its charms now. I suppose you are still carrying on the business. There should be an opening to do something between London and Sydney. Couldn't you work it so that you could gather up a number of girls desirous of emigrating who would in return for assistance guarantee to work 2 years here before they changed to something else or married, and get into immigration and get a trip as a chaperone or guardian or inspector or something. I wish I cd get to England once again, but I'm not strong enough to stand cheap travel and the prices otherwise are beyond me. The taxes here are frightful in addition to the cost of living being doubled and I believe trebled. For instance, shoes cost me more now per year than once I spent altogether on clothes for the period. Salt once a ha'penny per pound is now a penny ha-penny. In every little thing it is that way and it mounts up and up. . . .

Did you see the royal wedding? It was a great fairy story in real life, glass coach handsome prince and all only the woman raising the beggar instead of the Cophetua angle. Do let me hear something of how you feel and think these days. If you are passing Australia House please go in and ask about Australian books and if any of mine are procurable there.

Do you want parcels? How is the food situation? I have not sent to you as I know you have a family back of you and I concentrated on those who have no oversea connections. But I'd love to send you something if you need it. How about one of my blankets—worn, but clean, and would take no duty. If you shd note a second-hand copy of Virginia Woolf's *The Waves* lying around cheap I wish you would send it to me.

This is a dull letter because I seem to be writing to a blank wall till I can hear from you. I am in a dull mental state. There seems to be nothing ahead of me now but death, and I loathe and fear that. To be Irish I'm so afraid of death that I'm sure when I wake up some day and find I'm dead it will kill me with fright.

Does that Play Society still function? and do you still belong?

Does that Mr Rose with Farquharson still operate as a literary agent? Brent of BB still a mystery to the public: nothing to be announced yet. . . .

> Much love dear and hoping to hear from you
> [unsigned]

Carlton
Feb 2 1948

Dear Frank

Many thanks for your letter, information and yank hanky. Do you know a Ruth Auerbach? I noted in yesterday's *Sun* that she has arrived here and wd like to teach music in a school, that she was inspired to come to Australia by the fine men she met in *BCON* Osaka and who were so enthusiastic about that country.

I enclose a cutting from *Times Lit Supp* of last July 2. Please return when assimilated as I'd like to ponder it. I had thoughts in my mind for you but this expresses them. You will note that Alun Lewis was killed. You came through.

I add, hold on to your emotions. If you let your sympathies derange you, you become merely one more soul lost and destroyed by war and its aftermath. Otherwise, as one of the articulate, there is a compulsion within you to speak for those who also are sufferers, but cannot express themselves so well. This is not advice for those who would be successful but you will never be shriven unless you are true to what's in you. (I use the lovely old word shriven as meaning the attainment of harmony with your backbone and your soul.) If success comes, all right, but the ancients nailed Christ to a tree and the moderns shot Gandhi. Those men cd not have done other, and perhaps their final fate was less excruciating than Judas's or Peter's. I dunno. I only know that going against your inner grain is a fraying process.

Rough out incidents and thoughts, put down the details carefully, make a storehouse or a camel's hump to draw on in years of leaner experience and perhaps less power to feel. You won't be able to pump it all up in a hurry out of memory if and when the chance comes. You have a magnificent opportunity—and are you learning Japanese? . . .

You said an article about me in the *Herald*—I suppose you

meant Ian Mair in Melb *Argus*. I noted the old girlish picture
and did not read further. He is a chum of Glen's and she got
him to do it to keep my name from being lost.

I am tired and depressed but have often been depressed before
and so try not to give way to it. It is a matter of being
oversensitised—one cannot take in too much contrary stuff, but
those who are not sensitised are much worse. They often get
down in a rough way and moan and groan and kick against fate
more than we do. They haven't as much in them to fall back
upon. ... [remainder of letter missing]

8.35   To Rex Ingamells, Melbourne
Source: RIP

[nd, 15 March 1948?]

Dear Rex Ingamells

SOS. If you are not altogether gasping for breath with fatigue
consequent upon too many chores, etc, will you send me at yr
'early kind convenience' the authentic meaning of Jindyworobak. An ardent admirer of Jindy buttonholed me last night
and I, alas, cd give no concrete nutshell dictionary definition,
neither cd others. This man had procured six copies to give to
his fellow workers and quoted and testified at meetin' that it
is a great publication so I take on another chore. Also, where
is that tenth annual or whatever it was, that I wrote article for?
Have you scrapped it?

I know you are going flat out so no more but kind regds

from
Miles

8.36   From Rex Ingamells, Melbourne
Source: FP 40

431 Bourke St
16 March 1948

Dear Miles Franklin

'SOS' . . . 'early kind convenience' . . . Your wish is a command, and I scout delay.

'Jindy-worobak'—as the word appeared when it first hit my eye—appears in the glossary of Jim Devaney's *The Vanished Tribes*, where it is given the meaning 'to annex, to join'. I found it there in 1936, and have seen it dictionaried nowhere else, but Jim assured me it was a word of 'a Queensland Tribe'.

In adopting it for a special campaign, I reckoned it to have the following merits:

(1) It is *Aboriginal* and therefore apt in denoting interest in the indigenous.
(2) It is (or was) *outlandish* according to fashionable literary tastes, which deserved a shock.
(3) It has an apt *symbolism* from its meaning:
(a) denoting synthesis of our European cultural heritage with our Australian heritage. (I've expressed this variously—eg 'our English Mother Tongue and our Australian Mother Land')
(b) specifically 'directing the attention of Australian writers and artists to what should be their distinctive material.'

Point (3) here is the real answer you want, so please forgive me for the long prologue. In the first Jindy publication, *Conditional Culture* (1938), I gave 3b as the intent of the application. A few weeks later, in the first newspaper report on the Movement, 'The Jindyworobaks Come Forth' (Adelaide, *The News*), I gave the reporter 3a as the intent. Both are right, obviously bound up with one another. Some people assume that 'Jindyworobak', meaning 'to join', signifies the joining of the Club; and they can have that meaning too if they like, although it was never the basic one, and, according as Jindyworobak publishing and ideas have advanced, the Club has fallen into the background. Instead of worrying about a host of members, we are, in the Club sense, a small group of people.

No, the birthday *Review* isn't scrapped. Page proofs are in hand at the moment, and you will receive a copy of the book in a few weeks. Meanwhile, the tenth annual anthology has appeared. Didn't I send you a copy? I should've. I'll send one in a day or so. . . .

Sincerely
Rex

8.37 *To St John Ervine, Devon*
Source: FP 14

Carlton
May 12 48

Dear St John Ervine, Thank you for your generous consent to read my effort, MSS herewith—sent without cover to save postage at 1/6 per half ounce.

I am sorry your play was not a west-end commercial success as in such case we shd the sooner see it here. However, you are too well-established to be ignored by the more stable elements and I hope will pick up in the provinces.

We have in Sydney three theatres which run on a professional basis.

1. The Minerva where your other play appeared. This sometimes gives a more controversial piece among the assured overseas successes. For instance *Love on the Dole*, which failed, and *Mice and Men* which didn't quite. *Life with Father* helped them to recoup losses.

2. The Royal, which constantly stages *Rose Marie* with sometimes a sortie. *Born Yesterday* is there now and we had a season of Russian ballet.

3. The Tivoli, devoted to variety—the vulgarer inside the police regulations the more popular. I was there once with my

nephew during the war. He took a young woman too so my depression was not so noticeable as it might otherwise have been. The Tivoli has housed the Ballet Rambert and now awaits Vivien Leigh and Olivier. (Is this Olivier a son of Sir Sidney whom I met when a girl and when he was Governor of Jamaica?)

There are quite a few struggling amateur groups who give plays in suburban town halls or cubby theatres. The two leading are 1. under an Englishwoman named Doris Fitton, which had a great success with *Mourning become Electra* and she does Chekov, Hellman, Life of Oscar Wilde and so on. 2. The left-wing group concentrates on plays about and primarily for the 'red' proletarian. Are having a success with a valiant presentation of O'Casey's *The Star Turns Red*. That man has so much Irish genius that it cannot be entirely stodged even in a communistic sermon, which this play seems to be—as presented here. All these groups are as courageous as lions in tackling anything acclaimed overseas but never can bring themselves to local effort, and if they do kill it dead. Also the pederasters, from whom you suffer, are here too in imitating hordes. An instance of the courage for overseas things was that one group took Sydney Town Hall and produced Eliot's *Murder in the Cathedral*—and the Town Hall made a fine slap at a cathedral with the great steps for the actors to declaim on. The old hams who can't hold jobs with you get cushy jobs here. We have one conspicuous example. You shd hear him blether about Synge's *Riders to the Sea* and so on, but if there were even a super Synge here he'd never discern him.

When you go to Belfast again I wish you'd find out if the Misses Brett are still living. Charming people whom I used to meet at Lady Byles'. Miss Lucy Brett might remember me because she and I went to the Zoo one Sunday afternoon and in attempting to give Sandy the ape an orange on the end of her parasol, Sandy seized it from me and it was reduced to tatters, frame and all. It was a present Sir Charles had brought back from the East, with cloisonné handle. You can imagine my confusion, but I also remember Miss Brett's exquisite manners over the thing.

I see you do not accept my explanation of why I sent Bedford, and all you can say about my Marthaism is merited, but I think even your God wd think I've had enough punishment in this world and let me off in the next. I sent you a week ago another book (*B to BB*) a novel on Australia, rather a favorite with me. I wonder how much you'll dislike it. No more time, no more paper, my thanks. I'll write when I refind your note which at present is under a mass of pressing

[remainder of letter missing]

8.38   *To Mary E Dreier [Southwest Harbor, Maine]*
Source: FP 14

Carlton
June 3 48

My dear Mary Dreier

You don't know how nourishing it was to my over-affectionate heart to have your Christmas letter. USA and my friends there mean so much to me. Life there enveloped me in my most vigorous years and it is a bereavement to be so far away with all connections ceasing and receding; I suppose I was no more than one of the many people whom you see from other countries, who come and go without leaving mark or memory.

The voice of the USA, brandishing its supremacy and big stick at Russia and making England do what it wants, is very loud these days from radio and newspaper. I cling to the memory of my old associates and how gorgeous they were and know there are others equally splendid to-day. Can they prevail? They never do from generation to generation—but they leaven the lump and are responsible for real civilization, and on them depends man's upward climb. You have to live in a country to know its people. Otherwise it is all the noisy exploiteering elements which are heard abroad. I suppose we, if ever we are heard of at all, are known as a small inconsequent handful of ignorant backward mediocrities, descendants of criminals. But in the last two world wars our few precious boys were the farthest and first flung into the maelstrom to hold back the flood, while bigger powers hesitated and got ready: and then the first to the fray are entirely forgotten and disregarded. It is terrific to see those fields of graves all about the Pacific of Australian soldiers even unidentified. Your boys did not stay with us in dust though our earth is the cleanest in the world having lain fallow for perhaps millions of years. I saw on the newsreels those harrowing ceremonies with the flags and weeping mothers when the coffins were taken off the ships on arrival in USA. I think there is no excuse for war except lunacy. The warrior is never a hero to me. Soldiers, poor children, are the victims of their own mass hysteria rooted in fear—an inverted cowardice. They interned people for saying less than that in our war. So I had better get on to something more correct if not more constructive.

I have listened to Sir John Boyd Orr, food controller, Oliphant, scientist, Lord Beveridge, sociologist and one of our own men summing up the need for earth control, birth control and girth control. At the same time Cardinal Spellman and his man Friday, some prelate named Sheen, were telling us that Rome and Moscow are the only two powers in the world today and advising the Australian women to fill up their cradles. Another fellow, a papal legate, said blandly that each state of Australia is a province of Rome. Well, of course I don't know what such a small handful as we are can do about it, but Wall Street nabobs may put a crink in the tail of Rome and Moscow if they can't work up the populace to accept Rome instead of Moscow. I'd be for Moscow in the dog-fight if it could be clear-cut and the rest of the world unharmed onlookers. And if the world had really to be given over to USA or Joe Stalin as some very primary folks fear I'd be for the USA because I know the language and because I think they are more advanced in keeping their feet warm in winter and the flies out of their food in summer, and I love American trains. Wish I was aboard one of 'em now speeding across country like that time you took me to Shawandasee. . . .

We are severely rationed in milk and ordinary people haven't had cream since the war began. We are rationed in heating, no radiators or gas or electric fires allowed between 7.30 am and [numbers illegible] and we are having a cold winter due to a wet cold summer which did not allow the earth to warm up, the farmers say. A friend in a block of flats has just rung up to say an inspector has been in and found her with a prohibited radio on at 4 pm. I am wrapped in a rug with a hot water bottle at my feet to type this, but I have plenty of rubbish in my jungle garden that I am no longer strong enough to tame and old fashioned fireplaces because I live in a remote suburb among the hoi-polloi. If the sun doesn't shine tomorrow I'll light a fire but it is such a tiresome business and makes so much work for only one. Other cities have less coal than we because the miners won't work overtime any more and there are not enough of us to do the work in any case. Everyone insists on a full week and so no meat or bread from Friday till Monday, no post office nor many other things. The workers are deaf to the cries for more production. They are tired, if they worked till they were sapped their extra money goes in taxes and they have discovered that money is not the most valuable thing in life. They say if they produced as they are urged to do the result would soon be as after last war, they would be on the dole. Of course there always has been a crisis to urge on the workers and when they met it the masters kept on at the same old tricks. Even the most reactionary blimps have given up saying at every fresh strike that the workers shd be shot. People are really tired from the long strain, emotionally if nothing more. But it is a horrible thought that most of the peoples of the world never have enough to eat, and a worse, that nevertheless they keep on breeding like any other vermin. I have given up trying to save the world, I cannot even save myself, I have not sufficient wisdom.

Do you remember in 1923 you asked me what book I specially wanted to read on the train and I said Freud and you gave me a book of his essays which I still have. Today I am reading Dr Unwin's *Sex and Culture*, and getting a great deal of satisfaction from it because he is corroborrative of my views which I hold in spite of a world by majority vote given over to whoring and alcoholic drink. He says the human race cannot have great vital energy and unlimited sexual indulgence, it must choose one or the other, and that the puritan nations are living on the energy they banked in the past and will deteriorate if they keep on. He is a Cambridge man. Do you know him and how he ranks? You wouldn't think it would need a tome of reference to prove that obvious fact. There is one question I'd like to solve—why is it that in the most advanced nations, where women are in a slightly better position and where there are plenty of men so many of the finest women remain unmarried. I remember in USA once when a Hungarian asked me that question. He said all the most wonderful women were unmarried and that it was a dangerous symptom and spoke badly for American men. I remember totting up without stopping to delve the names of 100 women with whom I had contact in the work who were all unmarried. I started with Jane Addams, Mary McD, Dr Young, Lillian Wald and dozens and dozens down to less prominent women who nevertheless were obviously attractive physically and mentally. It was the same in Australia at that date our three most prominent women were unmarried two of them had been raging beauties. Of course in England the men were killed in war or emigrated but that was not so in America and Australia. There were lovely 'old maids' in my own family, stories of whose throngs of admirers still persist. I wish someone had gone around and questioned them seriously about thirty years ago. During the war one of my young friends about [number illegible] who had too many admirers was confiding in me and I said, 'well if you want to marry you shd do so while there are many men to select from, soon they'll be picked over. It is a fatal thing to have too many admirers.' She said spontaneously, 'Yes, old maids are always the most interesting and wonderful of all the women I know.' What is your theory on the matter?

If you were only here for tea we could theorise. . . .

[unsigned]

8.39   *To Sumner Locke Elliott, New York*
Source: FP 41

Carlton
October 31 1948

Well, Sumner, my dear, you've done it! *Rusty Bugles.* A poet's title, a challenge to go floating on the wind far and wide. When your aunt lamented to me that you were being sent away up

210

there, I rejoiced for your sake and envied you your chance of getting away from the segregation of our banal cities to a different banality and better segregation. See the result. What a pity you didn't have six years in all sorts of dumps if the results could have been proportionately rich.

I saw the play on Thursday evening last. Many of the sentences were lost to me partly through faulty articulation and because the little buzzers, excited by the immense publicity you've had, giggled in anticipation and at everything regardless, and drowned some of the dialogue. But they settled down after a bit and enough got through to me for me to recognise the best Australian play I have yet heard. The Australianness was so authentic, so original and actual, and so gifted. Humor and pathos succeeded each other artistically. The play shows how life and its tragedies catch all, even the most unlicked and empty, and call for pity rather than contempt for all caught in this unsolved mystery of human existence.

How I wish the play could have the advantage of the timing and pace of the best American commercial productions plus the clear articulation of actors long practised in getting every nuance across. However, the actors who took part were well-chosen and did magnificent work. They made the characters so actual and so lovable. I felt an affection for most of them especially Vic Richards, Darkey McClure, Cig Ape, the little ex-jockey (magnificent) and Dean Maitland. You made him so touching that I felt I had failed him myself when he went off and the letter came too late. Even the big vulgar lead-swinger was high-class comedy when he was shamed by his daughter's letter, even tho he was so much in character that he soon recovered. That telephone scene was gorgeously funny, so natural and evoked shouts of laughter. Spontaneous rounds of applause were frequent and hearty all through. Other spots that evoked much laughter were the men getting back when they thought they had got away, and Darkey McClure was ripping when he was drunk and finally repudiated help and staggered out alone. The piano scene was perfect with that sergeant (I did not get their names together) telling how his wife played this and that and the twiddly bits she put in. Lovely the man who wanted something by Bernard Shaw, and the fellow who got *Lady C's Lover* in triumph. And that YMCA hut man. I met him once coming home from San Francisco and he started to teach me to enjoy life and be happy—me of all people—can you imagine it—yes you can because you have captured the unbelievable opacity of such men's perspicacity. I loved the curtain call. Just that line of soldiers, each so different in appearance and character that it was a scene in itself, and standing stiffly to attention while Gor' Save was played as part of the scene and not as a mere regulation dismissal.

I wish you all sorts of luck and success. Don't stay away too long. Congratulations and love from

[unsigned]

8.40 *To Beatrice Davis, Sydney*
Source: FP 38

Carlton
Nov 11 48

Beatrice m' treasure, welcome home! Sydney's a dull hole without you. 189 Castlereagh St is aching for the return of the pride of the harem so I'll wait till you get yourself straightened out before plaguing you. Also you won't be as bold and brave when you get there as you imagine now in the dissatisfaction of being reefed from work and routine unpremeditatedly and inconveniently. But you'll work many days at home.

I'm quite all right so long as I do not use my right arm, so I sit in the dust and disorder. Dreary. To relieve the burden of contemplation of my nothingness and down-and-outness Mr Cousins kindly consented to aid me in a course of indecency in literature by the loan of Kinsey's tome on the sex habits of the male. My, oh my! how tastes differ.

Dymphna came and did shopping and cooking while I was in the first throes. She even cleaned the top of the stove better than I can, and we talked ourselves out.

Get one of your subservient male friends with a car to take you to *Rusty Bugles*. I loved it. A young man yesterday took

me to see the film of *Life With Father*. Not as good as the play.
I hope Elizabeth's baby is a girl.

[unsigned]

8.41   From Laurie Collinson, Brisbane
Source: FP 41

16/12/48

Dear Miles

It was very thoughtful of you to send me the English literary
papers. Thank you very much.

So far, my return to Brisbane has been uneventful. I have not
yet got a job, but am trying to get into the Public Service where
I hope to do the minimum amount of work for the maximum
pay. I feel the FAW should approach the government with a
view to its providing a number of sinecures for young writers
who have as yet nothing to show but their promise. As for
established writers—a minimum of ten pounds a week with no
strings whatever. Can you imagine it!

Several executive members of Unity Theatre have now read
Call Up Your Ghosts, and are very enthusiastic about it. It will
shortly be read at a General Meeting, and, dependent on the
opinion of members, will be considered for production. May
we have your permission to go ahead if all other considerations
are satisfactory? ...

At present I am reading a very interesting study entitled *The
Feminine Character* by Dr Viola Klein (Kegan Paul). The dust
jacket says 'this study surveys and co-ordinates the views of
recognised authorities on this topic in the fields of Biology,
Philosophy, Psychoanalysis, Experimental Psychology, Psycho-
metrics, History, Anthropology and Sociology . . . the conclusion arrived at is that the traits hitherto regarded as feminine
are rather sociologically than biologically determined' . . . which
sounds very sensible to me. I have been trying to obtain *The
Subjection of Women*, so far with no success. Do you know that
our Public Library hasn't even got a copy! I may come across

213

it in a secondhand shop. What other books would you suggest on the subject? I am tremendously interested.

My fond regards
Laurie

8.42   From Roland Robinson, Darwin
Source: FP 39

Dept Works and Housing
21.12.48

Dear Miles

I am really very sorry that during my last week in Sydney I was not able to be honoured by drinking out of the waratah cup. The week developed into an unholy rush and I came away with a lot of things left undone.

I flew up here and saw a lot of country but to really experience it you've got to rough it and travel by convoy as we did in the CCC days. Arriving at Darwin I interviewed an old friend (Mr Roderick who is Electrical Engineer for the NT) and he gave me a job on the staff. I miss a lot. I am in the town, wear a white shirt out of the heat and sun. White table-cloths in our mess. Bed linen issued to us. Dam'nd if I've been able to get into a decent conversation with any of these staff chaps. All they do is drink and keep up the white man's prestige with their white shirts saturated in sweat sticking to their backs. But I met, last night a lot of Gulf of Carpentaria natives who are on the two mission boats loading at the wharf. Some of them knew a native friend of mine. Queelpahmah of the Roper River. They brought out their bamboo drone pipe and we all sat on the wharf. I clapped my hands as they sang their songs for me and explained them to me. I sang a couple of Roper River native songs and they shrieked with delight and kept asking me to sing them and repeat the words. They are a mixed crew—from Wessel Is, Yerkala Mission, Milingimbi, Oenpelli and Alko Is. They told me all their native names—Boonumbīrra, Tootāruk, Maichēnba etc. One speaks perfect English and can read and write. He was educated at the Roper River Mission. On their next trip they are going to bring me bark paintings and painted baskets.

I have not yet met Bill Harney and have heard rumours that he has gone south. Probably he thought I was not coming up til after Xmas.

Darwin is quite a town: Public servants in white socks, shorts and shirts. Plenty of women and children, money, cars, beer and the quiet natives stroll about or sweep the gutters or else a whole tribe troops along the main street—lubras in bright coloured dresses, piccaninnies being carried on their fathers' shoulders— the dispossessed—who are still the most interesting people here.

When I have time and energy I'm going down to visit the luggers and their crews (Malays). The boats are now tied up to the mangroves for the wet.

But Miles, I know, I should not be in that office—I should be on that mission boat off to the Gulf. But I've never been so broke and I must stay here at least 6 months and get a roll on the hip again.

I suppose I'm late for Xmas but you know you have my very best wishes for Xmas and the New Year and I am always your respectful and admiring

Roland

8.43   *To Laurie Collinson, Brisbane*
Source: FP 41

Carlton
Dec 23 48

Dear Laurie

By all means present *Call Up Your Ghosts* if others agree to it. I don't think any regulations have been finally set up for amateur theatres' royalties. The FAW asks 10/6 or I mean pays 10/6 to read a one-acter and a guinea for a reading of a long play. Of course we got the prize out of the Melb production, and two guineas from Adelaide (I think the run was four nights) and a guinea from Katharine Prichard's club's production in Perth for *Ghosts*. You go ahead; we shan't let royalties ruin you. Dymphna and I wish we could see one of the productions. The one in Sydney has not come off yet but Christmas has stopped everything but Santa Claus ballyhoo.

I like that about characteristic being sociologically rather than biologically determined. Malinowsky said war was not biologically inevitable but sociologically induced.

As to books I can't remember the name of many. In my young days we used to set great store on Lester F Ward's *Pure Sociology* the Fourteenth Chap, but you may not find it in the library— shd be in University collections. *Sex and Culture* by Dr Unwin a more recent tome deals with sex indulgence. If you can't pick up a copy of the *Subjection of Women* I'll have to lend you my copy someday but it is very old, very precious, very precious through association and wd have to be treated like a priceless missal, but if your interest continues we'll see. You might take a glance through Oliver Schreiner's *Woman and Labor*. There are splendid new books that I don't know. You'll be able to instruct me. A lot of it is so sawdust-dull and such tripe.

Up to my eyes. No time for more. Good luck to you in the new year. Treasure the copy of *Ghosts* or it will be lost to history.

Special regards
[unsigned]

8.44   To John Kinmont Moir, Melbourne
Source: JKMC

Carlton
Dec 29 48

Dear Mr Moir

I am interested in all your activity. Those exhibitions are surely doing good work and take a lot of time and energy. If you still use that awful little ancient history photo of me I think it's about time you had a slightly more up-to-date one. I note in the reproductions in that little one I am gradually acquiring buck teeth of which I never had a suspicion. I shall watch with interest for the best books ever produced here from your press, but do choose your material with discernment.

I find that I'm inclined to shy from beautifully produced books because so often they are pompous shells and the matter does not live up to them. This feeling has come to me from my childhood when a tattered volume of Aesop was my delight and good works in stuffed-shirt-gilt-edged bindings were like those mausoleums that rich nonentities erect over their dead in a vain attempt to be what they are not. And today such a lot of treasure is to be found in paper-covered flimsies while many of the well-produced books are mere lumber.

And now will you carry out a little secret commission for me? First you must promise complete secrecy. Will you pass on the enclosed five pound note to Kate Baker in some pleasing way. I suggest that you tell her that one of your friends through the Bread and Cheese Club, who is an admirer of Tom Collins's work, wants her to have a little New Year gift in appreciation of all she has done to keep Furphy's books alive. Be sure, very sure, that there is no suspicion of me about the adventure. I do not wish her to be grateful to me. She misrepresented me because she misunderstood the situation over the biography: I have her letters correcting the mistake but of course this does not recall the aspersions cast upon me. However, that is a flea prick and I am so sorry to hear she is failing. Her memory and her purpose have lasted a long time in a remarkable and endearing way and it is sad that she seems to be failing at last. You will have to write to her, as she can't hear, so I enclose stamps for a registered letter. I shd be interested to know how you will put the matter so that there will be no idea that it is from me.

I wish I cd get an excuse to go to Melbourne, which I love, but I can't manufacture one at present, and also I hear that my dear old Federal Hotel, which suited me so well, particularly my purse, is now overrun by tourist trippers and I don't suppose I cd get in there or if so only at advanced rates. You must come to Sydney.

Good wishes for the New Year. Long may you wave. Remember me also to your wife and to Mr Pescott, whom I remember so pleasantly.

Miles

31.12.48

Dear Miles Franklin

You're a — good sort & sport & I'll cheerfully carry out your commission.

Have written Kate as per enclosed typed copy—registered the letter & enclose receipt. I'll be surprised if she rejects it.

Phoned a friend of hers today to ask how she was. She reports that K B is much better for her enforced rest.

You must come to Melbourne. If you aren't afraid of breaking conventions you can have my spare room in my *bachelor* home.

Let me know if you want any jobs done over. Do a lot of research for different people. Frank Clune is my most consistent client. His *Wild Colonial Boys* is a monument to his industry.

All good wishes,

Yours sincerely
J K

18 Braddon Flats
21st Jan 49

Dear Miles

I don't know if you have a play in for the Sydney NTL Competition. If you have, my request might as well be abandoned from the beginning. I have sent in an entry anonymously, telling them that an agent will be named to do any further dealings with them—receiving the returned script, or mayhaps the fifty quid. I don't want any connection with the play to be known as we public servants are not supposed to go in for out-of-office activities, and besides the play is a sling-

Ric Throssell and his mother Katharine Susannah Prichard, fellow writer and close friend of Miles Franklin, late 1940s (courtesy Ric Throssell)

off at Yankee foreign policies which might not be appreciated in some quarters.

Knowing you to have been suspected of some experience in the technique of anonymity, Miles, I wondered if you might feel inclined to take on the job for my play. I have thought of submitting it for the WA competition too, so as to give it a second chance, but I imagine success in either competition would automatically wipe it out for the other.

If you feel that it wouldn't be too much of a bother Miles

cd you let me know as soon as can do, & I'll send you the extra
copies & so on. Dorothy & I & the youngest Throssell are off
to Rio de Janiero in mid February so I'd like to get it fixed before
I go.

All the best to you
Ric

8.47 To Ric Throssell, Canberra
Source: FP 41

Carlton
Jan 22 49

Dear Ric

Certainly: I'll act as your 'fence' with glee at the opportunity
to muddy further my already cluttered spoor. Address to S M
Franklin as that is not so conspicuous or reminding as Miles.
You must instruct me precisely as to what I am to do as agent.
I advise you to plant one copy of your MS somewhere else
because my little shack is old and wooden and vulnerable to
fire.

You can be sure I'll keep the secret until released by yourself.
I've had practice and have gained some efficiency in the technique
required so that neither intimidation, bribes, inference, nor any
other wiles at smoking-out can avail. . . .

I envy you Ric. Is Portuguese a sort of bastard Spanish?
There's a tremendous awakening and wide range in that
continent.

Good luck
[unsigned]

Carlton
Good Friday 1949

Dear Roland, I shall now make a slap at answering your letter
which reached me around Christmas time.

I think it was glorious to fly up over the country after having
gone less luxuriously and so much slower by convoy.

I was most interested in your night with the Aboriginal men
on the mission boats and wish I could have been there. Perhaps
you have hopped off with them by now. You are certainly in
the right area to pursue your friendships with and studies of the
Aborigines, and it is a splendid and still unworked field.

The Aborigines you mention must be absorbing whiteman
customs to carry their children on their shoulders. I remember
my enthusiasm was always damped by the gins having to carry
the babies and all the gear while the stronger males strutted
unencumbered. The theory was that they were the hunters but
the women as far as I could learn had a lot of that to do too.
The same old pattern of cowardice and bullying of the weaker
in every breed and race of people. ...

I expect Sydney news will be very banal to you now. We had
a farewell party on Tuesday night for Dymphna Cusack. She
and her friend Florence James won the £1000 prize for novel
given by the *D Telegraph* some years ago. *Telegraph* has not yet
made any announcement about it. I was in the secret from the
start and read the story in first draft, but Dymphna told the
people at the party so it is no longer secret. Her friend F James
went to England two years since this July. Dymphna is sailing
on the 21st May but is struggling to finish another novel to enter
in *SMH* comp which ends 31st day of May.

Have not seen Harley since that day we visited him.

Ada Holman died on 3rd April. Hon Farrer, Pres of Legis-
lative Co and I spoke in memory of her last Sunday night. One
of my ever dwindling number of elders I am saddened by her
going.

Love me Sailor was put on as a play in a mighty tent behind the Stadium on Feb 11. The promoter was a company promoter sort who took down two young English people over it. They put in £19,000 pounds and lost it all. Too grandiose, and the silly babes had nothing in reserve in case of accident. The play was a little better than the book, but still not a draw. I was trying to get the tent bought up for a travelling Australian theatre. Don't know what has happened. . . .

Recently we had a man named David Nichol speaking at FAW. He was interesting because he said what I've been always saying, and when anyone thinks the same as ourselves we feel it is sheer geniass. He said England's identity is evaporating in Empire, that the hope in writing over there is coming from Scotland and Wales who have preserved their regional and personal identity. Ahaa! Aint I always saying that the way to be international is to work from the parish pump or gum tree out, with our own special contribution to the world pool!

[incomplete and unsigned]

8.49   *To Nettie Palmer, Melbourne*
Source: PP

Carlton
May 28 1949

Dear Nettie

I have just read your beautiful book. Hearty congratulations. This kind of book from a Mary Collum or a Lady Gregory and many others over there has a ready-made audience awaiting among all us English-speaking in London, USA, Paris and Australia because we are acquainted with the people written about. Quite the reverse when our remote, insignificant parochials have to be tackled. However, you have enough overseas birds to enliven your aviary and I hope the volume will be of interest beyond these shores.

I was surprised to find myself in such exalted company and please don't think me ungrateful to point out that I despise cooked pineapple and never used this fruit in jam in my life.

222

Only you could have carried off such reminiscences so expertly in this milieu. I hope you have many more.

I also trust you are well
Love from Miles

8.50   To Dymphna Cusack [at sea]
Source: FP 30

Carlton
May 31 [1949]

May you win, dear D. . . .

Yesterday I attended Lute Drummond's funeral service in Christ Ch. St Laurence on Geo St. Shortly after I last saw her she was stricken and put in hospital. Cancer in every part of her. That distortion of the face was because it was inside the skull. Her sister first had to have an eye out and then it went all over. Dear Lute, of course, knew as soon as she had that op under the arm, but never stopped in her stride. Horrible and long suffering, why shd such a radiant soul have to pass that way. All her belief was of colour and joy and love and beauty. I don't think she ever even frowned at anyone, or was blue or discouraged or discouraging. The church was nearly full—and oh the flowers! One of her prima donnas sang Kyrie eleison in the choir stalls in a very high soprano with a rattling tremolo. I think God shd have had mercy earlier, myself, and O, Rest in the Lord, might have been less rending. Saw many of the old C Crag group, lost sight of for years, among them Ida Leeson, looking thinner and frailer than ever. It was raining when we 'emerged' so I did not go to Rookwood. S Tomholt was there and we walked together back to town under the awnings to be out of rain and have a talk. He thinks even less of Les R than does M Morrell. He wasted a block or two insisting that it was a boy's choir which sang the Kyrie eleison—reliable reporter he'd be. He was at the back where he had not my view tho', and I think he is getting deaf. I said I had been seeing you off, and he said why was there all that queerness in not publishing, that you had won the prize with some friend. I discreetly said I didn't know, whereupon he said he'd heard that the *DT* were insisting upon the book being re-written beçause it was so red they couldn't possibly have anything to do with it.

Rubbish, I said, at that, so that the passers thought we were quarrelling.

Oh but, said he, she is a violent communist.

I halted at that to fight it out. Rubbish! they say I'm a communist because I like ideas later than Noah's.

I know you're not a communist but she goes to that filthy Fellowship of Writers, and it's a red committee. I go there too I said. I said that, like me, you believed in free speech for the other fellow as well as one's self. Then he said he wd have to contradict the idea that you were a communist, that you were so listed in some department. I said I disapproved strongly of C methods as I'd seen them applied, but I did not believe in witch-hunting people of that belief.

He said he did, that he is Treas of the PEN Club and won't allow a C in it.

But that is not Free Speech, said I.

He said he believed in free speech for everyone except the Cs.

I said yes, for anyone so long as you don't disagree with them, exactly like the Cs themselves.

He was rabid. So you see what it is when people who do not think have rabid ideas. And that is what Bart's policy has done for the Fellowship when writers were never more in need of a strong organisation. . . .

Have just received an invitation to a great Book Festival week to be held in Newcastle in Sept—I notice Godfrey's subject De Witt-Batty is on the letter-head, and the Mayor and Monsignor Peters, *et al*. Oh, how I shd love to go to that in company with you. And Godfrey is not here to tell it to. That is what life is in our far-flung community. And what is our life but meeting and parting and long regrets, to quote a tag from an old *Bulletin* verse. . . . You won't be able to take-in all the letters awaiting your arrival so I'll wind up. . . .

[unsigned]

Carlton
June 25 1949

Dear J K Ewers

I wonder where Leslie Rees got the notion that I might go to WA this year. I haven't seen him for a year at least. I've been longing to go for years, but the death of my dear little Mattie Furphy was a sad blow to the dream, which does not now look like ever coming true. At present I'm in misery with the cold, am comfortable only in bed or when walking about, and neither activity can be indulged in all the time. Why don't you come here and I'll give you tea out of my waratah cup. Not much to offer, but there are so many people in Sydney acquainted with your work that very likely you would not have time to seek me. . . .

With many thanks for your kind letter and to you and Mrs Ewers for your kind invitation.

Sincerely
[unsigned]

Carlton
Aug 4 49

Dear Rex

Glowry and Glammer be! When I need some small thing it falls into my lap like manna. Oh, that the thing wd work with big needs! A propos. I have been visited by one David Martin: you'll hear him as news commentator every now and again on Natl Stns at 7.15 pm. He did literary reviews on Reynold's. Has been into things from Spanish war to Welsh mines, India and so on. German-Dutch-Hungarian—handles English as well as Conrad and as infatuatedly. He asked me to make him a list of 20 books that he must read to understand Australia. The list was beginning to nag me and lo, here are your two brochures! I'll tell him to get both. Thank you for your generous inclusion of me.

Hope your big work is hatching healthily.

Suppose you'll be over this way again some time, and I'll see you.

No time for more but thanks and kindest regards.

Miles

8.53 From David Martin, Sydney
Source: FP 41

19 Augusta Street
Bankstown
5 VIII '49

Dear Miles Franklin

And so our correspondence develops . . . Your note is lovely and encouraging. I like to have letters like that, and from people like you. The books and bibliography you mention will be 'gone into'.

I have read both your books that we took away, even before Richenda managed to finish 'her' book. Of course, I do like both of them. *My Career Goes Bung*—what a title!—I thought I knew, but didn't. It shares with *Old Blastus* what seems to me your greatest strength: your deep identification with the people you criticise. I mean your criticism (if that be the right word for so subtle a thing) comes from the inside and from love.

(But I do think there must have been something very wrong with Australian manhood. Even with the seven great men who showed 'interest' in Miss S P Melvyn. Ah! if they had been Hungarians . . . (those middle-aged-spread Magyars and their revolting conceits!)—)

I am a poor reader of innermost thoughts and may not 'get it' all . . . I think the so deeply understanding ones are so often the deeply phoney ones. But that's a splendid book. I could wish

David and Richenda Martin in the late 1940s. Miles Franklin was delighted by the Hungarian-born Martin, a recent arrival in Australia (courtesy David Martin)

that your rebellion was more far-reaching because it defeated its purpose for *yourself*—*not* yourself as writer—by being bounded by your personal identification with the basic trends of the society which created your 'problems'. (In the Yiddish language, the word *problem* is colloquially synonymous with love-affair; 'Malke has a problem with Eli'—but I didn't mean 'problem' in this way.) The liberation of women isn't a rebel's but a revolutionary's job; it needs a deep-cutting incision. (48% of Soviet members of parliament are women—they don't make anti-feminine laws there as they do here despite women's franchise, that still-born gift to Aussie girls.) But if you had been anything but a rebel, if you had cut yourself loose—Richenda swears this is the right spelling—you wouldn't have been you and couldn't have written *Old Blastus*. (Though something else?) A gifted girl and a writer in pre-war-war Australia, my God! ...

Can't say I'd care for Blastus if I met him. Blooming cannibal in leather pants; a real Teuton. But this is a fine Australian novel and brings home to me the meaning of your scoffing at Mahony. *Blastus* hasn't a boring passage anywhere. It would be interesting to resurrect the children of these characters and see how they would play their parts now. A Dora and a kid like Lindsay's girl would be all right but Kate would be a confused sour-puss with all her virtue and strength (the papers would bewilder her) and the men would be like cabbages that were left and started 'shooting'—all leaf and the sap dried up. ...

Journalism is driving me mad and I shall break out again shortly. But, I fear, no more Gordons. The post-war rash of political lying, the anti-historical policies and attitudes of Dear Old England now, have poisoned song and simplicity. The next war will have no poets (good job, probably)—only caption-writers. Witch hunting doesn't go with boundary riding, I fancy.

Meanwhile: Up the infatuations—emotion. (How right you are!)

Yours
David Martin

I think that's the most tragic thing of all: Britain standing in the path of human advancement—in the name of 'freedom'! Where have we let ourselves get to since '42! D.

Carlton
Aug 19 49

Dear Beatrice

The temararious hour has come when I can go no further without
you. I have *Up the Country* and *Ten Creeks* sorted out ready
for the printer. *Prelude . . .* is to hand and I have read it word
for word. It is a tantalising story, pehaps I mean puzzling. It
is not thriller. R and M accepted it without a but or question
so it must be interesting. It is like a prophecy that has been
fulfilled: parts of it agree with what Dymphna writes out of
first impressions today.

I hope you can come and see it and talk secretly. Supposing you
were to leave the office a little earlier some afternoon and instead
of going home came here and had a snooze while I cooked our
chops and then you'd be fresh for an uninterrupted evening session.
I'm looking forward to having you for a night. Don't carry
anything but comb and tooth brush. I have even an old hair brush
which Dymphna always depended on and then took to scalding
herself before she left to save me. It resides in a paper bag free from
germs and dust. I have a diversified array of night attire ranging
from honest to goodness flannelette pyjamas to silks and woollens
which I got out for Henrietta. They'd be big enough for you. And
don't say you'll make washing because I haven't boiled for weeks
and just another pair of sheets when I start won't be noticed in
the copper. So!!! Also I want to introduce you to Nettie's bath mat
and you have not had tea from the waratah cup. . . .

It has been a bleak week for me with so many of my few
remaining elders going and an immediate contemporary like Mr
Cousins. When I got home from Rod Quinn's funeral a telegram
came to say Vida Goldstein had died on Monday night, a great
shock as she always encouraged me in my enterprises when I
was a girl.

With love
[unsigned]

Carlton
Aug 23 49

Dear David Martin

No more Gordons! There will be a place for poets until the
robots destroy man entirely. Poor Britain, as one of her sons
said to me, USA has her by the tail and she is helpless. If she
were let alone I'm sure she and Russia would worry out a
working understanding. What a theme for a satirical ballad-lyric
are all the peoples west of the Urals accepting oncoming
annihilation at the command of the $ to make democracy safe
for Big Business gangsters. . . .

H H Richardson is the most acclaimed novelist Australia has
yet produced. Furphy and Lawson best autochthonous writers.
I am always on the lookout for some writer, saturated with
Europe's infinite variety of genius, who will strain this sparse
last continent through his mind and give us a fresh view. He
might be you. Splendid if journalism drives you to the north
for a time. You have understanding and sympathy and complex
perception. You need not make it adulatious nor yet starkly
condemnacious from a superior altitude. C Hartley Grattan was
a clever sociological literary reviewer who, at the outset, had
more than surface interest in us, and has become an outside
authority on Australia, but we need also from overseas, poets,
novelists, and/or dramatists.

When you settled in a suburb of the mundane order which
will give you knowledge of Sydney's circumscribed domestic
mentality, why couldn't it have been Carlton, within speaking
distance: we could have had, in native idiom, a wongi or a
yabber-yabber occasionally. I am weary of writing letters to
contact a world outside of an isolation that is practically solitary
confinement.

I loved your letter, but in the double complexity—yrs and
mine—it generates more than I can write about. Fatuous praise
from the undiscerning I can turn aside with the ease of a rapier

against a broomstick, to be carped at by my soi-disant betters who are not, I feel, my biggers, is my usual fare, but penetration such as yours scares me in my covert. I'm so unused to it that response is hamstrung. Few women and no men hitherto have really rung the bell in commenting on *Career Goes Bung*. ...

Only two other private observations on *Blastus* have given it equivalent consideration. One was from a bishop, the other from an oversea journalist who said that the trouble with our novels about the bush (at that date) was that they were written by people too much on a mental level with the characters depicted, but in *Old B* you saw similar characters through a complex and cultured mind and the effect was very good indeed. It was written as a play and nearly got on the boards but for the outbreak of the talkie bonanza. So I turned it into a little novel for some old-timers who were clamoring for a story about the bush before they all were gone. I regard it as artists do a small canvas done in practice for a big mural. I claim nothing for it but actuality—verisimilitude. I wanted to get it on the air—no success with the mouldy hams and flat tyres who control that medium. ...

Yes. The Soviet is evidently trying to emancipate women to all men's pursuits, discoveries, philosophies, politics and religions, but still I wonder what really is in women if their egos could effloresce as men's have had the opportunity to do down the centuries. ...

Thanking you for your letter
[unsigned]

8.56 *From Beatrice Davis, Sydney*
Source: FP 38

A & Rs
26/8/49

Dear Miles

What a darling you are and how you cherished me at 26 Grey St! I can't tell you how lovely it was for me, and only curse myself for being such a dull sort of wreck. But I always feel a bit dull compared with you—and that is not to say that I am without wits by any means, you being *you*.

I was astonished and very proud to know that you have some faith in me as a critic—not necessarily of best-sellers alone. Goodness I wish I *did* have an infallible eye for best-sellers. That was a lovely story.

The MS will be perfectly safe, and I look forward to reading it. I hope soon to be able to tell you when publication will be possible.

Thank you for the taxi, too, Miles. *Really*, dear—

With my love
Beatrice

8.57   To Dymphna Cusack, London
Source: FP 30

Carlton
Sep 24 49

Dearest Dymphna

SMH this morning has come out with poem prize winners. Tom Moore first, Harold Stewart second, third divided between Raemonde Alain (female) and D M Rowbotham. Leon's (Gellert) article deals today with the MSS of the novels in which he is embedded, but only to the extent of garrulous complaints about the usual oaths and participles, particularly in war story section, which he very truly says have lost effect. No hint of any special MS but the secret must soon be out now.

You will want to know about my Newcastle trip. Was invited by the Cultural committee to the dinner and the Book Festival week. I gate-crashed into the A & R car driven by G Ferguson rep of Publishers, and in it were Idriess, Timms and one Iliffe in charge of sales who had put immense work into the exhibits. About 30 of committee, book-sellers, publishers' reps, and a few authors as decoration were given a lavish dinner by Ells at the Gt Northern where we arrived just in time to sit down. No towels in toilet rooms and I cd get no booking so I washed my hands and wiped them on my stockings and faced society without fixing a hair from the time I left home at 11.30. Lord Mayor presided and conveniently ate my oysters, with which the feast opened. I never had such a large helping of fowl and seized opportunity to wire into it. We had some toasts from Dr Mackaness, Dora Birtles, Mr Smith, school teacher, head of cultural committee, some little man head of writers there, a Mr Miller, Geo Ferguson and Timms replied in very few words. When the sec of writers said the whole thing was the work of writers Idriess who was colorless hitherto rose and threw up his arms in a wild spontaneous bushman's yell which was very effective and surprising. The publishers soon rectified the wild statement about authors however. Lord Mayor like Bendix when not battering something. Dora only one in nice evening dress. It was her return to her native town so I was glad she got some attention and the paper gave her the story in women's col next morning. This was Monday Sep 19. The L Mayor hurried everyone as he had to do opening in City Hall at 8. They had a dear little platform in a corner with a mike and enough chairs for the exhibits and a vast display of books in a great lower room. The L Mayor opened and hurried to another function, leaving little Smith at the mike, and he introduced the one speaker of the evening—Metcalfe. We who know our Metcalfe know what to expect. On Platform were Mackaness, Idriess, Timms, Dora, Smith, Metcalfe and I. I never saw a lovelier audience standing around there—2 or three hundred perhaps. A very few elders and some in their prime and down to school boys and girls. All so eager and expectant—they took my fancy, even I cd have talked to them. Metcalfe's address took an hour. He read it from a printed pamphlet. He went along at a dead level quiet voice, no expression, no emphases or animadversions or diversions—no short cuts, no jolly interpolations or human experiences and the subject was Mexican bulls!!!!!!!! He had been to Mexico to Unesco. He said he wd tell us of his trip. The people looked astonished at first but gradually the light died out of their faces and many drifted away behind the ramparts of books and the conversation at times threatened to swamp Met's drone, but he did not seem aware of defection. I had sunk myself in the coma which I have perfected through long years of my youth having been wasted and tortured by male addresses, but it presently dawned on me that this talk seemed to have nothing to do with book festival week. As he came towards the finish he said incidentally that much of the country around Mexico City was as barren and uninteresting as that on the way to N'castle, that the Mexicans despite bullfighting and other backwardness were immeasurably ahead of us in grants for libraries (they couldn't have been lower than us in quality of librarians surely and education). He praised English books and then said to my astonishment at the very end as if by an afterthought that we must also have Australian books. . . .

By my troth dear old Dr M was a shining light of culture by comparison. He was the big noise of the week—aside from Metcalfe. He took Beard's boy the only address I was asked to make but did not get there in time. Mr Beard wrote me a nice letter introducing himself through you. I said he couldn't have a better as all your friends were so nice. Next item on the programme was the L Mayor in his parlor where the drinks ran like a flood. From there to the supper room, immense amt of food provided by the cultural committee. At ten-thirty Irwin Page and wife came and extracted me and took me home and gave me a lovely bed. Next morning a fine breakfast, and Irwin attended to my bath and we had a yarn before he too left for work. Not on telephone and no one noticed where I went or with whom so when it suited me I ambled down town by bus and went to *Herald* where I met Lingard, Adrienne Cohen, Leo Butler, and the sec of the social editor was a lovely young girl. She was so excited when I mentioned you, said she was Bessie Wollard from N'castle Girls' High and thinks you were the most wonderful thing she ever met, entirely different from all others. Sent you best wishes in hopes you might remember her and got me to write my name on a piece of paper so she cd prove she had seen me and that I talked of you. Irwin then claimed me and took me to the sunken garden where I had been with you and Godfrey and told his dream for a bowl for concerts. He is a lovable thing and there is a wound in him that makes him endearing but vulnerable. . . .

Oh, sequel to Metcalfe's address. When we were on our way

home the men began—you never heard such disgust and disappointment. They had gone to labor and expense and worry over the Book Festival exhibits and had expected an address with a lead in it as to the cultural necessity of all books, of course, and with a special direction to the importance of our own books and writers. I said it served 'em right. That some of us had long known Metcalfe and why he was there—gave 'em Editha Phelps's quip and she was a classical cataloguer in one of the super-duper American Reference libraries—you remember about the genital organs of the male, not being used in library work but commanding more pay. I don't know G F's reaction as I was plumb behind him. He hung on to the wheel. Idriess with plenty of the gin which he pestered me to try let out a wild yell of laughter and said something to the effect that the said organs brought in two pounds a week extra to their owners but they needed something. I said you mean as compensation for the handicap. This further convulsed Iliffe in sheer boyish unsophisticated glee at such a wrecking statement. . . . Idriess said only that I was a girl he would tell me the real bulls-wool on the subject, but Timms was not amused—decidedly not. He is the heavy business man type—talked lovingly of Roast pork— carries his drink better than Idriess but it bloodshots his eyes and makes his face look apoplectic. He said with a self-satisfied and meant-to-be-daunting air, 'They're no weight to carry!' Ah, ha! I got a bite there. . . .

[unsigned]

8.58   From Dymphna Cusack, London
Source: FP 30

Australia House
16/10/49

Miles dearest, News of the *SMH* Comp this morning! So!! My thanks for letting me have the news so promptly. We are all disappointed but not surprised. For all its muddling, the *DT* Comp may yet be enshrined in Aust Lit for the guts to give a prize to a potential rather than an actual novel and one that would be unpopular with all the conservative-minded. Not that I think *Say No to Death* was a dead-shot prize-winner as it stood. I realise all its rough-nesses and inadequacies—those of a first draft. But—egoist or not—if there were nine MSS better than it in the *SMH* comp, then Aust Lit has nothing to fear for the future. I wouldn't mind being beaten by a *Capricornia* or *All that Swagger*, a *Battlers* or *Prelude to Xtopher*. But my toast and marg stuck in my throat to find myself not even an also-ran (Thank God!) to such puerile, pseudo Irishisms as the lesser half of the Park would be likely to turn out. 'Danno is a rotter of rotters!' Begorra and bedad. Any Irish-Aust unlucky enough to be called Danno in Aust would have no choice but to take to delinquency in a big way in sheer self-defence. T A G Hungerford I do not know at all. Do you?

His theme is novel and the ground unploughed—No mere stencil of all the Hibernian slop from Galway to Brooklyn such as the *Harp in the South* was and *Gold in the Streets* will most likely be. Let us hope they have really found some one in TAGH who will make an original contribution. ...

Florence and I signed our release from the *DT* last Thurs. Impossible to get at the root of the whole story but I agree with you that the whole truth isn't contained in their financial losses over publishing. They were obviously afraid as is indicated by the clauses in the release most carefully freeing them from any libel or legal actions etc etc. I think they are craven. I hope they are wrong. When we signed the mongrel-Irish rep here (all the charm and none of the guts of the Celt) smiled winningly and said: 'I wish it was a cheque for £75,000 like the football pools I was giving you' and I cracked. 'Maybe it is.' I am afraid it is too late for that. Two years ago it could have been but now I fear we have lost the market, and while the Eng are strongly anti-American they are short of paper, and the Americans have ceased to find themselves amusing when criticised in the role of universal saviours. We can only hope. But for all of it, I am more certain of my own track than ever. When *Say No* is off the stocks, I finish the Newcastle novel before that scene is too overlaid with impressions here. Beyond that I do not see. Anything I wrote with an overseas setting would be only as a visitor. The Eng mind is closed to me, however pleasant they are. I feel that the Roman Empire must have tottered to its doom in the same aloof unawareness as the Eng to-day who are lost in a dream of the revival of the great days of Empire. It is as tho' they wait a miracle. They dread the thought of war—particularly the women—but they do nothing to stop it. The Peace Procession to the Cenotaph had 2500 where France had 40 000. They are broader in general attitudes still than Aust—You cannot imagine such an act as you speak of in Vic ever being considered here. But then they don't care two hoots about religion here. Try publishing something not absolutely syco-phantic re the Royal family and you'd be thrown out of every pub office in [word illegible].

Had dinner with Christina Stead and Wm Blake at F's. Delightful people. He a 3-ring Barnum circus all to himself. Witty, caustic, brilliant, encyclopaedic; she gracious, charming, gentle, ruthless—the genius diverted from her true goal, I feel. He the American who cannot live in his country. She the Aus who remains emotionally fascinated by a background and world she doesn't understand. She insists she is still an Aust but the truth is they are both internationalists. I think that is where their great talents fall short of realisation. You must have yr roots down somewhere. In her 20 yrs abroad Xtina has achieved success such as she could never have achieved in Aust. She would never even have been pub there. They both have that same superb, egoistic sureness that XH hd. Permit no one else to criticise their MSS but each other. Read no reviews. They may be right. They are the darlings of reviewers but insist that both working full time and producing a book a year, they do not make enough to live on. So much for the pursuit of literature. I told them that in Aust they wouldn't even make enough to die on! Well, well, well, out of it all—the frustrations, the disappointment, the endless ploughing along, we achieve something for ourselves if for no-one else. I have not got round to saying the delight and anger yr letters telling of the N/cle fantasia, gave me. I boil when I think of you in the same category as Timms and Idriess, Mackaness. I am shamed and sick for our country when I think that writers of yr calibre must even be associated with them and that the fools of booksellers and publishers don't even know their own job. And, oh, joy and bitterness, the Metcalfe story! Maybe the 2nd half of his name conditioned him to bulls. Forever he will be for me MEXCALF. The fool, the snob, the nit-wit. All my love and deepest thanks, dearest friend. D.

8.59 From Myrtle Rose White, Sydney
Source: FP 42

Randwick
3/3/50

My Dear Miles

I cannot ever hope to convey my appreciation of your kindness & generosity in asking me into your home. You gave me great happiness. It was truly a Red Letter Day in my life. But I have a very guilty feeling that I did not quite play the game over your book. If you were reluctant for some reason to part with a copy—and I feel now that you were—I had no right to press the point—much as I coveted it. It was a lovely surprise to find it in my bag. I hugged it to me & thought—It can't be real! But if I am to keep it would it be too much to ask to have it autographed. Please Miles! I am getting a copy of *All That Swagger* for my daughter. May I have it autographed? I hope we can arrange a lunch or afternoon tea in the City the week after next—or would you come out here to lunch? Marie would love to have you.

   If not autographed—may I have a little personal note to place in *My Brilliant Career*? I shall never look upon it as wholly mine for many a day, because I want you to feel free to reclaim it if you want to. Do you know when I saw the cover it took me back over thirty years. A friend of mine in the Broken Hill library gave it into my hands saying 'You are going to love this'. I walked home through the moonlight dreaming of the treat in store. I do love books, and somehow I felt that yours was going to be a very special treat. It was. I do not know, or wish to know, the reason for its withdrawal from the public eye. I am sure it was, or is, a worthy one, and please forgive my blundering intrusion into your privacy and do please believe that I shall respect your wishes not to exhibit it. It shall be a special personal treasure wherein I can renew my acquaintance with a very wonderful woman when I dip into its pages.

I shall always pray God to give you that sweet understanding and peace I have been blessed with in the knowledge that there is no death. You know life could mean so much more to you if you could only let that truth steal in. . . .

Ever your sincere friend in the best of possible worlds, and if at any time I can assist you in any way—I am yours to command

With love
Myrtle Rose

PS So sorry I spoilt your Waratah Book with my nervous scrawl, and placing myself with the dear departed—not dead.

8.60 To Margery Currey, New York
Source: FP 22

Carlton
Mar 14 1950

Margery Darling

Some weeks since I received notice that there was a parcel for me at customs so I strutted off to the GPO and sat in a pew like a miniature Ellis Island or the Met. Library waiting till my number was called. I expected magazines and found three beautiful dresses, the man was lovely to me and let me off with one seventh of what you had valued them at tho he was particularly smitten on the blue white dotted one, but he said USA money was worth so much more than ours and I told him the dress I was wearing was the same as I had worn when I went to see you in 1932, which was quite true. So what a prize when I was in despair as to getting a new dress. A young woman condescended to make some tiny alterations and went into ecstasies. At first I thought she wouldn't condescend to 'alterations' but thank God she is a simpler soul from Tasmania who was excited about dresses from NY and thought the material better than any thing I cd get here. 'They're so nicely made' said she. And even more reviving than the dresses was the thought my dear of you still there warm and glowing and loving to send them to me in this world that is bleakly emptying of our generation. How am I to thank you. I have been a long time writing because I had a grandiloquent idea of getting snapped in the street in one of them to send you, but the irony of fate it has turned out perishing and deluging and I am shivering in old winter things. Never mind, judging by how long the others lasted me I am now set till the end of my days and can give more attention to world affairs and the chore of dying, which comes terrifyingly nearer and nearer. Today a lovely bundle of *Atlantics* arrived and I plunged into them instead of writing this earlier. I know the strength and trouble it takes to get parcels done up and sent, if nothing more, and I am so grateful. . . .

There is a movement for a Nobel prize for Lit to come here this year. I am among the three nominated by the literary groups but that is as far as it will go firstly because we all approve of Katharine Susannah Prichard and also she is an ardent communist and all her fellow religionists are pledged to her regardless of whether she wrote nothing but tracts and they are supporting her and promulgating her. It seems as if Churchill may be the winner of the Peace prize. Could irony be greater. A prize given from the proceeds of one of the first and biggest commodities of death dealing to the greatest old war bull of two generations who did more than any man to promote war— ask Ireland for his record, remember what an obstruction he was to woman suffrage—and a prize for peace!!!!

Wouldn't it! to use the current slang phrase.

Our Govt has a Commonwealth Literary Fund out of which it gives 100 pounds each year to each State University for ten lectures on Australian Literature. This year Perth University has invited me and wants me to give ten more to the Adult Education classes. I allowed myself to be persuaded and now wonder if I have the pluck to pull through. I feel the cold so terribly and there is no comfort in Australian houses—you get chilblains and

Miles Franklin in later life (undated photograph, ML)

flu in the perishing holes and I have never been physically comfortable in winter since I left the United States. . . .

I'm not sure of what will happen in the beyond so I must tell you what I think while I have the equipment to do so. I love you my dear. I was lying alone in my humpy the other night cogitating. I am still unable to sleep and often live alone from one month to the other now that commodities have grown so dear and strength so limited that I am unable to work for guests. I was going over my days in USA and totting up what I had got out of it. The things through affection are the only ones that ever meant anything to me. I hadn't the gifts for acquisitiveness. Affection plus intelligence is the most delightful mixture of friendship and friendship the warmest most permanent thing in this existence and I thought further that Editha, you and Ethel were my most beloved girl friends. Editha was unique, Ethel was so lovely and soft—not an inharmonious or suffering note in her and you my dear well, we had such a congeniality in impishness, audacity of thought and in every way you are a delight to remember and the blessing of it you still are there if only I cd see you once more. American money goes an awful long way out here if you cd only work some dodge to come. . . .

Ever and ever your loving
[unsigned]

8.61 *To Katharine Susannah Prichard, Perth*
Source: FP 21

Carlton
Ap 24 1950

Katharine dear

The official invitation from the Uni came lately so now I can talk about going (DV) and 'advert', as 'gents' say, to your kind invitation.

The doctor says I must give my talks and be silent in between as my throat isn't un-hoarsed yet, and I wd talk unless segregated, so I'm hoping for a cheap respectable room (Prof Edwards has the matter in hand) where I can go to earth. But I'm hoping you will let me refuge with you as much as possible, and if only you'd warm me up. I'm terrified of the cold as I can't keep warm in the winter without a fire of some sort, and you know what British hostels are—ice-boxes.

Physically and mentally I feel unable for the task, but can't let Henrietta down, nor you, the only person of tonnage who stands up for me. I'll do my best, but it will be very poor. The two lectures I like of what I have so far prepared are the opening one about first settlement, and the one on novels with Aborigines as the theme, in which I take *Coonardoo* and *Capricornia*.

Do tell me how to pronounce Wytaliba and gina-gina.

I really don't care if no one comes to hear me. I know what a bore the subject is to 99% of even those who read books. The students suffer us 'as another old fish who has to be listened to'. That's what they said about Mr Macartney. However, this too will pass.

I'm waiting impatiently for your Nobel honor to be announced. Worth a whole battalion to the political situation here at present, and of course I'd award it to you literally and literarrrrily for *Coonardoo* alone. How did you achieve that book? It is a black opal in the arid red heart of Australia when drought rules.

No news except that my young Brisbane friends of the New Theatre besieged me for Aus Plays, as they are eager to put one on, so I lent them, under penalty of wringing their necks if anything happened to it, Ric's printed play that you sent me. I hope this was right, and they will want to produce it.

I think the situation is working up to a 'pig-iron' tug-of-war. Glad McMahon Ball sounded a note of warning re Malaya. Are they mad enough to try to stop the billions of Asia with our half-a-dozen war-worn braves? However, I am so shattered that I am leaving it to the politicians and God. I don't care any more.

Too tired for more, love and good wishes
[unsigned]

May 23rd [1950]

My dear Miles,

. . .

Prof Ed. had told me you had consented to come, I was delighted, but did wait to hear from you first. Don't be ridiculous (at least I can recall this!) as if you have to do *me* justice! You will adorn whatever you touch, & I greatly look forward to listening—as a matter of fact, I thought you had once done this series in Hobart & wld only have to freshen up etc no idea you would feel you had to do v much work. Don't, anyhow. Talk in your own stimulating matter. That's what both Edwards & I hope you will do. Then the students will listen— their Profs & books can give 'em *facts*. You give them the breath & fire of life . . . To many, Aust Lit is *dull*. If you make the man Lawson, Furphy (& others) come alive and have *meaning*, that's the idea. Give us the old Tradition, which is even now giving place to new—new European strains—I do not *oppose*, but the nucleus(?) of the old should be retained & who better to magnify that on the slides of young minds than yourself. . . .

I saw Katharine a coupla times last week, but no answer. I thought she shld be back, & wondered if she went to Sydney & saw you.

I'll try again soon—

[unsigned]

Carlton
June 7 1950

My dear Henrietta

I set out yesterday to answer Perth letters, got off Prof Edwards
(voiced my fear of the Ocean waves and asked for something
cheaper in pubs so need not repeat that) and Mr Ewers and
left you and Katharine till today because yesterday I was
interrupted and went off in the evening to opening of Clive
Evatt's candidature plus his fiftieth birthday. It was at Hurstville. He is my state MP. Dr Evatt used to be my Federal, but
I lost him in rehash of electorate since when I am less well
Evatted. It was a funny meeting. Started inconsequentially, like
'The Cherry Orchard' or a Scriabin piece and wound-up
delightfully and cordially and with the chauffeur raging on the
pavement at the late hour. There was oodles of birthday cake,
a real eatable one and good coffee. I do not belong to any
political party but this bill of Menzies is sheer Hitlerism in
favor of Wall Street. I wonder who our new owners will be
(Asia eventually and inevitably) for the next generation. Uncle
Sam promises most physical comfort as they do at least know
how to keep their feet warm in winter and the flies out of
their food in summer, which no other that I know does. If
Menzies bill goes through you and I could be taken up for
friendship with Katharine.

I was so glad to get your earlier letter May 23 and know
how impossible it is to do what one has to do. I sit in the
middle of a mess because I have so little strength and had to
get my talks in shape. This nasty cold summer and winter have
paralysed me. It has poured again steadily since 3 am—is now
10. . . .

(Small plaint. I do wish all my friends hadn't taken to those
horrible new kind of pens—all the writing is now alike and what
was worse is now impossible to read or my sight and intellecks
are gone.) . . .

245

No, I refused two years' very kind invitations to Hobart because of the cold. I have taken Australian writing as a chronicle from the first fleet to now with the Australian novel as the heroine. I am very serious about it. Dull I suppose, but I found Cambridge dons dull before today, and the great Prof Moulton on Greek Tragedy depressing, and had to put up with it. We are as we are, and can't help it if we are bores, in fact bores are the basis of society and the most successful individuals in it. At anyrate I'll see something of you and shall be most circumspect as to not to disgrace you.

On Sunday my friend Malcolm Ellis named Greenway the big block of flats at Milson Point which are in course of construction. How interesting he made Greenway and on Macquarie also he can hold you with a skinny eye like the A Mariner. . . .

Well here's hoping I shan't be a pest and that I'll weather the weather.

With love and thanks
[unsigned]

8.64 To Clive Evatt, Sydney
Source: FP 42

22 June 1950

Dear Clive

I am so glad you are well and firmly in. When I went to vote I was met by two men, one with your dodger, the other with a liberal one. I said, Gentlemen, don't waste paper on me, I'm bent on preserving my habeas-corpus. Whereupon two women standing by with pencil and note book said, 'One for Evatt!' and that was that.

I loved the birthday party and hope you live as long as you want to and are happy.

Glen will keep you in touch with John's case. I have left him to you and her. Perhaps Alcohols-Anonymous would be helpful. . . .

Hearty congratulations and every kind thought to you and Mrs Evatt,

Sincerely
[unsigned]

8.65   To Sylvia, Victor and Ivy Pallot, Perth
Source: FP 43

Carlton
Aug 8 1950

My dear Silvia, also Victoire and Ivy

I arrived in Sydney at noon today. We touched down at Adelaide in a rosy dawn and then had to stop again at Canberra for 20 people who had been stranded earlier by a tyre on their plane going flat. Ooo, the cold and snow of my native mountains—it was 11 degrees on the grass they told me this morning.

They gave cups of tea during the night on the plane but I did not take any. Breakfast this morning on the Convair was cereal in cold milk, rolls and butter and marmalade and a fat chop rolled in breadcrumbs—coffee or tea and some kind of fruit juice. My neighbors met me and wanted to nurse me up for a week but my throat is endurable only when I'm silent so I must be alone. Sydney looks like a dump after Perth and so cold, no lovely Geraldton shrub or rosy banksia everywhere, and after that drive along the river every day you shd see what the miles of slums between the drome and city and between the city and my suburb look like, and it was so dry and dirty as if it had not been swept or washed since I went away. House cold and frumpy. There was no gas and no electricity. I had to light a fire and did not get the egg boiled till two. Slept till 8 pm exhausted. It is now nearly 11 and it has begun to rain. It is a terrible drop, really. I ran away from it when I cd endure it no longer, but have to start on it again now. I sneaked into the house and no one has found me out yet except the next door neighbor who got in things and says it's such a relief to 'hear your old voice' again. So that is friendly. Managed to get six eggs and two pounds of potatoes. . . .

You made everything lovely for me, retrieved me from disaster and defeat and I can never thank you all three enough. I made a lot of work and bother for you. I hope you are back in your own dainty bed by the time this reaches you, and not too tired. That was a lovely party, what a collection of exceptional women all of the first grade—Victor is right about Perth being the cream of the continent. . . .

[unsigned]

8.66 *From Beatrice Davis, Sydney*
Source: FP 38

A & Rs
14.8.50

Just to welcome you home, Miles, trailing clouds of glory— but no more sore throats, I hope. Many thanks for that splendid letter, and I was bursting with pride that you thought of me in the midst of everything. How devastating that you were ill; and what immense courage it must have needed to go on with the lectures! Henrietta told me how wonderful you were, & I wish I could have heard you making the academic ones sit up & take notice.

I do hope you're well again, & that the journey back had no bad effects. May I come to see you when you get your breath? Or will you have lunch?

P to W would have been out but for a calamitous error in production which made it look like a war time job done by Dymocks at their worst. I have been spitting execrations, with the result—I hope—that 2000 bound copies will be destroyed. This *entrée nous*. Shall tell you publication date when I know it.

Am wanting to see you, & to hear about WA.

Love
Beatrice

United Associations of Women
61 Market Street
September 8th 50

Dear Miss Franklin

As arrangements are now under-way for the Commonwealth
Jubilee Celebrations, our Council is anxious that the part played
by women in the development of our country should receive full
recognition in all phases of the celebrations.

We can reasonably assume that there will be many broadcast
sessions featuring episodes taken from Australian history. Little
Theatre Groups may also consider producing Australian plays,
and documentary films may be suggested as a good medium for
publicity.

It occurs to us that here will be an opportunity for bringing
before the public the question of women's fight for the franchise
and subsequently for economic and social equality.

We think it probable that you are already busy with scripts
and stories, but we wondered if you would have a few moments
to spare one day when you come to town to give us the benefit
of your advice about any way we can have the spot-light turned
on the early pioneers in the Woman's Cause.

I am always at the rooms on Fridays—some other days, too—
and would be very glad if you could call in one day. May I
telephone you about this?

With best wishes
Sincerely yours
Vivienne Newson
Acting President

Carlton
September 13 1950

Dear Mr Hardy

I was lent your *Power without Glory* for 36 hours gross, so spent yesterday reading it—right through without kangarooing. (I am not a popular writer so unfortunately can buy very few books.)

What an undertaking to keep all that straight! You depress me because you put in cold print what we hear all the time on every side, and I believe that integrity is the only thing that holds life on the rails, whether savage or civilized. You cheer me too because I believe in courage in facing facts and most people are cowards.

I'd like to remark one small detail. In the prewar 1914 era you have a character using bosker as a word of commendation. It was the universal vernacular word of the day. When I returned to Australia in the '20s bosker had been rubbed out for bonzer. You'll be too young to have known those times, how did you come by this item of accuracy?

I must not take up your time. This is merely to congratulate you and look forward to the other promised volumes. If you are ever in my vicinity I'd like a chat with you and I cd give you a cup of tea.

With heartiest wishes for your success

[unsigned]

Carlton
Oct 23 1950

Dear Mrs Newson

With regard to the advanced early women prominent at the beginning of the century, I lived in the bush and came in contact with them but rarely, though I knew Vida Goldstein and Rose Scott intimately.

I put some of what I knew in the article on Rose Scott which I wrote for the women's memorial volume published in honor of the Sesqui in 1938. Among my elders on the committee then I note sadly that some have gone including Dame Constance Darcy, Miss Sibella Macarthur-Onslow, Miss Jeanie Rankin. Still living are Dr Mary Booth, Miss Portia Geach, Margaret Preston, Mrs David Maughan, Dora Wilcox and Mary Gilmore. Dame Mary Gilmore has retained a vivid imagination and memory of what went on even farther back than the time of Federation and I am sure would be a good one to consult, also Dr Mary Booth and Miss Portia Geach.

I think women have slipped back since those days. This is inevitable following the states of war which have existed much of the time since. Women cannot hope to be in a dignified position as mothers of the race while the slaughter of males destroys the balance of the sexes and Asiatic women continue to swarm.

I am sorry your letter has been so long unacknowledged but I cannot keep up with correspondence.

Sincerely, with kind regards
[unsigned]

8.70   From Dan Clyne, Sydney
Source: FP 22

Ministerial Room
Parliament House
27th October 1950

My dear friend

Adverting to our recent conversation regarding the Commonwealth Jubilee Celebrations, I have made enquiries and have
ascertained unofficially that proposals are under consideration
by the appropriate Committees for competitions for a novel, a
non-fiction prose work, a short story and poems. It is also
proposed to hold competitions for an Australian play, amateur
theatrical groups, ballet, etc. . . .

I thoroughly enjoyed your recent visit to the House and was
glad to learn that you also enjoyed it and that you did not find
the steak too tough. You suggest tripe as an alternate dish. Well,
the general opinion is that quantity and quality here is first class.

I like your article on the Australian theatre. You blew holes
in the argument in favour of large auditoriums. In a community
that is not drama and ballet-conscious, they would be useless.
The scheme is as you suggest—cultural development and
building a number of small theatres. I return your article
herewith.

Glad that you agree with my views on current events, as
expressed in the debate in the Address in Reply.

Looking forward to seeing you again shortly
Yours sincerely
D Clyne

'Ardmore'
1st November, 1950

Dear Miles

At a recent meeting of The Vida Goldstein Memorial Committee, the Treasurer mentioned receiving a number of enthusiastic letters about V G, which were sent with subs. As we've
been planning some further publicity, I asked to see these letters.
The only one with *individuality* as well as goodwill was your
own, which was really touching. Later on, I'll hope to send you
a copy of the special (75 years' Jubilee) number of the PLC school
magazine *Patchwork*, which they tell me has some references to
V G as a brilliant early metric scholar and an organizer of an
early school debating society, the Magpies. I wish they'd print
the surviving photo of the Magpies at school.

News came of your lectures at Perth this winter, which seem
to have won past all hindrances—your throat trouble & chest
illness, ignored each time for the duration of the lectures, which
came over infallibly & delightfully. Your subject must have
uplifted you as well as your audiences.

. Mrs Singleton has written a very good letter to me about V G,
but couldn't put us in touch with any of the older suffrage people
with whom V G had worked in England in 1911 and, by
correspondence, later. If we're publishing something further
soon, to assist the memorial scheme, may we quote your letter
and/or perhaps call on you for a few lines of reminiscence?

I reproach myself, long after the event, for having worked
so little with V G—as you worked with Alice Henry, on the
contrary.

Hope Sydney's summer will be good to you in this what-a-
world.

Yours
Nettie P

Carlton
Nov 14 1950

Dear Nettie

You are welcome to use anything I said of Vida though I haven't a notion what I said or *how*. The *how* in a spontaneous and hurried note can put its writer to confusion when by some fluke it appears in print. I suppose most of those who met Vida in London are dead. I remember Christabel Pankhurst, Elizabeth Robins and Mrs Pethick-Lawrence; Jane Addams and Dr Hamilton from USA mentioning her, & Mrs C C Catt.

No, you were the wise or lucky one not to have gone working with dear Vida or anyone else in reform. Now you are a true and highly rated *litteratéur* (or *suse*) and I a mere charwoman no longer strong enough for that increasingly arduous incarceration. A propos: I hear you are to be congratulated very highly on your H H R book, which I haven't read yet. What are you going to do next? You are about the only one who can in the biographical field here, steer between the epitaphic brochure and the dangers of a suit for libel or some such. ...

This is a sample of the spontaneous composition to wreck the reputation of a *litteratéur* but not a charwoman.

Good luck to you, long may you wave
[unsigned]

Carlton
Nov 16 50

Dear David

Your letter uplifts me. That's the quality. Yes, do a small novel as you suggest. Look at the sensation D H Lawrence's *Kangaroo* caused and you are also a poet and have got more into the skin of the country. Bless you for thinking the bush is homely. I can understand how uninviting, how terribly strange and different and resistant it must have been to the first European exiles, and I don't expect newcomers now to see any beauty in our aridity and flatness after the high mountains (oh their exalting splendour) and the great rivers of Europe, Asia and America. Of course the bush to me is so homely, so friendly and inviting that when I go out in it, it takes me back to childhood and the longing to make cubby house and snuggle in it. Its magic enslaves those with the inner eye.

You must write down what you think of us while you are new enough to discern any differences which may exist. If you dally that will be fused with familiarity. I am great on first impressions. . . .

I've had a struggle to survive this last year. You said an enormously devastating thing to me last time you were here. However it was of service. Come and unsay it.

Re draft-evaders. I was thankful in 1914 that I was a woman (I am always glad of that) because had I been a man I wd have had to be a conscientious objector, and I doubt if I shd have had the courage to face up to what the American conscientious objectors had to undergo. They were tortured in a foul and monstrously cowardly way. They were the real heroes. It was the highest demonstration of courage. But circumstances veer. I doubt if conscientious objecting wd do any good today, the world is so upheaved and so altogether mad.

Richenda will, and you may find the Melbourne flat pleasant

after Putty. I never had children's books and am at a loss about them. Shall be interested to know what Jan reads.

Miles

Carlton
Nov 16 1950

Dear Professor Murdoch

I sent you my later book seeing that you recall my first attempt. Perhaps ever since I have been retreating from Moscow to fiasco. The other night at a dinner, the Chief Justice hailed me with the news that he had been sending my book to a friend in USA. It may serve to enlighten new Australians, who think they are hardly done by, how people of even two generations back struggled to make homes and fields in this enchanting but resistant land.

I wonder were you too a worshipper of G B S. I listened to Vance's and St John Ervine's tributes over the air. In view of you too having been patronised by Nettie I'll say this in confidence to you. Vance's tribute was almost first class—but first class ersatz and I was irritated by its condescensciousness. Who is Vance to say that Shaw had lived too long or to prate about the shrinkage of his flesh (for his age G B S retained his splendid looks unbelivably complete) or to say that all his friends were dead?

It is like poor H M Green who apologises for Lawson as a good substitute for a great man in our absence of such. To hear St John's deeply expressed love ('I loved him this side idolatry') was a relief. Shaw was far from lonely while one such friend remained. St John's tribute by contrast shows what the matter is with the higher Australian criticism. The critics feel they have to carp at people bigger than themselves to demonstrate efficiency and thereby merely illustrate their own inadequacy. ...

I'm so glad my dear Henrietta took me to see you and Mrs

Murdoch. I enjoyed the day so much. What a pity we didn't meet when we were young, we are so scattered in Australia. I always think that Furphy's was a sad case of isolation from his congenials, which he bore unfretfully.

With greetings to you and Mrs Murdoch,

Sincerely
[unsigned]

8.75   *To David Bradley, Perth*
Source: FP 43

Carlton
Nov 25 1950

Dear David Bradley

I loved your letter and am grateful to you for writing to me in such terms.

Friendships rest largely on some endowment enabling friends to make congenial exchange, just as much as on ages being exactly parallel. There are, of course, as one gets up in years, a few old friends like special books or pipes which none other can replace because these knew each other, were young together, but that is often the only cement. We overlap, a fifteener with an octogenarian, a twenty-one with a thirty, a forty with a sixty, in addition to the young finding most numerous companionship with their immediate contemporaries. This makes a fabric of thicker weave against the open sky of eternity to which we are exposed.

I had many special friends old enough to be my parents: when I'd find a rather elderly new one I used to be oppressed by his or her age because naturally I could not have enough of her before it was her time to go into that baffling silence.

I once complained to Jno A Hobson, the economist, who was a dear elder, that I found such pleasure with my elders but they slipped away and left me lonely. He said he was in the same position and added: 'The unusual always are, but as you grow older you will find the unusual young will seek you, and that balances it.' We had rich exchange. I had something to offer perhaps in untrammelled colonial zest and he used to suggest that I be invited to grave gatherings.

I think people shd be mixed in ages. Nothing is more saddening, almost gruesome than a concourse of the old. The young naturally are happier in crowds for they can play with each other, but even they like a sprinkling of granpas and mas and aunts and such as I have discovered in war work. So! . . .

Cordially
[unsigned]

8.76   To Ric Throssell, Rio de Janiero
Source: FP 41

Carlton
Dec 20 1950

Dear Ric

Your mother gave me your letter of June 6th when I was in Perth during July and Aug. We both made a mess of it, she by being down with a heart attack and I caught flu and instead of going to bed for a day or two went on the platform and bunged myself up permanently as far as my voice. However I pulled through, went out to your mother for one night and she managed to get to the afternoon that Silvia Furphy Pallot gave on the day I left. It was so disappointing as I cd not talk to yr mother as I wanted to do about politics and publishing. I am glad to hear she must be much better as she has been crusading for peace. I wish she wd not agitate herself.

First re your play *Highly Confidential* which I sent to London. The agent returned it as the time was not auspicious. It reached there just as Korea or whatever the current pustule in world affairs was disturbing people and he said it was too remote. The New Theatre in Brisbane or whatever it calls itself—the prime mover's chums of mine—were eager for an Australian play so I offered your printed one *Valley of the Shadows*. I was so disappointed when they preferred Laurent's(?) *Home of the*

Brave. It was put on at the Independent but I did not see it. You must just keep on and on writing plays and you are sure to break through at last as you have time as well as talent on your side. Then you can dive into the bottom drawer or the barrel as the Americans call the store of early plays. I've got Jim Lindsay safe. Also now there are prizes for Commonwealth jubilee plays and documentaries—stage and radio long and short. Your mother will send you the forms and formulas. If you want me to act as fence in putting anything in I shall be most happy to do so and there is still money in the kitty for postage. You never know when the judges will light on you though it is wearingly like a ticket in a lottery instead of a creative effort. ...

Kronk and all as I was I loved Perth. The little train across the Nullarbor is adorable. Your mother's friend met me in Coolgardie and had me shown the Golden Mile. Your mother gave me a white moss rose at the party—heavenly—had not seen one since a child in my grandmother's garden. The jarrah wood everywhere was a joy to me. And fancy they are still using it for palings and fowl houses and to burn. In the waiting room at Coolgardie there was a pile of it for us to put on as much as we liked. We still have remaining some of the privileges of emperors in this unique land but it is slipping away from us now. We dyed-in-the-gum-and-wattle British Australians are passing like the bandicoots and lyrebirds. A new race that made pies of kookaburras and little blue wrens.

Dymphna Cusack is making 'em sit up in London. First imprint of her joint novel is 24,000. David Martin says he never heard of such an edition since the Bible or How Green was my Valet. Her next eagerly accepted and good advance given and she has done a play. The RCs have taken control of politics here and are on the side of Menzies and the anti-habeas corpus bill. Hardy being prosecuted for his book *Power without Glory* because he among other things shows up the RC church. He is not a novelist, his book is like a royal commission on malfeasance made into a documentary but he is game and I have given my mite and went to his protest meeting. He is a good speaker. Only the reds in attendance except myself and Pixie O'Harris. There seem to be no old-fashioned liberalminded people believing in justice left—only extreme right and left. No hope for us as a satellite of US if US persists in attacking Asia.

I have no news. My love and good wishes to your family and self

[unsigned]

8.77   From Katharine Susannah Prichard, Perth
Source: FP 21

Xmas Eve 1950

Miles dear

I've just finished reading *Prelude to Waking*. A strange book, I tell myself, so clever, with many beautiful things in it. More by you, I imagine, than the other Brent novels. Indeed, I seem to hear your talking, behind the mask, as it were. It's unique in the attitude to current sex ideology—the over-emphasis on sex in literature & in life, to-day. Like the sword Excalibur!

Although, I think this emphasis is due to our social system which incites people to satisfaction of the grosser appetites. The sexual impulse in itself is natural, & should be innocent and free of any conception of evil. The ecclesiastical doctrines, priest-craft and so forth, have used it, & the notion of original sin, to defile a normal function of humanity: and exert control over the people—serving always the interests of property in women, as of all the means of existences. The power of RC Church for example rests on these superstitions of chastity, virgin birth, saintly renunciation of fundamental human qualities.

Nothing good—I mean of ultimate value to the Promethean struggle of the genus homo can come of a negation of his fundamental human qualities. They must be recognized. Negation leads only to the reaction—& over-emphasis which is destructive also.

One of the remarkable things that has been achieved in the Soviet Union, is that sex has been relegated to its proper place in life. Not exhalted as the be-all & end-all of existence; but recognized as a great & beautiful force for the fulfillment of men & women & the creation of finer beings than themselves. . . . I believe that sacerdotalism & capitalism are responsible for degrading our conception of sex relationships, and that relationship itself.

T'anyrate, darling, you don't have to worry about what the critics say. You have done very brilliantly what you wanted to! At least, I'm assuming that Brent is you in *Prelude to Waking*—though, maybe there may have been another finger in the pie when the book was planned. All I want to say is, there's fine writing in the book—and it's a strange, beautiful piece of work.

I've been getting all sorts of hostile comments from English reviewers for *Winged Seeds*. But I dont care a damn! I've said what I wanted to, and what they say doesn't disturb me in the least. I expect snorts & sniffles, and am pleased to have gone my wilful way, notwithstanding. My advance copies—have not yet *arrived*! Something must have happened to them en route. I want to send you one, when they do come.

I've been laid out this week. My beastly heart playing up again—but am having a course of injections supposed to help. Had to cut all engagements; but have quite enjoyed the excuse to stay quietly at home.

Do hope you are better! Its dreadful to think of you having that grief about Jack. If only he cd be induced to try the treatment I told you of. It has been miraculous in the case I mentioned.

Ric & his little family still well. He is the most sweet-natured lad, almost too fine for the world we live in. Love to you, Miles darling, and may the New Year bring you some rest and happiness

Katharine

December 28 1950

Dear Mr Chifley

... It was inspiring to listen to you in the Parliamentary broadcasts and I was specially thankful for your statement about the foolishness of sending our boys to every row around the world.

If we could bravely take a lead for peace I believe the world would recognise it as more helpful than the few unfortunate boys we can muster to fight. There is no excuse for the impending war. No matter what it purports to be in aid of it will end in disaster for all. American Big Business may fend off the day of reckoning by a false war-whoops and reduce Europe and other parts to a shamble but the day of conquest by violence and slaughter is past if mankind is to survive.

With hearty wishes for your good health and for Mrs Chifley in the New Year and may sanity preserve peace.

Sincerely
[unsigned]

December 29 50

Dearest Elsie Belle

You sent me the very thing I longed for—anything of or about Shaw. The lovely old darling had to leave us at last. I lapped up the book and pasted the little accompanying card in it. Did you hear St John Ervine's tribute over the air. It was heartwarming and he concluded that he loved Shaw this side idolatry. So did I. He was the great light of our age. In this book he lets us see why he seemed to be almost inhuman in his freedom from depression, anger, envy, grief—a high invincible soul. I knew him well on the platform but met him only four times personally and then briefly.

I still have the first books you sent me so long ago—*The Roadmender* and little books of Browning, De Quincey and one other. Among the Penguins if you ever come across Montague's *Disenchantment* I wish you wd send me a copy and the bill. I gave my copy to G B Lancaster in the days when we thought we cd get things again: such a waste for she was, I'm sure, too conservative to appreciate it.

I have no excuse but weariness of the flesh for not sending you the Christmas greeting I had: I got ahead of myself by collecting two wonderful little towels woven by the spastic children months ago—one for each of you—and I just got too feeble to pack them up. I did not buy one Christmas card. I find the commercialisation of Christmas an ordeal. I hadn't the money to participate and just didn't and it was a relief.

Do you ever go to the theatre these days. I went to *The Dark of the Moon*—some good things in it, tremendous piece of production with the rape right on the stage. I saw also the *Madwomen of Chaillot*, another big piece of production it also had flashes but not enough to justify it as a co-ordinated piece of thinking.

My love and thanks and good wishes, as ever
[unsigned]

8.80   From Eleanor Witcombe, Sydney
Source: FP 43

Cremorne
18/3/51

Dear Miss Franklin

Knowing of your interest in theatre—& indeed, in everything that is happening in the writing game—I've been hoping to get you along to see and pass an opinion on one of my plays. Unfortunately I have usually found that you were in WA, or that we were miles from any place convenient to you, and your health had not been good. However now I hope the time is propitious—Mrs Aylwood suggested it might be.

Next Saturday we, the Children's National Theatre, are commencing a Jubilee season of my plays. We will be playing *Smugglers, Beware*! for four Saturday afternoons at the St James Hall in Phillip Street, and then four Saturdays of *The Bushranger* before the company goes on a long country tour, while *Pirates at the Barn* is playing. We all, myself in particular, should be most pleased if you could come along one Saturday afternoon. Muir and Marg, I hope, are coming to see *Smugglers*. Perhaps you would like to come the same day?

If you find you are able to come on one of the dates, would you please let me know? We will then arrange for whatever seats you would like, as a guest of the Theatre.

Hoping we may have the honour of arranging this for you—

Yours sincerely
Eleanor Witcombe

8.81 *To Eleanor Witcombe, Sydney*
Source: FP 43

Sunday [April 1951]

Dear Eleanor Witcombe

Thank you so much for yesterday's treat, my first experience of a play for children. I came away refreshed and wishing I had your talents. It must be gratifying to hear the gales of youthful laughter. I laughed as I haven't done for ages. ...

I hope laughter will follow you all around the country. I'm sure it will be like taking Tommy to the circus, a *Punch* cartoon that depicted little Tommy as almost hidden by surrounding adult uncles storming the box office.

With every good wish
[unsigned]

Carlton
May 11 1951

Dear Myrtle Rose

Your letter came last night and if I do not answer at once it will be lost in the chaos. Thank you for the sweet book plate, and to think you put it in that old book, which I wish you would lose!

The Doctor friend, who had got a report of how John is, told me a fortnight since that he is very well, is in the free-est part of the re-pat hospital—could go out if he wished without trouble but he never does. He gives no trouble to anyone but seems to have lost initiative. ...

There is something mystifying about the statement that he is obsessed with a relative who died violently of drink. There is no trace of any such thing on his father's side, right back to his great-great grandfather. His father and I are (were) teeto-tallers, so was my other brother who died when John was about four. My mother's brothers were all completely temperate: I recently asked the sole remaining one, now 87, if he had ever been drunk and he said never in his life. I don't know his mother's people very well. ...

Yes, it is weary waiting on MSS, and our lives speeding away. Poor Joseph Furphy expressed it very well; I think I put it in the biography. This being read after death has no attraction for me.

I went to the Mitchell yesterday to read and ran into a jubilee opening of some exhibits upstairs. One of the Trustees fished me out and took me up much against my will as I had not been invited. They did not give me a seat and I was not well enough to stand so I sneaked out after a minute or two. Politicians and librarians were the muck-a-mucks. I didn't see one author. When the new library was opened, they had the same sort of University duds and officials on a stage, and the publishers and booksellers in a roped-in enclosure on chairs, and the few authors (even

Barnard and Eldershaw who were representing the Fellowship of Writers), walking about outside. They want only dead people in libraries. The living are too vulgar.

I was in bed Anzac week, caught a bad chill being dragged out of a hot bath to answer the door. It was a relief to lie there without telephone or door bell. I am not getting any better.

Thank you, my dear, for your kindly efforts. It was such a joy and help to see you over here, and as you are the young and enterprising one, I hope you will get over again. I don't think I'll ever go anywhere again unless I get this 'second wind' they talk about. At present I am 'winded'. . . .

Thanking you ever so much and with love
[unsigned]

8.83   *To Ian Mudie, Adelaide*
Source: FP 36

Carlton
July 5 1951

Ian my dear

I had your letter of March—can it be so long ago—and was delighted and cheered to hear of the muddle you were in. When my younger contemporaries are in the same state as myself it shows that it is universal not merely that I am on the brink or in the middle of senility.

I am wondering if the rains came and if your garden was saved, or at least the remnants of it and how you have gone on since. Here we are having another great wet just the same as last winter and there was no summer except about three days. Everything is soggy and mouldy. Anything steel rusts, the roofs leak and no help to be hired except by the wealthy wage earners. You are lucky to have your manpower in yourself and some more coming on in the boys.

Did *Come in Spinner* ever go to K S Prichard from you? Excuse me asking, but you were on the verge of despatching it when you wrote. I asked K S P after long weeks if she got it,

266

but that is many weeks ago and when she wrote she did not answer that question. I don't want to ask her again till I hear from you. It was inscribed by Dymphna and Florence is why I so much want to have it back. And did you ever come across the letter you said you wrote me about it? I am in exactly the same state. Letters piled everywhere. A new one coming in is speedily lost among the mobs. In going through one of the many piles I came on yours last night and pinned it on the wall for reply tonight.

I suppose you have seen the last *Meanjin* with D C's tale or rather a very mild part of it about the *Telegraph* mess. And wasn't Florence fine and rorty on the cultural cringe in Australia? I couldn't have been more uncompromising myself. My review was also in the same issue. . . .

Our Australia that we love is dissolving visibly. It will be a dammed, bulldozed area covered with those old foreign pines to make newsprint to advertise American inventions, our language gone, our gathering traditions disregarded like they were by the new Australians who made a pie out of kookaburras! Kookaburra pie!!!!

I haven't been well since last winter. The doctors can't find out the cause of the trouble so there is no good in me hypochondriacking about it. I have no strength at all—everything has had to go and I shiver all the time no matter if I'm wrapped in wool and fur. It is very dreary. I put people off from coming to see me as I don't like them to see the mess I'm in in my declining cottage—shabbier and shabbier and more and more unkempt.

I hope your Murray epic will see the light in due course. Writers with something to say have an ever increasing struggle against standardisation. Businessmen publishers think that best sellers can be written to formula and their businesses get more and more top heavy so they cannot take risks—must have sure fire things and that means dead to the artistic and free soul of man.

Guy Howarth is in London. I can't go to plays or meetings because I can't stand the cold so I am marooned and dull so will wind up with love and good wishes to you and Renee for ever

[unsigned]

Carlton
July 6 1951

Dear Mrs Evatt

Though I was excommunicated from the Doctor's parish some time ago, I shall be a member of his larger diocese again as soon as he is Prime Minister so I want to tell you how glad I was when he was chosen as leader, though of course there never was any doubt about it in the minds of the public.

I have waited till the rush was past before bothering you with one more letter of congratulation. There are signs that even the captains of industry are beginning to suspect that a nation cannot spend 40% of its budget on preparations for slaughter and at the same time sustain a boom in business profits, so it is to be hoped that any referendum designed to curtail our civil liberties will fail.

My kindest regards to the Doctor and yourself, and I trust you may both have continuing strength and zest to face the strain of office in these times, and the Doctor must not quite forget that he is also a writer. The Commonwealth can't let Mr Churchill reign alone as historian-statesman.

With every good wish
Miles Franklin

8.85   *To Warwick Fairfax, Sydney*
Source: FP 44

Carlton
Aug 3 1951

Dear Mr Warwick Fairfax

Our borné standards of division by having instead of being prevent the rich and the poor meeting together, but need not prevent my telling you how much I was entertained by your play. You have enough in it for one of the big family novels which, so far, have been the most successful in the novel form here.

Cheers, that you led the way in our empty dramatic spaces by placing your play here, not at the Court of Louis XV, or in Tut's Tomb, and then insisting it was an Australian play because written by an Australian.

I was particularly interested in the period, as that was the decade of my mother's girlhood. I have a scrap book in which she pasted fashions of '75, some of them ornate and striking. You were well served by those two beautiful girls for lead and *ingénus*. I hope you will follow with another play of recent times.

My excuse for intruding on you is my burning interest in Australian writing; I sometimes try a little myself—with not much success, however.

With all good wishes
Sincerely
[unsigned]

8.86 To Vance Palmer, Melbourne
Source: PP

Carlton
August 9 1951

Dear Vance

I have been much badgered about Brent of BB, as you can guess. Old acquaintances, whom I had thought to be normally intelligent, telephone me that they have known it was me for years. What were your clues? You were in London in 1926. Another: Do you remember asking me what sort of a café the Ambassadors was? No. Well, you did, and it's in a Brent book. These are piffling, others are gnatty, the kind that cares a whiff for Aus literature, only to be knowing in a whodunnit way. This species fixes me with a gimlet eye. You are Brent, I know. No reply. You don't deny it. That means assent. I looked the latest gnat in the face and said, This Brent racket is a disillusioning business. How so? I wish there were just one gentleman among Australian reviewers—just one, with enough literary and mental tonnage, indifferent to who Brent may be or who helps him, but who wd assess the books for what they are worth in the Australian literary field, and who had enough originality to save him from trying to bolster himself by gossip inquisitiveness. This tormentor had the grace to look uneasy and remarked lamely that a gentleman would be a queer bird in the newspaper world.

Then on Sunday I was listening to your session, which I miss only by mischance, and lo, there was the gentleman: great generosity to Brent and no breath of gossip-column—Lord-Castlerosse—knowallness to irritate me. Such a treat, such a surprise! It reminded me of an Indian guru who said he got all his power out of the air, that everything we needed was all about us, we had only to command it by the right spirit of receptivity.

I remember Nettie's first discovery of Brent, no buts or reservations—a Brent-like response to Brentism. Mother in those days used to get a Tasmanian paper and send the literary reviews on to me. They were good. I remember particularly one on Aldous Huxley.

Why did Geo Farwell disappear? Of the miscellany in his place I like Mr Phillips, but we atrophy for the stimulation of full criticism by people of consequence in a continuous forum, not these snippets which they have in the SMH with a letter of the alphabet to tag the writers, in case of accident I suppose; but it means nothing of stability to the general public. There is a man named Gellert, who has retreated from some poems he wrote years ago, to drivel in a labored and banal way about his ego. (Shades of dear old Beth Gelert, who with many a brach and many a hound attended Llewellyn's horn!) Such a stifling waste of columns, not only on Sat but on Sunday.

I hope you and Nettie are well, and both writing. I am fit for little so I keep to my lair, seeing and knowing nothing, a dreariness which I must not inflict on you.

Greetings and good wishes.

Miles

Georgian House
16th August 1951

Dear Miles

Glowry be! It did me much good to see you. I adore you, you know, and I wish I lived next door to you, or you lived next door to me, or that one of us had a helicopter, or something. I don't know any character, let alone genius, who so stimulates me with certainty that the Australian Spirit is vital, and bloody good. If only I'd been able to talk to you and hear you talk back when I was in the throes of writing *The Great South Land*, there wouldn't be half the arid and dull deserts that exist in the book. ...

This present splurge, apart from recording my adoration for you, which is no half-hearted thing, is to let you know that I've typed out the label for the parcel of *The Great South Land*, and that it is likely to leave our store for your address tomorrow. You should receive it, therefore, early next week. Of course, I want your reactions—and I know they'll be frank and not intended to please me, so much as to give me the priceless benefit of your point of view. ...

Ever thine
Rex

8.88   *To Rex Ingamells, Melbourne*
Source: RIP

Carlton
Aug 21 1951

Rex, my dear, it was miraculous of you to write to me so, just when I needed it and when you were much in my mind with lots of things for the 'next time'—the last having been all too short—and the wish that you would get a job in Sydney, seeing you love the trollop.

The postman has just left the great volume. I got it out of its wrapping in the sunlight, where I sit to write, and was astonished by the lovely paper, which I had not noted quite so acutely in the night light near the fire. Thank you for such a rich gift and for the dedication: yes, it wd be something to know who are the others: be sure that I am the least, for the glory of the Cross.

First I turned to 'The Mortal Moment'. That is a tremendous challenge and a new presentation of our lonely sentience.

There has never, or rather I shd say, there has not yet been another such major poem in or of or from this land. You have gone at it in so organized and scientifically documentated a manner as will stagger the little men who review and peck at their biggers. I know so few of your sources except Spencer and Gillen and Prescott. I would not dare give an opinion: I could only irritate you by my inadequacy. If you have brought it off you will be a nonpareil: and followed by a novel of comparable magnitude: how did one slender human in these harried and confused times manage so much? . . .

To come down from the heights: I sat that night and read your brochure by the dying fire, when I shd have been chasing sleep, and was alarmed at first because we might almost be plagiarists one of the other. But on second inspection, it wd seem that you took one bridle track and I another through the same scrub, and one of us stressed one thing and one of us another, but we have the same outlook and interpretation. It can't be helped. That field is pretty well-traversed now: it is interesting how the national mind has remained the same through the decades throughout the continent, because we each feel we own the whole continent, consequent upon our mobility and the fact that we so early occupied it all. That phase of one-family-ness will be scattered to glory on in-glory now with a new and unpredictable era of science plus machines. Our mark on this land will be obliterated as we wiped out the Aborigines—unless—unless and if only—two moonbeam phrases—good, or bad? 'Twould take a poet to interpret. Our ephemerality is the great tragedy—our fleeting moment of puny knowing, so inadequate to 'Keep with this land our Timeless Covenant'.

Congratulations and loving thanks for such a gift. More anon.

Miles

PS I suppose it was you sent me *Austrovert* as you are gratefully mentioned therein. Thank you for it. . . .

8.89   To Sumner Locke Elliott, New York
Source: FP 41

Carlton
October 3 1951

Sumner, my dear

I've been on the verge of writing to you for weeks but the chores are as much and more that I can manage in this brave new era of inflation which has got me quite deflated.

There has been a good deal in the gossip columns about you lately and your show *Buy me Blue Ribbons*. So you are making Broadway so early in your career—a vast engagement for one from far away so comparatively soon. But you were always precocious and got right into the theatre early like Noel Coward. . . .

The theatrical highlight of this winter here in the original line was Warwick Fairfax's play *A Victorian Marriage* but on in full canonicals as to costuming and scenes regardless at the St James by John Alden.

Poor Warwick, he put everything he knew into it, and hadn't the sense when he had the means to have it fully rehearsed and acted to take advantage of 'working-theatre' to trim and rearrange generally. Nevertheless it was an attempt for an Australian and it was also set here but away back so that was a kind of escaping the present milieu. . . .

We've had a referendum for or against the anti-communist bill. I'm glad it was defeated because I am sure that to kill off everyone of our few far-flung soldiers in Korea and millions of

GIs on top of them is sheer madness and will not stop communism if Asia wants to have that form of political belief.

You'll have no time for such meanderings so my dear, goodnight and all sorts of luck,

Ever yours
[unsigned]

8.90   To Arnold and Louise Dresden, Swarthmore,
Pennsylvania
Source: FP 35

Carlton
Nov 27 1951

Dear Things

Just a line to wish you a good Christmas together. I sent you some time ago a book on Aboriginal art which I thought may interest you. There has been great fun about the Aboriginal artists. An old friend who knows them well, a white man, was telling us recently that the administrators, in the interests of art, have difficulty in keeping track of who does the paintings. Namitajira will sign any of his tribes' work with the greatest goodwill and also honesty for they are natural practising communists. When a member of the tribe gets money or food all the others whack-in of natural right like the children of one parent. The administration supplied them with only a limited number of drawing boards each one numbered to try and keep order but that did not worry them, they beat out the white bark of trees and used that. It appears they have tremendous facility.

We have a dear soul out here now from your area. Professor Bruce Sutherland from, I always forget whether it is Pennsylvania University or Pennsylvania State University—it appears there are two. However, he is a Prof in the Dept of English Literature and gives a course on Australian Literature and is here on a Fullbright Scholarship to study it.

His wife is as nice as himself, but I have not yet seen the two daughters, of school age, who are going to one of the

Presbyterian Ladies' Colleges and are very happy in it. The other night at the dinner (annual) of the English Assoc, he proposed the toast of Australian Literature and I responded. He belongs to the Society of Friends sectarianly. When he goes home I hope he will some day go in your direction and tell you that he has seen me in the flesh. What would I not give to see you both in the same state. Life seems to me more and more cruelly baffling because of the silence of the dead. Life is so wonderful in some ways the terrestrial globe so delightful—men make an infernal mess and a slum of a cockpit of it: but if they didn't, if they ran it nearer to our dreams of what it shd and cd be, what then. We would still be getting old and have to relinquish it all, for what? Death would then be even more of an outrage than at present, when one is sometimes so sad and weary that it wd be a release and relief but for fear of it. You can still take pleasure in music. I can't afford to go to concerts and on the radio there is so much of clap trap: also one gets very tired of symphonies, no matter by what giants. Friends—congenial and loved friends would be the greatest joy and assuagement, but mine are scattered (what of them remain) and Big Business has made the world so big that none but a few politicians, entertainers and their molls and servants can afford the fares or secure seats on transports to go about it.

I have been reading *Ordeal by Slander* by Owen Lattimore. It should be required reading for every voter in Australia so the nincoompoops would see the mess they would have been in had Prime Minister got his witch-hunting Bill through to suppress communists, but it would have left us all in danger. I'd have no money to defend myself. I'd just have to go and die in jail. . . .

I thank you Louise dear for the papers so regularly sent. I know what a drag it is and an expense now with the postage (there has been a savage rise in ours), but you would feel rewarded if you knew how much the papers mean to me. They keep me from being quite as cut off as the prisoner of Chillon.

Oh dear, I don't suppose I'll ever, ever see you again and that makes me ache all over and so melancholy I should not write in such a mood.

So I had better wind up with every good wish for the

*Bruce Sutherland, literature professor and visiting Fulbright
scholar 1951–52, a late but true 'congenial' (ML)*

Christmas season. . . . The Sutherlands seem to be astonished at the implications of Christmas in the warm weather. They are like the Australian soldier in London at Christmas in the fog at Trafalgar Square saying what a silly time to have Christmas in the slop and cold.

[unsigned]

8.91 To Bill and Minka Veal, London
Source: FP 44

Carlton
Dec 26 1951

Dear Minka and Bill, I had an idea I started a letter to you but can't find it, so if I'm repeating myself put it down to fatigue, which is making hay of my memory. I sent you by slow mail a week or two back a mess of clippings about art shows—in which you may find something of interest.

First of all I was excited to hear you had met Jean Hamilton. She is a most wonderful person—Bill shd paint *her*. When I saw her she had titian hair and dancing green eyes and was the most harmoniously proportioned petite creature. I spent some of the happiest months of my life with her, and she is a very special dear friend. Do go around to her, and surprise her by a hug and tell her it's from me and that I love her still the same. I know how busy she is and how attractive, so that she never gets time to write many letters.

Do tell Bill to write real soon and set me right on a point of painting ethics. I have several people asking me to let them paint me for the Archibald, and I want to know wd it matter to let them all go ahead, or is it like marriage, must one be engaged to one at a time only? I am at present refusing all, but like matrimonial offers I suppose they will come again. I never took advantage of a man till he had proposed at least five times, and then I began to think up the excuses. Some of us had 'narrer shaves'. . . .

I haven't any news. You'll have heard that poor old Bert

Adamson dropped dead in the Domain talking on Russia, the land of his dreams. We have now buried poor old Rod Quinn three times—all a secretarian and political racket and how these fellows do spread themselves over a safe writer when he's safely dead! and how they do pay for pictures by dead artists who possibly starved to do them. First we interred the body after high or requiem mass. Then on the 2nd inst we went to Waverley again and choirs sang and Archbishop O'Brien orated, and C Roderick talked, and the Director of Education and the Mayor all had a go. Then a little later we were bidden to the Mitchell where the acting Gov-Gen and Doc Evatt, and Roderick again, presented to the institution a bust by Tom Bass, a gentle looking soul with a beard, who did not push himself, nor was he pushed. I shook hands with him afterwards and said, 'You're merely the sculptor, so we don't take any notice of you, but you'll be able to make your own birdroost for erection when you're safely dead.' Evatt was the best I've heard yet, as he did not make any political play at all. He detained me to ask what I thought of his remarks, and I approved, and he wanted to know was the bust a good portrait and I referred him to your portrait at the FAW (Bill) as a splendid likeness as well as a good painting.

I know nothing of painting so can't write on the subject nearest to you, but in cutting out the clippings I was struck by the constant way painting is in the news compared with writing. Kylie Tennant and Geo Farwell got first and second prize in the Jubilee Literary lottery, plays about Deakin and the old Bligh–Macarthur shindy. It doesn't seem to me that they can produce anything but a 'feature' or documentary from our historical figures. We are too near them, and they were comparatively too decent or not indecent or corrupt in a sufficiently large or exciting way to make good stage drama. Eureka, thank God, seems to be quiescent for the time as a subject. Vance P shared first and second in the 'feature' division with some Machin lady, and dear old Jno McKellar got third— with something on Burke and Wills—his first attempt at an air script. Vance also carried off the first prize for the short story, so literary life seems to be beginning at 65 for him—Gor' bless! . . .

You say you can swing a large cat in yr digs, which reminds

me of my dear old uncle from the wide open spaces who complained of the pokiness of his niece's town flat on the score that there wasn't room to swing a cat in it, and the niece said: 'How silly you are Uncle! What on earth wd you want to be swinging a cat for.' But the real luxury is your hot and cold water, if it is really hot. London must be modernizing itself. Mrs F Clune has taken to painting and enjoys herself very much. It must be an enchanting enterprise, so much more exciting than writing. A book I think would be of great freak interest, compiled by an artist, wd be to reproduce the portraits of our celebrities like Lawson and Quinn, etc. and beside them a reproduction of a photo taken at the same time. Think of it. Yours with love. . . .

[unsigned]

8.92 *To Kylie Tennant [Sydney]*
Source: FP 35

Carlton
Jan 5 1952

Dear Kylie

Only now can I squeeze a moment from the fatigue of the chores and general futility which besets me to congratulate you on your win in the Jubilee Literary Comp as well as for your scholarship to do the bees. I love bees and take as much interest in the flavors of honey as others do in liqueurs, so I'm all ears and interest awaiting that novel. I don't know what you could do to Deakin, or any of our public characters, to lift a play about him out of the documentary slough, because you will not be allowed to play too many drakes with dull facts. Have you any definite proposals or a date for stage production? I shall be waiting ready to applaud your success. . . .

   Loving congratulations and good wishes,

Ever yours
[unsigned]

Fairlight
[1952]

Dear Miles

It was so good to hear from you and be given such generous encouragement. Sometimes I wish I did not live so far away from everyone who is interested in books but then I remember how lucky I am to have good friends both in Laurieton and elsewhere. It was a good thing I collected the material for that bee book earlier because the poor apiarists are all burnt out this year so they tell me. . . .

Every now and then we have some scrap of news about you from Cam Morrisby who regards you as a valuable literary property belonging to the nation and puts you in a kind of mental glass case with a notice up in front, very reverent-like.

Charles Moses wrote to say he had had enquiries from Doris Fitton and the WA Theatre Council about the Deakin play. As I am yet to be convinced that it would not be terribly dull on the stage I am only dimly interested. . . . There. The baby is awake. Do let me know what you are writing and if there is any chance of your visiting us.

With love
Kylie

8.94   *From David Martin, Boronia, Victoria*
Source: FP 41

29-1-1952

Dear Miles

I've been so long in returning your play because I wanted to check my reactions by reading it twice with a goodish interval between.

First of all, it's a very brave play. As I see it, it raises the *whole* question of violence and war, and of women's part in what you consider an insane men's society. ...

The whole thing has a unity, it moves fast, there are climaxes which spring from within the action. In other words, it is very strong on the literary (purely) and philosophical plain, once one accepts your premises and your almost unfashionable absoluteness of approach. ...

I think these are some weaknesses:

Situations a little far-fetched and difficult, in as much as they won't sustain the viewer's illusion. ...

A subtler point is this: this is also a play of two generations—three really—but this important fact somehow fails to set up the tension it should. This is probably explained by the fact that, to you, there wasn't anything to choose between world war one and two. ...

While other centipedes can't get their pedes off the ground, you toss off plays and novels and what have you—magnificent! No one could possibly be so great a novelist as you are and be a great playwright too: at least it hasn't ever happened. *The Dead Must Not Return*, like everything substantial of yours I've seen, has a touch of genius about it: but it is not cast in a fully effective mould. ...

David

8.95 To David Martin, Boronia, Victoria
Source: FP 41

Carlton
Feb 3 52

Dear David, Thank you for giving me so much of your time and your illumination—illumination for which I faint in the mental atrophication of this sub-existence in which I am incarcerated. ...

I am glad when you say my simple idea. That means achievement on my part. I gave thought and applied rein, to shearing-off subtleties and involved ideas to keep to the one simple purpose of exhibiting the futility, the bestiality, the cruelty, the hell of war through the generations. You are still young enough and male enough to believe that wars are inevitable, that your own decades' war mattered, that there could still be a war that would matter and that in the light of the past would not show up as unnecessary. (Even Tojo and Churchill both have stated that the second world war was unnecessary although they take their stand on a surface instead of fundamentally as I do.) That is why I suggest through Flora that they each fought 'against aggression', I steered clear of any sectarian or political ideology, for such issues are mutable with each generation. I did not want to show the tension between the generations but their at-oneness as each generation is equally blasted, bedevilled and wasted by war. There is nothing in long perspective to choose between World War I and World War II and Korean War III, nor the Wars of the Roses, nor the Peninsular War, nor that of Waterloo, nor that of Xerxes when he crossed the Hellespont to wipe out braves as silly and as young as his own. Harry is quite naturally as affectionate as a father to Ernie, his brother's child whom he petted as a gentle little orphan, and Ernie, the gentle, clings to Harry as to a partner—mother more usually—as I have heard tortured soldiers screeching for their mothers. . . .

The clash of generations—another and separate theme: perhaps you see now why I suggested we shd collaborate on a play about New and Old Australians.

Of late I am touched most by great ideas simply put and most stirred when they are enfolded in a soft warmth of understanding and sympathy—pity instead of rage. If only I could get rid of my complexities, my far-flung deviousness, which sweeps me away in cross-currents when one life is sufficient only to get out one idea one aim.

One act plays about women—somehow I am more intimate with men. Men were plentiful, women a rarity in my youngest years and perhaps being a woman I was not so curious about them, thought I knew them as stupid and old (decent minded men and women bridle and think they each know all about the opposite sex through one stuffy pillow of a specimen).

If you are coming to Sydney I hope it will not be for the next month as I shd miss you perhaps. By the way have you the script of what you said on the air about being a new Australian. I was so disappointed that I missed it and I have had two such contradictory reports of it. I noted that *Spiegel* was on the regionals. Do you get any extra for that?

I must not take any more of your time but express my gratitude to you for sustenance.

I'm so tired, excuse dullness
Miles

8.96 From Eris O'Brien, Sydney
Source: FP 44

Neutral Bay
3-2-1952

Dear Miss B of B Bin

Thanks for your thoughtfulness in sending a letter to me about the death of Paddy Hartigan.

We all loved him. He found it hard to die—probably because he had always seen the good that was in the world and in the people in it. So he loved the world & its people. A letter, like yours, shows that they loved him too.

Just before he died I challenged him to write some new verse or to polish up unpublished verse: he was too tired to do it.

He has left quite a large number of unpublished poems— many of which need completing or polishing. A & Rs, I think, are considering publishing them.

We can't afford to lose people like 'John O'Brien'; so, I pray that the good Lord will let B of BB stay with us for many years. So, Miles Franklin, please help the said B of BB to survive & to do more work still.

I am going on vacation for a fortnight and I am taking with me a number of books on Genetics (which I suppose I shall not read); some spiritual books, which I shall read, and also, *Ten Creeks Run* which I shall read with delight.

With kindest wishes, sincerely yours
† Eris M O'Brien

Carlton
March 14 52

Dear J K O B E Esq

It is sweet of you to have said you miss me. Picture how that works from the other end where I arrived last night after a trip on the Riverina Daylight Express.

P R and Winnie were wonderful to me—not a bit changed from the early days of our meeting in London. I loved Alfred and the cow and everything about the place, which they run wonderfully—luxuriously. Win is a wonderful homemaker. But the drought from Melb to within an hour or so of Sydney is thorough. Not a speck of green all the way. It is almost too late for winter feed in the cold parts.

Do you remember the Coles of Yarra? I think they had the Towers (Rogers old place) after I left the district. Well, one of them, Tina, now Mrs Mitchell, a widow, is living at Bethanga Lower, and remembers me when I rode a black show mare and also a racing stallion who used to run at Randwick. It was a great meeting after fifty years. She has been 43 yrs at Bethanga. I saw on her walls the photo of a horse the Coles had got from my brother-in-law that I had ridden sometimes long ago.

I felt like a ghost yesterday as I came through Breadalbane and Yarra, where the old de Lisle homestead still looks cosy, and past Joppa Junction picking out the Towers and good old Lansdowne on the Hill and the tower of Bartlett's Brewery, where old Bartlett's boy played me Bach fugues; and I noted Riversdale, and I ran out in the Station yard where I came in the middle of the night in my youth. What a cramped place the Station seems today, and I used to feel it the base of all travel-beginning and romance long ago. There was the jail, which I visited in Gov Smith's time; and Kenmore has grown to a town. On past Marulan and the homesteads I put in *Pioneers on Parade*, and Professor David's rocks, like stranded whales; I don't think I can bear to look at it again. Too entirely empty

Miles Franklin with that 'wild man of letters' P R Stephensen at Bethanga, north-western Victoria, 1952 (ML)

of the old generation, too crowded with the ghosts of my girlhood. ...

I saw a paragraph about you in the *Argus* when I was on the train yesterday. I don't suppose there will be much in the papers here about your great exhibition. We are so stupidly provincial in our State compartments. Such things are of importance to the whole continent. Mr Spencer-Jackson's gallery should be a part of the great Australiana library you are gathering, like the Dixson gallery in the Mitchell. ...

I shall tackle the MS and when I get certain final items of research and reading attended to you may really read it if you have time. I don't expect it will be printable however. But I shall have got it off my chest. People are so stuffy and conventional.

Thank you for a glorious change and all your generous hospitality. It's a great comfort to have a newfound brother, so don't run out on me through overwork: I couldn't bear it.

Love from
Miles

P R Stephensen says *The Publicist* brings £1 a copy now from collectors—is that true? I am returning the photo in which you look as boyish but less cocksure than you did at 23. I have the other copy on which you wrote and which I will paste in the little book wh is not among my papers—I left it downstairs for you to autograph. You'll be glad of another copy of the state photo.

8.98   To Dymphna Cusack, London
Source: FP 30

Mar 15 1952

Dymphna, my dear, I had been hoping your silence was because of intense work and not a bout, and am distressed to hear you have had one—but there was a lengthening interval, and you had really been slogging. I envy you with the French language:

it is like suddenly being able to swim. Alas, 35 yrs since I attempted any French and I have grown rusty in reading it now.

I am thrilled by your continuing success—the French literary agent and getting away from Heinemann. Do you think the translator would be interested in *Prelude* or *Up the Country*? I wish they wd get out of the way and on to the explanatory volume to come. £150 advance on a translation is unbelievable—cheers!

Tom Ronan who won some sort of a prize previously got the £1000 for the Jubilee novel. D Niland second, and £300 third to a Mrs Dryvyneyde, an Australian-born now controlling the largest private school for boys in Vancouver. Her novel *Provoke the Silent Dust* sees pioneer life in Tas through the eyes of a woman who came from Eng as a Convict. Can you beat that! for expatriate escape in repatriation. D N's is called *The Big Smoke*. Ronan has just written me from the Katherine that I once told him that he had a wealth of personal experience and a talent for expression and his choice was to write for commercial standard or what he liked writing. So he has spent five years in turning out his job. I hope it is good, but he is no Xavier. We shall see. Heinemann has his MSS; it is 160,000 words. . . .

Yes, Strehlow is the one person of his academic knowledge who has been reared with the aborigines—invaluable, irreplacable in that field.

I chuckle to think of Heinemann's being furious they lost themselves *Caddie*. I hope it is a thriving success. It is good to have two strings to your bow, not to say many beaus on yr string.

I have felt lately I was dying of inanition as such as heart weakness so essayed a trip to Melb to see the crowd but it was too much for me. I had to lie down much of the time and missed numerous people on my list. . . .

Don't come home till it suits you.

I have two things: my essay and a play, which are my best, but I can't handle them from here, and have not the strength to battle. J K Moir, who was my host, is a remarkable man. He knows every Australian book and is collecting like Mitchell did for the Mitchell Library. He cd not get a house, so bought a shop in a half-slum street and puts all the books in it and lives in the back. Has a room for authors. He runs a salon where too many rabble take advantage of his generosity. He says I must have done a hell of a lot of research, which is high praise, also told Rex I it was terrific and no one else cd have done it. If Aus novels are so read overseas I wonder if this tale of their rise wd be interesting. More another day if I live. Ever my love.

[unsigned]

8.99 To Nettie Palmer, Melbourne
Source: FP 24

Carlton
22 Mar 52

Dear Nettie

It was so nice of you, Vance and Aileen to come to see me. I was in such poor form that the mere effort to try to talk was almost beyond me. I wish we cd have had some further private discussions because I have neither advisers nor association left and tho we agree fundamentally on principles, when I have to jump into space with an opinion I may be obstructing the machinations of my compeers because I may not have all the numbers of the sum desired. In that particular I miss Flora's good administrative mind which could always sift disputable matters down to a helpful formula. However, it doesn't matter now as I am withdrawing. . . .

I have been meaning to ask you if you know Gwen Meredith? I do admire her serial *Blue Hills*. I do everything I can to be near a radio at 1 pm every day. I do wish we got more than 10 mins of it every day. 'I would like to do a novel but when I consider D Cusack, Vance Palmer and you I sort of wilt at the idea of trying to compete.'!!!!

And at our local shops the grocer's wife cannot serve me often till she has discussed with the other housewives what this and that one did and should have done and what they thought shd have happened in *Blue Hills*. There is fame and popularity that I envy. (By the way I was so situated that I never heard one session of the prize serials.). . . .

Saw your brother Esmd in the Mitchell the other day. He is a dear. Were he a family physician the very sight of him arriving would save a patient from neuroses and fantods.

No more strength
Ever yrs
[unsigned]

8.100   To Mabel Singleton, Surrey
Source: FP 25

Carlton
Ap 1 1952

Mabel dear, Your kind letter to hand yesterday. Dear me, how time has gone for that play to have got there already, and how good of you to read it, tired and all as you are. The suggestion about Unity is a good one, but keep the play private to yourself for the present. I shd like to get it at least read here, where I could estimate if anything more shd be done. A play is like making a dress: one needs to be able to try it on to see where the seams should be let out or taken in. I have had it read by David Martin, who has had two of his plays put on here. He is also a novelist and poet. ...

I also got a woman to read it, who has acted lots of part and produced in the repertory and little theatre groups. I knew she would loathe the theme because she is conventional and one of those women who hunts with the male pack, but she knows 'theatre' as she puts it. I asked her only for the technicalities of putting it on and she says the mechanics are quite simple and well-knit that even a novice in production shd find no trouble with the play. She missed the point, of course, even more than I anticipated. She said no one is interested now in the forgotten soldier when he comes home. Nonsense! That was not the theme. It is my testimony against war, and how it wrecks men, and women are dragged down with them, and how some of the normal people like Myrtle and Ivor do well out of it. It contains a whole lifetime of experience and knowledge of wars and men in various parts of the world. . . . I think it is time for the stage to get down to the fundamental problems of the present, not this eternal pandering to *l'amour* and escape into fantasy and muddle-headed tripe, like *The Lady's not for Burning* and *A Sleep of Prisoners*, that has no clear meaning so people think it is profound.

I went over to Melbourne for a change to see if I could cheer myself up and to see some old friends once more. But I had not sufficient strength and had to rest most of the time. . . . My host, Mr Moir and Nettie Palmer were so alarmed at my weakness that they made me go to Nettie's doctor. Waste of money, as she only told me at 3 guineas what my nice Macquarie St men tell me for nothing. I've been gone over to the inch and X-rayed and charted. She said No work, no worry, no hurry. I know that, but what am I to do? . . .

I saw Mrs Champion, she is really, really old, still goes to Robertson and Mullens but they send her home early in the afternoon. Aileen looks after her, and she too has failed in the 9 years since I saw them. Got so small. Looks inches shorter, I think she has arthritis by the look of her, but of course wd not acknowledge it. Kate Baker was a triumph, 91 next month, and still going about by herself and tripping down steps in a half light without holding the side rail—looks so nice too. A Mrs Fairbairn had a dinner party for her to meet me, and Kate arrived apologising for being hungry because she said she had been around town all day and had had nothing to eat since a cup of tea at 11 am. She was also at a public meeting, memorial to Vic Kennedy at which a paper by her was read, and it was fine. I met B O'Dowd there too, for the first time, and he read poems in a magnificent booming way. One of my younger friends in his fifties, that I had not heard from, I found to be dead. That was a sad blow. I saw Em and Bell. Don't you make any mistake in addressing envelopes or mention anything unless Em tells you herself. It was very painful: they are on each other's nerves in a demented way. . . . Just as you hinted quietly long ago in London: poor Mary, what a turmoil she had to steer through and she so reflective and intellectual.

If they are not already using germs and everything else in Korea they soon will be, they are itching to release the A Bombs. My play holds, and is very mild, I don't care what any one says.

[unsigned]

8.101   To Henrietta Drake-Brockman, Perth
Source: FP 33

Carlton
April 15 1952

Dearest Henrietta

How gorgeous and reproach-arousing (reproach of myself) to have your letter just now. I owe you one for ever so long and have started so often to write but get as far as the envelope only when I am interrupted or strength gives out. I had the paper in the machine last night when two friends arrived and stayed till nearly midnight, which is no good to me. I cd hardly get up this morning. You will see that the envelope has yellowed and the cuttings staled. I meant to write from Melb. No strength. . . .

Can you and Geoff give me reliable information on a book by J M Hart called *The Pearlers*, dealing with Broome. I have read it and am told it was burned on the shore at Broome by irate townsfolk. Is that a fact? Is it recorded anywhere in news and what was the date? The book was published in 1933 I believe. I shd like to be sure of the burning episode.

Beatrice has gone. I shd miss her except that the effort to get to town is increasingly beyond me and I can do nothing to entertain people here. Everything in chaos. When Mrs Menzies has to commandeer Army girls and the Prime Min take them in his car to the races, and when the Maharajah Duleep Singh has to move to a hotel because the Ranee can't secure help, you know my chances.

I can't type more than half-an-hour without distress so will wind up this dull screed. I expect Prof Edwards will remove to USA. It is a wonderful place, and gorgeous people. I am trying to type finally my observations on Australian writing which

291

you'll at least have to glance through because of the dedication. Your name is in it: if you disapprove I can easily leave it out. Not that there is any probability of it being worth publication but I must finish it out of the ingrained habit of keeping my word. . . .

My love as ever
[unsigned]

PS I nearly forgot to mention *Models for Molly.* You have noted that it was dismissed from both competitions without a word of any kind. I have since shown it to Eleanor Witcombe, who writes and produces plays for children successfully. She has expressed her delight in it. Why had no one discovered it? Dialogue, everything all right, and she dotes on Mrs Fitzhugh, and deliciously period. But she is off to London and does only juveniles. I can't do anything about it. Can't be bothered any more. You must let me have real details of the one that got the West Aus prize. Something about the Governor's Stables was it not?

8.102 *To Jean Devanny, Townsville, Queensland*
Source: FP 32

[21 April 1952]

Dear Jean

So glad to have found you again. I thought you were lost till one day Delys blew in after absence, a good sight—and I asked after you and sent you the papers you mention. I have another roll ready now. . . .

Yesterday Vance reviewed your new book over the air. Do you hear such things on yr radio? In case you missed it, he said good things. Was enthralled with the first part about the Reef. The second part not so good because J D abandons the lyricism with which she treats the first half and robustly tells of the poverty of the life on the main land and round about. Read splendid bit about Julia Creek, and you certainly have got fine

292

character-drawing in the man who had no time for reading and tells how the place is going ahead. Also great about Normanton. I am longing to read it. . . .

Yes, Dymphna is going ahead. Has a third novel ready, which those who have read it say is her best, and also another book by an ex-barmaid, which she instigated, and has edited and written a preface. Her great good luck was to have been rejected by the *DT* and A and R's here and go to London. They cd have published an edition of 5000 instead of 25,000 to begin, and then perhaps have let it go out of print.

I am struggling like a fly in tar on a book, about Australian writing, what it is made of, and its struggles, wh I don't suppose will find a publisher, or sell if it does, but I must finish it now I've started.

You're all wrong when you say I was timid of your position. Aren't you, in your attitude about this, blaming me for your own outlook? You will recall how terrified you were that I shd put anything in writing lest you should get into trouble and that I was shocked that communists cd make you feel so unsafe. I don't know much about communism, but, as I said then, the antics of communists are more certainly alienating. You remember how the FAW was killed. Poor old Bart—I'm glad I never made an open rumpus now that he is dead. He died as he wd wish, for Russia, the country to which he wd have made Australia a burnt or any other sort of offering. Well, I don't fancy *any* political creed that does not allow me to love my own country first. If you remember I wasn't at all afraid to have you as my friend and guest nor to go and see you and enjoy you when I was being abused and put on a dossier for so doing. I still am an independent in politics and am against war—*all* wars. I shd be against even a war to emancipate women, because war never can be won. To contemplate war is to be defeated.. . . .

I wish I cd go up and spend a winter in Townsville and be near you. I'll bet you see as many congenial people as I do. . . .

[unsigned]

Carlton
May 9 52

Ian dear

If you have felt an extra warm glow around you lately—that's
me. When we're dead we shall not be able to tell our friends
we love them, so why withhold while we are alive? This outburst
comes of the fact that I'm finishing my essay on Australian
writing. It is not the book I had dreamed to write under the
title 'Australia Waits'. It was to have been my lovesong to my
land, but perhaps only the poets have the winged gift to give
such an offering—well—*wings*. Then I had to prepare those
talks for WA so instead of some high falutin dream I have
enlarged those. I selected the novel during our first 150 years
of history. It is a sort of biography of the novel to set forth
its trials in gaining a footing. But I can't live without my poets,
so I have dragged a word from one or two of them in at the
end as a sort of Panache. ...

So I got out yr collected poems a week ago to select those
two or three lines. It turned into a binge; I read them all, and
got lost and staggered off to bed in an intoxicated state such
as that Hope attributed to you, bewildered and overcome
because I felt I wanted to put in nearly everything.

A night or two since—three weeks later—I had to make up
my mind. I lay awake summing-up my utter futility. Everyone
belonging to me dead; my friends scattered in three continents
and even in Australia clean out of reach and I have accomplished
nothing and being of no consequence to any living soul. Then
I began to think—I always have the wings of thought if not
of poetry ready waiting—that the great joy is not so much to
be loved or expect love as to love and find joy in loving. Now,
who is there, I proceeded whom I can dote on with delight?
Up came Ian, and I was immediately restored from futility and
melancholy. Ian, plus dear Renee with him with enough warmth
and understanding to reach me too.

So next morning I set myself to choose the few lines without overimbibing again. So I thought the first 9 or fourteen lines of 'Corroboree' on p 12. This seemed so fitting to point my animadversions on the mediocrity which menaces us. But then intruded 'Earth' (p 14) the first seven lines heightens what I have been saying about love of Australia. But then I came to 'This is Australia'. Magnificent, an inspiring summing-up of all I'm trying to sheet home and I shut the book without another sip lest I drown again. . . .

How are you getting on? Is there a chink of light in your publication sky, or is it as closed as my own? At anyrate I'm thankful that Rex and Dymphna are having their moments for there are precious few for most writers except Neville Shute and Ion Idriess. Dymphna is for the moment well among best-sellers. Over 45,000 of *Spinner* sold already and *Say No to Death* getting wonderful reviews and there is talk of a friend of Jean Paul Sartre's translating it into French. . . .

A heartful of love to the four of you from
[unsigned]

By the way when last you wrote you were just going to post *Come in Spinner* to Katharine S Prichard. Do you remember if it went to her? It has not come back to me and I valued it for the inscription, and have no other copy. I have asked K S P but like you she forgot to reply to my question.

8.104   To Florence James, London
Source: FP 30

Carlton
June 3 1952

My dear Florence, You are on my must-be-written-to-or-bust list, have been for a month or two, but you know how it is. There are so many trivialities concerned with the mechanics of life to torment and occupy one these days. Florence Beaufoy telephoned me some days ago now to say you had written and she had to have some one with whom to share the exciting news about Julie's and Frances's success. They looked so clever and grown-up in those snaps, I did not recognise them. Congratulations! . . .

I wrote last, I think, and so have nothing in a letter from you to go upon. We have had several profs out here on Fulbright Scholarships to study our literature. One of them is lecturing at the University on Am Literature and has made a fine outburst in the *SMH* about the way we shd cherish our own writers and not be apologetic about them. Outsiders are saying now what I have been always saying, and what A G S said before me. Prof Sutherland who is studying our literature by way of special reading of A G S and his times, is the one I have met most. . . .

Colin Roderick asked him at lunch the other day, after five months' intensive reading at the Mitchell, in his opinion who was the best critic of our lit since A G S. Prof Sutherland said straight off the bat: P R Stephensen, that his *Foundations of C* was a grand thing, and also his study of A G S was first class. At the Journalists' Club someone remarked he must have been very occupied with the Uni people and he again said innocently he had hardly seen them, and added 'They are not interested in Aus Lit there and as that is what I am here to study they aren't any use to me.' !!!

I've just been told that the Dept of Eng at the Uni is impossible at present. Howarth very bitter because Mitchell made Milgate head in place of the deceased head. Now I understand that Milgate and Mitchell don't speak. And Howarth and Mitchell don't, Sutherland said it was awkward because he had to go to see Mitchell alone and the same to Howarth. They have such a small gauge they don't count except as obstacles. Also Clem Christesen is in a very disgruntled state of mind. One of his near friends said it was a great mistake for him to have resigned from Heinemann's: he shd have left it to them to make moves that cd be contested. . . .

I wish you were near. My friends are scattered far and wide, like the poem says (Mrs Felicia Hemans). This morning at daylight I was called next door by Arthur, whom you remember played with Julie, because he and Mum did not like the look of Dad. He was dead. I can't tell you what a blow it is to me.

He was with me in two great troubles, always generous and loving and good. It seems as if life is never to smile on me again. I wish something would happen just once to make me feel cock-a-whoop instead of down-the-drain. One cannot for ever row against Niagara. . . .

Prices go up, though unemployment is beginning. Therefore the recruits for Korea have increased and the old general who is making a campaign thinks it is he that is impressing the youth with the need for 'defence'. Poor young things, they are more frightened of unemployment than of war and you can't break the spell. They dither and say 'it won't be long now. There always has been war and always will be.' More madness rampant and the silly women echoing them.

No peace movement that has any connection with the communists can do anything except cause more friction, and how to get it separated fom the communists, I don't know. If they were game to lay down their arms I'd be with them, but they too have the same old cry that they have to meet aggression with aggression. Even the Quakers are half of them for war. The Communists don't care so long as capitalists get killed and the capitalists vice-versa. It is like the old cartoon of litigants one pulling at the head of the cow the other at her tail and the lawyer milking the beast comfortably. But it is the RC's that are milking the enmity of both sides for their own ends and growing stronger and bolder. The postmaster here remarked to me last week that we have given Australia away to refugees who complain that it is not good enough for them.

I may have something more interesting to say before long but I wanted to congratulate the girls and thank you for the papers and keep communications alive.

Ever your loving friend
[unsigned]

Carlton
July 27 1952

Dear, dear Magdalen, Art thou living yet? I am surrounded by large bags of letters each packed with scores of unanswered letters. It is no use, I shd need a secretary to keep abreast of correspondence and in Australia one has to do all one's own work. Even the rich can't get help, and with inflation, my tiny fixed income is enough only to buy food and fuel. Now postages are going to rise again savagely and I shall not be able to afford letters.

We'll have to start again from the beginning, as I do not know who wrote last. I know only that I love you still the same and that it would be a great and nourishing joy to see you again on this earth. I dare not hope that your little mother is still with you. I think other friends must have gone too. They have been silent a long time and there is no one to write and ask. They are Leonora Pease the school teacher, Miss Phelps's sister and Dr Josephine Young. The two last named were over eighty, so they must be gone. I heard Mr Ickes' death over the air: he always wrote to me. His first wife was one of my dear friends: she was Mrs Wilmarth's daughter, I suppose you remember, who owned the Auditorium Hotel. The Dresdens still write to me, and Mary Anderson sent me her book.

I have a wonderful letter here from you in which you told of all you had done to renovate your house. Those American houses make my mouth water to remember. You wd be shocked at my old shack, and now I have not the strength to do the work or keep the garden. It is a jungle, I live in fear of the rat inspector because you must not have rubbish about. You spoke of some trouble with your brother's health I think, in an earlier letter. The only relative of my immediate family left is a nephew who was a pilot in the air force. He is what they call a war neurosis case and is in a hospital with other wrecks through nerves. What I went through with him delirious, all alone for years, finally wrecked my heart. It is now 'fatigued'. I am all right so long as I do not indulge in physical exertion. Age too is telling. . . .

You are in the throes of your Presidential whoopee. Reading

of the conventions I remember 1912 when Mr Madill McCormick gave me a ticket to sit next in glory to the *Times* (London) correspondent, and I also had a ticket for the other party's convention when they elected Taft, father of one of the runners up this year. Those were days of great turmoil and excitement. So many dead, this tag-end of life is very sad, it calls for fortitude. If only one cd see old friends it wd be better but this scatter around the world is heart-breaking when only the rich and their attendants or entertainers and politicians and their henchmen can travel. ...

Do you remember Marjory Dell (used to be Mrs Floyd Dell) she still writes to me but only once in a blue moon. She went under a big operation, more extensive than yours, and I have several friends here the victims of those fibroid growths at present. I wonder why there are so many of them. ... Two neighbors, much younger than I, have recently died in their sleep. I suppose I'll go like that and no one to report me till the police are informed. It is terrible to have no friend to see you off and watch that you are put away decently and quickly.

We have had wild floods wrecking all the citrus fruits and the vegetables. The people on the land have a precarious time always. When it's not fire and drought it's floods; and how are you getting on with the Argentine ants?

There have been two novels very highly reviewed in USA: *Come in Spinner* and *The Sun in my Hand* by Dymphna Cusack. She is a great friend of mine and we wrote one novel in collaboration. She is in Europe now.

My one self-indulgence is to go to a newsreel once a week. There is often something of the Florida back places—men catching snakes or crocodiles, but there are too many of those water ski-ing so called beauties. I'm tired of the female form as a substitute for art or entertainment. Only one thing wd be worse—a similar display of men, but it being a man's world thank heaven we were spared that. Old men like to gloat on young women but elderly women wd be bored stiff with men and that wd lose a lot of customers for shows. My love as always and ever, your old friend

[unsigned]

Potts Point
24th July 1952

Dear Miles Franklin

Thankyou, again, very much indeed for having us all on Tuesday & for the lovely welcoming evening which I, for one enjoyed tremendously. Some time I'd love to take you up on your invitation to come again—I'm enclosing with this the Harold Mercer obituary which you said you had not seen.

Tonight I'm committed to inspecting—admiring???—and trying to make intelligent remarks about some pieces of surrealist sculpture in a draughty workshop at Kirribilli. Even in advance I'm nostalgic for the good Australian warmth & sense at Carlton.

Sincerely
Nancy

Carlton
Aug 12 1952

Dear Nancy Keesing, (it cd easily and gaily be contracted to Nanking)

Thank you for letting me see this, so typical of that generation of *Bulletin* Sydneyites and so warmly interesting—sad too as all things irrevocable are.

I'm afraid that was a very dull evening, made so by scrappiness and brevity, and uneasy because of the early rising ahead of some of the guests. Fri or Sat might have been more comfortable for them but we had to suit our Melbourne guest. It was good of you to come so far and I'm still here, as I said, but fares are so high and time so scarce that there is much better use to be made of both nearer base.

It is 40 years since I was in the thick of such shows as you outline, the trouble is that they have not changed.

Sincerely
[unsigned]

8.108   From Katharine Susannah Prichard, Perth
Source: FP 21

Greenmount
Aug 25 1952

Miles dear

I have finished reading your MS last week & took it back to Henrietta; but have been waiting for a free moment to write to you. First of all congratulations on it! I marvel at your patient research into the work of so many early writers & that all through something typically yourself is retained: the sparkle of your wit & forthrightness in criticism. There are pages and pages of brilliant writing. Particularly I liked your comparison of James & Furphy. My own sentiments exactly—and so good for the Jamesian devotees! I feel that the book must be published soon, & hope it will be. Henrietta thinks Angus & Robertson will be doing it. They ought to.

Needless to say, there are some points in philosophy where I don't agree with you. I don't like *you* referring to 'totalitarian & authoritarian' règimes; just as the newspapers do. The two words are contradictory, & neither accurate as far as a peoples' government in a Socialist State are concerned. Then too you seem to accept the military blah that Australian 'tradition' began with Gallipoli. It dates much further back, I think you'll agree when you think over this point, with Eureka & the strike struggles of the 90's & the whole democratic upsurge wh inspired Lawson & Furphy, gave rise to the Labour Party & all the social-reform legislation on wh Australia led the world. The 'unique importance of the common man', wh Grattan pointed out is charac-

301

teristic of Australia in literature, derives from this basis of aspiration & struggle for human rights. And by 'the common man', I don't think he meant, & I don't, just clodhoppers, but ordinary people of all sorts who work for their living & refuse to be treated like mere drudges.

And, darling, surely our literature doesn't suffer any longer from 'incipiency'? Your own work, Eleanor's, Dymphna's & even that of K S can stand with anything produced in other countries to-day. My books have been translated into French, German, Czech, Slav, Polish, Russian, Hungarian, Roumanian and Afrikaans—so, at least, they have done something to remove that slur from our literature. *Coonardoo*, by the way was published in 1929, and really was the first attempt to make a serious study of an aboriginal theme. . . .

Thank you so much for the papers, dear! Do tell Mabel Singleton how much I appreciated reading hers. And I'm always pleased to see a copy of the *New York Times*—though the supplement isn't as good as it used to be—as timid as most American writing these days.

I do hate to think of you not well & unhappy about Jack. It is a triumph through all your worries to have accomplished the lectures, & got them ready for publication. They'll be a great success I'm sure—although not likely to please the mugwumps. Still that won't bother you. You don't write to please them, do you?

Love to you, Miles dear
Katharine

8.109   *To Katharine Susannah Prichard, Perth*
Source: FP 21

Carlton
Sept 11 1952

Katharine me jool!

What a mess that poor cracked Wentworth has got himself into with the CLF, and then to attack you in the *SMH*, you the sacred white cow of all of us (no disrespect but only the highest respect intended, but you must excuse levity—can't help it in the face of such an ass).

I've got to lie low for Wentworth has me on his roll as a communist stooge and has already had the publishers assoc considering that they shd refuse to sell my books, and with my alleged *aliases*—well, I'm not strong enough for any shadow of controversy at present. Had to go to town yesterday and thought I'd really peg out last night. If I don't exert cunning I'll find myself shut in a hospital for a real rest. (This by way of explanation only—nothing the matter but a fatigued heart.)

But into the gap has charged our mutual white knight Alan Dalziel. He came in two days ago to read me from Hansard Les Haylen's reply in the house to Keon and Wentworth. How good it is that one of them is tory the other labor: I always contend that lit societies should be alertly political but strictly non-party. And Mr Menzies rose to this occasion. If *Meanjin* or *Southerly* doesn't print Haylen's outburst they are missing a real opportunity.

Wentworth went too far—*alias* Mrs Throssell indeed. He is so ignorant of literary privilege that he does not know that writers may indulge in nom-de-plumes to their hearts' content so long as genuinely as pen names and not nefarious. . . .

Dal says that Ric should confront Wentworth on the steps of Parliament in Canberra and punch his jaw and tell him to alias his mother as Mrs Thorssell. This says Dal would be a great aid to Australia and if Wentworth wd only take Ric up for assault it would make a real fool of W. Both sides wd be enchanted. I wish Ric would wait till he sees W coming up the steps and then walk down and soundly smack his face. It makes such a nice sound as I know, through having smacked the faces of tormentors in my day and it doesn't hurt but is much more humiliating than a crack on the jaw. If I had as magnificent an excuse as Ric's I'd enjoy going smack on W's cheek.

Les is going to have a question asked in Parliament about W's persecution of women who are an ornament to Aus Lit and in view of Wentworth's great energy going to waste suggest that he be given a commission in Korea where he really can show his prowess and courage.

I had some ideas on the CLF lecturers but will postpone it now lest I shd seem to criticise at this juncture.

I got your lovely letter dear. Have read only the first page yet such is my fatigue and such the interruptions and demands I have to meet, but thank you for words of cheer and as for us not agreeing on certain points I'll take that up when I get strength.

With many thanks ever and ever yr loving
[unsigned]

8.110   To Rex Ingamells, Melbourne
Source: RIP

Carlton
Sep 25 1952

Dear Rex

I've just come across your letter of 6th Aug about *Of Us now Living*—it was there all the time in a wrong envelope which put me off it. You say you don't think the person exists who wd claim to be accurately represented therein. You're an innocent babe not yet squz in the mill of novel making. I was so plagued when my first little effort appeared by the people from everywhere—strangers— who claimed the characters, and also by those of my own district who were enraged because they were in and those who said I had deliberately left them out. In my ignorance and inexperience I was baffled by this and it seared me so that I never recovered. I told my troubles to a gentleman who had written from Queensland, a sophisticated travelled man, elderly, I now understand. He pointed out that that was my triumph, the miracle of a child being so able in characterisation. He said he was off to the Rockies to shoot bear, and I never heard of him again. . . .

I loathe the 'modern' Australia, but perhaps that is my age— you should still be in the swim of it. The modern Australia as it appears in novels—take *The Harp in the South* etc., *Come in Spinner, The Sundowner, The Shades will not Vanish*, and so on. They are all *after* American models such as *A Tree Grows in Brooklyn*, *Grand Hotel* and *The Sundowner* is after Gavin Casey's *The Wits are Out*. It might very well have stood out from the MSS submitted in the Jubilee Comp and it is easy to see with that boost why it was made a book of the month in America. First of all it deals with RCs very nicely—a sure guarantee that it wd have nothing Red, and also no depth of thought and the women in it all indulge in unexpurgated brothelism in regard to their marital sexual affairs—right up to the fashion. He speaks of a cinch where it used to be a girth, but it may be that my discomfort is with the facts not with the presentation of them; it may be that Australia now is a poor ersatz USA, and these people are right artistically. *Sundowners* has all the old things in it, useless people like in *The Battlers*, and a race in shearing—all the way through I felt that it was observed by a man who had knocked about Australia but not by one who knew the bush, and then Ho! ho! my suspicions were verified when I came to the dark-eyed sheep.

The merinos are Nordics. The sheep's is the lightest eye known. When we youngsters wanted to jibe at our relatives we called them 'Old sheep eyes!' because they had those ice-blue eyes of the north which go as pale as the skies in strong sunlight. I don't suppose any one but myself cares, but I put it to my lovely old uncle down from his well bred flocks to enjoy his 90th birthday, and he took the words out of my mouth by saying, 'I don't believe even black sheep have dark eyes.'

You are feeling about in your mind with something more of the Singwood Diaries. If you really enjoy them and feel rich in them it is a scheme and a matrix from which you could turn in endless ways. It will keep coming up to you like a nice warm thought, like a meeting with a congenial friend when the day is over and after a while it will sprout so that you can direct it. Gestation from imagination is a wonderfully nourishing thing to living and to life. The moind! The moind! is truly a wonder. You have only to set it on a thought like a dog on a scent and it will keep expanding and progressing. . . .

I am so very very tired so excuse stodge.

With affection and thanks
Miles

8.111   To Beatrice Davis, Sydney
Source: FP 38

Carlton
Sep 30 1952

Dear Beatrice, Your exquisite handscript from Holland reached me in due time, but I had nothing to write in return. The winter was wet but not cold—only one or two bleak days—so mild in fact that I didn't even have a suspicion of a chilblain. The only trouble is that it will soon be the shortest day again. You can measure how much I miss you when I say that Roderick seems the flower of the flock to me there now, and I'm glad of his friendly welcome till he spoils it by some literary obtusity. No silvery soprano with a welcoming note when I ring-up but merely great caution as if I might be going to make some damaging statement or claim. But Pixie for Children's Week did a lively deed in assembling a noble array of publishers at the Fellowship, among whom George F was the flower of the flock as usual and indeed, and Frank Eyre of Oxford U Press condescenscious in keeping with his exalted sponsors. George had a yarn with me, drawn to me by our mutual bereavement in yr absence. I said there was not another like you in Sydney, he amended that to in Australia. Said something which I had previously heard about an enchanting and enchanted Frenchman. I said it wd be a great lark if a Frenchman shd capture you and G said he didn't mind as long as you brought him back to Australia. I asked wd he take him into the business. He said he wd if it was the only way of keeping you. He expressed himself as ready to put up with any appendages so long as he doesn't lose you, in which I heartily agreed. . . .

The latest excitement is that K S P has taken out a writ against Wentworth and *SMH* for £10,000 for libel. There has been a flurry in the cols of *SMH* about Wentworth's accusation in Parliament that the CL Fund was administered by and now almost exclusively for Reds. Les Haylen arose with a noise in defence and Menzies' smart-alecism was beautifully applied on the right side in this issue. Wentworth was pulled-up by Kylie Tennant and apologized humbly to her but in the correspondence cols took a slap at K S P as *alias* Mrs Throssell (sic). ....

Wentworth would have put me in the list too I'm sure only that I tackled him some years ago when he and I were guests at my young cousin's wedding. I told him that my GESTAPO had informed me that his OGPU had me blacklisted as a communist, and I *wasn't*. He said he knew I was not a communist, that I had too much sense. I said I was not, because the Cs did not go far enough in the woman question for me, but that Uncle Joe Stalin was my favorite whodunnit. Why? I said because he has taken women off the midden and put 'em into parliament, I didn't care why or how, but that made him the greatest whodunnit man living. I think myself that such Gilbertism is the way to meet such bigotry.

Oh, that I cd see London once again! People wd not accept *me* as Australian because I had not the distinctive accent. You shd have seen the class distinctions and the position of the lower orders before the first world war. And that assumption of superiority, but I lived & worked there long enough to grow used to the disadvantages and to enjoy the advantages and, in essence I love the English: they wear so well, and as G B S said their lunacy is of a less virulent kind. Considering the debacle of their pomp and empire I think they take it with great dignity, perhaps too quietly. As an American private said in the first war that they wd stand anything, that they stood too much. The Scots, the Irish, the French are all more appetising, perhaps more stimulating and enjoyable, but as a steady diet, day in and day out, in war and depressions, in coronation and royal marriage lunatic pageantry and general hum-drumery you know where you are with the English. And bless them for their insulated emotions, and after all there is no getting away from it, we are of them through language and tradition. ....

And now for New York. I wonder what you will make of that vortex in so short a time. I long to hear your findings on it all, and hope you will have the time and inclination and I the fares for just one collogue about it all.

With love from
Miles

Carlton

Sept 30 1952

Dear Helene Scheu-Reisz, What a joy to get your little note of
Sept 15 which reached me two or three days since. I hope I am
in time to catch you before you flit again.

It was with a sense of reprieve that I saw again the address
in Wien so familiar in the 41 Russell Square days. There is
something left after all: it will be happy as an international
embassy I am sure and how splendid to know you are still going
strong in your cosmic way.

I hope that dear little Wally is stronger than she was in
London, but she had a difficult and dreary time with that old
lady with her memory gone. So glad the Lancasters are still alive.
In these long separations from those with whom I associated
the gaps are growing too many. I never was very familiar with
the Cadburys but Miss Hodgson, whom you may remember at
41, sends me paper cuttings about them and that wonderful old
lady so recently dead. Seebohm Rowntree came often to the
Housing Council Rooms and I note that he has been co-author
of what sounds like a very interesting survey of conditions in
English life. I feel that the Housing Council when it lost the
spirit of Mr Aldridge sank to a mere clerkish adjunct of the
Ministry that deals with Housing. Instead of suggesting and
planning policy as in the old days it merely interpreted the maze
of regulations to the rural authorities whom they bemused. The
man who followed Mr Aldridge was conventionally minded, a
super clerk and has gone to South Africa. His ability lay in raking
in the fees and making the institution sound financially which
was entirely beyond our friend.

You lucky little going concern bundle of energy to be able
to commute between Vienna and New York and what an
interesting spread you have on family members. Son in London,
daughter in Minneapolis, your son's brother-in-law in Brisbane.
You may indeed come this way some day. There wd be little
hope of me going the other way with the deterioration in our

pound. I am not strong enough for cheap travel these days and have not the gifts to write a best seller to win American dollars. Did you have my big novel *All that Swagger*? I shall send you a copy if not, but I suppose it had better wait and go to Le Rochegasse when you return there next summer. ...

This is just to catch up the threads once more and very thankful to know you are still alive and well and happy in your work and family.

Yours cordially
[unsigned]

8.113   To Sybil Thorndike Casson, London
Source: FP 44

Carlton
November 9 1952

Dear Dame Sybil Thorndike

May I express my pleasure in your beautiful tribute to Elizabeth Robins printed in the *Listener* of July 1. I am so glad you specially mentioned her eyes. They were like an inner lantern shining out. The photograph reproduced has caught their fey illumination and she looked little older when I first met her at Henfield in 1911.

You don't know me but in the First World War when you were one of the glories of London I was an Old Vic addict and sometimes sat in the Manager's box when your parents would also be there. Those were great days. You were transcendent in *Medea* and *St Joan*. It was the actress with me then, rather than the plays, because you were so often the greater. I was absorbed in all you did, those new plays at some little theatre—was it near Swiss Cottage? and Grand Guignol. ...

I am writing to Elizabeth Robins' brother and sister-in-law concerning your tribute. In my youth I was intimately associated with them in the USA.

Your visit will be a great refreshment and I hope it will be a happy experience for you. Sure to be with your son here.

All the good wishes and good will in the world and grateful memories of what you were to me.

Sincerely
[unsigned]

8.114 From Jean Devanny, Townsville, Queensland
Source: FP 32

11/12/52

My dear Miles—More than pleased to hear from you. But what do you mean by saying you are too weak to go and sit in the Mitchell Library? You're not *old*, Miles—so I can only assume that that means you are ill. What you want is a good long change away from Sydney winters. Don't say you *may* go to Monaro in January. Just go, if you've got the chance. No good asking you to come up here at that time, Miles: this summer is *awful*. One of the hottest on record and just now I am almost prostrate. ...

Now—re that work you are doing. I am inclined to think I would agree with what Henrietta D B had to say about it— 'that there never has been and never would be, any thing like it'. That's your trademark—a brilliant whimsical originality. You may recall that I told you myself that your critical reviews of Australian writing were incomparably penetrating and simply *had to be published.* (By the way—I was very glad to see that the Brent of Bin Bin books were being reprinted at last. Have got them as they came out from library here.) ...

Now, if I have to go south I shall give you plenty of warning, Miles, but if you happened to go away for months—would you let me know? Just a line. Thanks for the last batch of papers. ...

Love from
Jean D

Randwick
17/12/52

Dear Miss Franklin

It's twenty past ten and I've just finished *My Brilliant Career* and I want to tell you how it delighted me, how readable it is, and how honestly it loves Australia.

My last year (last year) of teaching was with values like the M'Swats', and how I enjoyed to see them set down once and for all so that I could look at them steadily. ...

Pixie O'Harris mentioned some weeks back you were ill. I hope that's not so, now. Hope it's never so. Don't ever let it be so! 'It's all in the moind,' you know—or some of it is, and you must write lots more for Australians and not waste time shennanygan (why aren't we taught to spell words we use?) on the sick-bed.

I think *MBC* is your saddest book that I know, and your happiest; *Career Goes Bung* funniest and most educationalest; *All that Swagger* your bravest.

Please keep publishing. Please bring out the plays.

Sincerely
Ray Mathew

If I don't post this immediately courage will leave me.

9 'IF I LIVE': 1953-54

'My book is coming along if I live and can keep plugging.'

MILES FRANKLIN TO JOHN KINMONT MOIR,
12 OCTOBER 1953 (JKMC)

'I will subscribe to Overland *if I live.'*

MILES FRANKLIN TO MARJORIE PIZER HOLBURN,
? SEPTEMBER 1954 (MHP)

By 1953 it was evident that Miles was failing physically. But she clung to her independence. When friends wondered about a literary pension, she was offended. (She was in fact saving for the Miles Franklin Award, her last and best secret.) It was an increasing struggle to maintain the house at Carlton—'my humpy'—and Miles never ceased to lament the lot of Australian women, 'wood and water joeys' all. Fortunately there were good friends close by, Delys and Arthur Cross especially, who brought 'heaps of food'. Visitors included Jean Devanny (they went to the Show), Rex Ingamells, Katharine Susannah Prichard (one of the many who urged Miles to autobiography), and Jean Campbell, a new congenial. The loss of others seemed insupportable: two of Miles's oldest associates died in Melbourne in 1953, Elsie Belle Champion who first wrote to her in 1902, and Kate Baker, whom she met with Joseph Furphy in 1904. Miles had her say on the coronation, governors-general, the French, and Eisenhower. As usual book news absorbed most attention, as when J K Moir acquired Catherine Spence's birthday album, a rare and nostalgic item. By year's end, she was satisfied with the manuscript of what became *Laughter, Not for a Cage*. In search of a publisher, she turned first to Florence James in London.

Aged seventy-four, though now quite weak, she was resolute, pursuing publishers for *Laughter*, working on her 'autobiography', and helping other writers, everlastingly uninhibited in the expression of her opinions. A triumphant Royal tour in the early part of the year was to her the 're-garrisoning' of Australia; and she deplored the Petrov affair, the spy scandal which ensured the electoral defeat of ALP leader Dr Evatt in May 1954 and cast Australian politics in a conservative mould for nearly twenty years. Mid-June 1954, despite family lore that 'women don't die of hearts', she suffered a heart attack. Her last poignant letters are written from Beecroft, a northern Sydney suburb, where she was cared for by relatives. She died shortly after hospitalisation at Drummoyne on 19 September 1954, of coronary occlusion, a month or so before what would have been her seventy-fifth birthday. In accordance with her wishes, she was cremated and her ashes were scattered over Jounama Creek, Talbingo.

Miles Franklin never gave in. But by this time she was apt to make the conditional response—sad, sprightly, or simply defiant—'if I live'. Happily, she remained productive virtually until the end. *Laughter, Not for a Cage*, on the novel in Australia, appeared in 1956, and the classic *Childhood at Brindabella* in 1963. Two outstanding 'Brent' titles also appeared posthumously, under the A & R imprint. There would be more to come from a variety of manuscripts in the Franklin Papers. And still there were the letters. There can be no doubt that Miles Franklin became part of the literature of her country. Maybe she could have done so on the basis of her letters alone.

Line drawing of Miles Franklin by Louis Kahan Meanjin, *1965 (courtesy Louis Kahan)*

9.1   To Tom Ronan, Katherine, Northern Territory
Source: FP 44

26 Grey St
Carlton NSW
Feb 13 53

Dear Tom Ronan

Your letter of Oct last touched off a lot of interesting matters
if only we were near enough for a yarn. What you said of H L
setting a sad note for Australian writers hits the nail on the
head. It also shows the power of the man's art of communic-
tion. It was E J Brady who showed me that it [words illegible]
was artificial the one evening I saw him when I was a girl.
Shows how elders influence youngsters if the older has the key
and the youngster a listening heart or brain.

   Aus has got past the 'bush' stage and all the world has been
de-ruralised, as also the privileged classes have been deleisured
in the current disturbed ant-bed state. . . .

   So you have a wife and family since that wet night we had
a yarn here. That is a big achievement and puts you on a firm
basis.

   This week I heard a reading at the Fellowship of *Granite
Peak* a play by Betty Roland that was commended in the Jubilee
Play Comp. It is set in the Territory 150 miles from Alice
Springs. You would be better able to check on the local color,
and character than I. I did not note any glaring error like Jon
Cleary's *dark-eyed* sheep. . . .

   I'd love to go North but alas, expect it is a castle in the air.
Children I love, tho I'm not now strong enough for their perpetual mobility; but snakes, horrors! I'd keep on your heels like
any eager kelpie for fear of meeting one.

   Here is what I really wrote for. You say you have offered
a publisher the right to subedit your MS to their own liking.
Now, I thoroughly agree that 162 000 words is a bit extravagant for these days of paper shortage (tho I'll send you a review
of an American, longer), and as W B Griffin used to say, the
wisest man who ever lived cd write all he knew on a post card.

We can learn a lot by such shenannikins if we don't lose our sense of direction. So, let the publisher cut your MS by half but the point is don't consent without holding the right finally to agree or not to what has been done. Hold on to your essential self, swing to your inner pole of integrity in what you have to tell the world. There is a brazen and mistaken notion nowadays that the writer can be done away with, and any hack who can get his ideas botch them up for mass consumption. ...

Greetings to your wife and all good wishes from

[unsigned]

9.2 From Clem Christesen, Melbourne
Source: MA

27 March 1953

My dear Miles

Very many thanks for your note of March 24, and enclosure. Your continued support of *Meanjin* is tremendously appreciated. If you would permit me, I'd like to send you complimentary copies of the journal in future—as I do to Hugh McCrae, Louis Lavater, Harry Green and a few other stalwarts. It is a very little thing to offer, and we always have a few spare copies. So I am taking the liberty of returning your subscription herewith. If you should inherit a fortune later, you might care to make a substantial donation to our Sustaining Fund! ...

K S P is in Melbourne at present, and she was given an 'evening' last Saturday. Vance Palmer is in hospital, heart attack again. Judah Waten is very ill. Dymphna writes regularly. I hope to publish her 'Paris Journal' in the autumn issue.

Kindest regards.

Sincerely yours
C B Christesen

.

Carlton
Ap 2 53

Dear Clem

Please keep this pound. McCrae and Lavater are poets, Green
a University man. I have no such claims to consideration, and
have enough for a crust for a few years if we don't wake up
some morning to discover the pound has been wiped out and
we have to start from scratch. (All right for those of working
age, but a frightening prospect to some of the rest of us.) I'll
compromise. If I hadn't lost my purse I had intended sending
25/– to include an extra copy, which I'm needing to hurl at
a London publisher at whom I'm animadverting. If you can
spare me an extra that will reduce your receipts out of the
pound, and you need every penny you can get. . . .

Your news about Vance has upset me. I hope he is cherishing
himself and being cherished. We can't spare him. I have been
anxious about him since he mentioned when he was over that
he had had a coronary. They are dangerous things for men to
play around with but I understand that they can now be
dispersed.

Please, *please* keep the pound . . . .

Best wishes
Miles

Carlton
Ap 28 53

Dearest Dymphna

At last I'm typing you a note and I must just start up like a hare
about it as I can't remember when or what I wrote to you last.
I wonder if France is any more reconciled to Eisenhower. I'm
not to our new G-G, Slim, an old warcock, and I don't like his
bossy military statements, nor the look of him. A mild old dear
like Gowrie is much preferable. I hope your novel has continued
to go well. I am awaiting *SS* with excitement. I hear that the
paged proof copies are around the book stores. The books that
the lending libraries bind and reap a harvest ahead of the
booksellers without the expense of buying a copy.

Now for your letter of Mar 1. I'm also all agog for *Caddie*,
especially for your introduction. Your remarks about the unpopularity of Americans in Paris recalls the story of my dear
Editha Phelps of the unpopularity of the English 50 years ago
over the Boer war. . . .

I have sent your article in *Meanjin* to Sir Stanley Unwin.
You brave little darling about this French fight over Faites vos
Jeux. Le greatest Australian writer did not worry me as I am
intimate with the prefaces and *réclame* accorded Paul Wenz's
very simple stories, and I noted in the broadcast interview that
the interviewer went no deeper than our lesser reviewers here,
wh of course cd have been due to it being a broadcast affair.
And I am not at all surprised that they have behaved as they
have done in cutting the book and disregarding the contract.
I know the French, not in literature but in business, and a man
who knew them intimately and fought and bled with them said
they simply could not help ratting if it suited them, couldn't
indeed see that it was ratting according to our standards. What
has astonished me is that the edition has been withdrawn and
destroyed by court order. . . .

Town like Alice was the book the Queen was reading to learn about Australia before her postponed trip. Everyone is hankering for Neville's new book about Australia 30 years hence with the Q plump, and Menzies and Caldwell 80, still alive and playing chess together and bickering, and the Queen coming out here. Why! Inky was suspected because he said after the Statute of Westminster she was Q of Australia, and he advised her to come and live at Alice Springs. The irony and the grotesque quirks of time! People who never read a book are awaiting this last one. . . .

Jean Devanny has been down from Townsville, brought MS of her autobiography. It is inchoate. She does not realise the work it will mean to lick it into shape. She stayed a week with me. 5 years ago we went to Sydney Royal together so we went again. A great day. She said when she went to the show she wanted to see everything, and as I know every nook of it and love it that suited me. She cried crack first. I took her through the Hall of Industry and said there is A and R's stall. A fine display, mostly of course dictionaries and general books—they cd not take all the shop to a show. Only two novelists on display, two high shelves that caught the eye splendidly, one a line of Idriess, the other of Timms. Jean bowled up and rapped out 'It is disgraceful, a great firm like this displaying nothing but such trash as that!' The man, whom I don't know, got snakeheaded at once and said as roughly as a police sergeant, 'What nonsense you talk Madam, the concensus of all the editors and critics for 20 years is that they are the 2 greatest writers in Australia.' !!!! Glowry and Glammer be! I hear they are wondering whom they will get to replace these two money spinners. None on the horizon.

Kylie Tennant is the big picture on front of ABC weekly this week instead of a broadcast star musician or actor. That's fame. C Morrisby twittered the talk on 'Authors I have known'. I have not read her new novel. I hope it is really good. We've had gloriously warm days: it was 86 plus yesterday, warmest day since Nov. This compensates for the summer freezes. The FAW has dwindled to nothing. As Pixie O'H says, there are 5 morons to one writer on the Exec. Only real names you and Eleanor Dark. . . .

[unsigned]

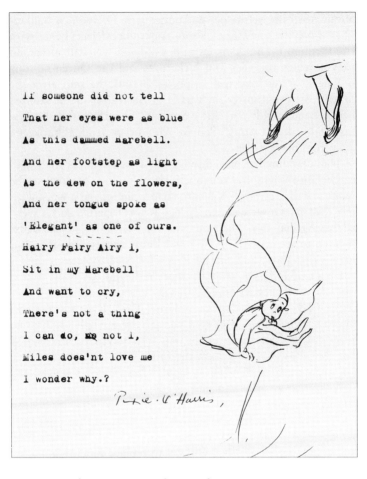

If someone did not tell
That her eyes were as blue
As this damned harebell.
And her footstep as light
As the dew on the flowers,
And her tongue spoke as
'Elegant' as one of ours.
Hairy Fairy Airy I,
Sit in my Harebell
And want to cry,
There's not a thing
I can do, no not I,
Miles does'nt love me
I wonder why.?

Pixie O'Harris,

'The Disappointed Fairy' by Pixie O'Harrris
(courtesy Pixie O'Harris estate, ML)

Carlton
May 3 1953

My dear K B–O B E

I hear that you have had your birthday and here I'm all behind
again. Many, many good wishes now for the next one in 1954.
I had this little note ready to send you for Christmas and did
not get round to it as my strength won't stretch to do things
these days. I am not made of such good material as you, apparently. I thought your birthday was in May and now I hear it's
gone in April.

I hope you are comfortable and keeping warm. If you have
a sweet tooth will you please get for yourself a big box of
chocolates on my behalf—those nice ones with the soft insides.
And you must eat them all yourself, or of course anything else
you may prefer, so long as it is in the line of self-indulgence,
not anything to do for Australian literature. Australian literature
is growing up now and beginning to fancy itself. I have just read
Lucinda Brayford by Martin Boyd, like the women of the '80s
he is divided between England and Australia.

My love and renewed good wishes
[unsigned]

9.6   *To E H Burgmann, Canberra*
Source: FP 27

Carlton
May 24 1953

Dear Friend

Thank you so much for the Christmas greeting from you and
Mrs Burgmann, and especially for the message which you wrote
in the coronation brochure. It is most valuable to have for

reference. But what a lot of patient work and knowledge you have put into it—seems a waste of your clear wide-seeing wise mind, when some of the pedants would have been less wasted on it. Better than the information was your comment in *Southern Churchman* to the effect that we could now put all thoughts of the coronation away from us for another fifty years. Such a charming and sensible way of wishing the Queen long life! In fifty years she will still be only at the beginning of the seventies, while we, sad thought, shall have left this entrancingly interesting life and globe—where? what? why?

The poor young Queen, loaded up like a living icon in a glass cage with all those gew-gaws and make-believe—a puppet for the Mountbattens. She can be used dangerously when you note the mushy sentimentality about a young woman so advertised and presented (*groomed*, the movie magnate's term) has on Mr Menzies, for instance. He positively drools. And those silly old prelates, each vying for even a walking-on part in the show, carrying a spur or a sword or a scent-pot! And the Arch-bishop acting God, yet he was terrified of the red dean with his crook and his smile and his peaceful statements, and strove to discredit him.

As they say in America, France still has the fashions for women and the British have the coronation. It is a tourist circus with the royal family the most finished performers before the camera in the world. None to approach them in soft charm of action. They have ceaseless practice from the cradle to the grave, assured, free from the worry and uncertainty and rivalry of unsubsidized practitioners. At anyrate it is a relief to see Elizabeth so enjoying her youth and exalted position, and the Duke a handsome consort. It is to be hoped he doesn't go off the rails light-o'-loving or die and leave her like poor brave old Queen Victoria to bear the burden alone. I regret to be the only one out of step, but such infinitesimal intelligence as I have refuses to be satisfied.

Still, what can we put in its place that would be better?. . . .

I enclose 10/- —my subscription to the *S Churchman*. I suppose I shd send it to the editor, but you are my sole link with the Church. It is my fault, I admit, but it has nothing for me—only you.

With every good wish for you and your family and my abiding affection,

[unsigned]

Carlton
July 31 1953

My dearest Dymphna, As I returned from posting my last letter to you, the telephone was ringing, and it was Caddie wanting to come to see me. A thing is no sooner said than done with her so I made a day a week ahead and there she was, punctual, plump and pleasant. I wasn't what she expected but she got used to me after a bit and took me on your word. There was never another person like you for cleverness, goodness etc, etc, and she therefore now seems to regard me as a sort of stuffed owl to be carefully set on the mantel and kept from the moths. Today she has just now departed after a second visit. She comes in time for lunch and leaves after afternoon tea. The real suburban housewife's visit. What I need is you, as my sense of humor is running away wasting. She is so matter-of-fact, no jokes with her. . . . I can help her in the anonymity, if she doesn't betray herself, or be betrayed by those near her, who may lose their heads and want to be in the limelight. A different matter shd she be slated.

She has sent you the first two reviews from *S.Sun* and *Telegraph*. The *Telegraph* very mild, and evidently the *Sun* has expanded a cable message by slabs from the book itself.

One of my friends, a politico, going on the *Sun* review, says it will be a bonanza for the interests who want to extend the swilling hours. We shall see. Poor Caddie is all taut expecting a siege from all quarters. I try to steady her apprehensions by saying she might like Smarty, Smarty, gave a party and all who wd be at it wd be dirty Arty. The husband, I understand, does not love the book, but I assured her that in Aus no families have any affinity with writers in their own brood unless they are of the Idriess and Timms variety of success plus innocuity—if there is such a word. '*You can't go home, again.*' She is worrying what to do shd she be asked—by *Truth* say, for an exclusive story. I have told her to accept no (probable) offers whatever. To say she will consider any and then write to you. It is easily done in days of air mail. Your word is that of the Medes and Persians. . . .

Re the Rosenburgs: Cardinal Mannix sent a message of his own, and the six protestant churches joined in sending a stirring protest. ArchB Mowll was abroad at the coronation but his deputy Hilliard signed in his stead. And lately there was a Rev McIntyre here from America, who says that in USA the Protestant Churches are a hot-bed of communism, and he began to say that it was the same here. He got it in the neck. I'm glad to say the Methodists cancelled his Sunday afternoon address at the Lyceum because of his attitude. . . .

Caddie is delightful about your reviews. She wd do battle and mayhem with any who do not fully appreciate you. She was shocked by the *DT*. I said I wish they had written longer and more virulently, as they merely criticise themselves, and I like people to be true to their labels.

She is most amusing about the jacket. Examines it minutely and says the picture of the girl is not exactly like her—could innocence of dustcovers go further!

Went to the Oliver lectures on K S P. He ranks her very high—third best Aus novelist, second only to Furphy, perhaps ahead of H H R. Then he lit into her—grammar and melodrama as severely as Marjory B once did me only he ranked K S P high and M B did not rank me at all; she merely tried to flatten me. . . .

Poor Caddie is so innocent that she asked me how much she'd have to pay the artist for the jacket picture. Then she wanted to know will she get her percentage on the full price of the book or only on what the bookseller gives. Ah, said I, the publisher hopes to whittle us down to the limited price but for the present it is on the retail price.

Well my dear, bless you and take care of yourself and keep up the good work.

ever your loving
[unsigned]

Carlton
Aug 24 1953

Dear Myrtle Rose

What an enchanting idea to go to you, if only I cd manage it! I long to see that country and never was there such an opportunity, but I don't feel able for such a trip. Everything is too much effort for me.

I deferred replying to yr letter till after Dame Mary's birthday party (88) at the Lyceum Club where we had that happy tea party with you. Well, it was a nice night and there were a lot there. Gavin Casey and Pixie O'Harris were the masters of ceremonies. It was all nice and informal. Gavin read the letters of congratulation from those who couldn't be present. Pixie called on one or two to say something, just from the floor. Dame Mary made a grand little speech in response and read a beautiful poem of her own on war, which I had not previously heard. She got many flowers, of course. A woman sang two of Henry Lawson's poems set to music by Varney Monk. I was called on to say something. I did, and then Dame Mary insisted on telling a yarn about me. Then a Henrietta Granville rose up and said no one had asked her to make a speech but she was going to. She looked younger than Dame Mary or I and spoke firmly and capably and then they told me she is 92. It was wonderful. I had never heard of her before. They say she lives alone and looks after herself.

Among those at the party were Kylie Tennant whom I had not seen for years. Her last book is great, they tell me. I have not had it yet. I have not seen Marie or Mrs Buchanan for ages. Was hoping they might be at the party.

Jean tells me she has cut 100,000 words out of her typescript. Yes, it is very heartrending to have one's work hanging about and getting stale and those we want to see it passing away. I can understand that you could not bear to look at the attenuated story but you must expect shocks when you see it in print, which perhaps you could have forestalled. . . .

Do you know that birthday book got out by the Spences long ago? Mr Moir has lately acquired Helen Spence's own copy and Mr Moir sent it to me to look at as I knew so many of the people in USA whose names were written in it. It has some lovely photographs of Adelaide in it. There wd be a copy in the Archives I suppose. . . .

How I wish I cd fly across to you and come back with you after a look at the people in Perth but don't feel strong enough.

Hoping you will really come on here and let us see you. A joyous welcome awaits you.

With love
[unsigned]

9.9 *From David Martin, Boronia, Victoria*
Source: FP 41

13 IX 1953

Dear Miles

Your letter warmed my heart. I was delighted by your good *opinion* of my poems, but more by your personal echo. Dame Mary and you had the same idea: she, too, wants to get hold of 'From Life' for Christmas cards. It seems a wonderful way for my poems to go to the people whose friendship and knowledge I value. Our society is split from top to bottom—and, as you know, I am not one to believe in spanning a chasm with a rose bush—but there is still—and always will and shall be— a comma on language and good feeling between people who love people.

I have lately finished a major work on which I began to toil when we last met. A narrative poem of nearly 3,000 lines. God alone (and perhaps not God) knows how or whether it will or can be published. However, Ned Kelly said 'Such is Life' when they put the noose round his neck, and I am no less a realist than he was, I hope.

Now I am reading a book that is fascinating to me, and would like, if you will, to tell me more about the author, you are almost bound to know him, or about him. Randolph Bedford. The book is an auto-biography, *Naught to Thirty Three*. He must have been a splendid fellow, and he is a splendid writer. A great-hearted Australian patriot. His book has awakened in me the old thirst of seeing more of this plain and mysterious continent. . . .

A mate of mine, Stephen Murray-Smith, a member of the Realist Writers Group in Victoria and a stalwart fighter for Peace, will be in Sydney at the end of this month for the great Convention against war. He very much desires to meet you, being an erudite admirer of your work. I shall tell him not to hesitate, but to ring you. He is a man who deserves respect. . . .

O'Dowd is dead. Nettie Palmer introduced me to him at his home about a year ago, but O'Dowd took hardly any notice of me, for which one cannot blame him. He did not, I think, realise that he was meeting a sort of poet. Fortunately Nettie has now all the material he could give her and she will do her usual thorough going job of a biography. I can appreciate O'Dowd in flashes, though there is an aristocratic touch about his democratic writing—maybe his classicism—which I can't assimilate. I don't know his work well enough, anyhow. Mary Gilmore wrote me that, in his day, he opened a window for many people, and I can well believe it. A Whitmanite, one of the real Australian Whitmanites. He has very moving letters from Whitman. Perhaps in the difference of American and Australian development since Whitman's day can be found the reason for O'Dowd's own latter-day silence and obvious disillusion. Australia needed, perhaps, a more rough and ready singer, or rather a man who could stick by the people even in its unheroic moods. . . .

I am becoming garrulous. Just the domestic news: We are well, though we all had 'the wog'. Jan and Richenda threw theirs off only slowly, but are well now. Richenda's arms are as strong upon mine, as ever. She still teaches, and I think the most advanced Lady's College has retrogressed since the days when H H Richardson went to the Methos. Or was it the Presbyterians she went to? Richenda doesn't care much for a goodly portion of her pupils. Spoiled, un-Australian upper class brats, reflecting already in their ways the demoralisation of their upper class homes, where money is the yard stick. Money plus Little Lord Jesus. You know.

And we hope you are well and determined. We are looking forward to seeing you, and I with hopes that it won't be long delayed.

Greetings!
David

9.10 From Jean Devanny, Townsville, Queensland
Source: FP 32

West End
1/10/53

Dear Miles—Your letter just arrived. Now, why not just pitch a few things into a bag and fly up here right now. The weather is now glorious, after a spell of horrible wind. What you need is a complete change. Don't think of anything, just drop a note to Del saying you are coming and take the first plane seat available. There should be plenty now that the tourist season is over. When I think of your melancholy, with rain and wind and here the sun is glorious, my little house is surrounded with sparkling shining foliage. Talk of shadows, of death's mean hand: Miles, don't let anything stop you. I am just over a rotten spell of cold in the head myself and need a few days on the island. *Do come.* . . . No nonsense: stay as long as you like. Never mind about books or anything. Or you could bring your manuscript if you liked. Don't bother about the typewriter. You can use mine because I am not using it now. . . .

I won't bother to deal with anything else now. I want to get this away by midday mail. *Miles come.* It will be the making of you, to get out of that cold melancholy house. This is the best time of year. The sun will eat into your bones and rebuild you. I am sweating, at eleven in the morning.

Jean

Carlton
Oct 3 53

Jean dear

What a child of impulse, you are, but all the same it is nice to know you have asked me. I'll send Hal some USA papers which may interest him.

No, no 'Nanette'. I must sit here and get that book finished or I cd not be anything but uneasy even in your paradise. Another three weeks would see me through only I have to break off to lecture to 300 students and teachers at one of the colleges. That will take fully a week out of me what with preparation, doing the deed and recovering. Then I have to tackle the dreary hardship of getting a publisher.

If I cd pick a time to do what I'd like my dream would be to clear out when the thing was published and let the pettifoggers pettifog in my absence. It wd be fun if we cd get them out as twins and then disappear together. What is most likely that we *shan't get them* out as twins.

Katharine came up from Victoria for the Peace and War conference. It was well attended I believe. Dal, Col Shep and I went on the last night, a big rally at the Leichardt stadium. We were behind the speakers high up and cd not hear without strain and I had spent my youth in such boredom that I did not strain too greatly. I saw K S P sitting down near the platform. Both Dal and the Col were dead tired and I always am so we escaped early and did not meet anyone. The hall was well filled and they got over £700 in the appeal for expenses. Del went to all sessions so did not come to see me this week, also they have colds. She was thrilled and said the expenses came in well.

I had to go in to take Jean Campbell to lunch—she was FAW delegate from Melb. That made it a long day.

I am keeping away from A and R till I get this finished so if you get impatient about the result of your MSS you can write to her direct. I told her to communicate with you direct when I left the parcel.

Del will tell you my news not that there is any.

With love dear and thanking you but I must sit right here in my own lair for this job.

[unsigned]

9.12 *To John Kinmont Moir, Melbourne*
Source: JKMC

Carlton
October 17 1953

Dear J K

I've fished up one of yr letters to begin, out of the large boxful of lately-come. Others have retreated to Bluebeard cupboards and will be found again some day. I can't keep up.

I heard that K B had gone, on the air, a short crude notice and never a line in any Sydney newspaper that I have seen. You speak as if it was some final illness took her off. Did she not sink gently with age weakness? I hope she had no pain. I felt sad at her passing. There can be only a few people around Perth, including his daughter and daughter-in-law, that now live, who knew Furphy. I know of no other here except N Lindsay.

Tom Moore's anthology seems to be a success. There is another by Marjory Pizer of old Ballads, looks good too. My book is coming along if I live and can keep plugging. I get so very few hours per week to finish it. For example two weeks ago two days went in the death of my dear little neighbor next door. Her daughter came in at dawn to say her mother had just gone. It was a great shock as she had promised a day earlier if she were the one to find me dead that she wd let none see me; and she had the phone too and said if I cd crawl to that and let her know she wd be in any minute. It is a great gap without her. Then Katharine Prichard came, and one must see a friend whom one may never see again, then Jean Campbell came, and that was a great pleasure that I couldn't miss. There have been numbers of others, and last night the Howarths had a lovely party for Prof M Miller at which I was present. I had been so busy trying to get a bit done that I did not eat much all day knowing that the Howarths always prepare a rich banquet. I had such a pain around my heart that I never touched anything but a teaspoon of brandy and that did not restore me. I was very dull and uncomfortable but managed to carry on. Prof M is a dear, and you will get the list of all who were present as we signed on purpose. Then he and I walked home together to his hotel near my station and when I was on the train I remembered I had had nothing to eat, and probably it was wind. So when I got home I had a cup of tea and two slices of bread and there was no more pain and I went to bed and was perfectly comfortable all night except that I regretted that I hadn't had some of the beautiful food—there were even mushroom patties!!!

I am to have lunch with Prof Miller and Beatrice Davis next Tues.

The Spence diary would not have come from Mary Fullerton. They had no connection with her. If it was not from some member of the family it could have been from Alice Henry, who worshipped Miss Spence, but I think A H would have sent it to me with various other treasures like the autographed copy of B O'Dowd's poems and some of the tiny A G S *Bookfellows*. . . .

Every good wish, & *yes* you can do something for me—take care of yourself—have a rest.

Yrs affectionately
M F

Carlton
October 29 1953

My dearest Mabel

I have two letters from you to answer, the last written on Oct 8. I am glad you were having a day's rest and saw a play. Constant work at our age is not only terrifically wearying but so deadening. One needs a little relief. . . .

I am also sending you a little book of poems. I think you will like some of them I do. It is by a new Australian—Hungarian by birth, German mother tongue though he knows many languages. His wife is an Englishwoman of Quaker persuasion.

You ask me what I think of the story or something that looks like that but I can't make out what it is nor where you live exactly. After much trouble and labor I can manage to guess what a good deal of your letter means but not any proper names. You mention a Lady someone—I don't know who or what. I'm sorry to keep nagging about your writing, but it always looks to me as if you sat down for hours and curled and crooked it to make it illegible. Strange hand for such a noble straightforward person.

Fountains Abbey is one of the places I have always longed to see. I hate life being such a short fleeting thing, there is time for little in it except scratching for a living for most of us, yet those who have wealth and complete leisure spend it in trying to find things which kill time.

I am particularly upset tonight because I have just read in a Melbourne paper that Elsie Belle Champion died on Oct 20. It does not say of what. Old age I suppose as she was very old but I had such a nice letter from her a little while ago with no hint of illness or decay. She worked until January last. I knew her for forty nine and a half years. When the other members of the family went they always sent me a telegram or an airmail letter, but Aileen did not inform me this time. She looked frailer than Mrs Champion so perhaps did not feel up to it. They were such an attached family. Aileen will be desolate now. Kate Baker also went a week or two ago. You know how death upsets me. There is no use in trying to comfort me. I just suffer anguish at each loss and feel it a mortal blow. . . .

There is a new anthology of Australian ballads out which contains some of Mary's. I have not seen which yet as it is nearly a pound—books are terribly dear, no wonder people can't buy many of them. The people with the money are not the kind who buy poetry: they prefer grog or going to the races. Well, at anyrate it does not look as if I'm going to starve for want of food. I [words illegible] is a chef at one of the colleges and at the end of the cooking week they have to dispose of what food is left over. My share tonight is six eggs, a bream fish, some fowl fried in batter, 2 loaves of smoking hot bread, a cinnamon loaf, a tumbler of lemon butter, a big Apple Dutch tart, short-bread biscuits and you should see the dozen jam puff tarts and tomorrow they are coming with a chook and salad. Sometimes it is soups and stews as well as bread and Madeira cake and jam rolls. . . .

I wish I could see you but know I never shall again. Men have made a mess of the world with their belligerence and lust.

Ever your loving
[unsigned]

9.14 *To Henrietta Drake-Brockman, Perth*
Source: FP 33

Carlton
Nov 13 1953

Henrietta me darlint, me darlint

I send you one of my American handkerchiefs that I've been treasuring for years. Its funny hem and those little fat leaves are supposed to make it a swell. So tribute to the fair swell. I had our sweet Beatrice for a night and she tells me you are full to the gunwale with family affairs for Christmas. So be happy, and don't dare write to me or anything till you are back in line again. Enjoy it all to the fullest.

Saw Geoff Burgoyne at the Eng Ass dinner—we were Beatrice's guests. Met the new editor of *SMH* and liked him.

Two nights ago two of the gentlemen of my harem took me to dinner and to a church, the lure being a Hungarian Jew from mid-Europe who is now a Presbyterian parson at Thirroul on S Coast. He spoke at some Dowling's kirk which is the oldest kirk in Sydney. The Thirroul gentleman's subject was religious drama in Australia. Religious drama bores me to the vitals but he had the right view that it must be Australian religious drama, that we must not look to Europe for our plays. Also in his drama group he has put on a play by Dymphna both in Newcastle and Thirroul. The young folk want to start a group where he spoke. He said the Greek pre-Christian great plays were really religious dramas and he went on to say we must look to the Aborigines and their myths for a similar kind of thing. And then he got most enthusiastic about a book, a lovely, lovely book, he thought it cost a pound, but it was really worth it, it was such a lovely book, about Aboriginal legends, that they could start with as plays, and it was the Langloh Parker legends. No one knew anything about them. So I stepped into the picture then and said they were brought to light again by you and you had a book of Aus plays coming out that they could work on as soon as they cut their teeth. It is good to have plays in print. . . .

By the way, when you come into circulation again I'd like to know if your radio plays in Perth are on their own bat, or are they chosen by Les Rees and the hierarchy here? Someone has suggested to me that my play shd be cut down to an hour for radio. I thought perhaps you could get hold of a radio script of an hour play, only as a loan, as a model—for Miles not Molly.

I have finished my essay at last, and after Christmas must see about publication. I'm winded at present, and so is every one else. I go to my aunt for Christmas dinner—she is 86 and then to my Uncle, 91, for the rest of the day. He has just come down from the western plains and the grasshoppers to be with his daughter for the season. It is a regular routine, and very precious, because it can't last much longer for any of us, and we slightly younger ones may give out first. You never can tell.

I'm wondering if you had any oil shares. If it booms and you get very rich I'll be able to go about saying you were my washerwoman once. How is your dear mother?

And now a heartful of love and good wishes to you and each member of the family, and happy Christmas, and hoping to hear from you before the N Year has too long a beard.

[unsigned]

9.15 To Jean Campbell, Melbourne
Source: FP 44

Carlton
Nov 27 53

Dear Jean

I've been struggling like a fly in tar ever since your letter came to get a moment to reply. First of all to acknowledge safe re- turn of play *Models for Molly* and glad you liked it, and very good of you to have read it. I think, too, it wd go on the air if *abridged*, but the snag is that some lout of a reader calling himself an actor would want to leave out everything except himself.

I'm sorry I can't make out the name of your novel—looks like (see [word illegible]). Of course I don't know your work but don't think he wd yet know you had spoken to someone with an idea later than the Ark. In days before the Russian scare I've had publishers flattering me and for no known reason suddenly turn like enemies. They are a strange breed of cattle— the commercial ones. If they don't think a thing will be a best- seller they daren't touch it these days, and make many mistakes even in that category.

Confidential. Dymphna Cusack was turned down for every- thing that she took overseas and had published, even *Caddie* was refused, and she was treated like you in London and that's why she changed from H-mann to Constable. Would you like to send your manuscript overseas? D's collaborator is a scout for Constable, and would read it. I could put you in touch. Keep on going. Don't give in till you've been laid out with a wet fish across your face or something like that. It's a chancey business and there is no use in being sensitive. Go to!

No time for more but thanks and affection
[unsigned]

9.16 From Katharine Susannah Prichard, Ainslie, Australian Capital Territory
Source: FP 21

Dec 2 1953

Miles darling

Safely arrived, & chewing over my lovely time with you! Such a treat just to hear you talk. I do love the wit & play of your so original mind. Nobody makes me laugh so much. And I've had Dodie & Ric chortling over some of your bits & pieces—so delightfully Miles, gay, intrepid & unique!

Only hope you weren't too tired by my being there, & having things to do about meals—and so on. Hate to think of having impeded your work, or destrained on your time. Although, those days with you will always be a precious memory for me. ...

Quite warm here to-day, which pleases me; feel as if I'd never get this last winter out of my bones. Do wish you cd have come for a visit while I'm in Canberra. The place itself is such a smug, un-Australian version of all that it ought to be. Only the blue divine mountains, & the gums still undisturbed on Mt Ainslie behind us, assuring me that this is still Australia. Out & away from the neat suburbs & stucco of official buildings there remain the rounded sunburnt hills, & the Molonglo—by its very name, though shrouded in willows, reminds us of the earth and a tradition deeper than the fantasy of a federal city here. The earth & the tradition are part of us, belong, at least—though filched from the aborigines.

Love to you—my dear, incomparable Miles—and thank you again for so much stimulus—and the happiness of being with you,

Katharine

The little bottle of skin perfume is to refresh you on hot days— & make you think of me.   K S.

9.17   To Ethel Ruby Bridle, Tumut, New South Wales
Source: FP 47

Carlton
Feb 10 1954

My dearest Ethel

I hope you are not anxious about the well-being of those lovely photos. They are carefully packed ready for return as soon as I get to the post office to register them. . . . The photo of you is just what I wanted, and it is a pet. What on earth age were you on it, and weren't you dressed as a bridesmaid—and to whom? I showed it to Pixie O'Harris yesterday and also another artist and Myrtle White, the author of *No Roads Go By.* We went to see the Archibald exhibits in company. You won all hearts. You wonder what I wanted it for. Well, Pixie and a publisher are chivying me into writing my autobiography and I have weakened sufficiently to start on the first ten years of my life—the memories of a completely happy childhood in segregated and unique circumstances of days that are wiped away in progress. And you come in as you took me to the only session of Sunday school I ever attended, when I was put outside for the duration with some dirty boy named Willie. I think he was a moron or an outlaw. You also took me to the Sunday School pic-nic where a big rough girl grabbed my pint pot and said it was hers. . . .

I long to see you but know what an impossible effort it is for us both to get about.

[unsigned]

9.18   To P R Stephensen, Melbourne
Source: FP 28

Carlton
Feb 17 54

Dear P R

Koo-koo-koo-ha-ha-haa! for kookaburras versus satyrs. An appetising mouthful! The Social-literary-historical angle is vividly
interesting to me because it was my period before I reached
prisoner of Chillon [word illegible] where I am now immured.
More interesting and reviving are the flashes of the old—or
rather young—'Inky' who similarly retreated from London a few
months before me. He is still here, still deeply humorous though
perhaps not so exuberantly, hilariously so. Release him further.
Let him rip. This I trust is a single swallow presaging a flock.

Also plunged into *The Viking*, a major opus indeed. I have had
only scrappy moments to sample so long and impressive achievement, but read with easy avidity. Did you hear Stewart Howard
reviewing it over the air in a session on 2GB sponsored by A and
R? He said he had no admiration for Clune, wished he had never
learned to string one sentence after the other, but he would say
that Stephensen's typewriter was responsible for all the writing
in this case and gave it a boost. Repeated longer in *SMH* and
more adapted to that journal's style.

What has become of that novel that you read in MSS to me
while wearing a grey Ascot topper? You wd now have more
perspective, and, if you retain the zest and verve that was in that
first draft, it should outdo all the other chronicle opera.

I thank you so much for the volume. I have nothing with
which to respond at present.

One grows so balanced with experience that well, one is in
danger of being so poised that he or she stays in that position
statically. This thought occurred to me as I listened to so many
of the royal speeches about the Queen of Australia and our own
Queen of Australia being here. It was considered an almost
subversive doctrine when you pointed out that by the Statute
of W she had become that and that it was a question of England

340

abandoning us because she could do no other. The politicians pontificate a generation or two later what the foreseeing discern in their unstatic days. . . .

I hope Win is well and you are flourishing, ever

[unsigned]

9.19   To Bruce Sutherland, State College, Pennsylvania
Source: FP 44

Carlton
Mar 18 54

Dear Bruce

I much enjoyed your letter of Jan 29 and enclosures. First of all many thanks for the continued *Atlantic Monthly*, which is extravagant of you, but very delightful. I revelled in the article on Jeanne d'Arc. She has been one of my uplifts since as a girl of 15 Mark Twain's version of her came into my hands. He made her come alive and was a revelation after the dull droning of her case in a 'brief history of England', on which, I to that date, had been drug up.

I long to send you books, but seeing their expensiveness and my penury I don't want to duplicate. I am therefore relieved that Colin is not forgetting you, as he has the resources of Angus and Robertson back of him, free of charge. I saw him about a month ago when he was busy confounding some pedant profs (who had gone astray with him), with a Scab Act. Incongruity exhilarates my sense of humor, and the necessity for a Scab Act was a basic fact in the settling of this country, and all those bush activities which are so familiar to me. . . .

I suppose you hear of us only as wasteful descendants of riff raff—which of course we are from one angle—and you'd think that USA was all Rosenburg horrors and Ike acting Hindenburg to McCarthy's Hitler, as one London paper has put it, but last night when I was undergoing my usual insomnia I sent myself when young back across America. Oh, the sweetpeas and opulence of Redlands California, and Los Angeles when Hollywood

341

was a big name on a rough hillside. Then the beauty of Salt Lake City and its Wasatch(?) mountains, then the Rockies with Hanging Lake, to reach which I astonished the guides by hanging on to my horse's tail and making him tow me up as we used to do beyond Canberra. It was a new trick to them. I had been lent a lovely red roan polo pony belonging to some rich lady at the rich hotel. So they thought I sat special and handed me a rifle and insisted that I shoot something. We were riding up the pass where the Shoshone rapids come down, and in them was a little log about the length of two fence posts. I just pulled the trigger and by chance the bullet hit it. I suppose I had previously fired a gun as many as half a dozen times, and at a fixed target. I loathed the repercussion or percussion of the beastly instruments. All my denials were no good after that. I got an offer to go in a circus and the strong man of a vaudeville act proposed to me. Such a nuisance! But how gorgeous were Mt Sopris and the Roaring Fork. Then there came up memories of the rich meals in Wisconsin and Michigan farm houses, rollicking days at Madison University; days driving down the Merrimac and on Long I Sound getting automobiles full of ripe wild grapes in Connecticut, floating down the Missouri on a paddle wheeling, and on L Michigan on the Sitchee Manitou[?]! What a country! & all a going concern. The joy of the Twentieth Century, and trips up the Hudson to Toronto and Quebec, and those Santa Fe crossings. To wake up in the warm dry air and look across the vast plains to blue mountains! Heaven can offer nothing more satisfying and exciting, and the people! All ranks from the rich and cultured down to the workers, everywhere I went, I used to say I had only to present myself and the Americans did all the rest, and adopted me and kept me in cotton wool. If only I had had the qualities to acquire and be on the make what a success I could have been. But I love the beautiful land and its people for ever, and in eternity if there is identity there. . . .

I had hoped for one book to be out this February, promised faithfully for over a year. It is in galley but postponed again to make way for a changed schedule to get out a gift book of the royal corroboree here, and what an orgy of spending it was. Looked at from the angle of power politics I chuckle to note that as an icon Elizabeth outglittered all others. The RCs gave in and whooped too, as they astutely recognised here a bulwark against communism or any other advanced ism. ...

Don't you bother to write me proper letters. Follow my lead in swift rough draft, off-the record yaps—that's the way to keep in touch, and it would be a great refreshment to me to know that I still had friends (so many of my elder ones have gone and are going) in that great land to whom I could speak without reserve, and who wd trust me similarly in return. Don't fear you'll be quoted or taken from context or misrepresented, and my will reads that my papers are to be destroyed and those that are not—those that I allow to remain—are to be sealed-up and not seen for twenty years after my death. ...

My love and good wishes to Doris and you and the girls
[unsigned]

9.20 Draft letter to Helen Heney, Sydney
Source: FP 45

[March 1954?]

Dear Miss Heney

Your article (*SMH* Mar 27/54) was a relief. I shd like to be a member with you in the soc for decent burial of the past. For any mere mortal like this patterson Person to produce such an affronting and offensive repulsive study of the matchless Emily she must be singularly without a sense of humor (I wish I cd rent to her a little of my hilarious joy in the incongruous which is lying idle) for it wd seem to be that she was abnormally eschatologically and this Lesbianism I thought that was *vieux jeu* women now mouldily disintegrating. In the 20s and 30s one could not enjoy one's friendships without this foul aspersion. I'm so glad that you point out that *The Well of Loneliness* terms do not fit Emily's century nor indeed my girlhood in every way and [we] were also well healthily able to live without Freudian 'complexes' of the freudians. As for friends and families destroying letters it cd be nothing more than these people's limitations as that of a case I know a woman destroyed a long correspondence innocent with J Furphy when she was about to be married as her family had thought it very dangerous to correspond even as innocently as the Furphyian way with a married man and when she was about to be married she got rid of the beautiful letters as if putting behind her a life of 'looseness'.

The mere P Person wd seem to be the one who is etc and singularly wanting in a sense of humor so to exhibit her.

I have been go[ing] to tell you for some time how much I enjoyed yr writing in Cam and the later one about the woman st with the blacks. You have a brilliant power to give the inter-acti[on] of character on character. I am always interested in you and your sister because when I was a girl your father was always so kind and encouraging to me.

9.21 Telegram from Dymphna Cusack, London
Source: FP 30

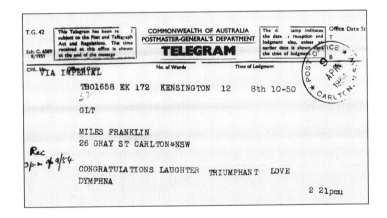

9.22 *To Mary Alice Evatt [Canberra]*
Source: EC

Carlton
Ap 24 54

Dear Mrs Evatt

. . . It would seem that the Lord is on the side of Mr Menzies, first the bonanza of the Queen's visitation, now the spy melodrama. I hope it will not make a farce of the election by reducing it to a shoddy imitation of McCarthy's mighty antics. I was amused at the newsreel last week. That very good take of the Mascot incident was on the screen. Its end with the European migrants raging brought spontaneous laughter from the prosaic souls around me. They had no knowledge of that fury and it was merely funny to them. Just like the loony foreigners! How wonderful if the affair could be conducted on a similarly common-sense level, which we'd like to think of as typically Australian. Never mind about our lacks in the inner life or of high culture, continually dinned in our ears, if only we could behave without fear or hysteria or mere opportunism now. . . .

I hope to hear the Doctor in Hurstville on 6th prox but will have to feel better than I do at present to get there.

With all good wishes and kind regards
Sincerely
Miles Franklin

9.23 *To Dymphna Cusack, London*
Source: FP30

Carlton
May 1 54

Dymphna, my pet

Your gorgeous telegram came in due time and you can guess that I've bunged myself up very efficiently for the present when

I tell you I seemed too far gone for it to matter. Then followed your uplifting letter. You know how it is when we get adverse criticism, we think it may be merited, and that gives the blues, and when our loved friends praise us it is more than sweet, but we wonder if it is merely their affection for us which softens their gaze. But there is always something in your critiques that delights me and reaches a spot or strikes a chord of mutual understanding that is very releasing. So I revel in, 'Indeed it is a celebration, not a criticism.' I have been thinking of it as a toot and a fanfare and a rhapsody but celebration is le mot just. In another letter you told me something N F said of me which pleased me more than almost anything I've ever had. . . .

The Parliamentary Opposition has almost thrown in its bundle, as if an election is an unnecessary expense in face of Menzies' great luck, first the bonanza of the royal visitation and now a Russian spy melodrama in his own backyard. I have no way of knowing the facts but now I wish it had been handled with a little more politesse on the part of our elected representatives. Good manners to the powerful are related to fawning, but good manners to the down-and-out and the hated and the outcast or vanquished foes—well they are *really* good breeding, and how exquisitely they show up in actuality and in records.

Tonight Geoffrey Thomas is having a meeting about his theatre for playwrights 'Australian' and I had my hair done to go but the bus to the station stopped, the taxi has no 'phone and my doc today warned me I must go *very* quietly, and so I can't risk it. I don't want to sprawl out in a public meeting. I am loosing all the ear fleas I can in regard to the Elizabethan theatre becoming a great refuge for the old Shakesperean hams and shysters, unless a hostile eye is kept upon it.

Now back to the essay. Will you please post it to me at your convenience, surface mail. I have made some alterations in the MS since that copy. I don't care if it is not printed in England. At present I cannot do anything. I note what you say about where it should end. It is for you to carry on with the next period. You should rough out your ideas for the vol on the retreat from glory theme before you become too embedded in the life over there. There is a lot of contempt for people who stay six weeks in a place and then write a book on it, but I have always held that in that six weeks you get something that you can never recapture and those differences one sees at first are very stimulating and entertaining. . . .

The only panic angle which may arrest the hydrogen bomb is the delightful suggestion that it can render men sterile at long range. No thought of devastation, or killing women and children wd deter, but *that* possibility is underlying men's thought on it now. If it wd render all Mongol Asia impotent for a generation Mother Earth might be able to cleanse herself somewhat. This is the bomb I bring out when my men friends say that the women, as the way out, will have to unite and withhold their favors unless men abandon war. . . .

[unsigned]

9.24   To Eris O'Brien, Canberra
Source: FP 44

Carlton
May 15 1954

Your Grace

You will have forgotten your letter to me a long time ago now, and may attribute this one to an idiosyncrasy similar to that of Mr Toots, who married Susan Nipper, and delighted to address letters to great men.

I regret that you are farther away, but Canberra after a royal visitation and with the two richest prelatical personalities of the Commonwealth settled there will begin to feel its ripening entity. The wags call me the literary bishop of Monaro, an office no doubt obliterated by your presence unless you graciously allow me the parish of Monaro while you have the National Capital and the whole Commonwealth.

I wanted to thank you for your kind words about cherishing Brent of Bin Bin and for putting it so tactfully—such a relief in contrast to the baiting and badgering I have endured. I hope you re-enjoyed *Ten Creeks Run* which you were about to re-

read on a vacation. Another story is imminent in the series, in which I cannot deny complicity, and I wonder what you will think of it.

I was helped greatly by *The Foundation of Australia* in the first chapter of another kind of toot I have just finished and hope that in Canberra the weight of administration may have slackened so that you can follow that splendid historical volume with others. . . .

I mustn't end with a dirge or a threnody so wish you health and satisfaction and a very long life in your elected way of life.

Yours very sincerely
[unsigned]

9.25 To Magdalen Dalloz, Jacksonville, Florida
Source: FP 41

Carlton
June 2, 1954

My dearest Magdalen

The cuttings about the Fifth Av Easter parade which you mailed on Ap 21 reached me this morning. It is 23 years since you and I enjoyed ourselves in that throng, chief delight of which is that we old friends were together once again after separation by the whole world and the great war.

You beat me to it as I have hoped to write to you for weeks but my heart has gone phut and everything is beyond me these days. Now that I have reached the allotted span I don't know whether it is the end or whether it is worth while to struggle on. My mother lived till nearly 88 but at over 80 she was much stronger than I have been for four or five years now.

I have been wondering how you got on since your mother left you and if your sister and you are still together. I was saddened very much by the passing of Prof. Arnold Dresden in April. Do you remember him in Chicago? He was Pres. of the American Mathematical Assoc. and also was a distinguished musician. He, it was, that started all that good music in parks in Chicago and often when I was young I had to go traipsing on icy winter Sunday nights to some outlying park as representative of the W T Union League, under which auspices he carried out his proposition. . . .

I have long been hankering for a dictionary. We are not allowed any more dollars under the appropriation to import them and the University of Perth, where I saw the book, had not one in stock or would have presented it to me. Would you find out how much it is and I cd send you enough Australian money to get exchange and you cd get it and use it and so make it second hand and write in pencil in it a birthday present to me, and that wd be a private personal matter. It is *The American College Dictionary* edited by Barnhardt—a Harper's publication. That shd be enough to identify it. . . .

June 4   Yesterday your letter dated 31 March but postmarked Ap 21 also came to hand but I was interrupted and cd not get on with it. I am glad the family are filling in the blank.

Now to your letter. So you are Polish (½). The Poles are all the go at present. I was put in the charge of one on my last train journey and he took care of me as if I been an escapee or something and we had a most interesting time. I have used my space or I'd tell you. I'd like to know why your father came to USA. You never told me.

Indeed, in those old days we were so swallowed by our work and causes that private life got pushed out of consideration. . . .

[unsigned]

Sorry about the arthritic knee. I waked up one morning about 8 weeks ago with a swelling as big as an ostrich egg under one knee the leg too stiff to bend and I cd hardly get about. It went away but now I remain stiff to get up and down whereas before I cd get up and down off the floor like a cork. Growing old is a pest.

at Mrs G Perryman's
22 Murray Road
Beecroft
July 23rd 1954

Dear Vance

I had your book ready to read when I was taken with a heart attack five weeks ago; so I have not read it but I am glad it is out & know it will be a great success. You will have said all the things you oughter. I have said all the things I oughtenter in a book which is coming. At any rate there is now no one living except you and me who has felt the 'nineties' emotionally and the heady joy of the balladry about our very own country.

I was really very ill till rescued by the Doctor & a roster of friends who saved me from hospital. I could not have survived a hospital. Then my sweet younger cousins rallied round & would not let me go to the bone-yard which was a wonderful saving feeling when I was so ill.

Two of them brought me to this beautiful quiet suburb where I have the minutest & tenderest attention. The Dr & my nurses think I am getting better but I have never been really ill before and I do not feel that way, so as you have had a heart attack will you please take time to tell me how long you were in bed & what they did to you & how you felt.

I feel like a poisoned pup which makes food abhorrent & the Dr says it is because of the constant drugging I have had to quieten my heart. Perhaps you were not so wild & fierce as I am & reacted more like a civilized citizen.

I do not know whether it is worth struggling to survive so will you please tell me lots about your illness, any details I would be pleased to receive.

I am too dopey for more except love to you and Nettie & the girls & added good wishes for your book.

Miles
per Phillis Moulden

Wednesday
[nd, pm 2 Sept 1954, Sydney]

Dear Marge

I am very interested to have the copy of H L's letter. He used
to look at me with his soft eagle eyes & assert that I was a
greater writer than he. Also Furphy. And A G S used to say in
a sardonic way that I was a genius & he only a parasitic critic.
It embarrassed me as flattery then & as I matured I thought
it had been the attitude of middle-aged men to a young female.
I have never gained self-confidence & my writing fills me with
a sense of tortured failure. Critics don't see the underside or
innerness of what I attempt. It must have been interesting to
see that Lawson stuff. But it takes a lifetime to search & pick
out the gems.

This week end is to be full of relatives from the country so
we'll have to wait yet tho I long to see you. I've had no visitor
of my own since D Martin, no strength for more.

My love & interest as always if I live

Miles

Beecroft
Sep 3 54

Pixie dearest dear

You little know, I perceive, by your letters, how near I still
am to tumbling into the grave. My wonderful little cousin is
bent on salvaging me & what a task it is, and what that girl
does!

I've only last week started to read my letters, & the newspaper. I have not had my clothes on yet. Sit up a few hrs wrapped in eiderdowns.

I thank you for all your expensive extravagant gifts darling. You mustn't send any more.

Tell Ray Mathew not to worry about his play, I always feel worse than he does. That being so, why do we go on? Writing is an affliction worse than TB for TB can be cured. Cassons or anyone else out of question for me at present. *I remember* is reposing in my cousin's deed box. For if it be a book worth publication is a good idea—if I live.

The essay on novels has to come first. B D will come out about that if I am well enough. I'll tell you about it if ever I see you. For the present please say nothing. Must keep my strength for that and as you are so busy don't worry about me for the present. I loved both your letters. As for peace messages surely the madness of the male rampant can go no further. Peace or Perish! The human race has reached such a crisis in politics & science that to survive we must abandon the *idea* of war.

Lovely gum trees here and many many birds. No strength for more. To get out here you get out at Beecroft Stn and take a cab 2/–. It is a long expensive journey so do not bother. I had a kind message from Mr & Mrs Allan Moses. I hope their baby came all right and is flourishing. No strength for more. This has knocked me out. Love to Robin.

My love as always dear, & many thanks
Miles

Jounama Creek, Talbingo, NSW, Miles Franklin's birthplace,
where her ashes were scattered in accordance with her wishes
(photo by Muir Holburn, courtesy Marjorie Pizer Holburn,
ML)

BIBLIOGRAPHIC NOTE

The main sources of Franklin correspondence have been noted in the Introduction. The *Guide to the Papers and Books of Miles Franklin in the Mitchell Library* issued by the Library Council of New South Wales, Sydney, 1980, lists correspondents alphabetically. A listing is also available for Franklin materials at the National Library of Australia, Canberra. There is an internal guide to the microfilm edition of the records of the National Women's Trade Union League of America.

There have been three biographical studies of Miles Franklin to date: Marjorie Barnard *Miles Franklin* (1967, reissued UQP, 1988), a graceful literary study predating the release of the Franklin Papers; Verna Coleman *Miles Franklin in America: Her Unknown (Brilliant) Career* (1981); and Colin Roderick *Miles Franklin: Her Brilliant Career* (1982). My entry on Miles Franklin in the *Australian Dictionary of Biography* vol. 8 (1981) was revised for Heather Radi (ed.) *200 Australian Women* (1988).

Except for the 1890s generation, it is too soon for many biographical studies of Miles Franklin's friends to have appeared, although memoirs and autobiographies are increasingly available; for example, *Point of Departure: The Autobiography of Jean Devanny* (ed. Carole Ferrier, 1986) and David Martin *My Strange Friend* (1991), and there is much work in progress. Notable exceptions are Ric Throssell *Wild Weeds and Wind Flowers: The Life and Letters of Katharine Susannah Prichard* (1975) and Craig Munro *Wild Man of Letters: The Story of P R Stephensen* (1984). Recent biographies of Miles Franklin's 'elders' include: John Barnes *The Order of Things: A Life of Joseph Furphy* (1990); Diane Kirkby *Alice Henry: The Power of Pen and Voice. The Life of an Australian-American Labor Reformer* (1991); Susan Magarey *Unbridling the Tongues of Women: The Life of Catherine Helen Spence* (1985); and W H Wilde *Courage a Grace: A Biography of Dame Mary Gilmore*

(1988). On C Hartley Grattan, see *Perspectives on Australia: Essays in Australiana in the Collections of the Harry Ransom Humanities Research Center*, ed. Dave Oliphant, University of Texas at Austin (1989). The best reference for Miles Franklin's women friends in America is *Notable American Women 1607–1950* (4 vols, 1971–80).

For Miles Franklin's publications to date, see Debra Adelaide *Bibliography of Australian Women's Literature 1795–1990* (1991), plus *The Net of Circumstance*, published in London in 1915 under the extraordinary pseudonym 'Mr & Mrs Ogniblat L'Artsau'.

Additional letters by and/or to Miles Franklin appear in the following collections: *Henry Lawson Letters 1890–1922*, ed. with intro. and notes by Colin Roderick (1970); *Letters of Vance and Nettie Palmer 1915–1963*, selected and ed. by Vivian Smith (1977); *Letters of Mary Gilmore*, selected and ed. by W H Wilde and T Inglis Moore (1980); A W Barker *Dear Robertson: Letters to an Australian Publisher* (1982); *Diary of a New Chum and Other Lost Stories, Paul Wenz*, ed. and transl. Maurice Blackman (1990); *As Good As A Yarn With You: Letters between Miles Franklin, Katharine Susannah Prichard, Jean Devanny, Marjorie Barnard, Flora Eldershaw and Eleanor Dark*, ed. Carole Ferrier (1992).

CHECKLIST

1: 1879–1906

1887
1.1   Stella Miles Franklin [SMF]/Sara Metta Lampe,   FP113x**
      Brindabella, 17/6/1887

1893
*1.2   Charles A Blyth/SMF, Brindabella, 17/6/1893   FP6

1896
*1.3   Thos J Hebblewhite/SMF, Goulburn, NSW,   FP6
      8/9/1896

1899
1.4   SMF/Angus & Robertson, Bangalore,   ML MSS 314
      30/3/1899
1.5   SMF/Henry Lawson, Bangalore, 19/11/1899   FP6

1900
*1.6   Henry Lawson/SMF, Sydney, Wednesday [January   FP6
      1900]
1.7   SMF/Henry Lawson, Bangalore, 17/10/1900   ML DOC
                                                      2211

1901
1.8   SMF/J B Pinker, Bangalore, 6/2/1901   FP80
1.9   SMF/J F Archibald, Bangalore, 5/9/1901   FP7
*1.10   Linda Franklin/SMF, Talbingo, Monday   FP49
      [16/9/1901]
1.11   SMF/A G Stephens, Bangalore, 10/10/1901   MA
1.12   SMF/Uncle—?, 'Stillwater' [Thornford],   FP50
      21/10/1901
1.13   SMF/J B Pinker, Bangalore, 18/11/1901   FP80

1902
1.14   SMF/Ethel Curlewis [Turner], np, nd [Sydney 1902?] ML MSS 667
*1.15   Ethel Curlewis [Turner]/SMF, Sydney,   FP8
      17/5/1902
*1.16   Rose Scott/SMF, Sydney, 22/6/1902   FP8
1.17   SMF/George Robertson, Bangalore, 20/7/1902   ML MSS 314
1.18   SMF/Rose Scott, 'Stillwater', 19/8/1902   RSC
*1.19   Telegram Rose Scott/SMF, Sydney, 20/8/1902   FP8

*   letter to Miles Franklin
**   Franklin Papers & volume number. See Abbreviations for other locations

1903

*1.20	Sarah Lampe/SMF, Talbingo, 30/3/1903	FP49
*1.21	Rose Scott/SMF, Sydney, 22/5/[1903, pm]	FP8
1.22	SMF/George Robertson, Sydney, Friday [mid 1903?]	ML MSS 314
*1.23	A G Stephens/SMF, Sydney, 29/7/1903	FP7
*1.24	S M E Franklin/SMF, np [Penrith], 29/10/1903	FP48

1904

*1.25	Joseph Furphy/SMF, Shepparton, Vic., 17/2/1904	FP9B
1.26	SMF/Rose Scott, Melbourne, 3/3/1904	RSC
1.27	SMF/Joseph Furphy, GPO [Melbourne], 23/3/[1904]	FC
1.28	SMF/Mrs E W O'Sullivan, Melbourne, Tuesday [April 1904?]	ML MSS 1603
*1.29	Kate Baker/SMF, Guildford, Vic., 17/4/1904	FP9A
*1.30	Aileen Goldstein/SMF, Melbourne, 24/5/1904	FP10
*1.31	Mae Gillespie/SMF, Thornford, NSW, 16/6/1904	FP10
*1.32	Vida Goldstein/SMF, Sydney, 16/10/1904	FP10
1.33	SMF/Joseph Furphy, Penrith, 15/11/[19]04	KBP

1905

1.34	SMF/A G Stephens, Penrith, 30/3/1905	FP55
*1.35	A G Stephens/SMF, Sydney, 31/3/1905	FP7
1.36	Draft letter SMF/T W Heney, Penrith, 1/4/1905	FP55
1.37	SMF/George Robertson, Penrith, 22/6/1905	ML MSS 314
*1.38	Edwin Bridle/SMF, Wilga Vale, NSW, 24/11/1905	FP47

1906

1.39	Postcard SMF/Linda Graham, Auckland, NZ, 12/4/1906	FP111
*1.40	Edwin Bridle/SMF, Wilga Vale, NSW, 23/5/1906	FP47
*1.41	Linda Graham/SMF, np, nd, [Goulburn, mid 1906]	FP49
*1.42	Postcard Vida Goldstein/SMF, Melbourne, 11/8/1906	FP10
1.43	Postcard SMF/Linda Graham, [S. California], 20/8/1906	FP111
*1.44	Sarah Lampe/SMF, Talbingo, 24/9/1906	FP49
*1.45	[He]Lena Lampe/SMF, Talbingo, 6/10/1906	FP49
*1.46	Edwin Bridle/SMF, Wilga Vale, NSW, 10/12/1906 [pm]	FP47

2: 1907–1915

1907

*2.1	Margaret Dreier Robins/SMF, Chicago, 29/10/1907	FP10
2.2	Postcard SMF/S M E Franklin [Winnetka, Ill.], 14/11/1907	FP111

1908

| 2.3 | Postcard SMF/S M E Franklin, Chicago, 9/3/19[08] | FP111 |
| 2.4 | Postcard SMF/S M E Franklin, Stannington, Conn., 20/8/1908 | FP111 |

1909

| 2.5 | SMF/Blackwoods, Madison, Wis., 2/8/1909 | FP80 |

1910

| 2.6 | SMF/Blackwoods, Chicago, 4/4/1910 | FP80 |

1911

*2.7	Margaret Dreier Robins/SMF, Chinsegut-Hill, Fla., 18/4/1911	FP10
2.8	SMF/S M E Franklin, New York, 27/6/1911 [pm]	FP111
*2.9	Helen Marot/SMF, New York, 30/9/1911	WTUL (LC)
2.10	SMF/Helen Marot, Chicago, 4/10/1911	WTUL (LC)
2.11	SMF/Isabella Goldstein, Chicago, 13/10/1911	VGP
2.12	SMF/NWTUL Executive Board, Chicago, 30/10/1911	WTUL (LC)

1912

| 2.13 | SMF/Eva O'Sullivan, Chicago, 8/5/1912 | ML MSS 544 |
| 2.14 | SMF/Rose Scott, Chicago, 9 and 21/12/1912 | RSC |

1913

2.15	SMF/Margaret Dreier Robins, [Chicago] 17/6/1913	MDR
2.16	SMF/Rose Scott, Chicago, [19/7/1913]	RSC
2.17	SMF/S M E Franklin, Chicago, 2/8/1913	FP111
*2.18	Press cutting Demarest Lloyd/SMF, [Boston, 14/10/1913?]	FP12
2.19	SMF/Annie Franklin, Chicago, 21/11/1913	ML DOC 2866

1914

2.20	SMF/Dorothea A Dreier [Chicago], 27/2/1914	DDP
2.21	SMF/Raymond Robins, Chicago, 11/6/1914	RR
2.22	SMF/Leonora O'Reilly, Chicago, 25/7/1914	OP *WTUL*
2.23	SMF/Demarest Lloyd, Chicago, 26/9/1914	FP12

1915

2.24	SMF/Leonora O'Reilly, Chicago, 5/1/1915	OP *WTUL*
2.25	SMF/Jane Addams, Chicago, 6/1/1915	WILPF
2.26 –27	SMF/Leonora O'Reilly, Chicago, 9/8/1915, and enclosure SMF/Emma Steghagen, Chicago, 9/8/1915	OP *WTUL*
2.28	SMF/Lola Lloyd, Chicago, 9/9/1915	FP13
2.29	SMF/Kate Baker, Chicago, 23/9/1915	KBP
2.30	SMF/Eva O'Sullivan, Chicago, 23/9/1915	ML MSS 544
2.31	SMF/Leonora O'Reilly, at sea, 6/11/1915	OP *WTUL*

3: 1916–18

1916

3.1	SMF/Alice Henry, London, 23/3/1916	FP114
3.2	SMF/Leonora O'Reilly, London, 14/5/1916	OP *WTUL* ⋅
3.3	Postcard SMF/J M Franklin, London, 8/7/1916	FP111
3.4	SMF/Alice Henry, London, 26/9/1916	FP114
3.5	SMF/Agnes Nestor, London, 21/10/1916	ANP
3.6	SMF/Emma Steghagen, London, 31/12/1916	WTUL (LC)

1917

3.7	SMF/Alice Henry, London, 1/3/1917	FP114
3.8	SMF/'Dear Friends', London, 28/6/1917	ANP
3.9	SMF/Rose Scott, London, 2/7/1917	RSC
3.10	Postcard SMF/S M E Franklin, nr Ostrovo, 24/7/1917	FP108

1918

3.11	SMF/Alice Henry, London, [26/2/1918]	FP115
*3.12	Postcard Alejander Stamenkovic/SMF, Salonika, 12/4/1918	FP13
3.13	SMF/Emma Pischel and others, London, 8/5/1918	FP114
*3.14	Alice Henry/SMF, Chicago, 20/5/1918	FP114

4: 1919–26

1919

4.1	SMF/Alice Henry, London, 6/2/1919	FP114
4.2	Postcard SMF/S M E Franklin, [London], 18/3/1919	FP108
4.3	SMF/Agnes Nestor, London, 20/6/1919	ANP
4.4	SMF/Eva O'Sullivan, London, 5/8/1919	ML MSS 544
4.5–6	Postcards SMF/J M Franklin, Ireland, August 1919	FP113X
4.7–8	SMF/Alice Henry, London, 26/11/[1919] and enclosure from Lady Byles, London, Wed.	FP114
4.9	SMF/Alice Henry, [London], 12/12/[1919]	FP115
4.10	SMF/Rose Scott, London, 28/12/1919	RSC

1920

*4.11	Margaret Dreier Robins/SMF, Chicago, 14/4/1920	MDR
4.12	SMF/Margaret Dreier Robins, London, 7/5/1920	MDR
*4.13	Alice Henry/SMF, [Chicago], 9/6/1920	FP114
4.14	SMF/Alice Henry, Newport, 10/7/[1920]	FP114

1921

4.15	SMF/George Robertson, London, 16/4/1921	ML MSS 314
*4.16	George Robertson/SMF, Sydney, 16/6/1921	ML MSS 314
4.17	SMF/Alice Henry *et al*, London, 18/10/[1921]	FP11

1922

4.18	SMF/Alice Henry, London, 23 and 25/5/1922	FP114
4.19	SMF/Jane Addams, [Yorkshire] 6/8/1922	WILPF
4.20	Draft letter SMF/Phyllis Neilson-Terry, [London], 18/9/1922	FP88

1923

4.21	Postcard SMF/S M E Franklin, Stratford-on-Avon, 13/5/1923	FP108
*4.22	S M E Franklin/SMF, Sydney, 14/8/1923	FP48
*4.23	Postcard Olive Aldridge/SMF, London, 26/10/1923	FP14
4.24	SMF's visiting card with message to George Robertson, Sydney, nd	ML MSS 314

1924

*4.25	Marion Mahony Griffin/SMF, Melbourne, 7/1/1924	FP15
4.26	SMF/Rose Scott, Sydney, 2/2/1924	RSC
*4.27	Dr Mary Booth/SMF, Sydney, 4/3/1924	FP15
4.28	SMF/Margaret Dreier Robins, Sydney [13/3/1924]	MDR
*4.29	S M E Franklin/SMF, Sydney, 17/3/1924	FP48
*4.30	Telegram Vida Goldstein/SMF, Melbourne, 27/3/1924	FP10
*4.31	S M E Franklin/SMF, Sydney, 4/4/1924	FP48
4.32	SMF/George Robertson, at sea, 16/4/1924	ML MSS 314
4.33	SMF/Mary Fullerton, London, 10/6/1924	MEF

1925

4.34	'J Verney' [SMF]/Editor *Royal Magazine*, London, 22/6/1925	FP88
4.35	Postcard SMF/S M E Franklin, Exeter, 23/8/1925	FP108
4.36	SMF/Marian Dornton Brown, London, 24/11/1925	FP15

1926

4.37	'H F Malone' [SMF]/Jonathan Cape, London, 19/1/1926	FP86
4.38	SMF/Eva O'Sullivan, London, 5/4/1926	ML MSS 544

5: 1927–1932

1927

*5.1	Mary Fullerton/SMF, London, 3/3/1927	FP16
*5.2	Lady Byles/SMF, London, 22/6/1927	FP6
*5.3	Kate Baker/SMF, Melbourne, 11/3[?]/1927	FP9A
*5.4	P S Watson/SMF, Melbourne, 22/8/1927	FP12
*5.5	G B Lancaster/SMF, Longford, Tasmania, 24/8/1927	FP20
5.6	SMF/Alice Henry, Sydney, 26/12/1927	FP114

1928

5.7	SMF/Kate Baker, nr Kiandra, NSW, 12/2/1928	KBP

*5.8	Mary Fullerton/SMF, London, 27/3/1928	FP16
5.9	SMF/Mary Fullerton, Sydney, nd, and 12/6/[1928]	FP119
5.10	SMF/Alice Henry, Sydney 13/8 and 20/8/[1928]	FP115
*5.11	Lady Byles/SMF, London, 12/9/1928	FP6
*5.12	Alice Henry/SMF, Santa Barbara, Cal., 13/10/1928	FP114
5.13	'Brent of Bin Bin'/Mary Gilmore, [Sydney], 2/12/1928	FP119
5.14	SMF/Alice Henry, Sydney, 23/12/1928	FP114

1929

5.15	SMF/Mary Fullerton, Sydney, 1/1/[1929]	FP119
5.16	SMF/Mary Fullerton, Sydney, 2/1/[1929]	MA
5.17	SMF/Margaret Dreier Robins, Sydney, 6/5/1929	MDR
5.18	'Brent of Bin Bin'/Nettie Palmer, [Sydney], 22/7/1929	PP
*5.19	Mary Fullerton/SMF, London, nd, and 30/7/1929	FP16
*5.20	Lady Byles/SMF, London, 28/10/[1929]	FP6
5.21	SMF/George Robertson, Sydney, 6/12/1929	ML MSS 314
*5.22	Dr Josephine Young/SMF, Chicago, 8/12/1929	FP20
*5.23	Marion Mahony Griffin and Walter Burley Griffin/SMF, Sydney, 24/12/1929	FP15

1930

*5.24	Telegram Margaret Dreier Robins/SMF, Florida, 24/1/1930	MDR
5.25	Telegram SMF/Margaret Dreier Robins, Sydney, 30/1/1930	MDR
*5.26	Mary Fullerton/SMF, London, 27/3/1930	FP16
5.27	SMF/George Robertson, Sydney, 15/5/1930	ML MSS 314
5.28	SMF/Mary Fullerton, [Sydney], 20/5/1930	FP119
*5.29	Katharine Susannah Throssell [Prichard]/SMF, Perth, 1/6/1930	FP21
*5.30	Lady Byles/SMF, London, 14/8/[1930]	FP6
*5.31	Dan Clyne/SMF, Sydney, 29/10/1930	FP22
5.32	SMF/Margaret Dreier Robins, Sydney, 30/10/1930	MDR
5.33	SMF/Margaret Dreier Robins, Sydney, 8/11/1930	MDR

1931

5.34	SMF/S M E Franklin, Sydney, 21/1/1931	FP108
*5.35	S M E Franklin/SMF, Sydney, 12/4/[1931]	FP48
5.36	SMF/S M E Franklin, London, 12/11/1931	FP108
5.37	'Brent of Bin Bin'/Nettie Palmer, London, 18/11/1931	PP
5.38	SMF/Alice Henry, London, 21/12/[1931]	FP114

1932

5.39	SMF/Helene Scheu-Riesz, London, 5/1/1932	FP20
5.40	SMF/Margaret Dreier Robins, London, 4/3/1932	MDR

5.41	SMF/S M E Franklin, London, 9/3/[1932]	FP108
5.42	SMF/C Hartley Grattan, London, 18/3/1932	FP23
*5.43	S M E Franklin/SMF, Sydney, 10 and 11/4/1932	FP48
5.44	'Brent of Bin Bin'/A G Stephens, [London], May 1932	MA
5.45	SMF/Eva O'Sullivan, London, 4/5/1932	ML MSS 544
5.46	'Brent of Bin Bin'/Kate Baker, [London], June 1932	KBP
5.47	SMF/S M E Franklin, London, 8/6/[1932]	FP108
5.48	SMF/C Hartley Grattan, London, 21/7/1932	FP23
*5.49	P R Stephensen/SMF, London, 25/7/1932	FP86
5.50	'Brent of Bin Bin'/P R Stephensen, [London], August 1932	FP86
5.51	SMF/Agnes and Mary Nestor, at sea, 11/11/1932	FP24

6: 1933–1938

1933

6.1	SMF/Margery Currey, Sydney, 4/1/1933	FP22
6.2	SMF/Norman Lindsay, Sydney, Wednesday [Feb 1933?]	HLC
6.3	SMF/C Hartley Grattan, Sydney, 29/3/1933	FP23
6.4	SMF/G B Lancaster, Sydney, 19/4/1933	FP20
*6.5	C Hartley Grattan/SMF, New York, 27/4/[1933]	FP23
6.6	SMF/Mrs F E [J A] Hobson, Sydney, 30/4/1933	FP23
6.7	SMF/Henry Handel Richardson, Sydney, 30/5/1933	FP25
6.8	SMF/Nettie Palmer, Sydney, Wednesday [mid 1933]	FP24
*6.9	Henry Handel Richardson/SMF, London, 2/9/1933	FP25
6.10	SMF/C Hartley Grattan, Sydney, 25/10/1933	FP23
6.11	SMF/Jean Hamilton, Sydney, 6/12/[1933]	FP26

1934

6.12	SMF/Alice Henry, [Sydney], 1/4/1934	FP11
*6.13	Alice Henry/SMF, Melbourne, 15/4/1934	FP114
6.14	SMF/Virginia—?, Jean Hamilton and Mary Fullerton, Sydney, 14 and 15/5/1934	FP25
6.15	SMF/Mary Fullerton, Sydney, 22/5/[1934]	FP16
6.16	SMF/Jean Hamilton, Mary Fullerton and Mabel Singleton, Sydney, 8/6/1934	FP26
6.17	SMF/Mary Fullerton, Sydney, 15/6/1934	FP16
*6.18	Mary Fullerton/SMF, London, 26/6/1934	FP16
6.19	SMF/Carrie Whelan, Sydney, 15/8/1934	FP20
6.20	SMF/Mary Fullerton, Sydney, 14/9/1934	FP16
6.21	SMF/Rose Schneiderman, Sydney, 13/11/1934	FP15

1935

| 6.22 | SMF/C Hartley Grattan, Sydney, 14/3/1935 | FP23 |
| 6.23 | SMF/E H Burgmann, Sydney, 28/3/1935 | BP |

*6.24	Nettie Palmer/SMF, London, 9/5/1935	FP24
6.25	SMF/Nettie Palmer, Sydney, 13/4/1935[?]	FP24
6.26	SMF/Governor of NSW, Sydney, 27/5/1935	FP27
6.27	SMF/Harold Ickes, Sydney, 21/9/1935	FP12
*6.28	Walter Burley Griffin/SMF, Lucknow, India, 25/11/1935	FP27
6.29	SMF/Margaret Dreier Robins and Raymond Robins, Sydney, 16/12/1935	FP10

1936

6.30	SMF/Alice Thatcher Post, Sydney, 31/1/1936	FP27
6.31	SMF/Elsie Belle Champion, Sydney, 31/1/1936	FP8
6.32	SMF/Harold Ickes, Sydney, 14/2/1936	FP12
6.33	SMF/Alice Henry, Sydney, 11/3/[1936]	FP11
6.34	SMF/Ambrose Pratt, Sydney, 2/5/1936	FP27
*6.35	Telegram P R and Winifred Stephensen/SMF, Sydney, 22/7/1936	FP28
*6.36	Lucy Spence Morice/SMF, Adelaide, 22/7/1936	FP22
*6.37	Vida Goldstein/SMF, Melbourne, 24/7/1936	FP10
6.38	SMF/Lucy Spence Morice, Sydney, 10/8/1936	FP22
6.39	SMF/Margery Currey, Sydney, 18/8/1936	FP22
6.40	SMF/Henry Handel Richardson, Sydney, 9/9/1936	FP25
6.41	SMF/Eleanor Dark, Sydney, 14/10/[1936]	FP26
*6.42	Eleanor Dark/SMF, Katoomba, NSW, 15/10/1936	FP26
6.43	SMF/C Hartley Grattan, Sydney, 23/10/[1936]	FP23
6.44	SMF/Guy Innes, Sydney, 23/10/1936	FP24
6.45	SMF/Vida Goldstein, Aileen Goldstein and Elsie Belle Champion, Sydney, 4/11/1936	FP10
*6.46	Dan Clyne/SMF, Sydney, 8/12/1936	FP22
6.47	SMF/Xavier Herbert, Sydney, 18/12/1936	FP28
6.48	SMF/Nettie Palmer, Sydney, 31/12/[1936]	FP24

1937

6.49	SMF/Mollye Menken and family, Sydney, 12/1/1937	FP29
6.50	SMF/Emma Pischel, Sydney, 22/1/1937	FP15
6.51	SMF/Alice Henry, Sydney, 5/2/1937	FP11
6.52	SMF/Kate Baker, [Sydney], 11/5/1937	KBP
6.53	SMF/Vance Palmer, Sydney, 30/5/1937	FP26
*6.54	C Hartley Grattan/SMF, Townsville, Qld, 11/7/1937	FP23
6.55	SMF/Paul Wenz, Sydney, 14/7/1937	FP29
6.56	SMF/Carrie Whelan, Sydney, 22/7/1937	FP20
6.57	SMF/Lucy Spence Morice, [Sydney], 31/8/1937	FP22

1938

6.58	SMF/Mary Fullerton, Sydney, 10/1/1938	FP17
6.59	SMF/St John Ervine, Sydney, 15/2/1938	ML MSS

6.60	SMF/Xavier Herbert, Sydney, 8/3/1938	FP28
6.61	SMF/Leonora Pease, Sydney, 12/3/1938	FP13
*6.62	Alice Henry/SMF, Melbourne, 3/7/1938	FP11
6.63	SMF/Nettie Palmer, Peak Hill, NSW, 31/7/1938	PP
*6.64	Mary Fullerton/SMF, London, 30/8/1938	FP17
6.65	SMF/C Hartley Grattan, Sydney, 6/9/1938	FP23
6.66	SMF/Alice Henry, Sydney, 11/10/[1938]	FP11
6.67	SMF/Kate Baker, Sydney, 27/10/1938	KBP

7: 1939–45

1939

7.1	SMF/Mabel Singleton, Jean Hamilton and Mary Fullerton, Sydney, [7 and 8/4/1939]	FP25
*7.2	Michael Sawtell/SMF, Sydney, 3/7/1939	FP32
7.3	SMF/R G Menzies, Sydney, 5/7/1939	FP32
7.4	SMF/Kate Baker, Sydney, 16/7/1939	FP9A
7.5	SMF/Mary Fullerton, Sydney, 9/8/1939	FP119
*7.6	St John Ervine/SMF, Devon, 23/8/1939	FP14
*7.7	Jean Devanny/SMF, Sydney, 26/8/1939	FP32
7.8	SMF/Jean Devanny, Sydney, 30/8/1939	FP32
7.9	SMF/Kate Baker, [Sydney], 6/9/1939	KBP
7.10	SMF/H N Smith, Sydney, 4/10/1939	FP29
7.11	SMF/John Kinmont Moir, Sydney, 14/10/1939	JKMC
7.12	SMF/Mary E Dreier, Sydney, 28/12/1939	MDP

1940

*7.13	Henrietta Drake-Brockman/SMF, Perth, 22/2/[1940]	FP33
7.14	SMF/Dymphna Cusack, Sydney, 7/3/[1940]	FP30
7.15	SMF/Henrietta Drake-Brockman, Sydney, 29/4/[1940]	FP33
7.16	SMF/Eleanor Dark, [Sydney], 8/5/1940	FP26
*7.17	Nettie Palmer/SMF, Melbourne, 25/5/1940	FP24
7.18	SMF/Nettie Palmer, Sydney, 31/5/1940	FP24
7.19	SMF/Katharine Susannah Prichard, Sydney, 6/6/1940	FP21
7.20	SMF/Mary Fullerton, Sydney, 30/6/1940	FP119
7.21	SMF/May and Phil Meggitt, Sydney, 6/7/1940	FP34
*7.22	Tom Inglis Moore/SMF, Sydney, 15/7/1940	FP29
7.23	SMF/Alice Henry, Sydney, 17/7/1940	FP11
7.24	SMF/Margaret Dreier Robins, Sydney, 17/9/1940	MDR
7.25	SMF/C Hartley Grattan, Sydney, 18/9/1940	FP23
7.26	SMF/Mary Fullerton, Sydney, 26/9/1940	FP119
*7.27	Katharine Susannah Prichard/SMF, Perth, 14/10/1940	FP21
7.28	SMF/Mary Fullerton, Sydney, 21/11/1940	FP17

1941

7.29	SMF/John Kinmont Moir, Sydney, 8/2/1941	JKMC
7.30	SMF/Dr H V Evatt, Sydney, 11/3/1941	EC
7.31	SMF/Arnold and Louise Dresden, Sydney, 16/3/1941	FP35
7.32	SMF/Mary Fullerton, Sydney, 20/4/1941	FP18
*7.33	Mary Anderson/SMF, Washington, 30/6/1941	MAP
7.34	SMF/Desmond Fitzgerald, Sydney, 13/7/1941	FP33
7.35	SMF/Ian Mudie, Sydney, 20 and 21/7/1941	IMP
7.36	SMF/Mary Fullerton, Sydney, 22/9/1941	FP18
7.37	SMF/Eleanor Dark, Sydney, 8/10/[1941]	EDP
*7.38	Eleanor Dark/SMF, Katoomba, NSW, 10/10/1941	FP26
7.39	SMF/Mary Alice Evatt, Sydney, 25/11/1941	FP35

1942

7.40	SMF/Alice Henry, Sydney, 29/1/1942	FP11
*7.41	Alice Henry/SMF, Melbourne, 2/2/1942	FP11
7.42	SMF/Grattan family, Sydney, 10 and 19/2/1942	GC
7.43	SMF/Margaret Dreier Robins, Sydney, 19/2/1942	MDR
7.44	SMF/Ian Mudie, Sydney, 17/3/1942	FP36
*7.45	Ian Mudie/SMF, Adelaide, 19/3/1942	FP36
7.46	SMF/Ian Mudie, Sydney, 23/3/1942	FP36
7.47	SMF/Ian Mudie, Sydney, 21/4/1942	FP36
7.48	SMF/Mary Fullerton, Sydney, 23/5/1942	FP18
7.49	SMF/Katharine Susannah Prichard, Sydney, [nd, June 1942]	FP21
*7.50	Katharine Susannah Prichard/SMF, Perth, 9/6/1942	FP21
7.51	SMF/Alice Henry, Sydney, 18 and 19/6/1942	FP115
7.52	SMF/Clem Christesen, Sydney, 28/7/1942	MA
7.53	SMF/Dymphna Cusack, Sydney, 6/10/1942	FP30
*7.54	Dymphna Cusack/SMF, Newcastle, NSW, 12/10/1942	FP30
7.55	SMF/Godfrey Bentley, Sydney [October 1942]	FP37
7.56	SMF/Tom Inglis Moore, Sydney, 14/10/1942	FP29

1943

7.57	SMF/Mary Anderson, Sydney, 24/3/1943	MAP
7.58	SMF/Frank Ryland, Sydney, 21/4/1943	FP37
7.59	SMF/Mary Fullerton, Sydney, 4/7/1943	FP18
7.60	SMF/E J Brady, Sydney, 10/8/1943	FP37
*7.61	Vida Goldstein/SMF, Melbourne, 18/8/1943	FP10
7.62	SMF/Clem Christesen, Sydney, 2/9/1943	MA
7.63	SMF/Kate Baker, Sydney, 28/9/1943 plus enclosure: Joseph Furphy's Centenary	VKP
*7.64	Nettie Palmer/SMF, Canberra, 6/10/1943	FP24
7.65	SMF/Dymphna Cusack, Sydney, 13/10/1943	DCP

7.66	SMF/Nettie Palmer, 19/10/1943	FP24
*7.67	Hilda Esson/SMF, Melbourne, 15/12/1943	FP38
7.68	SMF/Mary Anderson, Sydney, [rd 15/12/1943]	MAP

1944

*7.69	Harold Ickes/SMF, Washington, 27/1/1944	FP12
7.70	SMF/Mary Fullerton, Sydney, 24/3/1944	FP18
*7.71	R G Howarth/SMF, Sydney, 20/5/1944	FP33
7.72	SMF/R G Howarth, Sydney, 22/5/1944	FP33
7.73	SMF/E H Burgmann, Sydney, 6/7/1944	FP27
*7.74	E H Burgmann, Goulburn, NSW, 10/7/1944	FP27
7.75	SMF/Ian Mudie, Sydney, 31/8/1944	IMP
*7.76	Frank Ryland/SMF, [Australian Army, 11/10/1944]	FP37
7.77	SMF/Colin Roderick, Sydney, 22/11/1944	PP
7.78	SMF/Kate Baker, Sydney, 24/11/1944	KBP
*7.79	Jean Hamilton/SMF, London, Xmas 1944	FP26

1945

7.80	SMF/Catherine Duncan, Sydney, 22/2/1945	FP38
7.81	SMF/Lucy Spence Morice, Sydney, 18/4/1945	FP22
7.82	SMF/Elisabeth Christman, Sydney, 20/4/1945	FP24
*7.83	Elisabeth Christman/SMF, Washington, 20/7/1945	FP24
7.84	SMF/Clem Christesen, Sydney, 22/7/1945	MA
7.85	SMF/Dymphna Cusack, Sydney, 9/8/1945	FP30
*7.86	Telegram Hilda Esson/SMF, Melbourne, 30/8/1945	FP86
7.87	SMF/Hilda Esson, Sydney [September? 1945]	FP38
*7.88	J B Chifley/SMF, Canberra, 10/9/1945	ML MSS 3659/1
7.89	SMF/Mary Fullerton, Sydney, 16/9/1945	FP19
7.90	SMF/Frank Ryland, Sydney, 28/9/1945	FP37
7.91	SMF/J B Chifley, Sydney, 14/10/1945	FP39
*7.92	Arnold Dresden/SMF, Swathmore PA, 5/11/1945	FP35
7.93	SMF/Mabel Singleton, Sydney, 16/11/1945	FP25
7.94	SMF/Phil and May Meggitt, Sydney, 17/12/1945	FP39
*7.95	P R Stephensen/SMF, Warburton East, Vic., 17/12/1945	FP28
*7.96	Dymphna Cusack/SMF, Hazelbrook, NSW, 20/12/1945	FP30

8: 1946–1952

1946

8.1	SMF/Kathleen Monypenny, Sydney, 5/2/1946	FP22
8.2	SMF/Winifred Stephensen, Sydney, 11/2/1946	FP39
8.3	SMF/Mary Fullerton, Sydney, 25/2/1946	FP19
8.4	SMF/Mabel Singleton, Sydney, 27/2/1946	FP25
8.5	SMF/P R Stephensen, Sydney, 4/3/1946	FP28

8.6	SMF/Tom Inglis Moore, Sydney, 31/3/1946	FP29
*8.7	P R Stephensen/SMF, Warburton East, Vic., 24/4/1946	FP28
8.8	SMF/Dymphna Cusack, Sydney, 14/6/1946	DCP
8.9	SMF/Dymphna Cusack, Sydney, nd [1946]	DCP
*8.10	Pixie O'Harris/SMF, Sydney, 29/7/1946	FP35
*8.11	Dymphna Cusack/SMF, Hazelbrook, NSW, 14/8/1946	FP30
*8.12	Beatrice Davis/SMF, Sydney, 21/8/1946	FP38
*8.13	Henrietta Drake-Brockman/SMF, Perth, 2/9/1946	FP33
8.14	SMF/Raymond Robins, Sydney, 4/9/1946	FP39
8.15	SMF/Henrietta Drake-Brockman, Sydney, 9/9/1946	FP33
8.16	SMF/Dymphna Cusack and Florence James, nd [Sept/Oct 1946]	FP30
8.17	SMF/Leisa Gunnell, Sydney, 4/11/1946	FP35
8.18	SMF/Rika Stoffel, Sydney, 16/11/1946	FP15
8.19	SMF/C Hartley Grattan and Marjorie Grattan, Sydney, 19/12/1946	FP23
*8.20	Marjorie Pizer/SMF, Sydney, 17/?/[1946]	FP39

1947

8.21	SMF/Emmy Lawson, Sydney, 13/1/1947	FP39
*8.22	Aileen Goldstein/SMF, Melbourne, 23/2/1947	FP10
*8.23	Rex Ingamells/SMF, Melbourne, 18/3/1947	FP40
*8.24	Beatrice Davis/SMF, Sydney, 3/5/1947	ML MSS 3659/1
8.25	SMF/Emma Pischel, Sydney, 6/5/1947	FP15
8.26	SMF/Aileen Goldstein, Sydney, Sunday, [22/6/1947]	FP10
8.27	SMF/Anne Barnard, Sydney, 1/8/1947	FP40
*8.28	Florence James/SMF, London, 7/10/1947	FP30
8.29	SMF/Florence James, Sydney, 16/11/1947	FP30
8.30	SMF/Katharine Susannah Prichard, Sydney, 20/11/1947	FP21
8.31	SMF/Glen Mills Fox, Sydney, 28/11/1947	FP40
*8.32	Vida Goldstein/SMF, Melbourne, 22/12/1947	FP10

1948

8.33	SMF/Jean Hamilton, Sydney, 11/1/1948	FP26
8.34	SMF/Frank Ryland, Sydney, 2/2/1948	FP37
8.35	SMF/Rex Ingamells, Sydney, [15/3/1948?]	RIP
*8.36	Rex Ingamells/SMF, Melbourne, 16/3/1948	FP40
8.37	SMF/St John Ervine, Sydney, 12/5/1948	FP14
8.38	SMF/Mary E Dreier, Sydney, 3/6/1948	FP14
8.39	SMF/Sumner Locke Elliott, Sydney, 31/10/1948	FP41
8.40	SMF/Beatrice Davis, Sydney, 11/11/1948	FP38
*8.41	Laurie Collinson/SMF, Brisbane, 16/12/1948	FP41

*8.42	Roland Robinson/SMF, Darwin, 21/12/1948	FP39
8.43	SMF/Laurie Collinson, Sydney, 23/12/1948	FP41
8.44	SMF/John Kinmont Moir, Sydney, 29/12/1948	JKMC
*8.45	John Kinmont Moir/SMF, Melbourne, 31/12/1948	FP34

1949

*8.46	Ric Throssell/SMF, Canberra, 21/1/1949	FP41
8.47	SMF/Ric Throssell, Sydney, 22/1/1949	FP41
8.48	SMF/Roland Robinson, Sydney, Good Friday 1949	FP39
8.49	SMF/Nettie Palmer, Sydney, 28/5/1948	PP
8.50	SMF/Dymphna Cusack, Sydney, 31/5/[1949]	FP30
8.51	SMF/John K Ewers, Sydney, 25/6/1949	FP42
8.52	SMF/Rex Ingamells, Sydney, 4/8/1949	RIP
*8.53	David Martin/SMF, Sydney, 5/8/1949	FP41
8.54	SMF/Beatrice Davis, Sydney, 19/8/1949	FP38
8.55	SMF/David Martin, Sydney, 23/8/1949	FP41
*8.56	Beatrice Davis/SMF, Sydney, 26/8/1949	FP38
8.57	SMF/Dymphna Cusack, Sydney, 24/9/1949	FP30
*8.58	Dymphna Cusack/SMF, London, 16/10/1949	FP30

1950

*8.59	Myrtle Rose White/SMF, Sydney, 3/3/1950	FP42
8.60	SMF/Margery Currey, Sydney, 14/3/1950	FP22
8.61	SMF/Katharine Susannah Prichard, Sydney, 24/4/1950	FP21
*8.62	Henrietta Drake-Brockman/SMF, Perth, 23/5/[1950]	FP33
8.63	SMF/Henrietta Drake-Brockman, Sydney, 7/6/1950	FP33
8.64	SMF/Clive Evatt, [Sydney], 22/6/1950	FP42
8.65	SMF/Silvia, Victor and Ivy Pallot, Sydney, 8/8/1950	FP43
*8.66	Beatrice Davis/SMF, Sydney, 14/8/1950	FP38
*8.67	Vivienne Newson/SMF, Sydney, 8/9/1950	FP41
8.68	SMF/Frank Hardy, Sydney, 13/9/1950	FP43
8.69	SMF/Vivienne Newson, Sydney, 23/10/1950	FP41
*8.70	Dan Clyne/SMF, Sydney, 27/10/1950	FP22
*8.71	Nettie Palmer/SMF, Melbourne, 1/11/1950	FP24
8.72	SMF/Nettie Palmer, Sydney, 14/11/1950	FP24
8.73	SMF/David Martin, Sydney, 16/11/1950	FP41
8.74	SMF/Walter Murdoch, Sydney, 16/11/1950	FP31
8.75	SMF/David Bradley, Sydney, 25/11/1950	FP43
8.76	SMF/Ric Throssell, Sydney, 20/12/1950	FP41
*8.77	Katharine Susannah Prichard/SMF, Perth, 24/12/1950	FP21
8.78	SMF/J B Chifley, [Sydney], 28/12/1950	FP39
8.79	SMF/Elsie Belle Champion, Sydney, 29/12/1950	FP8

1951

*8.80	Eleanor Witcombe/SMF, Sydney, 18/3/1951	FP43
8.81	SMF/Eleanor Witcombe, Sydney, Sunday [April 1951]	FP43
8.82	SMF/Myrtle Rose White, Sydney, 11/5/1951	FP42
8.83	SMF/Ian Mudie, Sydney, 5/7/1951	FP36
8.84	SMF/Mary Alice Evatt, Sydney, 6/7/1951	EC
8.85	SMF/Warwick Fairfax, Sydney, 3/8/1951	FP44
8.86	SMF/Vance Palmer, Sydney, 9/8/1951	PP
*8.87	Rex Ingamells/SMF, Melbourne, 16/8/1951	FP40
8.88	SMF/Rex Ingamells, Sydney, 21/8/1951	RIP
8.89	SMF/Sumner Locke Elliott, Sydney, 3/10/1951	FP41
8.90	SMF/Arnold and Louise Dresden, Sydney, 27/11/1951	FP35
8.91	SMF/Bill and Minka Veal, Sydney, 26/12/1951	FP44

1952

8.92	SMF/Kylie Tennant, Sydney, 5/1/1952	FP35
*8.93	Kylie Tennant/SMF, Sydney, [1952]	FP35
*8.94	David Martin/SMF, Boronia, Vic., 29/1/1952	FP41
8.95	SMF/David Martin, Sydney, 3/2/1952	FP41
*8.96	Eris O'Brien/SMF, Sydney, 3/2/1952	FP44
8.97	SMF/John Kinmont Moir, Sydney, 14/3/1952	JKMC
8.98	SMF/Dymphna Cusack, [Sydney], 15/3/1952	FP30
8.99	SMF/Nettie Palmer, Sydney, 22/3/1952	FP24
8.100	SMF/Mabel Singleton, Sydney, 1/4/1952	FP25
8.101	SMF/Henrietta Drake-Brockman, Sydney, 15/4/1952	FP33
8.102	SMF/Jean Devanny, Sydney [21/4/1952]	FP32
8.103	SMF/Ian Mudie, Sydney, 9/5/1952	FP36
8.104	SMF/Florence James, Sydney, 3/6/1952	FP30
8.105	SMF/Magdalen Dalloz, Sydney, 27/7/1952	FP41
*8.106	Nancy Keesing/SMF, Sydney, 24/7/1952	FP44
8.107	SMF/Nancy Keesing, Sydney, 12/8/1952	FP44
*8.108	Katharine Susannah Prichard/SMF, Perth, 25/8/1952	FP21
8.109	SMF/Katharine Susannah Prichard, Sydney, 11/9/1952	FP21
8.110	SMF/Rex Ingamells, Sydney, 25/9/1952	RIP
8.111	SMF/Beatrice Davis, Sydney, 30/9/1952	FP38
8.112	SMF/Helene Scheu-Reisz, Sydney, 30/9/1952	FP20
8.113	SMF/Sybil Thorndike Casson, Sydney, 9/11/1952	FP44
*8.114	Jean Devanny/SMF, Townsville, Qld, 11/12/1952	FP32
*8.115	Ray Mathew/SMF, Sydney, 17/12/1952	FP44

9: 1953–1954

1953

9.1	SMF/Tom Ronan, Sydney, 13/2/1953	FP44
*9.2	Clem Christesen/SMF, Melbourne, 27/3/1953	MA

9.3	SMF/Clem Christesen, Sydney, 2/4/1953	MA
9.4	SMF/Dymphna Cusack, Sydney, 28/4/1953	FP30
9.5	SMF/Kate Baker, Sydney, 3/5/1953	FP9A
9.6	SMF/E H Burgmann, Sydney, 24/5/1953	FP27
9.7	SMF/Dymphna Cusack, Sydney, 31/7/1953	FP30
9.8	SMF/Myrtle Rose White, Sydney, 24/8/1953	FP42
*9.9	David Martin/SMF, Boronia, Vic., 13/9/1953	FP41
*9.10	Jean Devanny/SMF, Townsville, Qld, 1/10/1953	FP32
9.11	SMF/Jean Devanny, Sydney, 3/10/1953	FP32
9.12	SMF/John Kinmont Moir, Sydney, 17/10/1953	JKMC
9.13	SMF/Mabel Singleton, Sydney, 29/10/1953	FP25
9.14	SMF/Henrietta Drake-Brockman, Sydney, 13/11/1953	FP33
9.15	SMF/Jean Campbell, 27/11/1953	FP44
*9.16	Katharine Susannah Prichard/SMF, Ainslie, ACT, 2/12/1953	FP21

1954

9.17	SMF/Ethel Ruby Bridle, Sydney, 10/2/1954	FP47
9.18	SMF/P R Stephensen, Sydney, 17/2/1954	FP28
9.19	SMF/Bruce Sutherland, Sydney, 18/3/1954	FP44
9.20	SMF/draft letter Helen Heney, Sydney, [March 1954?]	FP45
*9.21	Telegram Dymphna Cusack/SMF, London, 9/4/1954	FP30
9.22	SMF/Mary Alice Evatt, Sydney, 24/4/1954	EC
9.23	SMF/Dymphna Cusack, Sydney, 1/5/1954	FP30
9.24	SMF/Eris O'Brien, Sydney, 15/5/1954	FP44
9.25	SMF/Magdalen Dalloz, Sydney, 2 and 4/6/1954	FP41
9.26	SMF/Vance Palmer, Sydney, 23/7/1954	PP
9.27	SMF/Marjorie Pizer Holburn, Sydney, 2/9/1954 [pm]	MHP
9.28	SMF/Pixie O'Harris, Sydney, 3/9/1954	ML DOC 3233

INDEX

I xxv, xxi, 4, 41, 95, 187, 191, 261, 274, 315, 359, 383; II 6, 7, 9, 11, 16, 17, 18, 25, 41, 47, 78, 98, 99, 100, 102, 122, 217, 218, 290, 315, 323, 332, 335

Baker, Richard (1854–1941) botanist and curator, II 3, 56, 149

Ball, William MacMahon (1901–86) prof pol science, Univ Melb 1949–68, II 243

'Banjo' *see* Paterson, A B

BARNARD, Anne, student, 5 ls 1946–7, II 190

Barnard, Marjorie Faith (1897–1987) librarian, writer and historian, I 261, 300; II 6, 27, 28, 60, 130, 132, 149, 266, 326; *see also* 'Eldershaw, M Barnard'

Barrymore, Freda, journalist (eg *Australasian* 13/10/1945), I 361

Barton, (Sir) Edmund (1849–1920) first PM Aust 1901–03, I 11

Bass, Tom (1916–) sculptor, II 278

Batty, Francis de Witt (1879–1961) Anglican bishop, II 224

Baume, Frederick Ehrenfried (1900–67) journalist, media commentator, II 13

'Baylebridge, William', *pseud* Charles William Blocksidge (1883–1942) poet, I 302, 303, 304, 305, 316, 381; II 77

Baynton, Barbara (1857–1929) wrote *Bush Studies* (1902), I 231

Beach, Sylvia (1887–1962) publisher, Paris, I 31

Beard, Mary (1876–1958) US feminist historian, II 100

Beaufoy, Florence (1897–1987) theosophist, Sydney, II 295

Bedford, Randolph (1868–1941) writer, politician, publicist, I 357; II 329

Benet, Stephen (1898–1943) US writer (incl 'John Brown's Body'), I 233, 356; II 67

Bennett, (Dr) Agnes (1872–1960) medical practitioner, I 103, 120

Bennett, Arnold (1867–1931) English writer, reviewer, I 232

BENTLEY, Godfrey, journalist, Newcastle and Sydney, d 1947, 28 ls 1942–46, II 4, 84, 86, 87, 117, 224, 234

Beveridge, (Sir) William (1879–1963) f of the welfare state, II 208

Birtles, Dora (1904–91) writer, II 233

Blackwell, Alice Stone (1857–1950) American suffragist, I 111, 117

BLACKWOOD, William and Sons Ltd, publishers, Edinburgh, Scotland, publishing correspondence 1902–47, I 3, 4, 12, 19, 22, 58, 63, 64, 183, 203, 247, 261. 266, 267, 268, 306

Blake, William (Bill), b US, *pseud* William Blech, h Christina Stead (*q.v.*), II 237

Blamey, Sir Thomas (1884–1951) commander allied land forces SW Pacific under Gen MacArthur (*q.v.*) WWII, II 48

BLYTH, Charles A, Scottish graduate, tutor Brindabella, 25 ls 1887–99, I 3, 5

'Boldrewood, Rolf' *pseud* Thomas Alexander Browne (1826–1915) writer, I 31

Bondfield, Margaret (1873–1953) British trade unionist and Labour cabinet minister 1929–31, I 116; II 130

BOOTH, (Dr) Mary (1869–1956) physician, feminist and welfare worker, Sydney, 13 ls 1924–52, I 21, 26, 28, 78, 120, 131, 168, 205, 358; II 251

Bottomley, Horatio (1860–1933) British jingo journalist, politician, I 162, 302

Boyd, Martin (1893–1972) expatriate novelist, I 183, 201, 208-9, 221; II 323

Bracken, Brendan (1901–58) Conservative MP, UK, II 77

BRADLEY, David (1925–) lecturer in English, Univ WA 1948–57, emeritus prof Monash, 2 ls 1950, II 257

Bradman, (Sir) Donald (1908–) cricketer, I 355

BRADY, Edwin James (1869–1952) journalist and traveller, settled Mallacoota, Vic, 3 ls 1943–45, II 94, 180, 317

Brailsford, Henry Noel (1873–1958)

CASSON, (Dame) Sybil Thorndike (1882–1976) British actor, 6 ls 1926–52, II 309

Catt, Carrie Chapman (1859–1947) US suffragist, peace leader, I 89, 155, 241; II 254

Chamberlain, Neville (1869–1940) Conservative PM UK 1937–40, II 50

CHAMPION, Annie B, sr H H Champion (*q.v.*) 7 ls 1916–27, I 101, 111,

CHAMPION, Elsie Belle (1870–1953) prev Goldstein, m H H Champion (*q.v.*) 1898, prop Book Lovers' Library, Melb, 10 ls 1902–53, I 31, 79, 96, 187, 201, 234, 249, 309, 312, 347, 348, 367; II 262, 290, 315, 334

Champion, Henry Hyde (1859–1928) b India, English socialist, journalist, arr Melb 1890, I 30, 36, 71, 79, 96, 111

Chekov, Anton (1860–1904) Russian playwright, writer, I 220

CHIFLEY, Joseph Benedict (1885–1951) ALP PM Aust 1945–9, w Elizabeth res Bathurst NSW, 3 ls 1945–50, I xxii; II 134, 138, 262

Childs, (Mrs) E M, of NY, I 242-3

Chomley, Charles Henry (1868–1942) expatriate ed *British Australasian* (London 1884–1948), I 116

CHRISTESEN, Clement Byrne (1911–) editor, author, publisher, f literary magazine *Meanjin* Brisb 1940, Melb 1945–, 63 ls 1941–53, II 83, 97, 130, 296, 318, 319

CHRISTMAN, Elisabeth (1881–1975) sec-treas NWTUL 1921–50, 13 ls 1932–54, I 124, 312; II 68, 89, 126, 128

Churchill, (Sir) Winston Spencer (1874–1965) British statesman, II 3, 19, 21, 50, 77, 92, 240, 268, 282

Cleary, Jon (1917–) wrote *The Sundowners* (1952), II 304, 305, 317

Cleary, William James (1885–1973) chair ABC 1934–45, II 76

Clune, Frank (1893–1971) popular author, incl many works ghosted by P R Stephensen (*q.v.*), I xx, 275, 364; II 44, 83, 118, 218, 340

Clune, Thelma Cecily (c1902–92) prev Smith, w Frank Clune (*q.v.*), I 275, 364; II 279

CLYNE, Dan (1879–1965) NSW MLA 1929–56, Speaker 1941–47, friend J M Franklin (*q.v.*) 19 ls 1930–53, I xxii, 238; II 252

Clynes, John Robert (1869–1949) trade union leader (UK), Home Sec 1929–31, I 155, 157

Cobden-Sanderson, Thomas James (1840–1922) London book-binder, printer, I 160

Cockburn, (Sir) John (1850–1929) SA politician, medico, suffragist, I 78

Coleridge, Samuel Taylor (1772–1834) English poet, I xviii, 194

'Collins Tom', I 95, 96, 261, 262, 303, 315, 359, 361; *see also* Furphy, Joseph

COLLINSON, Laurence (1925–86) writer and playwright, 5 ls 1948–9, II 150, 213, 215

Collisson, Marjorie Chave, sec British Commonwealth League, London, I 244, 245, 249, 263

Colum, Mary (1884–1967) Irish-American writer, II 222

Comans, Katherine, (1857–1915) prof history Wellesley, US, II 82

Consett-Stephen, Nancy *see* Stephen

Commonwealth Literary Fund, (CLF) est 1908, expanded 1939, I xxiv; II 119, 125, 137, 151, 152, 169, 240, 304, 306

Cottrell, Dorothy (1901–57) first novel *Singing Gold* (1928), I 198, 204, 205

Cousins, Walter G, dir publishing and chair A & R 1933–49, d 1949, II 8, 120, 212, 229

Coward, (Sir) Noel (1899–1973) English writer esp of comedies, II 43, 273

Cowling, George Herbert (1881–1946) prof English Univ Melb 1928–43; for the objectionable article, see *Age* 16/2/1935, I 315

dictator, I 287, 293, 326; II 33, 34, 50, 51, 199

Hjelmar, Marie, Danish politician, I 145

HOBSON, Florence E, m J A Hobson (*q.v*) 1885, 6 ls 1932–37, I 116, 200, 237, 249, 286; II 113

Hobson, John Atkinson (1858–1940) economist, wrote *Imperialism A Study* (1902), I 116, 132, 200, 237, 238, 287, 288, 338; II 113, 257

Hodge, Margaret, b 1860 UK, Syd 1897–1910, co-principal with H Newcomb (*q.v.*) Shirley College, Edgecliff, I 103, 107, 142, 143, 145, 160, 167

Hodges, Frank (1887–1947) sec Miners Fedn (UK) 1918–24, I 155, 157

HODGSON, Miss E, b 1871, long-serving sec NHTPC, ret Leeds, Sheffield, 22 ls 1921–53, I xvii, 166; II 180, 181, 308

HOLBURN, Marjorie *see* PIZER HOLBURN, Marjorie

Holburn, Muir (1920–60) journalist, poet, pres FAW (NSW branch) 1948–50, II 5, 156, 179, 264, 353

Hollis, Dr, pr Leslie Thomas (1865–1898) medical practitioner,MLA Goulburn, NSW 1891–8, I 6

Holman, Ada (1869–1949) journalist, w W A Holman (*q.v.*), I 98, 112, 120, 179, 205; II 151, 193, 197, 198, 221

Holman, William Arthur (1871–1934) premier NSW 1913–20, I 179; II 40-1

Hooper, Sydney Benjamin (c1869–1959), bank manager, partner P R Stephensen, V Crowley (*qq.v.*) *Publicist*, I 381; II 4, 65, 72, 73, 75, 83

Hooton, Harry (1908–61) anarchist poet, Newcastle, II 4, 85

Hoover, Herbert (1874–1964) engineer (in WA 1897–8), pres US 1929–32, I 215

Hope, Alec Derwent (1907–) poet, prof English ANU 1951–67, II 117, 294

Hore-Ruthven, (Hon Sir) Alexander

see Gowrie Lord

Howard, Stewart, journalist, II 340

HOWARTH, Robert Guy (1906–74) lecturer Univ Syd 1933–55, prof English Univ Cape Town 1956–71, f ed *Southerly* 1939, active English Association (the 'Eng Ass', f Syd 1923) 111 ls 1940–54, II 72, 109, 111, 130, 267, 296, 333

Hubener, Gustav, visiting German literature prof, I 314

Hughes, Charles Evans (1862–1948) Republican pres candidate US 1916, I 111

Hughes, Randolph (1890–1956) author *C J Brennan* (1934), I 318

Hughes, William Morris ('Billy') (1862–1952) PM Aust 1915–23, II 59, 75

Hungerford, Tom (1915–) first book *The Ridge and the River* (1952), II 236

Huxley, Aldous (1894–1963) wrote *Those Barren Leaves* (1925), I 209; II 135, 270

Hyndman, Henry Mayers (1842–1921) f British socialist, I 79

Ickes, Anna (1873–1935) prev Wilmarth, m Harold Ickes (*q.v.*) 1911, feminist, civic reformer, legislator, I 148, 322, 325

ICKES, Harold L (1874–1952) Progressive lawyer, Chicago, US Sec of Interior 1933–46, 18 ls 1913–46, I 322, 330; II 102, 298

Idriess, Ion (1889–1979) travel writer, II 25, 120, 132, 232, 233, 235, 237, 321, 326

Ifould, William Herbert (1877–1969) NSW State Librarian 1912–42, I 366

'Ike', *see* Eisenhower, Dwight D

Iliffe, Bert, A & R distribution manager, II 232

INGAMELLS, Rex (1913–55) b SA, poet, publisher, f Jindyworobak movement 1938, 60 ls 1946–54, I xxi; II 151, 152, 183-4, 203, 204-205, 225, 271-2, 288, 295, 304, 315

Inge, William Ralph (1860–1954) Dean St Paul's, London 1911–34,

I 245
INGLIS MOORE, Tom *see* Moore,
  Tom Inglis
'Inky', *see* Stephensen, P R
INNES, Guy Edward Mitchell
  (1882–1954) b Ballarat, journalist
  and writer, London, (Aust
  Newspaper Cable Service,
  1926–35, Aust Assoc Press,
  1935–40) 30 ls 1932–40, I 280,
  345, 346, 353, 361
Irving, Henry Brodribb (1870–1919)
  British actor-manager, w Dorothy
  Baird, I 112
'Isadora' *see* Duncan, Isadora

JAMES, Florence (Heyting) (1902–)
  b NZ, writer and ed, collab D
  Cusack (*q.v.*) *Come in Spinner*
  (1951) 90 ls 1946–54 (incl some
  with Cusack), I xxi, xxv; II
  149, 151, 175, 191-2, 221, 236,
  267, 295, 315
James, Henry (1843–1916)
  expatriate US writer, I 314, 346;
  II 301
Jauncey, (Dr) Leslie Cyril
  (1899–1959?) wrote *The Story of
  Conscription in Australia* (1935),
  I 345, 348
Jefferies, Richard (1848–87) British
  naturalist and writer, I 7
Jephcott, Sydney (1864–1951) poet,
  II 119
Joan of Arc (1412–31) French
  heroine, II 341
Johnson, Agnes, WTUL Chicago, I
  113, 119, 124
Johnson, Amy (1904–41) flew alone
  Croydon, UK to Australia, 1930,
  I 326
Johnson, Samuel(1709–84) English
  lexicographer, II 170
Jones, Inigo (1872–1954) 'the
  weather man', II 43
Jones, Jenkin Lloyd (1843–1918)
  minister religion, social reformer
  US, II 171
Jones, Phyllis Mander (1896–1984)
  Mitchell Librarian 1946–57, II 154
Joyce, James (1882–1941) wrote
  Ulysses (1922), twice banned in
  Aust, I 318; II 8, 59

Kaeppel, Carl Henry (1887–1946)
  scholar, teacher, writer, I 358
KEESING, Nancy (1923–93) writer,
  with Douglas Stewart (*q.v.*) comp
  Australian Bush Ballads (1955), 4
  ls 1952, I xxi, xxii; II 300-01
Kellor, Frances, associate M Robins
  (*q.v.*), I 148
Kennedy, Victor (1895–1952)
  writer, II 290
Kent, Duke of (1902–42), 4th son
  George V (*q.v.*) killed aircrash, II 19
Keon, Standish Michael (1915–)
  anticommunist Labor MHR, Vic,
  II 303
Kidgell, Stella, sr Ada Holman
  (*q.v.*), I 179
Kidman, (Sir) Sidney (1875–1935)
  'the cattle king', II 85
Kinsey, Alfred Charles (1894–1956)
  main author *Sexual behaviour of
  the human male* (1948), II 212
Kipling, Rudyard (1865–1936)
  imperial poet, author, I 47; II 27
Kisch, Egon (1885–1948) visiting
  Czech antifascist lecturer, 1934, I
  313, 341; II 31
Kitchener, (Lord) Horatio Herbert
  (1850–1916) British soldier, War
  Minister, I 353
Klein, Viola, wrote *The feminine
  charcter, History of an ideology*
  (1946), II 213
Knefler, Mrs, US associate SMF, I 269

Lambert, Elisabeth, pr US journalist,
  II 106
LAMPE, (He)Lena (1868–1964)
  aunt SMF, 20 ls 1906–53, I 16,
  50, 51, 308; II 57, 336
Lampe, John Theodore (1857–1931)
  br S M E Franklin (*q.v.*), I 50
LAMPE, Sara Metta (1860–1925)
  aunt SMF, 6 ls 1887–1925, I 5,
  48, 179
LAMPE, Sarah (1831–1912)
  grandmother SMF, 13 ls
  1897–1912, I 14, 25, 50, 51
Lampe, Theodor Oltmann
  (1844–1924) great uncle SMF, res
  Wachendorf, Germany, I 15
Lampe, Theodor (1882–1968) b
  Uenzen, Germany, SMF's German
  cousin, I 326

384

Lampe, William Augustus ('Gus')
(1862–1959) uncle SMF, farmer
central NSW, I 54; II 336
'LANCASTER, G B', *pseud* Edith
Joan Lyttleton (1874–1945) b Tas,
expatriate novelist, works incl
Pageant (London and Syd, 1934)
24 ls 1927–45, I 132, 141, 189,
283, 286, 293, 357; II 6, 263
Lanchester, G H and WR, (pr
George Herbert, Winifred Rose
Lanchester), II , 308
Lang, John Thomas ('Jack')
(1876–1976) Labor premier NSW
1925–7, 1930–2, I 255, 256,
258; II 71
Lang, Mary (1914–) wrote *Strange*
battalions and other poems
(1933), I 300, 305, 307
Langley, Eve (1908–74) wrote *The*
Pea Pickers (1942), II 94
Langloh, Parker K *see* Parker
Lathrop, Julia (1858–1932) pioneer
US social worker, reformer, I 218
Lattimore, Owen (1900–89) Asia
specialist, early victim
McCarthyism, II 275
Laval, Pierre (1883–1945) French
politician, Vichyite, II 75
Lavater, Louis (1867–1953)
prominent critic, Melb, II 101,
318, 319
Lawrence, David Herbert
(1885–1930) wrote *Kangaroo* in
Aust, 1922, I 231, 282, 287,
292, 347, 356, 359; II 8, 255
Lawson, Bertha (1876–1957) prev
Bredt, m H Lawson (*q.v.*) 1896, I
11, 168
LAWSON, Emmy, ret office-worker,
NHTPC, 36 ls 1946–53, II 180
LAWSON, Henry (1867–1922)
writer and poet, 16 ls 1899–1902,
I xx, xxi, 3, 9, 10, 11, 13, 21,
167, 168, 173, 381; II 4, 9, 71,
78, 88, 95, 100, 157, 174, 230,
244, 256, 279, 301, 317, 327, 351
Lawson, Will (1876–1957)
bohemian and balladist, II 132
Leeson, Ida Emily (1885–1964)
Mitchell Librarian 1932–46, I
337, 345, 349, 366; II 11, 88,
154, 223
Leigh, Vivien (1913–67)

Shakespearean actor, 1st w L
Olivier (*q.v.*), II 206
Lenin, Vladimir (1870–1924)
Bolshevik leader, I 142; II 75
Levin, Sam, US trade unionist, I 198
Lewis, Alun (1915–44), Welsh-born
poet, d Burma, II 202
Lindsay, Jane (1920–) dr Norman
Lindsay (*q.v.*) wrote *Kurrajong*
(1945), II 137, 141
LINDSAY, Norman (1879–1969),
artist and writer, 1 1 1933, I 231,
264, 265, 278, 279-80, 281, 282,
284, 315, 329; II 137, 176, 332
Lindsay, Nicholas Vachel
(1879–1931) US writer, I 250
Linklater, William (also 'Billy
Miller') (1867–1959) NT identity,
writer, I xxii; II 9, 10, 78
Litvinoff, Maksim (1876–1951)
Soviet statesman, I 122
LLOYD, Demarest (1883–1937)
Chicago playboy, Christian
Scientist, 36 ls 1912–21, I 58,
81, 82, 88, 115, 381
LLOYD, Lola Maverick
(1875–1944) 1st w W B Lloyd
(*q.v.*) WTUL 'ally', pacifist, 1 1
1915, I 81, 94, 116
Lloyd, William Bross (Bill)
(c1875–1946) br Demarest Lloyd
(*q.v.*), I 58, 116, 139, 152, 332
Loch, Frederick (1889–1954)
farmer, served Gallipoli, author
The Straits Impregnable (1916),
expatriate writer, I 111
Locke, Agnes, sr Helena Locke
(*q.v.*), I 127
Locke, Helena Sumner (1881–1917)
writer, mr Sumner Locke Elliott
(*q.v.*), I 123, 127
Locke, Lilian Sophia (1869–1950)
Melb labour organiser, sr Helena
Locke (*q.v.*), I 127, 201
Loraine, Robert (1876–1935) British
actor–manager, I 143
Low, (Sir) David (1891–1963)
expatriate cartoonist, I 132,
141, 143
Luffman, Laura(ette) Bogue
(1846–1929) writer, feminist, I 42
Lyons, (Dame) Enid (1897–1981)
politician, w J A Lyons (*q.v.*), II 7
Lyons, Joseph Aloysius (1879–1939)

385

Labor 'rat', PM Aust 1932–39, I
258; II 7

M A B see Maynard M A B
Maas, Nuri, see Mass
MacArthur, Douglas (1880–1964) US
general, commander Allied forces
SW Pacific WWII, II 4, 136
Macarthur, Mary (1880–1921)
British labour organiser, I 116
Macarthur-Onslow, Rosa, dr
Elizabeth Macarthur-Onslow
(1840–1911), II 251
McCarthy, Joseph (1909–57) US
senator, anticommunist crusader,
II 341, 345
McCarthy, Molly, II 161
McCartney, Frederick Thomas
(1887–1980) bibliographer, II
122, 179, 243
McCay, Adam Cairns (1874–1947)
bohemian journalist, II 13
McCormick, Ruth Hanna (Mrs
Medill McCormick), WTUL 'ally'
Chicago, I 123
McCrae, Hugh (1876–1958) poet,
II 29, 318, 319
MacDonald, James Ramsay
(1866–1937) PM UK 1924
(Labour) 1929–35 (National from
1931), I 238
Macdonald, Louisa (1858–1949)
principal Women's College Univ
Syd 1891–1919, I 120, 121
McDowell, Mary (1854—1936)
settlement worker, social
reformer, Chicago, I 136, 160,
162, 200, 332; II 210
McIntyre, Rev, American evangelist,
II 326
Mackaness, (Dr) George (1882–1968)
head Eng dept Syd Teachers
College 1924–46, anthologist, I
310, 311; II 233, 237
McKay, Adam see McCay
McKay, Stanley, pr showman, b
Tumut (1877–1974), I 163
McKell, (Sir) William (1891–1985)
ALP premier NSW 1941–47, gov
gen Aust 1947–53, II 182
MacKellar, John, b 1881, poet,
Melb, II 278
McKinnon, Thomas Firmin
(1878–1953) and w Emma Louise

(1884–1964) prev Powell,
journalists, I 297, 299, 304
Macky, Mrs, pr Mrs Anne Macky, f
dir New Conservatorium, Melb,
1918, I 161
McLean (?John, US trade unionist),
I 112
MacLeish, Archibald (1892–1982)
US poet, II 90
McMillan, Lady, pr Helen Marial,
Lady McMillan (1863–1937) I 121
McMillan, Margaret (1860–1931) f
open air creche Deptford, London,
WWI, I 103, 106, 107, 116
McMillan, Rachel (1859–1917) sr
M McMillan (q.v.) educational
reformer, I 103, 106, 116
Mair, Ian, journalist II 170, 203
Malinowski, Bronislaw (1884–1942)
Polish anthropologist NG,
Melanesia, II 216
'Malley Ern', II 5; see also Harris,
Max
'Malone, H F', pseud SMF, I 178
Malone, Nell, expatriate friend SMF
Chicago, London, I 110, 116
Maloney, Elizabeth, WTUL
Chicago, waitresses union, I 148
Malraux, André (1901–76) wrote La
condition humaine (1933), I 318
Malyon, Edith, friend P S Watson
(q.v.), I 348
Mander, Mary Jane (1877–1949)
wrote The story of a New
Zealand river (1920), I 254, 255
Mann, (Rev) Rowena Morse,
American preacher, I 86
Mann, Thomas (1875–1955) Nobel
prizewinner 1929, works incl
Buddenbrooks (1900), II 5
Mannin, Ethel, b 1900, prolific
British author, first novel 1922,
II 14
Mannix, (Cardinal) Daniel
(1864–1963), II 326
Mansfield, Katherine (1888–1923)
pseud Katherine Beauchamp, NZ
expatriate writer, I 287
MAROT, Helen (1865–1940) sec
NY WTUL 1906–13, reformer
and writer, 2 ls 1911, I 66, 67
Marshall, Alan (1902–84) wrote I
can jump puddles (1955), 118
MARTIN, David (1915–)

386

Hungarian-born writer and peace activist, 79 ls 1947–54, w Richenda, sn Jan, I xxii, xxiv; II 151, 152, 225, 226, 227, 230, 255, 256, 259, 280, 281, 289, 328, 329, 351

Mason, Ethel (later Nielsen), close friend SMF Chicago, I 87, 114, 136, 148, 341; II 37 242

Mass, Nuri (1918– -) author, editor, incl A&R, II 132

MATHEW, Ray (1929–) playwright, expatriate from 1961, 3 ls 1952–3, II 311, 352

Matthews, Harley (1889–1968) war poet and vintner, Moorebank, NSW, I 382; II 73, 75, 90, 117, 134, 135, 160, 183, 193, 221

Matthews, Susan May (1877–1935) child welfare inspector NSW, visited USA with Aust Industrial delegation 1927, I 201

Maughan, Mrs (Lady) David, Jean Alice (1882–1957) prev Barton, II 251

'Maurice, Furnley', *pseud* Frank Wilmot (1881–1942) poet, manager Melb Univ Press, I 247; II 77, 111, 156

Maynard, Frieda Byles (1895–1940) dr Ken and M A B Maynard (*qq.v.*), I 152

Maynard, Ken, h M A B Maynard, relative S A Byles (*qq.v.*), I 151, 152, 170, 324, 325, 375

Maynard, M A B (?–1944) settlement worker, Chicago, London, I 119, 324, 325, 375; II 49

Meagher, James Anthony (c1895–1975) b Dublin, solicitor, II 117

MEGGITT Phyl and May, 'my precious Meggitts', teacher, nurse, London, Newport, Wales, later Cheshire, 10 ls 1914–53, II 34, 141

Melba, (Dame) Nellie (1861–1931) soprano, I 69, 109, 244

Mencken, Henry Louis (1880–1956) the original 'muckraker', II 127

MENKEN, Mary Shaw (Mollye) b 1891, Rose Scott's niece, m Jules Menken, economist, London, 12 ls 1928–53, I 179, 245, 263, 264, 352-3

MENZIES, (Sir) Robert Gordon (1894–1978) Liberal PM Aust 1939–41, 1949–65, 7 ls 1939–46, II 10, 20, 24, 50, 57, 58, 71, 197, 245, 259, 303, 306, 321, 324, 345, 346

Meredith, Gwen (1907–) wrote radio serial *Blue Hills* (1949–76), II 288

Metcalfe, John Wallace (1901–82) NSW State Librarian 1942–59, II 233-5, 238

Micklem, (Rev Dr) Philip Arthur (1876–1965) incumbent St James Syd 1917–37, m Evelyn Auriac, 1932, I 358

Miles, John Bramwell (1888–1969) gen sec Communist Party Aust 1931–48, II 195

Miles, T S, I 21

Miles, William John, (1871–1942) businessman, rationalist, employer P R Stephensen (*q.v.*), I 342, 348; II 58, 65. 72, 101

Milgate, Wesley, (1916–) appt prof Eng Univ Syd 1951, ANU 1961, II 296

'Miller, Billy' *see* Linklater

Miller, Edmund Morris, (1881–1964) prof Univ Tas, with F T Macartney (*q.v.*) comp *Australian Literature* (1940), II 333

Miller, Frieda Segelke (1889–1973) Philadelphia WTUL, 2nd dir US Women's Bureau 1944–52, lifelong companion Pauline Newman (*q.v.*), I 145

Millet, Jean Francois (1814–75) painted 'The man with the hoe' 1863, I 223

'Mills, Martin' *see* Boyd

Milton, John (1608–74) Puritan poet, II 167

Miranda, Beatrice(1881–1964) singer, I 161

Mirsky, prof, pr D S Mirsky, Univ London, I 288

Mitchell, (Prof) Alexander George (1911–) wrote *The Pronunciation of English in Australia* (1946), f vice-chancellor Macquarie Univ, II 43, 198, 296

Mitchell, Margaret (1900–49) wrote

I 103, 107, 142, 151; *see also* Hodge

Newman, Pauline, WTUL organiser, Philadelphia, I 145

NEWSHAM, Isabel, graduated BA Univ Syd 1900, associate Alice Henry (*q.v.*) Chicago 1906–12, medical stenographer California 1926, 29 ls 1912, 1937–54, II 29, 99, 102, 103

NEWSON Vivienne Elizabeth (c1892–1973) editor, vice-pres United Associations of Women (*q.v.*), II 249, 251

Nichol, David, pr Nichol Smith, prof English Oxford 1929–46, Adelaide 1950–1, II 222

Nicolson, (Sir) Harold (1886–1968) British diplomat, historian, I 346

NIELSON-TERRY, Phyllis, b 1892, actor, niece Ellen Terry (*q.v.*) London, 2 ls 1922, I 163

Niland, D'arcy Francis (1917–67) wrote *The Shiralee* (1955), II 287

Northcliffe, (Lord) Alfred (1865–1922) British newspaper prop, I 108, 162

Oakes, Russell (1910–52) soldier, playwright, II 118

O'BRIEN, Eris (1895–1974) Catholic archbishop Canberra-Goulburn 1953–67, historian, 3 ls 1952–54, I xxii; II 278, 283, 347

O'Casey, Sean (1884–1964) Irish dramatist, I 231; II 206

Odets, Clifford (1906–63) US playwright, wrote *Till the day I die* (1935), I 341

O'Dowd, Bernard (1886–1953) poet, I 41; II 118, 119, 290, 329, 333

'O'HARRIS, Pixie' (Rona Olive Pratt) (1903–91) b Wales, children's author/artist, 34 ls 1941–54, I xxi; II 4, 165, 166, 259, 306, 311, 321, 322, 327, 339, 351

Olander, Victor (1873–1949) pres Lake Seamen's Union, Chicago, I 161; II 89

Oliphant, (Sir) Mark (1901–) physicist, later gov SA 1971–6, II 208

Oliver, Harold James (1916–82) later f prof English Univ NSW 1960–81, II 326

Olivier, (Sir) Laurence (1907–89) British actor, II 206

O'Reilly, Dowell (1865–1923) poet and politician, sn Thomas O'Reilly (*q.v.*), fr Eleanor Dark (*q.v.*), II 60

O'REILLY, Leonora (1870–1927) WTUL rebel, trades school teacher NY, 28 ls 1911–16, I 80, 87, 89, 90, 91, 92, 99, 108, 123, 127, 140

O'Reilly, (Canon) Thomas (1819–81) incumbent St Philip's, Syd 1869–c81, II 60

Orr, (Sir) John Boyd (1880–1971) nutrition expert UK, Nobel prize 1949, II 208

Osborne, (Dr) Ethel (1882–1968) medical practitioner, industrial hygienist, I 263

O'SULLIVAN, Agnes Ann, prev Firman, milliner, m E W O'Sullivan (*q.v.*) Melb 1878, 1 1 1904, I 16, 26, 28, 32, 138, 179

O'Sullivan, Edward William (1846–1910) Protectionist MLA Queanbeyan NSW 1885–1904, later Belmore, Minister Public Works 1899–1904, I 3, 32, 74, 179, 137

O'SULLIVAN, Evelyn Inez (Eva) (1880–1957) public servant, dr Agnes and E W O'Sullivan (*qq.v.*), 18 ls 1912–49, I xxiii, 97, 132, 74, 132, 137, 178, 260, 367

O'Sullivan, Tossie, sr Eva O'Sullivan (*q.v.*), I 137, 138

O'Sullivan, Vera, sr Eva O'Sullivan (*q.v.*), I 261

Oxford and Asquith, Lord *see* Asquith, H H

Packer, (Sir) Frank (1906–74) prop *DT* Syd, II 178, 196

PALLOT, Sylvia Judith (1875–1967) dr Joseph Furphy (*q.v.*), sn Victor (1903–) and (?Ivy Pallot), 21 ls 1950–3, I 40; II 151, 247, 258

Palmer, Aileen (1915–88) dr Nettie and Vance Palmer (*qq.v*) poet, ambulance officer Spain 1936–8,

390

(1911), I 181, 265; II 37, 46, 216
Schwimmer, Rosika (1877–1948) b
Hungary, feminist and pacifist,
I 90
Scott, Charles Prestwich
(1846–1932) ed *Manchester
Guardian* from 1872, I 222, 249
Scott, Melinda, British-born, vice-
pres NWTUL 1915, I 124
SCOTT, Rose (1847–1925) feminist,
56 ls 1902–24, I xxiii, xxvi, 3,
21, 23, 24, 26, 38, 76, 80, 103,
120, 131, 142, 167, 179, 190,
274; II 60, 94, 149, 189
Scullin, James Henry (1876–1953)
Lab PM Aust 1929–31, II 161
Shain, Jean, II 24
Shaw, George Bernard (1856–1950)
dramatist, wrote *The Intelligent
Woman's Guide to Socialism,
Capitalism, Sovietism and Facism*
(1928), I 131, 142, 143, 200,
205, 241, 245, 366, 371; II 19,
22, 211, 256, 262, 307
Shaw, Molly *see* Menken
Shawn, Ted, US dancer, m Ruth St
Denis (*q.v.*), I 159
Sheen, John Fulton (1895–1979)
American Catholic priest,
broadcaster, II 208
Sheepshanks, Mary (1872–1952) co
ed *Ius Suffragii,* international
women's suffrage news (London,
1906–29), I 116
Shepherd, Miriam, sec international
congress working women convened
M Robins (*q.v.*) Washington 1919
(congresses also Geneva 1921,
Vienna 1923), I 144
Sheppard, (Col) Alexander William
('Shep') (1911–) Syd bookman,
II 331
Shute, Neville, *pseud* Neville Shute
Norman (1899–1960) wrote *A
Town Like Alice* (1950), II 295,
320-1
Simonds, Frank Herbert
(1878–1936) US journalist, I 329
Singleton, Denis Gordon (1911–)
OBE, sn Mabel Singleton (*q.v.*), w
Eileen, I 249, 301; II 34, 78
SINGLETON, Elizabeth Ethel
Mabel (1877–1965) b UK, prev
Jupp, businesswoman, m Robert

Singleton 1904 [d 1913, Melb],
companion Mary Fullerton (*q.v.*)
London 1922–46, 153 ls
1934–54, I xv, xxvi, 74, 184,
186, 222, 249, 301, 302, 351; II
7, 77, 140, 157, 159, 253, 289,
302, 334
Sitwell, (Dame) Edith (1887–1964)
English poet, wrote *Victoria of
England* (1936), I 336
Slessor, Kenneth (1901–71) poet,
II 164
Slim, (Sir) William (1891–70) gov-
gen Aust 1953–60, II 320
Smillie, Robert (1857–1940)
Scottish miners leader, socialist, I
155, 157
Smith, (Miss) A A (c1863–1919)
social reformer, London, I 122,
134, 136, 139
Smith, (Sir) Charles Kingsford
(1897–1953) pioneer aviator,
with Charles Ulm 1st flight across
Pacific (1928), I 326
SMITH, H N, b c1874, English
businessman, 6 ls 1924–44, II 19
Smith, Tilden, literary agent,
London, I 230
Smythe, Nora, suffragette, I 116
Spellman, Francis Joseph
(1889–1967) US Cardinal (1946),
II 208
Spence, Catherine Helen
(1825–1910) SA writer, social
theorist, I xxiv, 274, 275, 338;
II 125, 315, 328, 333
Spencer, (Sir) Walter Baldwin
(1860–1929) prof biology Univ
Melb 1887–1919, anthropologist,
I xxvi, 184, 222, 249; II 272
Spencer-Jackson, II 286
St Denis, Ruth (c1877–1968) 'first
lady of American dance', I 159
Stalin, Josef (1897–1953) Soviet
dictator, II 136, 196, 208, 307
STAMENKOVIC, Alejander ,
soldier, 1 l 1918, I 124
Stead, Christina (1902–83)
expatriate writer 1928–1974, I
382; II 164, 237
Steffens, Lincoln (1866–1936) US
author, editor, one of the
'muckrakers', I 87, 356
STEGHAGEN, Emma, NWTUL

393

office Chicago, prev boot and shoe workers union, 8 ls 1915–17, I 67, 92, 93, 94, 114, 127, 140, 218

Stephen, Nancy Consett (1859–1943) Red Cross worker, OBE 1934, II 94-5

STEPHENS, Alfred George (1865–1933) critic and ed *Bulletin* Red Page 1894–1906, *Bookfellow* 1907–25, 27 ls 1900–32, I 4, 16, 19, 20, 27, 29, 39, 41 42, 213, 214, 259, 261, 262, 274, 275, 290, 359; II 29, 30, 69, 98, 296, 333, 351

Stephens, Constance *see* Robertson, Constance

STEPHENSEN, Percy Reginald ('Inky') (1901–65) 'wild man of letters', ed *Publicist* 1936–42, interned 1942–45, 37 ls 1932–54, I xxii, 184, 264, 265 , 266, 267, 273, 275, 279, 281, 282, 283, 284, 293, 299, 303, 305, 307, 315, 317, 318, 320, 321, 342, 343, 344, 346, 348, 352, 371; II 3, 4, 13 , 29, 30, 58, 60, 65, 71, 77, 135, 144, 149, 152, 160, 162, 163, 284, 285, 286, 296, 340

STEPHENSEN, Winifred, prev Lockyer (1886–1971) b UK, dancer, m P R Stephensen 1947, 17 ls 1945–54, I 299, 335, 345; II 57, 69, 77, 135, 152, 154, 284, 341

Stetson, Mrs *see* Gilman

Stewart, Douglas (1913–85) b NZ, poet, ed *Bulletin* Red Page 1940–61, II 5, 93

Stewart, Harold (1916–85) poet, co-perpetrator 'Ern Malley' hoax, 1944, II 232

STOFFEL, Henrika, music teacher Deventer, Holland, 16 ls 1924–53, II 49, 177

Strachey, Lytton (1880–1932) wrote *Eminent Victorians* (1918), I 151, 336

Street, (Lady) Jessie (1889–1970) feminist, II 127, 149, 164

Strehlow, Theodor George Henry (1908–78) b Hermannsburg cent Aust, linguist and scholar of Aboriginal Aust, II 287

Sullivan, Mark, wrote *Our Times. The United States 1900–1925* (2 v 1927–8), II 171

Sullivan, Olive, WTUL office Chicago, I 119, 124

SUTHERLAND, Bruce (1904–70) literature prof, Penn, Fulbright scholar Aust 1951–2, w Doris, 6 ls 1952–54, I xviii, xix, xxvii; II 152, 274, 276, 277, 296, 341

Suttor, (Sir) Francis (1839–1915) pastoralist, pres NSW Legisl Council 1903–15, I 32

Swanwick, Helena (1864–1939) British suffragist, lecturer, I 151; II 186

Tagore, (Sir) Rabindranath (1861–1941) Indian poet, nationalist, II 26

Tate, Harry (1873–1940) British music-hall comedian, II 19

Tauber, Richard (1891–1948) British tenor, I 313

Tawney, Richard Henry (1880–1962) British historian, I 151

Taylor, Laurie, expatriate artist, I 141

'Telly', *Daily Telegraph*, Syd *see also* Packer

Temby, Henry Stanley (c1890–1965) sec CLF from 1938, II 32

TENNANT, Kylie (1912–88) writer, 4 ls 1941–52, II 27, 64, 278, 279, 280, 306, 321

Tennyson, (Baron) Hallam (1852–1928) 2nd gov-gen Aust, I 31, 250

Terry, (Dame) Ellen (1882–1976) English actor, I 200

Thaw, Evelyn Nesbit (1884–1967) of angelic demeanour, Thaw case NY 1906, I 125

Theodore, Edward Granville (1884–1950) ALP Treasurer Aust 1929–31, II 196

Thomas, Geoffrey, arr Aust c1950, est Experimental Theatre for Playwrights, II 346

Thomas, John Henry (1874–1949) sec railwaymens union (UK) 1918–24, cabinet minister

1929–31, I 157

Thorndike, Sybil see Casson

THROSSELL, Ric (1922–) diplomat, writer, sn Katherine Susannah Prichard (*q.v.*), 41 ls 1949–54, I xvii; II 6, 133, 218, 219, 220, 243, 258, 261, 303, 338

Thwaites, Frederick Joseph (1908–79) romantic novelist, wrote *Broken Melody* (1930), I 31; II 92

Tickell, J E, sec Australian Book Society est FAW 1945, II 164

Timms, Edward Vivian (1895–1960) wrote historical romances incl *Forever to Remain* (1948), II 232, 233, 237, 321, 326

Tojo, Hideki (1884–1949) PM Japan 1941–4, II 282

Tolstoy, Leo (1828–1910) Russian writer, I 220

Tomholt, Sydney (1884–1974) dramatist, drama critic *SMH*, II 198-9, 223

Travers, Pamela Lyndon (1906–) expatriate, wrote *Mary Poppins* (1934), I 318

Trist, Margaret (1914–86) b Qld, writer, worked ABC, II 164

Turgenev, Ivan (1818–83) Russian writer, I 259

TURNER, Ethel Mary (1870–1958) works incl classic *Seven Little Australians* (1894), m Herbert Curlewis 1896, I xxi, 19; II 7

UNCLE ?, I 17

Uncle Theo see Lampe, John Theodore

Uncle Gus see Lampe, William Augustus

United Associations of Women, f Syd 1929, 5 ls 1948–53; see NEWSON

Unwin, (Dr) Joseph Daniel (1895–1936) head Cambridge House, England, wrote *Sex and Culture* (1934), II 135, 186, 209, 216

Unwin, (Sir) Raymond (1863–1940) British townplanner, I 142

Unwin, (Sir) Stanley (1884–1968) British publisher, II 320

Unwin, Thomas Fisher (1848–1935)

British publisher, I 179

Ussher, Kathleen, b 1891, expatriate, wrote *Hail Victoria!* (1934), I 111, 179, 231, 232, 234, 254, 289, 306

Ussher, Mrs, mr Kathleen Ussher (*q.v.*), I 134, 179

Valéry, Paul (1871–1945) French symbolist poet, I 318

VEAL, Hayward (Bill) (1913–68) conducted Meldrum School of Painting, Syd, w Minka, 5 ls 1951, 277

'Verney, J' *pseud* SMF, II 175

Vernon, Edgar, b 1874, cousin SMF, I 28

W, A P see Pankhurst, Adela

Wadham, (Sir) Samuel (1891–1972) prof ag science, Univ Melb, I 358

Wald, Lilian D (1867–1940) nurse, settlement worker Chicago, II 210

Walker, Amy, WTUL Chicago, I 115

Wallace, Helenus Hope Scott ('Nene') (1878–1951) Rose Scott's nephew, I 21, 31, 353, 366

Walton, Miss, Australia First, Syd, II 69, 71, 75

Ward, Harry Frederick (1873–1966) wrote *The Soviet Spirit* (1944), II 171

Ward, Lester F (1841–1913) wrote *Pure Sociology: a treatise on the origin and spontaneous development of society* (NY, 1911), II 216

Waten, Judah (1911–) communist, writer, 1st book *Alien Son* (1952), II 318

Watson, Leo, br P S Watson (*q.v.*), I 358

Watson, Nancy Lister, w P S Watson (*q.v.*) d 1928, I 172, 188, 197, 204

WATSON, P S, ret squatter 'Gregory Downs' Qld, Christian Scientist, d 1936, 5 ls 1911–30, I xxii, 172, 188, 197, 329, 337, 347, 358

Wedgwood, Camilla (1901–55) anthropologist, principal Women's College Univ Syd 1935–43, II 104, 105

Weinstock, Anna, Boston WTUL, I 145

Wells, Mrs H G (Amy Catherine, prev Robbins) d 1927, I 120

Wentworth, William Charles (1907–) anticommunist, Liberal MHR 1949–77, I 358; II 150, 152, 161, 195, 196, 197, 302, 303, 306, 307

WENZ, Paul (1869–1939) French-Aust writer, station owner Forbes, NSW 10 ls 1937, I 362, 367; II 320

West, (Dame) Rebecca (1892–1983) British writer, feminist, I 200, 318

WHELAN, Carrie, feminist, California, d 1937, 17 ls 1929–37, I 4, 46, 49, 241, 308, 364

WHITE, Myrtle Rose (1888–1961) wrote No Roads Go By (1932), 22 ls 1950–54, II 151, 238-9, 265, 327, 339

White, Patrick (1912–89) first novel Happy Valley (1939), I xix; II 8, 151

Whitman, Walt(er) (1819–92) US poet, wrote Leaves of Grass (1855), II 329

Wilcox, Dora (1873–1953) b NZ, poet, playwright, II 251

Wilkie, Alan (1878–1970) toured Aust performing Shakespeare, 1920s, I 199

Wilkins, Miss, pseud US writer Mary Eleanor Wilkins Freeman (1862–1930) works incl A New England Nun and other stories (1891), I 7

Wilkinson, Aunt, I 50

Willard, Anna, Chicago, I 148

Williams, (Mrs) Mary Jamieson, temperance worker, feminist, d 1947, I 263

Wilson, Woodrow (1856–1924) US Pres 1913–21 (2nd w Edith B Galt, m 1915), I 113, 124, 374

Windon, Rose, I 353

Wingfield-Stratford, Esmé Cecil (1882–1971) English cultural historian, works incl Victorian Tragedy (1930), Victorian Sunset (1932) Victorian Aftermath 1901–1914 (1933), I 336

Winter, William, US public broadcaster, incl for ABC, II 182

Wise, Bernhard Ringrose (1858–1916) barrister and politician, NSW Agent-Gen Lond 1915–16, I 112

WITCOMBE, Eleanor (1923–) playwright, wrote screenplay for film 'My Brilliant Career' 1979, 13 ls 1951–2, I xxi; II 152, 263, 264, 292

Wood, (Dr) Thomas (1892–1950) English composer, wrote Cobbers (1934), I 314, 356

Woodcock, Lucy (1889–1968) teacher, II 164

Woolf, Humbert (1886–1940) poet, public servant, London, II 208

Woolf, Virginia (1882–1941) writer, works incl The waves (1931), Three guineas (1938), drowned herself, II 8, 54, 201

Yeats, William Butler (1865–1939) Irish poet, II 53

Young, Jeanne Forster (1876–1955) wrote Catherine Helen Spence (1937), I 366

YOUNG, (Dr) Josephine E, b c1856, medical practitioner, Chicago, 22 ls 1928–49, I 60, 159, 227, 244; II 210, 298

Zeisler, Fanny Bloomfield, American musician, I 86